Blackland Prairies of the Gulf Coastal Plain

D1603231

Blackland Prairies of the Gulf Coastal Plain

Nature, Culture, and Sustainability

Edited by

Evan Peacock and Timothy Schauwecker

THE UNIVERSITY OF ALABAMA PRESS

Tuscaloosa and London

Typeface: Trump Mediaeval

∞

The paper on which this book is printed meets the minimum requirements of
American National Standard for Information Science-Permanence of Paper for Printed
Library Materials, ANSI Z39.48-1984.

Library of Congress Cataloging-in-Publication Data

Blackland prairies of the Gulf coastal plain : nature, culture, and sustainability /
edited by Evan Peacock and Timothy Schauwecker.
     p.   cm.
Includes bibliographical references and index.
ISBN 0-8173-1263-3 (cloth : alk. paper) — ISBN 0-8173-1215-3 (pbk. : alk. paper)
1. Prairies—Southern States—History. 2. Paleoecology—Southern States. 3. Gulf
Coast (U.S.)—Environmental conditions. 4. Human ecology—Southern States.
5. Indians of North America—Southern States—Antiquities. I. Peacock, Evan, 1961–
II. Schauwecker, Timothy, 1967–

QH104.5.S59 B43 2003
304.2'0976—dc21

2002011022

British Library Cataloguing-in-Publication Data available

This volume is dedicated to the memory of Joye Peacock-Murphy
and Robert Graham Jeffrey
and
with continuing best wishes for
Geraldine Jeffrey
and
Sidney McDaniel

Contents

Figures   ix

Tables   xii

1. Introduction: The Nature, Culture, and Sustainability
of Blackland Prairies
Evan Peacock and Timothy Schauwecker   1

PART I: NATURE

2. Paleoenvironment and Biogeography of the Mississippi
Black Belt: Evidence from Insects
Richard L. Brown   11

3. Terrestrial Gastropods from Archaeological Contexts
in the Black Belt Province of Mississippi
Evan Peacock and Rebecca Melsheimer   27

4. The Application of a Small-mammal Model in
Paleoenvironmental Analysis
S. Homes Hogue   48

5. A Comparison of Three Methods of Paleoenvironmental
Analysis at an Archaeological Site on the Mississippi
Black Prairie
Evan Peacock and Mary Celeste Reese   64

6. Louisiana Prairies
*Michael H. MacRoberts, Barbara R. MacRoberts,
and Lynn Stacey Jackson*   80

7. Blackland Prairie Landscapes of Southwestern Arkansas:
Historical Perspective, Present Status, and Restoration Potential
*Thomas L. Foti, Scott Simon, Douglas Zollner,
and Meryl Hattenbach*   94

8. A Plant Community Classification for Arkansas's
Blackland Prairie Ecosystem
Douglas Zollner, Scott Simon, and Thomas L. Foti   110

9. Plant and Soil Interactions in Prairie Remnants of
the Jackson Prairie Region, Mississippi
L. P. Moran, D. E. Pettry, and R. E. Switzer   146

PART II: CULTURE

10. Prehistoric Settlement Patterning on the Mississippi
Black Prairie
Janet Rafferty   167

11. Water-resource Controls on Human Habitation in the
Black Prairie of North-Central Mississippi
Darrel W. Schmitz, Charles L. Wax, and Evan Peacock   194

12. Osage Orange Bows, Indian Horses, and the Blackland
Prairie of Northeastern Texas
Frank F. Schambach   212

PART III: SUSTAINABILITY

13. Rediscovery and Management of Prairie Remnants
of the Bienville National Forest, East-Central Mississippi
Dean Elsen and Ronald Wieland   239

14. Plant Assemblage Response to Disturbance at a
Blackland Prairie Restoration Site in Northeastern Mississippi
Timothy Schauwecker and John MacDonald   246

15. Restoration of a Prairie Remnant in the Black Belt of Mississippi
*Sherrill Wiygul, Kay Krans, Richard Brown, and
Victor Maddox*   254

16. Priorities for the Future: Planning for Sustainable Multiple Use
Thomas W. Schurch   262

17. Conclusion: Theory and Applications in the Study of
Human/Nature Interactions
Evan Peacock and Timothy Schauwecker   279

References Cited   283

Contributors   337

Index   343

List of Figures

1.1.   Blackland prairies on the Gulf Coastal Plain   3

2.1.   Black Belt (solid gray) and Jackson Prairie (hatched) in Mississippi and Alabama   12

2.2.   Obsorn Prairie in Oktibbeha County, Mississippi   13

3.1.   Archaeological site 22OK904, Oktibbeha County, Mississippi   31

3.2.   Comparison of bleached (Protohistoric) and unbleached (Historic) gastropods from 22OK904   35

3.3.   Protohistoric gastropod assemblage, 22OK904   36

3.4.   Historic gastropod assemblage, 22OK904   38

3.5.   Modern gastropod assemblage, 16th Section Prairie, Oktibbeha County, Mississippi   39

3.6.   Modern gastropod assemblage, cedar glade, Chickasaw County   40

3.7.   Archaeological and modern gastropod assemblages from the Mississippi Black Prairie   41

4.1.   Archaeological sites 22OK793 and 22CL814, Mississippi Black Prairie   50

4.2.   Percentage of small-mammal NISP at Black Belt archaeological sites   59

4.3.   Percentage of small-mammal MNI at Black Belt archaeological sites   59

4.4.   Ratio of rodent/rabbit to carnivore, Black Belt archaeological sites   61

4.5.   Small-mammal representation, Black Belt archaeological sites   62

5.1.   Yarborough (22CL814) and Lyon's Bluff (22OK520) archaeological sites, Mississippi   67

5.2.   Impression of persimmon leaf in daub from the Lyon's
       Bluff site   72

5.3.   Casts of acorn from daub, the Yarborough site   74

6.1.   Distribution of Louisiana prairies   82

6.2.   Native American mounds on Jefferson Prairie, Morehouse
       Parish, Louisiana   85

6.3.   Aerial photograph of Keiffer Prairies, northern Louisiana,
       ca. 1940   91

7.1.   Blackland soil associations of southwestern Arkansas   95

7.2.   Generalized model of the geology, soil, vegetation, and
       topography of a cuesta in southwestern Arkansas   96

7.3.   Vegetation of southwestern Arkansas as mapped by Sargent   99

7.4.   Original distribution of blackland prairies and associated
       communities in southwestern Arkansas   104

7.5.   Landscape sites containing concentrations of blackland
       communities in southwestern Arkansas today   105

8.1.   Hypothesized blackland community distribution along
       soil-moisture and soil-depth gradients   142

8.2.   Hypothesized model of blackland plant community states
       and ecological processes   144

9.1.   Location of Jackson Prairie study areas, south-central
       Mississippi   147

10.1. Clay and Oktibbeha counties, in the Black Prairie of
       northeastern Mississippi   168

10.2. Site sizes for archaeological sites in the Mississippi
       Black Prairie   174

10.3. Distribution of longer-duration archaeological sites in
       Oktibbeha and Clay counties, Mississippi   177

10.4. Intensity of site use as measured by frequency of
       ceramic diagnostics   178

10.5. Distribution of shorter-duration archaeological sites in
       Oktibbeha and Clay counties, Mississippi   185

10.6. Number of shorter- and longer-duration assemblages by
       cultural period   186

10.7. Distribution of shorter-duration archaeological sites in

	eastern Oktibbeha County, Mississippi, in relation to chalk soils	191
11.1.	Black Belt of Mississippi and Alabama	196
11.2.	Surface-water features of the Black Prairie region	197
11.3.	1860 map showing place-names mentioning springs on the periphery of the Black Prairie	198
11.4.	Terrace deposits on the Black Prairie	199
11.5.	Possible Chickasaw water-collection pit at Tupelo, Mississippi	201
11.6.	Levee for a constructed impoundment	203
11.7.	Examples of Black Prairie "bottle cisterns"	204
11.8.	Depiction of hand-boring process and implements	205
11.9.	Distribution of deep artesian wells on the Black Prairie in 1928	206
11.10.	Hand pump used on the Black Prairie	207
11.11.	Windmill at West Point, Mississippi, manufactured in the late 1850s	208
11.12.	Rotary drilling rig mounted on a 1940s Studebaker truck	208
11.13.	Electrically powered, aboveground, rod-type pump	209
11.14.	Water association storage tank	209
12.1.	Mississippian world	213
12.2.	Gateway location of the Spiro site	215
12.3.	Biogeography of the Spiro, Nagle, and Sanders sites	220
12.4.	Probable range of Osage orange (*Maclura pomifera*) at the time of European contact	230
12.5.	Western part of the Spiroan trade network	231
13.1.	Location of Bienville National Forest, south-central Mississippi	240
14.1.	Location of Osborn Prairie, Oktibbeha County, Mississippi	248
14.2.	Number of pin-frame touches plotted as a function of actual biomass	250
15.1.	Starkville High School biogeography students conducting studies	260

List of Tables

2.1.   Lepidoptera in the Black Belt with localized distributions elsewhere in Mississippi   18

3.1.   Gastropods from Protohistoric and Historic contexts in the Mississippi Black Belt   34

4.1.   Indigenous fauna and certain preferred habitats for the Black Belt in Mississippi   53

4.2.   Small-mammal species from the Josey Farm and Yarborough sites   57

4.3.   Percentages of small-mammal NISP and MNI for archaeological sites in the Black Belt   60

5.1.   Pollen from the Yarborough site (22CL814)   69

5.2.   Charred plant remains from Late Mississippian contexts at the Yarborough site (22CL814)   70

5.3.   Plant impressions in daub from the Yarborough site (22CL814)   73

5.4.   Presence/absence of taxa revealed by different methods of environmental analysis at the Yarborough site (22CL814)   75

6.1.   Floristic information for four Louisiana prairies   87

6.2.   Longevity information for four central Louisiana prairies   87

6.3.   Rare Louisiana plant species that occur in prairies   89

9.1.   Common species in prairie openings in the Bienville National Forest of the Jackson Prairie region, Mississippi   149

9.2.   Study sites in the Jackson Prairie region of Mississippi   151

9.3.   Common flora in the Jackson Prairie remnants   153

9.4.   Midseason aboveground biomass production of the Jackson Prairie study sites   156

9.5.   Selected surface-soil properties in the Jackson Prairie study sites   157

9.6.   Root features of common prairie species at Harrell
       Prairie Hill   158

9.7.   Nutrient contents of diagnostic prairie species at Harrell
       Prairie Hill   158

9.8.   Family distributions in the Harrell Prairie Hill seed bank   159

9.9.   Emerged flora in the Harrell Prairie Hill seed bank   160

9.10. Selected soil properties of seed-bank soils at Harrell
       Prairie Hill   161

9.11. Correlation analysis between flora emergence and selected
       soil properties   161

10.1. Ceramic chronology for the central Tombigbee River valley   170

10.2. Pottery in assemblages from longer-duration sites   176

10.3. Pottery in assemblages from shorter-duration sites   179

14.1. A comparison of pre-treatment and post-treatment mean
       number of pin-frame touches via paired t-test   251

14.2. Sixty-year average, monthly precipitation, and departure from
       average for Mississippi State University weather station   252

14.3. Species with significant response to burning and mowing   252

16.1. Implementation options, strategies, and sources   268

Blackland Prairies of the Gulf Coastal Plain

1 Introduction

The Nature, Culture, and Sustainability of Blackland Prairies

EVAN PEACOCK AND TIMOTHY SCHAUWECKER

For centuries the prairie ecosystems of North America have held a special fascination for naturalists, historians, artists, and travelers. The extraordinary biotic richness, the endemic species, the sweeping vistas, the terrifying conflagrations, and the complex Native American cultures are but a few of the characteristics that continue to capture the popular imagination and invite scientific inquiry. That inquiry has tended to be segmented along disciplinary lines: botanists study plants, pedologists study soils, archaeologists study artifacts, and so on. Yet the prairies themselves cannot be understood in all their complexity unless practitioners of the different disciplines learn to communicate with one another. Does the nature and scale of prehistoric land use matter to a restoration ecologist? Can an archaeologist benefit from what a hydrologist has to say about soil-water retention capabilities in a prairie setting? Are historical land-use data relevant to modern conservation efforts? The answer to all of these questions is yes. We all can benefit from what others are doing, regardless of our special interests, if we can learn to bridge the interdisciplinary gaps that make communication difficult. This volume is an effort to build those bridges, or at least to sink a few pilings in that direction.

The North American grassland formation extends from Manitoba to Texas and from the Rocky Mountains to Indiana with a prairie/forest mosaic to the northeast and southeast (Packard and Mutel 1997). Weaver and Fitzpatrick (1934) were among the first to describe the North American prairie. Their survey covered midwestern (Nebraska, Iowa, Missouri) grasslands and described two major climax consociations. The big bluestem (*Andropogon gerardii*) and the little bluestem (*Schizachyrium scoparium*) consociations accounted for about 80 percent of the total grassland. The big bluestem type was found on wetter lowland soils and the little bluestem on dry upland soils. The *Stipa spartea* and *Sporobolus heterolepis* consociations were found on dry ridges and slopes and on dry uplands, respectively, and were minor in area compared with the bluestem types. Numerous subdominant grasses, sedges, and forbs were scattered among the dominant grasses. In the mid-1900s researchers focused on further descriptions of the North American grassland biome and its intricacies (Dodd 1968; Weaver 1954).

North American grasslands evolved under the influences of a combination of climate, fire, and grazing (Whittaker 1975). Climate is most important in the western edge of the biome, where the rain shadow of the Rocky Mountains causes a dry, short-grass prairie. Fire and grazing become more influential to the east. Lightning unaccompanied by precipitation can cause natural fires. Native Americans actively managing the landscape for hunting and other purposes also set fires. Tall- and mixed-grass prairie is associated with these fire-prone areas. Buffalo herds that once roamed the Midwest also contributed to habitat modification by grazing close to the ground. In river bottoms, hardwood vegetation resisted fire and, with the grasslands, formed a mosaic of vegetation that became increasingly woody to the east.

Less well known, both to the scientific community and the public, are the "blackland prairies" of the southeastern United States. The southern extensions of the North American prairie association are scattered across Texas (Collins et al. 1975; Diamond 1985), Arkansas (Foti 1974, 1989; Schauwecker 1996), Louisiana (M. MacRoberts and B. MacRoberts 1997a; M. MacRoberts et al., this volume), Mississippi (Morris et al. 1993; Schauwecker 1996; Leidolf and McDaniel 1998), Alabama (Jones and Patton 1966; Schuster and McDaniel 1974), and Georgia (Figure 1.1). These grasslands are found scattered among hardwood and pine/hardwood communities in the Gulf Coastal Plain. *Schizachyrium scoparium* (little bluestem) is generally the dominant associated grass. Many of the forbs found in the Midwest occur, as do some endemics and southern species.

Blackland prairies are found on limestone formations laid down in the shallow sea that covered the southeastern United States ca. 30 million years ago (DeSelm and Murdock 1993). Calcareous grasslands of this kind are isolated on the Gulf Coastal Plain in Texas, Arkansas, Mississippi, and Alabama. The general term describing these grasslands is "blackland" in Texas and Arkansas (Foti 1989); they are known collectively as the "Black Belt" (Mohr 1901; Stauffer 1961) or "Black Prairie" (Jones and Patton 1966) in Mississippi and Alabama. Early European travelers to these states were captivated by the parklike appearance of the grassland patches. For example, in 1708 Thomas Nairne described the Black Belt in northern Mississippi as "pleasant

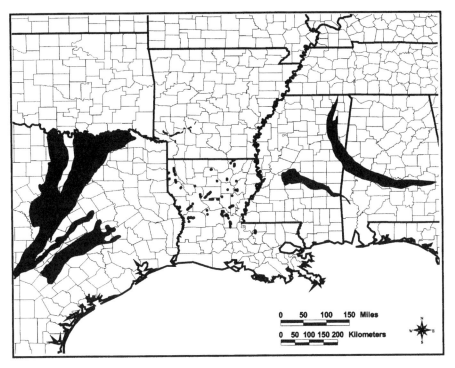

Fig. 1.1. Location of blackland prairies on the Gulf Coastal Plain of the southeastern United States as defined by floristics and pedology. (Louisiana prairies are not to scale.)

open forests of oak chestnuts and hickerery so intermixt with savannas as if it were a made landscape" (Moore 1988:57). David Taitt described the same province in Alabama as "appearing more like the works of art than of nature" (Taitt 1772). A number of early researchers understood that fossils from the underlying Cretaceous deposits were marine in origin (e.g., Adair 1930 [1775]; Nutt 1805, in Jennings 1947). More often than not, these fossils were explained by reference to the biblical Flood (e.g., Moore 1988:59—but for a more precocious account, see McGuire 1834:93, who said, "My own observations . . . have satisfied me, that the prairies once constituted the boundary of the Atlantic Ocean"). The extraordinary fertility of the alkaline soils was recognized early on: the Black Belt, for example, was a focus of slave-based cotton farming for planters leaving Virginia and the Carolinas following depletion of the soils from tobacco agriculture. A map showing slave populations in 1859 highlights the Black Belt as clearly as if it were a geologic map (Fogel 1989:Figure 10). During the American Civil War, the Black Belt was known as the "grainery" or "Corn Belt of the Confederacy" (Wilson 1981).

A more unfortunate characteristic of the blackland prairie ecosystems is their vulnerability. Historical data indicate that these communities have suffered various types and degrees of anthropogenic disturbance (Collins et al. 1975; Foti 1974; Jones and Patton 1966; Peacock 1992; Peacock and Miller 1990). The northeastern Mississippi Black Belt and the southwestern Arkansas blackland prairies once covered about 300,000 ha (estimated from Jones and Patton 1966) and 148,000 ha (Roberts 1979), respectively (cf. Foti et al., this volume; Schauwecker and MacDonald, this volume). Heavy agricultural pressure has reduced native prairie in both regions; today, very little remains. Small patches (0.5–5.0 ha) of relict prairie can be found in abandoned pastures, along roadsides, in power line rights-of-way, and in public and private natural areas. Prairie patches in Louisiana have undergone similar degradation (MacRoberts et al., this volume). If ignored, these relict patches will continue to degrade, and the southeastern arm of the central North American grasslands will likely be lost. Understanding the community composition of these small prairies is of paramount importance for their perpetuation and restoration.

Unlike most of their midwestern counterparts, southeastern prairies developed on limestone formations. Our historical database concerning their flora and fauna is limited (e.g., as to the extent of bison in the Black Belt physiographic province—Johnson et al. 1994), as is our contemporary understanding of these ecosystems. Only a handful of ecological site descriptions exist for the Mississippi and Arkansas blackland prairies, for example. Also poorly understood are the similarities and differences between blackland prairie systems. While several prairies in southwestern Arkansas and northeastern Mississippi have been surveyed floristically (Foti 1989; Jones and Patton 1966; Leidolf and McDaniel 1998; Schuster and McDaniel 1974), comprehensive descriptions and gradient analyses have been lacking. Quantitative investigations in the southeastern coastal plain of Texas identified seven different grassland types associated with climate and soil gradients as one moves from east to west (Diamond 1985; Diamond and Smeins 1988). These prairies are from 1 to 6° latitude south of the Mississippi prairies. Thirty-year average yearly rainfall data indicate that the east Texas prairies receive 85.6 cm of rain, Arkansas prairies 129.2 cm, and Mississippi prairies 141.9 cm (National Oceanic and Atmospheric Administration [NOAA] 1999). The average daily temperature is 3.7°C higher in Texas than in Mississippi (NOAA 1999). Perhaps most important, Texas prairie physiognomy is more flat and lowland in character than that of Mississippi prairies. Foti (1989) suggested that the Arkansas and Mississippi/Alabama prairies should be similar based on these climatic and edaphic factors. The direction of the geologic outcrop is one major difference between the sites in Arkansas and Mississippi. Both areas are found on cuestas of Cretaceous limestone, but they generally face south in Arkansas and east-northeast in Mississippi.

General lack of knowledge concerning such variability was one reason we organized a multidisciplinary conference on blackland prairie ecosystems. This conference was held on May 19 and 20, 2000, at Mississippi State University, and most of the papers in this volume were presented there. The papers are organized into the three categories proffered in the title: nature, culture, and sustainability. This has been done primarily for the convenience of readers interested in particular aspects of the natural or cultural history of blackland prairies. In practice, such divisions are arbitrary, and we hope this volume will stimulate interdisciplinary communication rather than a focus on particular natural or cultural characteristics of blackland prairies. The categories actually serve to emphasize some particularly important connections: under the section Sustainability, for example, are papers on planning (by Tom Schurch), education, restoration, and conservation efforts (Dean Elsen and Ronald Wieland; Tim Schauwecker and John MacDonald; Sherrill Wiygul, Kay Krans, Richard Brown, and Victor Maddox). As Redclift (1991) has pointed out, "sustainability" means different things to different people: when combined with "development," it becomes what Wilbanks (1994:541) has characterized as an "oxymoronic" slogan rather than "a basis for either theory or action." However oxymoronic it might sound, sustainable development—if such a thing is achievable in the long term—is preferable to uncontrolled development in any event. Owing to their unique geological and geomorphological characteristics, blackland prairies tend to be a focus for particular kinds of development. The Black Prairie of Mississippi, for example, was seriously considered as a site for the Superconducting Supercollider because of its geological stability. The impermeability of the chalk substrate has led to the emplacement of large landfills in recent years. Hundreds of catfish ponds have been excavated in the Black Belt in Alabama and Mississippi because the chalk substrate, besides being impermeable, obviates the need for liming the water. Whether such development is "sustainable" in the long term remains to be seen: assessing its impacts necessitates adopting the holistic approach advocated in this volume.

Under Nature, Richard Brown uses insect biogeography to posit past prairie connections between the Midwest and the Southeast. The use of archaeological faunal remains for paleoenvironmental modeling is covered by Evan Peacock and Rebecca Melsheimer (terrestrial gastropods) and S. Homes Hogue (small-mammal remains). Peacock and Mary Celeste Reese compare three different types of data on plant remains from archaeological contexts, examining questions of bias and interpretive scale and how they affect attempts to mesh different data sets at a particular site. Michael MacRoberts, Barbara MacRoberts, and Lynn Stacey Jackson provide a much-needed overview of the little-known blackland prairies of northern Louisiana. Their paper demonstrates how historical data help to inform us about the development of contemporary ecological settings. Tom Foti, Scott Simon, Douglas Zollner, and Meryl Hattenbach offer a similar overview of blackland prairies in southwestern Arkansas, following which Zollner, Simon, and Foti present a plant community classification for the Arkansas prairies, a valuable contribution toward the management of those fragile ecosystems. Louis Moran, Dave Pettry, and Richard Switzer discuss the role of soil in shaping the floristic makeup of the Jackson Prairie in south-central Mississippi.

Under Culture, Janet Rafferty considers how environmental constraints shaped prehistoric settlement patterns on the Mississippi Black Prairie. Darrel Schmitz, Charles L. Wax, and Evan Peacock complement Rafferty's work by discussing the influence of the most critical resource—water—on Black Prairie settlement patterns to the current day. Frank F. Schambach presents a sophisticated, broad-scale analysis of how the natural resources of blackland prairies helped to shape Native American lifeways over most of the last millennium.

About half of the papers in this volume focus on the Black Belt prairie of northeastern Mississippi. We hope the range of topics on the Black Belt—entymology, archaeology, hydrology, biology, ecology, land management, public education—will demonstrate how the collaborative efforts of practitioners in different disciplines, using different approaches and different scales, can yield a greater appreciation and understanding of prairie landscapes in a given area.

Acknowledgments. We would like to thank the participants in the blackland prairies conference held at Mississippi State University, especially those who contributed papers to this volume. The conference was sponsored by the Department of Biological Sciences, the Cobb Institute of Archaeology, and the Anthropology Program at MSU. We would like to thank Dr. Donald Downer, Gloria Blankenship, Joanne Cotton, and Tom Tidwell, all with the Department of Biological Sciences at MSU, and Dr. Joe Seger, director of the Cobb Institute of Archaeology, for their support. Evan Weiher helped initiate the conference, and Kathy Elliott and Homes Hogue helped with the local arrangements. Ron Wieland provided a base map used to help construct Figure 1.1. The authors would like to thank Jason Giessow of DENDRA Inc., Encinitas, California, for additional help with the figures. Janet Rafferty read and provided comments on Chapters 5 and 17. We would like to thank the reviewers of the manuscript for their constructive criticism. Timothy Schauwecker would like to thank Erinn Holloway for her love and encouragement. We are grateful to Kristin King for her hard work as copyeditor, no easy task in a multidisciplinary work such as this. We also would like to thank the many researchers who, over the years, expressed an interest in a conference on the unique black-land prairie ecosystems of the Gulf Coastal Plain. We hope this volume will repay that interest in some small manner.

I NATURE

2 Paleoenvironment and Biogeography of the Mississippi Black Belt

Evidence from Insects

RICHARD L. BROWN

GRASSLANDS IN THE SOUTHEASTERN UNITED STATES

Grass-dominated communities occur in a variety of edaphic and climatic conditions in the southeastern United States, as reviewed and characterized by DeSelm and Murdock (1993). A diversity of upland grasslands are present in the upper Coastal Plain and interior areas of the region, including serpentine barrens in the Piedmont (Radford 1948), barrens and cedar glades on limestone in Kentucky, Tennessee, and elsewhere (Dicken 1935; Quarterman 1950, 1986; Somers 1986; Baskin et al. 1994; Chester et al. 1997), the Grand Prairie on alluvial soils in Arkansas (Foti et al., this volume; Zollner et al., this volume; Irving et al. 1980), and the blackland prairies, which occur in Texas, Arkansas, Mississippi, and Alabama (Foti 1989; DeSelm and Murdock 1993; Schauwecker 1996; Leidolf and McDaniel 1998).

THE BLACK BELT OF MISSISSIPPI AND ALABAMA

The largest of the blackland prairies, as well the most southeastern grassland of the tall prairie type, is the Black Belt of Mississippi and Alabama (Figure 2.1). This crescent-shaped region has a width up to 40 km and extends more than 500 km from McNairy County, Tennessee, south across east-central Mississippi and east to Russell County, Alabama; it covers more than 14,141 square km (Brent 1973; Harper 1943; Schauwecker 1996; Schiefer 1998). The Black Belt is situated near the northeastern and northern border of the Gulf Coastal Plain in Mississippi and Alabama, respectively, and underlies the eastern border of the Mississippi embayment. The Black Belt was formed on soils that

Fig. 2.1. Black Belt (solid gray) and Jackson Prairie (hatched) in Mississippi and Alabama. Dots indicate sampling sites for insect survey.

originated from Demopolis chalk of the Selma group, which dates to the Upper Cretaceous (Stephenson and Monroe 1940; Kaye 1974).

Much of the Black Belt includes a mosaic of three plant communities: open prairie, chalk outcrops, and forest (Leidolf and McDaniel 1998) (Figure 2.2). The open prairie and chalk outcrops include many species widely occurring in the eastern United States, but which in Mississippi are restricted to the Black Belt or also to the Jackson Prairie in the central area of the state, for example, *Agalinus auriculata* (Michx.), *Silphium terebinthinaceum, S. laciniatum* L., and *Rhamnus lanceolata* Pursh. The Black Belt also includes species that occur primarily in the Great Plains, for example, *Bouteloua curtipendula* (Michx.), *Agalinus oligophylla* Pennell, *Heliotropium tenellum* (Nutt.), *Neptunia lutea* (Leavenw.), *Dalea candida* Michx., *D. purpurea* Vent., *Arnoglossum plantagineum* Raf., *Galium virgatum* Nutt., *Aster sericeus* Vent., *Evax prolifera* Nutt., *Crataegus engelmanni* Sarg., and *Spiranthes magnicamporum* Sheviak.

Six forest communities have been identified in the Black Belt: xeric post-oak ridges, mesic oak-hickory forests, bottomland hardwood for-

Fig. 2.2. Obsorn Prairie in Oktibbeha County, Mississippi, with *Schizachyrium scoparium,* little bluestem, in foreground bordered by Demopolis chalk exposed by erosion and *Juniperus virginiana* mixed with woodland in background.

ests, water tupelo swamps, mixed hardwood gallery forests, and prairie cedar woodlands, the latter appearing to be a recent feature resulting from the absence of fire and grazing (Leidolf and McDaniel 1998). *Quercus durandii* Buckl. and *Carya myristiciformis* (Michx.) are relatively common in oak-hickory forests in the Black Belt, although these species are rare or localized elsewhere in their ranges.

Lowe (1921) considered prairie to be historically more extensive than forest. Based on analysis of a land survey of Sumter County, Alabama, in 1832, Jones and Patton (1966) concluded that 23.4 percent of the 112,588 ha in the Black Belt of that county had few or no trees, 14.5 percent had relatively dense forest (296 trees/ha), and 62.1 percent had forest of intermediate density, with some of the latter having savanna vegetation. They further showed that open prairie was associated with alkaline soils, whereas dense forests were associated with acidic soils. Jones and Patton also reported that areas designated as prairie in the 1832 survey ranged in size from 7 to 2024 ha. Most of the Black Belt was converted to agriculture by the late 1800s, leaving only small remnants of prairies, forests, and chalk outcrops, with many of the latter being highly eroded.

HISTORY OF GRASSLANDS IN
THE SOUTHEASTERN UNITED STATES

According to Axelrod (1985), extensive grasslands developed in mid-continental North America about 75 million years before present (B.P.) during the driest part of the Tertiary, which resulted in a restriction of forests and woodlands and a radiation of grasses and forbs. Geographic ranges of grasslands contracted and expanded many times during the glacial and interglacial periods of the Quaternary period (Braun 1928; H. Delcourt et al. 1986). Between the warm, dry late Altonian stadial, which ended about 28,000 years B.P., and the Farmdalian interstadial, which ended about 23,000 years B.P., prairies, glades, and other grasslands were present across the Great Plains (Watts and Bright 1968; Watts and Wright 1966; Graham and Heimsch 1960), an open parkland of jack pine was present in the Ozarks (King 1973), and xeric oak-pine forests and dry prairies covered the eastern side of the Mississippi Alluvial Valley (P. Delcourt 1978). Fossil pollen records indicate that prairies or glades also were present in northwestern Georgia before 30,000 years B.P. (Watts 1973).

During the Wisconsin glacial maximum (20,000–15,000 years B.P.), woodlands and grasslands in the Central Plains and upper Atlantic Coast were replaced largely by a boreal forest between approximately latitude 34°N and the tundra bordering the Laurentide ice sheet (Axelrod 1985; Whitehead 1967; Watts 1980a; H. Delcourt 1979; P. Delcourt and H. Delcourt 1993). South of latitude 33°N, much of the southern Atlantic and Gulf coastal plains were covered by the southeastern evergreen forest, of which oak species were an important component; however, peninsular Florida was occupied by sand scrub that was not replaced by the evergreen forest until about 10,000 B.P. (Watts 1975; P. Delcourt and H. Delcourt 1993). Boreal species of spruce and larch extended south along the Mississippi Alluvial Valley to the Tunica Hills of Louisiana, separating jack pine populations in the Appalachian Mountains from those in the Ozarks and Great Plains (P. Delcourt and H. Delcourt 1977, 1993; P. Delcourt 1978).

The southern Great Plains in Texas and northern Mexico have been cited as areas where open grasslands may have been present during the glacial maximum (Ross 1970; Hoffman and Jones 1970), but prairie vegetation was present in other areas of the eastern United States. The dominant vegetation in southeastern North Carolina during full glaciation was probably an open jack or red pine forest with a savanna having many heliophytic herbs (Frey 1953; Whitehead 1967); similarly, in central South Carolina, a mosaic of jack pine, spruce, and prairies was present (Watts 1980b).

As the glacial ice retreated from 16,000 to 10,000 years B.P., the boreal forest migrated northward and prairie vegetation moved into the central and southern Great Plains (P. Delcourt and H. Delcourt 1993). Scattered grasslands in oak woodland became established in the Great Plains sometime after 8,300 years B.P., but the regional open prairie, as described by the early settlers, was not formed until less than 5,000 years B.P. (Axelrod 1985). The southeastern evergreen forest maintained its floristic composition and geographic range with no major relocations of warm temperate taxa (P. Delcourt and H. Delcourt 1993). Wells (1970a) presented evidence that a mosaic of sclerophyllous oak woodland and small patches of prairie, with herbs characteristic of the prairie in the upper Midwest, was present in southeastern Georgia and north-central Florida about 8,500–5,000 years B.P. After 5,000 B.P., the upland herb communities in Georgia and Florida were eliminated, and longleaf pine forest replaced oak. Longleaf pine and associated savannas eventually extended from eastern Texas to southeastern Virginia.

During the Hypsithermal interval of postglacial warming and drying between 9,000 and 4,000 years B.P., the prairie region extended farther eastward from the Central Plains states, forming a prairie peninsula extending northward through Illinois into the Great Lakes region and southward into southeastern Missouri (Transeau 1935; King and Allen 1977; Axelrod 1985; P. Delcourt and H. Delcourt 1993). Relict prairies in southern Ontario have many species of Homoptera (Hamilton 1998), sawflies (Goulet 1998), and Lepidoptera (Lafontaine 1998) that are disjunct from the Great Plains. Evidence that a prairie corridor extended from the Great Plains to the upper Atlantic Coast is provided by species of *Euxoa* (Noctuidae) (Lafontaine 1982) as well as by the presence of bison and prairie chickens in Historic times.

Given the dry conditions that promoted expansion of grasslands during the period 7–5 million years B.P., it is possible that prairie vegetation became established in the Black Belt of Mississippi and Alabama as well as in other inland locations in the Gulf Coastal Plain following the mid-Tertiary retreat of the Mississippi embayment. If prairie vegetation was present in the Black Belt at the end of the Tertiary, it is probable that it persisted in varying degrees of size and continuity throughout much of the Pleistocene. Prairie vegetation appears to have been historically restricted to certain soil types, rather than being climatically determined. Core samples of pollen and plant macrofossils from Goshen, Alabama, about 32 km south of the Demopolis chalk where prairie vegetation occurs, do not show evidence of prairie vegetation from 33,000 years B.P. to present (P. Delcourt 1978).

Although core samples for pollen have not been taken from within the Black Belt, vertebrate fossil assemblages from 33,000 to 16,000 years B.P. document a rich fauna of grazers (e.g., six species of *Equus*, mammoth, buffalo, and camel) and browsers (e.g., mastodon, sloth, peccary, and deer) (Kaye 1974). Fossils of the horselike animals were more abundant than fossils of all other animals combined. Notably, fossils of three of the six species of *Equus* occurring in the Black Belt have been found elsewhere only in the Great Plains. Likewise, the extinct bear, *Arctodus simus,* occurred in the Great Plains and western states, and the only records from the eastern United States are from Pennsylvania and the Black Belt. This combination of browsers and grazers, with the latter dominating, suggests that grasses with a mixture of trees and shrubs covered the Black Belt during the Sangamon interglacial and Wisconsin glacial stages. Additionally, the presence of western species of vertebrates suggests that a grassland or savanna corridor existed between the Great Plains and the Black Belt before the Wisconsin glacial stage.

INSECT SURVEYS IN THE BLACK BELT

Records of insects from the Mississippi Black Belt before 1990 are relatively few and scattered. Most collections consist of various insects found during the 1920s in Oktibbeha County or of moths found during the period 1967–1972 in Lee County. During the period 1990–1995 the Mississippi Entomological Museum conducted a survey of selected insects in prairie and oak-hickory forest habitats of the Black Belt in Chickasaw, Clay, Oktibbeha, Lowndes, and Kemper counties. Since 1995, collections of insects in the Black Belt have concentrated primarily on sites in Oktibbeha County. In addition to collections by hand and net, samples were obtained from malaise traps for flying insects, blacklights for nocturnal insects, and pitfall traps for ground-crawling insects. Quantified samples of macrolepidoptera were taken at two prairie remnants and an oak-hickory forest to determine abundance and diversity. More than 35,000 specimens of bees, moths, and selected beetles, in addition to a large number of other insects, have been collected in the Black Belt since 1990. A survey of the bees in the Black Belt is in progress.

Data to determine distributions of species in areas outside the Black Belt were obtained primarily from published records, holdings in the Mississippi Entomological Museum (more than 900,000 specimens of insects from Mississippi, Alabama, Tennessee, Arkansas, and Louisiana), and the collection of Bryant Mather (more than 190,000 specimens of moths from Mississippi). The combined records of these two collections are based on extensive surveys in 9 of the 11 physiographic regions of Mississippi; only the Pontotoc Hills adjacent to the Black Belt in northeastern Mississippi and the Barrier Islands have been poorly sampled. These data were supplemented by collection records of John G. Franclemont, Morton S. Adams, D. G. Ferguson, Ed Knudson, J. Bolling Sullivan, Howard Grisham, and Tim McCabe, and by specimen data obtained at the following institutions: Auburn University, Cornell University, Florida Division of Plant Industry (Collection of Arthropods), Louisiana State University, Kansas State University, University of Georgia, University of Kansas, and the U.S. National Museum.

UNIQUENESS OF THE BLACK BELT FAUNA

SPECIES RICHNESS

Uniqueness of a fauna in a physiographic region is due to several combined factors, including species richness and the presence of uncommon and localized species, endemic species, and species with disjunct distributions. The moth fauna exemplifies the species richness of the Black Belt. Collections in prairie and forest habitats of the Black Belt have yielded 1,021 species of moths as well as many species yet to be identified; this number represents slightly more than half of the species of moths known to occur in Mississippi. Of the total collected, 780 species were collected in prairie sites, although some of these feed on hosts in forests and peripheral habitats. Quantified samples of selected larger moths, the macrolepidoptera, were taken in two prairie sites and one oak-hickory forest site on six dates, and all species were identified and counted. These 18 samples included 544 species and documented higher species richness in the oak-hickory forest than in the prairie. The samples from a forest at Crawford, Mississippi, included 282 species, whereas the six samples from the adjacent prairie site in Crawford included 171 species and those from the Osborn Prairie in Oktibbeha County included 130 species.

LOCALIZED SPECIES

Although species richness of moths is lower in the prairie than forest habitat, 50 of the 59 uncommon and geographically localized species were collected most frequently in prairie sites (Table 2.1). Most of these species have broad geographic ranges in the eastern or southeastern United States and into the Great Plains, but in Mississippi many are restricted to the Black Belt. Some occur also in the Jackson Prairie region and in Gulf Coastal counties (Hancock, Harrison, Jackson). The arctiid moth, *Cycnia inopinatus* (Hy. Edw.), for example, is considered uncommon throughout its range from New Jersey to Florida and west to South Dakota and Texas (Covell 1984). However, *C. inopinatus* is abundant in the Black Belt, where more than 100 specimens have been collected. Elsewhere in Mississippi, this species is known from one specimen from the Jackson Prairie and three specimens from the Gulf Coast.

Of the 59 species identified as having localized distributions in the

Table 2.1. Lepidoptera in the Black Belt with localized distributions elsewhere in Mississippi

Lepidoptera Species	Number MS Records	Distribution	Hosts
Arctiidae			
Crambidia pura B. & McD.	51 BB, 1 JP	E, GP	lichens* (1)
Cycnia inopinatus (Hy. Edw.)	103 BB, 1 JP, 3 GC	E, GP	*Asclepias* spp. (1)
Cosmopterygidae			
Triclonella determinatella (Zell.)	16BB	GC, GP	unknown
Crambidae			
Argyria nummulalis Hbn.	48 BB, 5 JP, 1 GC	E, GP	grasses* (3)
Crambus new species	42 BB	BB endemic	grasses*
Hileithia rehamalis (Dyar)	6 BB	GP	unknown
Mecyna submedialis (Grt.)	20 BB	GP	unknown
Thaumatopsis edonis (Grt.)	65 BB, 4 JP	E, GP	grasses*
Thaumatopsis pexella (Zell.)	10 BB, 1 JP	E, GP	grasses* (3)
Elachistidae			
Elachista ciligera Kaila	1 BB (f)	BB endemic	grasses or sedges*
Epiplemidae			
Callizzia amorata Pack.	6 BB (f), 1 M	E, GP	*Lonicera canadensis* Bartr. (4)
Gelechiidae			
Dichomeris citrifoliella (Cham.)	3 BB	GC, GP	*Citrus* spp., *Xanthoxylum* spp. (5)
Dichomeris costarufoella (Cham.)	8 BB, 1 M	GC, GP	*Rudbeckia* sp. (5)
Dichomeris gleba Hodges	1 BB	GP	*Eupatorium* sp. or *Solidago* sp.? (5)
Dichomeris glenni Clarke	4 BB (f)	GC, GP	unknown
Dichomeris mimesis Hodges	3 BB	GC, GP	unknown
Helcystogramma ectopon Hodges	4 BB	GP	unknown
Naera fuscocristatella Cham.	38 BB	GP	unknown
Neodactylota liguritrix Hodges	12 BB	GP	unknown
Geometridae			
Apodrepanulatrix liberaria (Wlk.)	1 BB, 2 JP	E	*Ceanothus americanus* L. (6)
Erastria coloraria (F.)	4 BB, 1 JP, 3 GC, 1M	E, GP	*Ceanothus americanus* L., *Rubus* spp. (7).
Eusarca fundaria (Gn.)	3 BB, 3 GC	GC, GP	unknown
Leptostales ferruminaria (Zell.)	37 BB (f)	E, GP	unknown
Lytrosis heitzmanorum Rindge	17 BB (f)	GP	*Quercus* spp.*
Pimaphera sparsaria (Wlk.)	37 BB (f), 4 M	SE	unknown
Tornos cinctarius Hulst	2 BB, 4 GC	AC, GC	Asteraceae*
Noctuidae			
Agnorisma bollii (Grt.)	2 BB, 12 JP	E[a], GP	unknown
Amolita roseola Sm.	38 BB, 6 JP, 14 GC, 3 M	AC, GC	grasses*
Catocala alabamae Grt. (7)	3 BB, 3 JP, 4 GC, 1 M	SE	*Prunus angustifolia* Mar., *Crataegus*
Cucullia alfarata Stkr.	1 BB	E	*Aster ericoides* L. (8)
Hemeroplanis habitalis (Wlk.)	113 BB (f), 2 JP, 2 GC, 1 M	GC, GP	unknown
Homohadena infixa (Wlk.)	2 BB (f)	E, GP	*Juglans nigra* L. (7)
Leucania subpuncata (Harv.)	1 BB, 11 GC	AC, GC	grasses*
Lithophane lemmeri (B. & Benj.)	2 BB	AC, GC	unknown

Black Belt, 20 have unknown hosts, 15 are known or suspected (based on known hosts of related species) to feed on Asteraceae, and six feed on grasses (Table 2.1). Three localized species are known to feed on thorny plants: *Catocala alabamae* Grt. on Chickasaw plum and haw-thorn, *Ceratomia hageni* on Osage orange, and *Dichomeris citrifoliella* (Cham.) on prickly ash.

Table 2.1 (cont'd)

Lepidoptera Species	Number MS Records	Distribution	Hosts
Phytometra ernestinana (Blanch.)	194 BB, 2 JP, 1 GC, 3 M	AC, GC, GP	unknown
Plagiomimicus pitychromus Grt.	10 BB, 4 JP, 3 M	E, GP	*Ambrosia trifida* L.(9)
Properigea tapeta (Sm.)	3 BB, 22 GC, 2 M	AC, GC, GP	unknown
Schinia grandimena Hdwk.	3 BB	GP	Asteraceae*
Spargaloma sexpunctata Grt.	6 BB (f), 1 JP, 1 M	E, GP	*Apocynum* spp. (10)
Nototontidae			
Schizura badia (Pack.)	4 BB	E	*Viburnum* spp. (11).
Pyralidae			
Tampa dimediatella Rag.	11 BB, 5 JP, 38 GC, 5 M	AC, GC	unknown
Sesiidae			
Euhagena emphytiformis (Wlk.)	1 BB	AC, GC, GP, W	*Gaura filipes* Spach, *Erigeron* sp. (12, 16)
Sphingidae			
Ceratomia hageni Grt.	327 BB, 42 JP, 127 M	E[b], GP	*Maclura pomifera* (Raf.) (13)
Proserpinus gaurae (J.E. Sm.)	3 BB	SE, GP	*Oenothera* spp, *Epilobium* spp. (13)
Tortricidae			
Ancylis semiovana (Zell.)	3 BB	E, GP	unknown
Cudonigera houstonana (Grt.)	19 BB	W, AC. GP	*Juniperus* spp. (14)
Epiblema iowana McD.	2 BB	GP	*Ratibida pinnata* (Venten.)
Epinotia nonana (Kft.)	1 BB	E[c], GP	unknown
Eucosma fiskeana Kft.	3 BB	AC, GC, GP	Asteraceae*
Eucosma fulminana (Wlsm.)	55 BB	GP	Asteraceae*
Eucosma giganteana (Riley)	104 BB	AC, GP	*Silphium* spp. (15)
Eucosma graciliana Kft.	36 BB	AC, GP	Asteraceae*
Eucosma matutina (Grt.)	8 BB, 1 JP, 1 M	E, GP	Asteraceae*
Eucosma ridingsana (Rob.)	13 BB	GP	*Gutierrezia* spp. (15,17)
Phaneta annetteana (Kft.)	5 BB	E, GP	Asteraceae*
Phaneta autumnana (McD.)	13 BB	E, GP	Asteraceae*
Phaneta canusana Wright	10 BB	AC, GP	Asteraceae*
Phaneta stramineana (Wlsm.)	12 BB	AC, GC, GP	Asteraceae*
Phaneta verna Miller	41 BB	E, GP	Asteraceae*

Note: Number of Mississippi (MS) records represents those known from the Black Belt (BB), with species more abundant in forest than prairie indicated by (f), Jackson Prairie (JP), Lower Gulf Coastal Plain (GC), and remainder of Mississippi (M). Distribution in the United States outside the Black Belt is indicated by E (east of Mississippi River), W (west of Mississippi River), SE (southeastern states), GC (Lower Gulf Coastal Plain), AC (Atlantic Coastal Plain), and GP (Great Plains). References for hosts are given at the bottom of the table; suspected* hosts are based on known hosts of related species.

[a]*Agnorisma bollii :* Southern Ohio to Mississippi, western Arkansas, Kansas.

[b]*Ceratoma hageni :* localized from Texas to Missouri and east to Ohio and Mississippi, the latter with records from three counties outside the Black Belt and Jackson Prairie.

[c]*Epinotia nonana:* only Michigan and New York in East.

(1) Forbes 1960; (2) J.G. Franclemont, Department of Entomology, Cornell University, personal communication 2000; (3) Fernald 1896; (4) Brower 1974; (5) Hodges 1986; (6) Rindge 1949; (7) Covell 1984; (8) Poole 1995; (9) Crumb 1956; (10) Forbes 1954; (11) Forbes 1948; (12) Eichlin and Duckworth 1988; (13) Hodges 1971; (14) Powell and Obraztsov 1977; (15) Heinrich 1923; (16) R. Brown, unpublished data; (17) Hetz and Werner 1979.

ENDEMIC SPECIES

Two species of beetles are known only from the Black Belt of Mississippi and Alabama. *Cyclotrechelus hypherpiformis* (Freitag 1969) (Carabidae) is a large, flightless ground beetle that was described from prairies in Dallas County, Alabama, and unknown sites near the campus of Mississippi State University. This beetle is common in prairie remnants at Osborn and Crawford, Mississippi. The May beetle, *Phyllophaga davisi* Langston (Scarabaeidae), historically was known only from the Black Belt and adjacent areas in Oktibbeha County, Mississippi, where adults were recorded as feeding on oak (Langston 1927). This species was recently collected near the Alabama River in Monroe County, Alabama, about 60 km south of the Black Belt. This species probably was originally endemic to the Black Belt with a subsequent dispersal southward in Alabama. Although adults of *P. davisi* feed on oak leaves, larvae of all *Phyllophaga* feed on roots of grasses; thus a mixed habitat of grasses and forest favors this species.

Two species of moths are known only from the Black Belt. An undescribed species of *Neodactria* (Crambidae), a relatively large moth, has been collected only at the Osborn Prairie. Species of *Neodactria* and related genera, commonly known as sod webworms, feed on the lower leaves and stems of grasses, but the grass host of the new species is unknown. *Elachista ciligera* Kaila (Elachistidae) was described from a single specimen collected in the oak-hickory forest adjacent to a prairie remnant at Crawford, Mississippi (Kaila 1996). All species of *Elachista* with known hosts feed on grasses and sedges.

Disjunct Species

Disjunctions between the Black Belt and the Great Plains have been documented recently for some insects, and additional disjunctions are noted here (Table 2.1). The bee, *Xenoglossodes albata* (Cresson) (Anthophoridae), occurs in prairie remnants in Oktibbeha and Lowndes counties, where it is a pollinator of prairie clover, *Dalea purpureum* (Vent.) (MacGown and Schiefer 1992). In the Great Plains, this bee occurs from Colorado to Texas and South Dakota and as far east as Illinois. Four species of longhorned beetles (Cerambycidae) are disjunct between the Black Belt and the Great Plains: *Ataxia brunnea* Champ. & Knull (Minnesota to Illinois and Texas), *Mecas rotundicollis* (Thom.) (Oklahoma to Arizona and south to Guatemala), *Tetraopes femoratus* Lec. (throughout the Great Basin and Great Plains south to central Mexico), and *Tetraopes texanus* Horn (Missouri, Oklahoma to northern Mexico) (Schiefer 1998). Hosts of *A. brunnea* and *M. rotundicollis* are unknown, but species related to both feed on a variety of herbaceous plants. Hosts of *T. femoratus* and *T. texanus* are milkweeds, *Asclepias* spp., and in the Black Belt both species were found primarily on *A. viridis* Walt.

Ten species of moths (Lepidoptera) have been collected in the Black Belt that occur elsewhere only in the Great Plains and western areas. These include four species of Gelechiidae—*Dichomeris gleba* Hodges (Illinois, northwestern Arkansas, Missouri), *Helcystogramma ectopon* Hodges (Nebraska), *Naera fuscocristatella* Cham. (western United

States), and *Neodactylota liguritrix* Hodges (Texas); three species of Tortricidae—*Epiblema iowana* McD. (Missouri and Illinois, Iowa, Minnesota), *Eucosma fulminana* (Wlsm.) (Wisconsin, Illinois, Iowa, Kansas, Texas), and *Eucosma ridingsana* (Rob.) (Texas to Manitoba, west to Washington and California); one species of Crambidae—*Hileithia rehamalis* (Dyar) (Arizona to Texas); and one species of Noctuidae— *Schinia grandimedia* Hardwick (Kansas to Texas, west to Colorado and New Mexico). The preceding species are associated with the prairie habitat, and five are known or suspected to feed on members of Asteraceae (Hardwick 1996; Heinrich 1923; Hodges 1986). A single species of Geometridae, *Lytrosis heitzmanorum* (Rindge 1971), is disjunct between scrub oak habitat in the Black Belt near Tupelo, Mississippi, and similar habitat in central Missouri, northwestern Arkansas, and eastern Texas.

Species of insects that occur only in the Black Belt and either Jackson Prairie or the Gulf Coast within Mississippi also occur in the Atlantic Coastal Plain, the Great Plains, or both. No species of moths are known to be disjunct between the Black Belt and either Jackson Prairie or the Gulf Coast. Many species of insects are known to have a Gulf Coast–Great Plains distribution without occurring in the Black Belt.

DISCUSSION

Various authors, as reviewed by Axelrod (1985), have noted that relatively few plants and animals are endemic to the Central Plains, but rather the Plains biota originated from other areas of the United States. One refugium for grassland species during the Wisconsin glaciation may have been the Black Belt. Grass-feeding leafhoppers now occurring in the Great Plains are thought to have survived the Wisconsin glaciation in southern Texas and northern Mexico as well as in isolated grass patches elsewhere, although grasslands in the southeastern United States were not mentioned specifically (Ross 1970). Howden (1966) considered the majority of the 200 *Phyllophaga* species in North America to be derived from two Pleistocene refugia, one in Mexico and one in the southeastern United States. Larvae of all species of *Phyllophaga* feed on roots of grasses, and adults feed on foliage of herbaceous plants and deciduous trees (Ratcliffe 1991). Of the 32 species of *Phyllophaga* in Nebraska treated by Ratcliffe, four occur either in the southern Great Plains or southwestern United States, and 21 occur in Mississippi and other southeastern states. Nebraska and the Black Belt share 17 species, and although these species occur in other areas of Mississippi, some are more abundant in the Black Belt than elsewhere (Paul Lago, Department of Biology, University of Mississippi, personal communication 2000).

The possibility that the Black Belt was a Pleistocene refugium for grassland species is supported by its distinctive moth fauna, which includes many localized species that are uncommon in their ranges outside of the Black Belt. Of the 59 species listed in Table 2.1, two are endemic in the Black Belt, 10 occur only in the Great Plains and the Black Belt, and 38 occur in the Great Plains, Black Belt, and other locations in the eastern United States. The faunistic affinity of the Black Belt with the Great Plains is supported by these shared species.

The flightless ground beetle, *Cyclotrechelus hypheripiformis*, was placed in a species group by itself because its relationships with other species were unclear (Freitag 1969). However, Freitag considered *C. hypheripiformis* to be phylogenetically close to the *C. seximpressus* species group. The four species in the latter group occur in the Great Plains; one of these species occurs from Texas to Alabama on the Gulf Coast. If these two species groups are sister taxa, this phylogenetic relationship would indicate a past connection of similar habitat between the Black Belt and the Great Plains that was occupied by the ancestral species and subsequently broken to isolate the derived *C. hypheripiformis* from western relatives.

Hosts of other endemic species suggest that the Black Belt was formerly a mixture of prairie and forest. The hosts of *Elachista ciligera* and the new species of *Neodactria* are unknown, but all other species in these genera feed on sedges or grasses. Adults of *E. ciligera* are small, weak fliers, and the larvae probably feed on a grass or sedge occurring in the oak-hickory forest where the moth was collected. The larger *Neodactria* probably feeds on grasses in prairie remnants. The near endemism (accounting for a single distribution record outside the Black Belt) of *Phyllophaga davisi*, with grass-feeding larvae and oak-feeding adults, also suggests that a mosaic of grasslands and woodland has been present in the Black Belt since the species was separated from its sister species.

The abundance of thorny plants in the Black Belt was suggested to reflect a selective adaptation to Pleistocene vertebrate browsers (Kaye 1974), an idea supported by Janzen (1986) for areas with thorny plants elsewhere. Three localized species of moths feed on thorny plants, including *Ceratomia hageni*, which feeds only on Osage orange (bois d'arc), *Maclura pomifera* (Raf.) and which is one of the most abundant species in the Black Belt based on quantified diversity studies. This large and distinctive moth is also common in the Jackson Prairie but has been recorded from only three other counties in the remainder of Mississippi. Elsewhere in the United States, *C. hageni* is locally common in Kansas, Arkansas, Missouri, and Texas (Hodges 1971). In recent years it has been recorded from southern Iowa east to Ohio and south to northwestern Georgia (further information is available at http://www.npwrc.usgs.gov/resource/distr/lepid/moths/usa/1029.htm). The native range of this moth relative to areas where it has dispersed along with its host has been speculative. Osage orange occurs as a naturalized species in most states east of the Rocky Mountains and in California and Washington (see details at http://www.csdl.tamu.edu/FLORA/b98/check98.htm). Field guides and other general references indicate that Osage orange is native to portions of Arkansas, Oklahoma, Texas, and Louisiana (Elias 1987; Grimm 1966; Peattie 1953). Based on fossil evidence, Osage orange ranged as far north as Ontario during warmer interglacial periods (Peattie 1953). Pollen identified as *Maclura-Celtis* type was found with a suite of pollen types indicative of dry prairies in core samples dated to pre-Wisconsin at Nonconnah Creek in southwestern Tennessee (P. Delcourt 1978; P. Delcourt et al. 1980). However, pollen from these two trees could not be differentiated with light microscopy (Paul Delcourt, personal communication 2000).

Opinions have differed regarding the extent of the native range of Osage orange since the last glacial period. Shambach (1995, this volume) has proposed that the native range was restricted to the Bois d'Arc watershed of the Red River valley in northeastern Texas. His restriction of the range is based on the Spiroan Indians' use of the wood to make bows at the Sanders site on Bois d'Arc Creek and the tribe's monopoly of the wood trade, which brought great wealth. Schambach (this volume) further suggests that the introduction of horses in the late 1600s may have been responsible for expansion of the range of Osage orange.

Early (2000a) provided an extensive treatment of historical records of Osage orange to support a broader native range extending to the Little Missouri River and Arkansas River valleys and as far east as Arkansas Post in southeastern Arkansas. These historical records document two habitats where the tree was most frequently seen, bottomland hardwood stands and margins of prairies on black prairie soils. Early (2000a) argued that the slow growth rate of Osage orange made its cultivation by Native Americans counterproductive, and that there is no evidence to document cultivation and spread of Osage orange by either Native Americans or early Euroamerican settlers.

The well-established and localized population of *Ceratomia hageni* in the Black Belt, in contrast to other areas in the eastern United States, suggests that Osage orange is native to the Black Belt rather than having been dispersed to the Black Belt by humans or modern horses. It is proposed here that one or more of the three *Equus* species that moved from the Great Plains to the Black Belt before the Wisconsin glaciation expanded the native range of this tree. The Osage orange is also known as "horse apple" because of modern horses' preference for the fruit, and it is likely that now-extinct horses also fed on the fruit. As discussed by Janzen (1986), horses are excellent dispersal agents of seeds: horses can travel long distances, and some seeds will remain inside horses for months. The dispersal of *C. hageni* from the original range of its host in Texas and Oklahoma to the Black Belt may have occurred in short jumps following the dispersal route of the *Equus* horses carrying seeds of Osage orange, rather than by wind-aided dispersal over the distance between the two areas.

As discussed previously, climatic and floristic changes south of latitude 33°N were moderate during the Wisconsin glaciation, and evidence from disjunct species indicates that the Black Belt served as a refugium for grassland species. Thus, both *Ceratomia hageni* and Osage orange could have survived the glaciation and persisted as relict populations. Humans could have carried Osage orange from the Black Belt to other areas in Mississippi and neighboring states without a coincident dispersal of *C. hageni,* a hypothesis supported by current incongruent distributions of the moth and Osage orange in the eastern United States. If Osage orange persisted as a relict population in the Black Belt, as proposed here, it is likely that this tree also persisted in relict populations in Arkansas and Louisiana, as supported by Early (2000a).

Two alternative hypotheses can be made to explain the disjunction of plants, insects, and extinct vertebrates between the Black Belt and the Great Plains: (1) organisms dispersed from the Great Plains to the Black Belt across barriers of non-grassland habitat, or (2) organisms dispersed from the Great Plains to the Black Belt along a corridor or archipelago of savanna, parkland, or other grassland at one or more times and became isolated when barriers of unfavorable habitat arose. Although wind-aided dispersal may account for occurrence of some species in the Black Belt, it is unlikely that many species of midwestern grazing vertebrates could have crossed large areas of non-grassland habitat. If a grassland corridor or archipelago existed for these vertebrates, it is likely that insects also dispersed by this route rather than being wind blown and landing in the Black Belt by chance. Whereas the grazing vertebrates probably arrived in the Black Belt after the Illinoian glacier, which extended farther southward than the Wisconsin, the flightless ground beetle endemic to the Black Belt may have originated from an ancestral species that occupied the Black Belt and Great Plains before the Illinoian because of the degree of morphological difference from related midwestern species.

Geographical locations of pre-glacial corridors between the Black Belt and the Great Plains are speculative, and any grassland corridor would be dependent on absence of natural barriers that would impede animal dispersal. A grassland corridor between the Black Belt and the Great Plains could have existed across Arkansas by way of the Grand Prairie or Arkansas River valley before the last glacial period. During this time the Mississippi River encompassed two major complexes of braided stream terraces extending from Cairo, Illinois, south to Louisiana (Saucier 1974), and these would not have prohibited movement of vertebrates into Mississippi. During the last glacial period, a coniferous forest extended along the Mississippi Alluvial Valley to Tunica Hills, Louisiana; this forest would have created a barrier for some grassland species. The post-glacial warming resulted in a regression of the coniferous forest, but the Mississippi River, enlarged from melting ice, replaced the forest as a barrier. Whether a pre-glacial corridor for dispersal might have existed from the northern end of the Black Belt across Tennessee to Missouri or Kentucky, or from the Black Belt across southern Mississippi and Louisiana, is unknown.

The Black Belt may have served as a refugium for species that dispersed to the Great Plains after the retreat of the Wisconsin glacier, but no post-glacial connection of grasslands between the two areas has been documented. It is possible that the prairie peninsula of the Great Plains (Transeau 1935), which existed between 9,000 and 4,000 years ago, extended from Missouri or Illinois across Tennessee as an archipelago of fragmented grasslands to the Black Belt. Prairie-like barrens occur on the western Highland Rim and Central Basin of Tennessee (DeSelm 1988), but the barrens in counties due north of McNairy County, where the Black Belt ends, have fewer western taxa of plants than those in the cedar glades of the Central Basin. Cedar glades extend from Indiana across the central areas of Kentucky and Tennessee into northern Alabama and are near the northern and central portions of the Black Belt. Many of the plants in the glades are geographically/ evolutionarily allied with species whose ranges are west of the Mississippi River (Baskin and Baskin 1986).

CONCLUSIONS

A large number of plants and insects in the Black Belt of Mississippi are disjunct from populations in the Great Plains. Based on these disjunct species and other species with localized distributions, the Black Belt was probably dominated by grasses and herbs, especially Asteraceae, with a mixture of thorny shrubs and forest before the Wisconsin glaciation. These disjunctions are hypothesized to have occurred after Black Belt populations became isolated from Great Plains populations by barriers of non-grassland habitat that replaced one or more earlier corridors or archipelagos of grassland habitat.

Acknowledgments. I thank Terry Schiefer, David Pollock, and Joe MacGown for their efforts in collecting and processing specimens from the Black Belt. Bryant Mather contributed many identified specimens and distributional data for moths in Mississippi. Don Davis, Ron Hodges, Doug Ferguson, Tim McCabe, Alma Solis, Dave Adamski,

Sam Adams, Bernard Landry, and John Franclemont provided identifications of moths and distributional data. Mike Pogue, U.S. National Museum; Paul Lago, University of Mississippi; Wayne Clarke, Auburn University; Vicky Moseley, Louisiana State University; John Heppner, Florida State Collection of Arthropods; Cecil Smith, University of Georgia; Sonny Ramaswamy, Kansas State University; James Ashe, University of Kansas; Ed Riley, Texas A&M University; E. Richard Hoebeke, Cornell University; J. Bolling Sullivan, Beaufort, North Carolina; and Howard Grisham, Huntsville, Alabama, provided additional distributional data and access to collections. John Kaye provided much information on vertebrate fossils. Robert T. Allen, William E. Miller, Terry Schiefer, Jack Reed, and Clarence Collison provided valuable comments for improving the manuscript. The Mississippi Agricultural and Forestry Experiment Station, Mississippi State University, State Projects MIS-6538 and MIS-311020, and the National Science Foundation, Grant Nos. BSR-9024810 and DEB-9200856, provided funds for this research.

3 Terrestrial Gastropods from Archaeological Contexts in the Black Belt Province of Mississippi

EVAN PEACOCK AND REBECCA MELSHEIMER

INTRODUCTION

The role of Native Americans in shaping pre-European landscapes is little understood. The myth of American Indians as "natural conservationists"—as people in balance with nature in both a spiritual and a practical sense—remains very strong indeed (Denevan 1992; Peacock 1998a), despite archaeological and historical evidence to the contrary (e.g., Krech 1999; Redman 1999). There is an enormous popular literature to that effect, the bulk of which advocates a return to, or an embracing of, a more respectful attitude toward the natural world (e.g., Bierhorst 1994; Olson 1995). Without denigrating that worthy message, we believe that it is important to more accurately portray the effects of pre-industrial humans on the landscape, for three main reasons. First, to better understand native cultures as they existed before contact it is necessary to understand what sorts of environments they inhabited, why those particular environments were chosen, and how they were exploited. Second, to understand long-term plant and animal community dynamics, the role of humans as modifiers of those communities must be explored (cf. Goudie 2000). Finally, the perennial question facing all ecological reconstruction efforts—reconstruction of what?—remains a legitimate one (e.g., Kline and Howell 1987; Powers 1987) that must be answered on a case-by-case basis, taking into account the goals of the reconstruction effort (Apfelbaum and Chapman 1997) as well as any and all paleo- and neoecological data that pertain to those goals.

When landscape evolution in the Eastern Woodlands of North America is discussed, far too often aboriginal populations either are left out of the picture altogether or some passing mention is given to historical accounts of fire use by Indians. These historical accounts offer only the briefest glimpse of the very end of at least 12,000 years of land use by human populations that, at particular times and places, reached considerable size. Those populations systematically exploited a vast range of terrestrial and aquatic resources. Plant domestication had appeared in some parts of the Eastern Woodlands by 5,000 years ago, and intensive, maize-based agriculture by 1,000 years ago. Hundreds of thousands of archaeological sites in the Southeast alone yield testimony to a long-term human presence in the region. Yet in ecology, history, biology, geography, and other disciplines that consider human/nature interactions at a landscape scale, papers still appear every year with that most inaccurate of modifiers—"presettlement"—attached to descriptions of pre-European landscape conditions (e.g., Beach 1994; Foster et al. 1992; Nelson et al. 1998). It has recently been argued, based on the ubiquity of archaeological remains, that this practice should be avoided in any discussion of Holocene environments in the New World (Peacock 1998a:18).

Environmental archaeology provides a forum for tying together different kinds of data from different disciplines to address questions of long-term human/nature interactions. Unfortunately, environmental archaeology is still woefully underdeveloped in the Southeast. In recent syntheses, either the environment is portrayed as a backdrop against which broad cultural patterns emerged (Smith 1986) or human effects on the landscape are minimally mentioned (Steponaitis 1986:388). The backdrop is provided by paleoenvironmental reconstruction (something of a misnomer—see Peacock and Reese, this volume), which itself was present "only in embryo form until rather recently" in the Southeast (Watson 1990:47). As Reitz (1993:129) put it, "many archaeologists in the southeastern United States still appear to be operating under the influence of environmental possibilism and preprocessual research interests more appropriate to the 1940s than the 1990s." Environmental archaeology earned no place in The Development of Southeastern Archaeology (Johnson 1993), which quite accurately focused on culture history and processual archaeology, the dominant regional paradigms (Dunnell 1990). In that historical overview, papers discussing biotic remains from archaeological contexts concentrated primarily on methodological and subsistence issues, although there is some coverage of the effects of husbandry practices on plant evolution (Gremillion 1993; cf. Smith 1992). Reitz (1993:126–127) noted that with the advent of the systems-oriented New Archaeology of the 1960s, a goal of zooarchaeological studies became "to study fundamental relationships between humans and their environment, with primary emphasis on the biological aspects of environment." Generally speaking, these "relationships" were explored in functional terms; that is, the orientation was on ecological systemics as opposed to evolutionary analysis and explanation. Such a functional orientation, characteristic of processual archaeology, impedes the study of change through time as the transitions between units, whether natural or cultural, are necessarily seen as a change in state (Dunnell 1986; Plog 1974). Probably the most sophisticated use of environmental data in southeastern archaeology has been in settlement pattern analyses that correlate site locations with soil types, distance to watercourses, hypothesized vegetative conditions, and so on. Even these studies are mostly cast in a functional light, however, as settlement patterns considered to be characteristic of a given period or phase are presented as "snapshots in time" that might encompass centuries.

It is safe to say that evolutionary archaeology has not yet made much of an imprint on the discipline in the Southeast (see the discussion of "interpretation versus explanation" in O'Brien 1996). If and when it does, it should incorporate more sophisticated analyses of both cultural and natural phenomena, dealing with each as a continuum rather than as a series of static condition states that can only be linked via description and/or functional arguments. Human-induced environmental changes, and cultural responses to those changes, may profitably be included in such analyses. The only concessions to an essentialist mode of thought are the use of species as analytical classes and a uniformitarian approach to the use of habitat data. The former is defensible at the time scales involved in archaeological research in the Southeast (cf. Peacock and Reese, this volume). The latter seems to provide consistent results when different environmental data sets are compared (e.g., P. Delcourt et al. 1986) but bears further consideration as environmental archaeology in America matures.

Interestingly, in the few cases where paleoecologists have specifically looked for the mark of humans on the prehistoric landscapes of the southeastern United States, they have found it. Sedimentation rates, along with data on pollen, microscopic charcoal, and plant macrofossils, show steadily increasing anthropogenic pressure on the environment beginning about 5,000 years ago, coincident with the beginnings of native horticulture. That pressure is indicated by the depletion of local forest resources (Williams 1993), the proliferation of early-successional plant taxa (e.g., H. Delcourt 1987), and accelerated soil erosion (e.g., P. Delcourt et al. 1986). These conditions have been seen in the highlands of Kentucky (P. Delcourt et al. 1998), the southern Appalachians (H. Delcourt and P. Delcourt 1997), and the Little Tennessee River valley (Chapman and Shea 1981; Chapman et al. 1982; H. Delcourt 1987; P. Delcourt et al. 1986). Unfortunately, such examples are very rare because biotic remains are usually very poorly preserved in the highly active and generally acidic soils of the Southeast. Pollen, for example, is quickly degraded in the bacteria-rich, seasonally wet and dry soils of the region (e.g., Whitehead and Sheehan 1985). Alternative paleoenvironmental data sources must therefore be tapped if site-specific environmental conditions are to be modeled with any success (Hogue, this volume; Peacock 1993; Peacock and Reese, this volume).

An opportunity has recently arisen to begin modeling anthropogenic environments that existed in the Southeast before modern impacts. Salvage excavations have been carried out at late prehistoric and Protohistoric sites on the western edge of the Black Belt physiographic province in the vicinity of Starkville, Mississippi. These sites were extensively excavated in advance of highway construction (Rafferty and Hogue 1998). Of particular interest are several sites dating from the Middle Mississippian period (ca. A.D. 1250) and later. The Mississippian and Protohistoric periods coincide with a prehistoric subsistence regime that included maize as a staple component in local diets (e.g., Hogue 2000), meaning that landscape alteration by clearing and cultivation must have been taking place at some scale. Owing to the alkaline chalk substrate of the Black Belt, faunal preservation at many of the sites is quite good (Hogue, this volume). In particular, thousands of land snails have been recovered from carefully controlled contexts. This paper focuses on the use of gastropod shells from archaeological sites to model past environmental conditions and how these conditions changed through time in the Black Belt of Mississippi.

NATURAL AND CULTURAL BACKGROUND

The Black Belt physiographic province (also referred to as the Black Prairie) stretches in a narrow arc through northern Mississippi and eastward into central Alabama (Figure 3.1). It is characterized by a chalk substrate, rolling topography, and small, intermittent streams (Cleland 1920; Jones and Patton 1966; Rankin 1974; Rankin and Davis 1971; T. Wilson 1981). Landscape conditions in the Black Belt today consist primarily of open grasslands broken by stands of cedar on the hilltops and thin hardwood belts along the streams (Myers 1948; T. Wilson 1981; Schauwecker and MacDonald, this volume). Rich, alkaline soils developed on the Cretaceous chalk bedrock, leading to intensive agricultural pursuits in the province early in the Historic period (Fogel 1989).

The Black Belt in Mississippi has an impressive archaeological record, with hundreds of sites already recorded in surveys conducted thus far (Blakeman 1985; Johnson and Sparks 1986; Johnson et al. 1984; Johnson et al. 1991; Rafferty 1996, this volume). Although a number of these sites have Woodland-period occupations (ca. 200 B.C.–A.D. 1000), apparently a concentration of Mississippian-, Protohistoric-, and Historic-period aboriginal sites exists in the Black Belt. In particu-

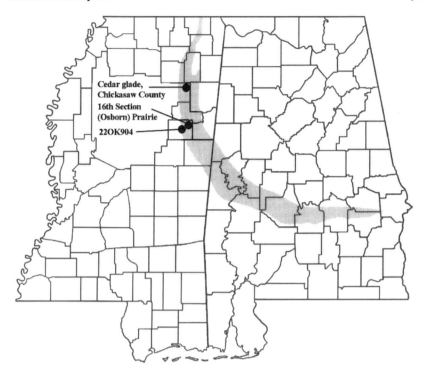

Fig. 3.1. Location of archaeological site 22OK904, Oktibbeha County, Mississippi, and modern sampling sites for terrestrial gastropods.

lar, there is one dense cluster of such sites in the vicinity of Starkville, Mississippi (Atkinson 1979; Galloway 1994; Hogue 2000; Hogue and Peacock 1995; Rafferty, this volume) and another farther north in the vicinity of Tupelo (Atkinson 1987; Galloway 1994; Rafferty 1995; Stubbs 1983). The settlement pattern represented appears to be one of individual farmsteads: the economic and political relationships between such small sites and larger mound centers in the area are topics of continuing interest (Hogue and Peacock 1995).

It is difficult to explain why the Black Belt uplands, with their limited water resources (Peacock 1992; Rafferty, this volume; Schmitz et al., this volume), should have been a focus for prehistoric settlement following the advent of agriculture. Jay Johnson suggested that the cedar glade ecosystems of the province were attractive deer habitat and that human populations shifted away from large river valleys into the chalk uplands late in the Mississippian period to take advantage of that faunal resource (Johnson 1990; Johnson and Sparks 1986; Johnson et al. 1984; Johnson et al. 1991). This model was questioned by Peacock, who argued that the cedar glades characterizing the province today are a result of Historic-period land clearance, subsequent erosion of the fragile soils, and invasion by cedar (Peacock 1992; Peacock and Miller 1990), and thus have no bearing on prehistoric or Protohistoric settlement patterning (cf. Hogue and Peacock 1995; Peacock and Rafferty 1996). This archaeological debate mirrors a similar one from the geographical literature concerning the effects of Native American burning on the Black Belt landscape (Rostlund 1957; Tower 1961).

The key to understanding how the Black Belt environment shaped Native American lifeways, and how Native Americans themselves altered the landscape, lies in constructing a picture of environmental conditions at a large number of sites of different ages in the province and then mapping the magnitude and rate of environmental change through time. The recovery of thousands of land-snail specimens from archaeological sites in the Black Belt provides us with an opportunity to begin this process.

LAND SNAILS AND ARCHAEOLOGY

The analysis of gastropod remains is standard practice where environmental archaeology is well established (Evans 1972; Lowe and Walker 1997). It is commonly employed in Europe (Evans 1972), Mesoamerica (Pohl and Bloom 1996), Polynesia (Hunt and Kirch 1997), and elsewhere in the world. Land snails are essentially site-specific indicators and, since they were rarely eaten or otherwise exploited, assemblages are generally not affected by cultural biases (see discussion in Bobrowsky 1984). Land-snail analysis has been used to establish overall environmental conditions that existed at particular locales and times (Klippel and Turner 1991), to investigate climatic fluctuations (Baerreis 1990), to establish the nature and magnitude of prehistoric human environmental disturbances (Hunt and Kirch 1997), and to understand how prehistoric mounds and other earthworks were constructed (e.g., Bell 1990). The method has been used in the United States to a limited extent (Barber 1988; Baerreis 1973, 1990; Bobrowsky 1984; Bobrowsky and Gatus 1984; Mead 1991), most often to explore past environmental conditions. Only rarely has it been applied in the Southeast, despite many decades of extensive archaeological excavations and the fact that molluscan remains are a common constituent of many prehistoric and Historic-period sites in the region.

ANALYSIS OF LAND SNAILS FROM 22OK904

Site 22OK904 is a small, Protohistoric site located on the western edge of the Black Belt near Starkville, Mississippi (Figure 3.1), that dates from about A.D. 1550 to 1650 (Rafferty and Hogue 1998; Rafferty and Peacock 2000). People in the area during that time practiced agriculture, but the extent to which the inhabitants of this particular site were engaged in the practice is not yet known. It is postulated that the site represents a single-family farmstead of relatively short occupational duration (Rafferty and Hogue 1998).

Snails were derived from a variety of contexts at the site, including the fill of pit features and postholes, and from general strata. They were recovered by water-screening the soil through 0.64-cm (1/4-inch) mesh and window mesh, and also by flotation—that is, by immersing dirt in water and pouring off the floating materials into a fine mesh screen. Any materials that did not float were subsequently handpicked out of the remaining sediment. The assemblage is quite rich and the snail shells are in an excellent state of preservation owing to the alkaline substrate and to the excellent and painstaking field and lab recovery techniques used. A minimum of 35 gastropod taxa have been identified from the site (Table 3.1).

Each shell was cleaned thoroughly; the aperture received particular attention to allow for the observation of internal structures. Afterwards, the shells were examined under a microscope at 10 to 30X magnification. The snails were identified using diagnostic features listed in various guides (e.g., Archer 1948; Burch 1962; Pilsbry 1939–1948; Walker 1928) and by reference to comparative specimens provided by the Smithsonian Institution. Quantification was based on the presence of the aperture. A few taxa thus identified are outside the ranges displayed in Hubricht (1985). The distinguishing characteristics of those taxa are discussed at the end of this paper. Nomenclature follows Turgeon et al. (1998).

One potential problem with shallow sites like 22OK904 is distinguishing between recent and archaeological subfossil remains. To address this problem, shells that were completely bleached were tallied separately from those showing even the slightest trace of color, surface markings, or translucency. The results were reassuring, as there is scarcely any overlap between the taxa in the bleached and unbleached categories (Figure 3.2). Had we been dealing with a mix of recent and ancient material that could not be distinguished, there should have been a more even distribution of taxa between the two categories. Clearly, there are two distinct faunas from the site, one Protohistoric and the other presumably Historic and probably modern. This is supported by stratigraphic relationships: essentially, the deeper one goes in the deposits, the greater the dominance of those taxa making up what we will call the Protohistoric assemblage.

RESULTS

The Protohistoric assemblage is dominated by *Hawaiia minuscula*, at about 42 percent. That is followed by *Helicodiscus singleyanus* at a little over 15 percent, then several species of *Gastrocopta*, includ-

Table 3.1. Gastropods from Protohistoric and Historic contexts in the Mississippi Black Belt

	22OK904, Protohistoric	22OK904, Historic	16th Section Prairie, Oktibbeha County	Cedar Glade, Chickasaw County
Anguispira alternata ssp.		3		
Anguispira spp.	1	3		
cf. *Columella edentula*		8		
Daedalochila leporina				1
Daedalochila triodontoides	1	2		
Euchemotrema leai		2		
Euconulus chersinus	1	7	1	48
Gastrocopta abbreviata	95			
Gastrocopta armifera	131	1	4	5
Gastrocopta cf. *clappi*	11			
Gastrocopta contracta	10	1		
Gastrocopta contracta climeana	2			
Gastrocopta corticaria		1		
Gastrocopta cristata	2			
Gastrocopta pellucida			5	
Gastrocopta pentodon	38	7		
Gastrocopta procera		110	18	4
Gastrocopta riparia		19		
Gastrocopta sterkiana		2		
Gastrocopta tappaniana	4			
Gastrocopta sp.	50	16		
Glyphyalinia indentata	43			72
Hawaiia minuscula	409	3	5	1
cf. *Helicodiscus nummus*				1
Helicodiscus parallelus	2			
Helicodiscus singleyanus	156			
Mesomphix sp.				10
Oligyra orbiculata	2			3
Paravitrea cf. *clappi*				1
Polygyridae		1		
Punctum minutissimum	2			
cf. *Pupisoma dioscoricola*		3		
cf. *Pupisoma* sp.		1	2	
Pupoides albilabris	2	729	137	16
Pupoides cf. *modicus*		2		
Pupoides sp.		116		
Rabdotus dealbatus		1		
Rabdotus sp.		1		
Succinea sp.			6	7
Ventridens demissus			1	
cf. *Vertigo alabamensis*			12	
Vertigo cf. *tridentata*		1	1	
Vertigo cf. *conecuhensis*		1		
Vertigo oralis		1		
Vertigo ovata		1		
Vertigo rugosula		5	1	
Zonitidae	8		1	17
Unid.	1	1		
Total	971	1049	194	186

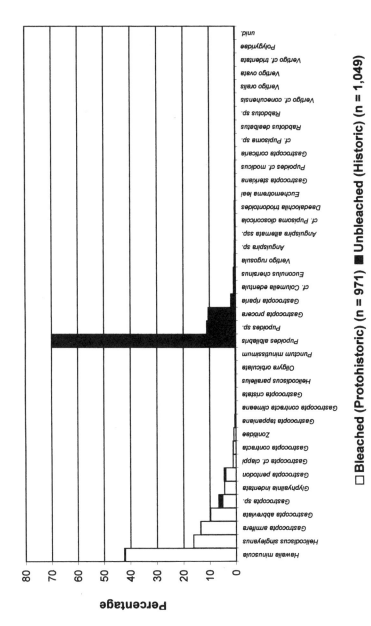

Fig. 3.2. Comparison of bleached (Protohistoric) and unbleached (Historic) gastropods from 22OK904.

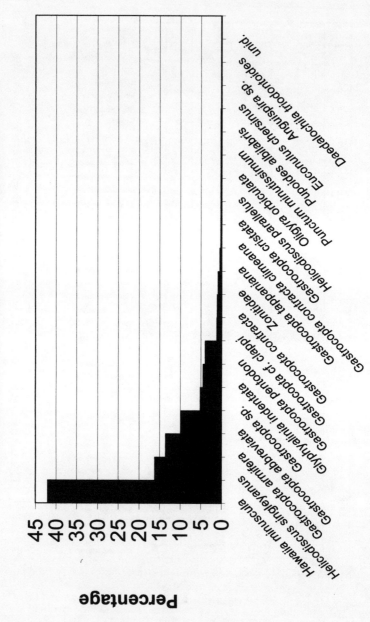

Fig. 3.3. Protohistoric gastropod assemblage, 22OK904.

ing *armifera, abbreviata,* and *pentodon.* There are a fair number of *Glyphyalinia* (= *Retinella*) *indentata,* at about 5 percent of the total. The remaining taxa each make up 1 percent or less. Only two specimens of *Pupoides albilabris* are included in the Protohistoric assemblage (Figure 3.3).

The Historic assemblage from the site could hardly be more different. It is overwhelmingly dominated by *Pupoides albilabris,* at about 70 percent. The true proportion is probably even higher, as about 10 percent of the assemblage consists of *Pupoides* fragments that we did not assign to species but which are likely *P. albilabris* (Table 3.1). *Gastrocopta procera* makes up about 10 percent of the assemblage, followed by a host of other taxa that are represented by only one or a few individual specimens (Figure 3.4).

Obviously, landscape conditions at 22OK904 have been greatly altered over time. The site was on a small knoll which, at the time of excavation, supported several large oak and hickory trees as well as a cedar component. It was surrounded by open pasture. To help interpret the Protohistoric snail assemblage, litter samples were taken from two other locations in the Mississippi Black Belt: the 16th Section Prairie in Oktibbeha County (a.k.a. the Osborn Prairie—Brown, this volume; Schauwecker and MacDonald, this volume) and a cedar glade in the Tombigbee National Forest in Chickasaw County (Figure 3.1). One kg of litter and soil to a depth of a few centimeters was taken at each locale. These samples were washed through 500-micron screen and all shells were picked out of the remaining detritus. The 16th Section Prairie sample produced 194 snails, whereas 186 were obtained from the cedar glade sample (Table 3.1).

The resultant gastropod assemblages are markedly different. The open prairie assemblage is dominated by *Pupoides albilabris,* at about 70 percent, followed by *Gastrocopta procera* at nearly 10 percent, then a minimum of 11 other taxa represented by one or a few specimens (Figure 3.5). The cedar glade assemblage contains *Glyphyalinia indentata* at 38 percent, *Euconulus chersinus* at 26 percent, undifferentiated *Zonitidae* at 9 percent, *Pupoides albilabris* at 8 percent, then 9 other taxa in decreasing frequency (Figure 3.6).

Figure 3.7 shows differences in the relative proportions of different taxa from the four assemblages: the Protohistoric and Historic assemblages from 22OK904 and the modern litter samples from the 16th Section Prairie and the cedar glade. The Historic assemblage from 22OK904 and the 16th Section Prairie assemblage are quite similar. The main difference is the greater number of taxa at 22OK904, something that may be attributable to differences in sample size. The overall similarity is somewhat surprising, given that the site had been wooded for many decades before excavation, while the prairie locale was open.

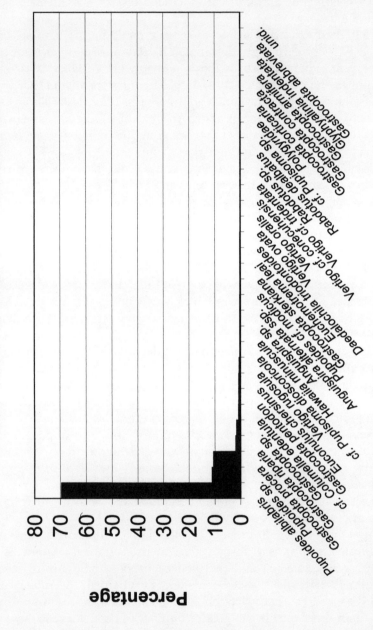

Fig. 3.4. Historic gastropod assemblage, 22OK904.

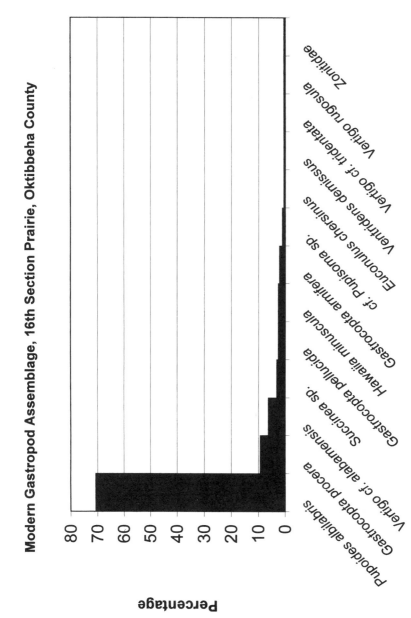

Fig. 3.5. Modern gastropod assemblage, 16th Section Prairie, Oktibbeha County, Mississippi.

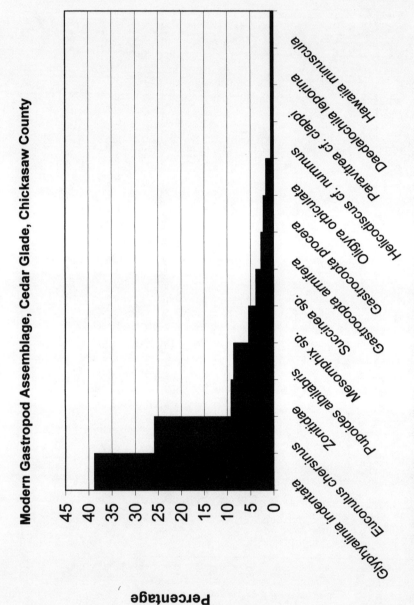

Fig. 3.6. Modern gastropod assemblage, cedar glade, Chickasaw County.

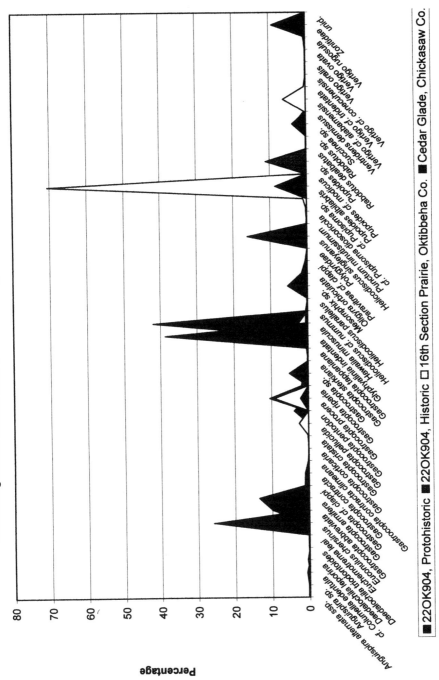

Fig. 3.7. All archaeological and modern gastropod assemblages from the Mississippi Black Prairie.

The main differences between them that probably are *not* due to sample size are the presence of taxa in the prairie sample that are not present at 22OK904. These include *Vertigo alabamensis, Succinea* sp., *Gastrocopta pellucida,* and one specimen of *Ventridens demissus.* Hubricht described *Vertigo alabamensis* as being found "under rotting leaves in a ravine." It has not been reported in Mississippi before, and its identification must be considered tentative until it can be verified. The *Succinea* sp. cannot be confidently identified to species based on shell characteristics alone, though it can be suggested based on environmental conditions that we are dealing with *S. indiana,* the xeric amber snail (Hubricht 1985:15). *Gastrocopta pellucida* is usually found in "open grassy places or in open woods" (Hubricht 1985:10). *Ventridens demissus* is a leaf-litter snail, usually found in cedar glades but tolerant of a wide range of habitats (Hinton 1951:49). While these and other taxa may ultimately be useful in reconstructing ground cover at archaeological sites in the Black Belt, available habitat information is limited. A great deal of work must be done for the ecological requirements of these taxa to be more fully understood. The Protohistoric assemblage from 22OK904 is unlike any of the three modern samples (Figure 3.7).

ENVIRONMENTAL RECONSTRUCTION
AND LANDSCAPE CHANGE

The literature holds clues as to what the site may have looked like in the past and what caused the transition to a completely different fauna. The more common snails, such as *Helicodiscus singleyanus, Gastrocopta armifera,* and *Gastrocopta abbreviata,* are characteristic of open, sunny, grassy locations, including cedar glades (Hubricht 1985). *Hawaiia minuscula,* the dominant taxon in the Protohistoric assemblage, apparently can tolerate a wide range of environmental conditions (Hinton 1951). However, Hubricht (1985:29) describes it as "A species of bare ground," and states that he "never found it in leaf litter" but only on bare ground. This suggests that the site was bare during the period of Protohistoric occupation, a reasonable enough conclusion given the amount of trampling that takes place at any habitation site. The site locale was thus a "habitat island" (Butzer 1982:189), a spot with floral and faunal characteristics unlike those of the surrounding landscape. As Rafferty (this volume) has shown, well over 100 sites recorded in eastern Oktibbeha and Clay counties alone can be assigned to the Mississippian or Protohistoric periods, and many other sites go back much further. Only very small portions of those and surrounding counties have yet been surveyed for archaeological sites. Extrapolating from what we have discovered, there are undoubtedly thousands of such sites in the Mississippi Black Belt. While these sites were not, of course, all occupied at the same time (Rafferty, this volume), they are a ubiquitous feature of the landscape. They imply not only a particular habitat type that occupied a great deal of the landscape in the past—an anthropogenic habitat type that may have no modern analog—but also millennia-long, continuous human pressure on the limited forest resources of the province as wood was obtained for fuel, house construction, and so on.

The transition from that pre-modern anthropogenic habitat type to what is seen today may be understood from Theler's study (n.d.) of a Pleistocene gastropod assemblage from the Burnham site in Woods County, Oklahoma. There, a transition from strata dominated by *Hawaiia minuscula* to strata containing *Gastrocopta procera* and *Pupoides albilabris* was interpreted as representing a shift from mesic to xeric conditions attributable to climate change. A similar suggestion can be made for 22OK904, where *Gastrocopta procera* was the second most abundant snail in the Historic assemblage following *Pupoides albilabris*. Rather than being due to climate change, however, the shift at 22OK904 may be attributed to human-induced erosion and soil loss, with a concomitant drop in soil moisture retention capacity.

SUMMARY

This initial analysis of archaeological snails from the Mississippi Black Belt has demonstrated a significant shift in landscape conditions through time. The question is when did that shift begin? Was it entirely a phenomenon of the Historic period, or did the extensive prehistoric and Protohistoric agricultural settlement of the Black Belt uplands initiate landscape transformation? When all of the snails from all of the sites currently being studied are analyzed, we hope to be much closer to answering that question. It is obvious that the potential for answers exists.

Beyond the analysis of prehistoric faunas, a great deal of work must be done in collecting modern samples with adequate habitat data so that archaeological assemblages may be more precisely interpreted. Such a study, headed by the senior author, is currently under way in the Black Belt physiographic province of Mississippi. This paper represents the beginning of a long-term research project which, by all indications, promises to provide a very accurate picture of human-induced environmental change in the Black Belt, whether that change was prehistoric/Protohistoric, Historic, or both.

Theoretically, an evolutionary approach should provide a means for linking archaeological and paleoenvironmental data into a single explanatory framework in a nonessentialist fashion. A few recently published studies demonstrate how artifacts or artifact assemblages from the Southeast can be ordered through time without recourse to essentialist units such as phases or cultural periods (e.g., O'Brien et al. 2001; Peacock 1997; Rafferty 1994). Biotic remains retrieved along with artifact assemblages can be ordered by association, provided adequate contextual control is maintained. As a result, continuous change through time may be observed in landscape indicators such as land snails. The potential thus exists for observing coincident changes in the two data sets and testing hypotheses concerning human-nature interactions. For example, fossil oyster shell began to be used as a tempering agent in ceramics in about the mid–sixteenth century in the Black Belt (Rafferty 1995). That technological change occurred at a time when prehistoric agriculture had been practiced on the chalk ridges of the province for two to three centuries (Peacock 1993; Peacock and Rafferty 1996; Rafferty 1995, this volume). The availability of fossil shell may have been a contributing factor in the adoption of that material as a tempering agent. Such availability may have been directly related to the amount of exposure of the fossil beds via erosion. If that erosion was human-induced, then we are seeing an interesting example of how anthropogenic environmental changes influenced material culture. This hypothesis should be testable when more land-snail assemblages from sites of different ages are analyzed.

As discussed above, change through time in indicators of human environmental disturbance has been reported from a few other archaeological locales in the Southeast. Those studies, groundbreaking as they are, were hampered by the use of essentialist units in ordering the archaeological and associated biological data. In both the cultural and environmental spheres, the stuff of interest is variability. That is precisely what is being masked when cultural periods of whatever stripe— stages, phases, and the like—are used as analytical units. To say that change took place from Woodland to Mississippian, for example, is important but of limited utility in understanding how and why that change occurred. Only when variability is accommodated by dealing with both cultural and environmental changes as continua will we move beyond the confines of environmental possibilism and systemic functionalism. We would argue that this is only achievable by adopting an explicitly evolutionary approach, something we hope to employ as more land-snail assemblages from the Black Belt are analyzed.

DISCUSSION OF PROBLEMATIC SPECIES

Identifying snail species based on their shells can be a very difficult process. A number of characteristics used for classification refer to the soft bodies of snails. Obviously these cannot be employed in the analysis of archaeological specimens. Additional difficulties arise from the general similarity of the shells of some taxa. There may be few deviations between different species of the same genus or family. At times, there is no way to differentiate between them based on shell characteristics alone, as with the members of the genus *Succinea*. These identification problems can be especially vexing when shells are fragmentary and missing diagnostic features, as is often the case with archaeological gastropod remains.

Another difficulty is the identification of juvenile shells. The descriptions of snail species are based on adult specimens. Many features integral to the identification process are only visible in adults. Chief among these are size and number of whorls. In addition, some snail species exhibit a great deal of phenotypic plasticity in the traits commonly used for identification (e.g., the number/configuration of "teeth," or apertural folds). For accurate identification, attention must be paid to a range of features and comparisons made to museum specimens whenever possible.

During the course of this research, some identifications were made that did not conform to known snail ranges as illustrated in Hubricht (1985). This fact, coupled with the identification difficulties just described, makes it necessary to present the criteria on which the more difficult/problematic specific identifications were made. Voucher specimens are stored at the environmental archaeology laboratory at the Cobb Institute of Archaeology, Mississippi State University. Some basic terminology follows. The aperture is the opening for the snail. A fold is a denticle, or "tooth," located on the outer or basal lips of the aperture. A lamella is a denticle located on either the columellar (inner) or parietal (outer) lips. Callouses, or shell thickenings, may also occur within the aperture. A crest is a raised ridge on the last whorl behind the outer lip, usually set off from the outer lip by a constriction.

A snail commonly identified in this study is *Gastrocopta procera*. Identification of *G. procera* is based on the presence of an angulo-parietal lamella with a bifid tip, a columellar lamella, a subcolumellar lamella, a long, deeply placed lower palatal fold, and a small, less deeply placed upper palatal fold. *G. procera* typically ranges from 2.2 to 3 mm in length. Whereas the study area is well within the range given for this species by Hubricht (1985), identification of similar species from 22OK904 is based on their deviation from the *G. procera* type, some of which have not been previously reported in the Black Belt province in Mississippi, or whose occurrence is relatively rare. The main difference between each of these is the size, number, and placement of lamellae in the aperture. All have five to six whorls and a reflected lip. Their shape is elongate-conic and they have a crest behind the lip.

Gastrocopta riparia has a lower palatal fold that is much shorter and less deep than that found in *G. procera*. It also lacks a callous beneath the columellar lamella, which is shorter than in *G. procera*. *G. riparia* measures 2.3 to 3 mm in length. This species has been reported from Black Belt counties in Mississippi and Alabama, but apparently that is the northern edge of its range (Hubricht 1985:Figure 52). *Gastrocopta sterkiana* differs by having a more bifid tip of the angulo-parietal lamella. Unlike *G. riparia*, it has a strongly developed callous beneath the columellar lamella. *G. sterkiana* is typically 2.2 to 2.9 mm in length. Its reported range is relatively distant from the Black Belt area: it was previously recorded in Texas, Arkansas, and Oklahoma (Hubricht 1985). *Gastrocopta corticaria* has only five and a half whorls. It has a highly variable angular lamella which, if present, is very small and barely united with the parietal lamella. The only other denticle present is a small columellar lamella. It also is generally smaller, measuring only 2.5 mm in length. It is shown by Hubricht (1985:Figure 53) in one Black Belt county in Alabama.

Gastrocopta armifera also was commonly found, and the study area is well within its range (Hubricht 1985:Figure 44). It is described here because there are other species very similar in form. The shell is ovate-conic in shape, with a reflected lip. It has six and one-half to seven and one-half whorls. A large number of denticles are found in the aperture. There is a strongly developed columellar lamella. The angular lamella is united with the parietal. Some divergence is evident, but the angulo-parietal lamella is not bifid per se. There is a lower palatal and a smaller upper palatal fold. Size varies on these denticles, but they are always present. A very small subcolumellar lamella and suprapalatal fold may be present. *G. armifera* is 3 to 4.8 mm long. *Gastrocopta abbreviata* has the same shape and teeth except that the columellar lamella is shorter and the basal fold is more pronounced. It is within the size range of *G. armifera*, measuring 3.3 to 4.2 mm in length. The Black Belt is the eastern edge of its range (Hubricht 1985:Figure 50). *Gastrocopta clappi* also is similar to *G. armifera*. It differs in lacking the forward branch of the angulo-parietal lamella seen in *G. armifera*. It is 3.5 to 4 mm in length. Its reported range is in northern Alabama and Tennessee (Hubricht 1985:Figure 64); the specimens reported herein therefore represent a range extension for this species.

Gastrocopta contracta is similar in overall appearance to *G. armifera* but is much smaller with different denticles. It has five and one-half whorls and a reflected lip. The aperture is triangular in shape. There is a large, twisted angulo-parietal lamella. The columellar lamella is large. There is a small upper palatal with a larger lower palatal fold. Together, these teeth almost close up the aperture, making it difficult to see inside. It is 2.2 to 2.5 mm in length. A subspecies is *Gas-*

trocopta contracta climeana, the distinguishing characteristic of which is a parietal tooth that is L-shaped.

Vertigo tridentata has five whorls and a narrow aperture. It is oval-shaped. It has four denticles: an angulo-parietal, a columellar, a lower palatal, and an interpalatal at the fold. It measures from 1.8 to 2.3 mm. Hubricht (1985) found only fossil specimens of this taxon in Mississippi.

Vertigo conecuhensis is oval-shaped as well with five and one-half whorls. There is no basal fold. All of the denticles are strongly developed, with the parietal, angular, lower palatal, and upper palatal interlocking. There is a columellar lamella. It is 1.5 to 1.8 mm in length. Its range according to Hubricht (1985:Figure 94) is limited to the lower coastal plain of Alabama. Its presence in modern samples from the Black Belt thus represents a major extension of its natural range or may be the result of a recent introduction.

Euconulus chersinus has a beehive shape with six to eight whorls. The aperture is trapezoidal and the shell is umbilicate and tightly whorled. There are no denticles found in this shell. It ranges in size from 2.4 to 3.4 mm.

Euchemotrema leai was formerly known as *Stenotrema leai aliciae* (e.g., Hubricht 1985:Figure 427). It is distinguished from other members of the genus by the lack of a basal lip notch.

4 The Application of a Small-mammal Model in Paleoenvironmental Analysis

S. HOMES HOGUE

INTRODUCTION

Few of today's environments and landscapes have not been influenced by human development or culturally modified to some extent. The activities of past human populations have led to continuous alterations of the landscape, creating new ecological niches and habitats. Ethnohistorical and ethnographic documents have furnished some evidence for these activities. Plains Indians, for example, may have been responsible for deforestation in central North America (Wells 1970b). Similar forest destruction has been proposed for the Piedmont region in the southeastern United States. Here, Native Americans repeatedly burned off large portions of forestland to create grazing lands for deer populations (Hudson 1976:19). Additional sources suggest that burning forests and brush was a hunting technique used to concentrate game in one area for killing (Hudson 1976:19). Forest growth is further affected by cutting wood for fuel (Dimbleby 1978:53) and in the establishment of footpaths used for trading, hunting, and gathering (Ellen 1989:23). All of these human activities have altered the environment (Ellen 1989), but probably the most detrimental human behavior affecting the prehistoric southeastern United States was the process of clearing land for maize cultivation. Globally, the process of plant cultivation has led to enormous changes in the structure of biotic associations. Field clearance alone has actuated the destruction of forests and native grasslands as well as other natural habitats (Ellen 1989:22–23).

This paper examines the application of a small-mammal model to document prehistoric environmental change in the Black Belt physiographic region in Mississippi. The study's major emphasis is on documenting changes in small-mammal faunas in response to prehistoric agricultural clearing. To assess these changes, a small-mammal model is developed and applied to archaeological faunal assemblages recovered from the Black Belt region of east-central Mississippi and west-central Alabama. Previous works by Scott (1982, 1983), where small-mammal data were used for environmental reconstruction, provide a basic framework for developing the model used in this study. Habitat preferences for small mammals indigenous to the study area are included in the model. The small-mammal model is then applied to assess possible environmental changes for two small Mississippian-period (A.D. 1000–1540) sites located in the Black Prairie physiographic zone: the Josey Farm site (22OK793) (Rafferty and Hogue 1999) located just north of Starkville, and the Yarborough site (22CL814) located in nearby Clay County (Solis and Walling 1982).

DEVELOPING A SMALL-MAMMAL MODEL FOR LANDSCAPE DISTURBANCE

Small mammals are defined as those mammal species weighing about 5 kg (11 lb) or less. The faunal inventory compiled for this study includes all mammals whose weight range falls within this category, although several species such as the raccoon, gray fox, red fox, and bobcat can exceed this weight. From an evolutionary perspective there are specific advantages to being small. These include (1) ease of concealment from predators and low energy expenditure for escape; (2) a wider range of potential food types, since small mammals are typically generalized feeders; (3) adaptability to a wide range of habitats; and (4) the characteristic of r-reproduction, a high rate of population increase that favors a rapid response to environmental change (Pianka 1988; Fleming 1979:1–2). The last characteristic is especially critical to this study, as an increase in small-mammal frequency in response to newly disturbed habitats, such as deforestation for agricultural fields, should be reflected in the archaeological record. Vigne and Valladas (1996), for example, found that large increases in the number of bones of the genus *Mus* (house mouse) in owl pellets from a cave in Corsica were correlated with periods of Roman agricultural clearance on the island.

Modeling past environments has been a valuable focus for archaeological research. Landscape alterations associated with prehistoric agriculture are generally manifested archaeologically in ethnobotanical remains (Cowan and Watson 1992; Gremillion 1997) and by site placement in relation to cultivable land (Ward 1965; Waselkov 1997). However, landscape alterations may be inferred from a change in the composition of fauna, specifically small terrestrial mammals. Scott (1982, 1983), for example, used small-mammal faunas recovered from archaeological sites in Alabama and Mississippi to document prehistoric

Fig. 4.1. Locations of archaeological sites 22OK793 and 22CL814, Mississippi Black Prairie.

agricultural practices. An important study by Grayson (1991a) at Gate-cliff Shelter, Nevada, demonstrated that small-mammal faunas derived from noncultural deposits were very similar to faunas from cultural strata, leading him to question the use of small-mammal faunas for subsistence-oriented research. In another study, Grayson (1991b) reviewed the biogeographic history of small mammals in the Great Basin and demonstrated that small isolated populations are more prone to extinction than larger ones. Studies in applied zooarchaeology also have provided insight into prehistoric environmental conditions with the intent of recreating natural habitats and improving wildlife management (Lyman 1996).

Central to the research presented in this paper are two studies by Scott (1982, 1983). In Scott (1983), faunal remains of prehistoric pre-agricultural and agricultural faunal assemblages were compared from a multicomponent site known as Lubbub Creek (1PI85) located in Pickens County, Alabama. The site is located within the Black Belt physiographic zone that extends southeast from Mississippi (Figure 4.1). The pre-agricultural small-mammal assemblage identified at Lubbub Creek consisted of 32 identified specimens (NISP) representing a minimum number of 14 individuals (MNI). The small-mammal faunal assemblage associated with the agricultural occupation at the site had an NISP of 282 representing 56 MNI. One problem worthy of consideration here is sample size. It is generally held that some faunal samples are too small to provide adequate representation and that differential preservation may lead to bias toward larger mammals. Moreover, when two or more assemblages are compared, samples should be similar in size and representation (Reitz and Wing 1999). Despite the size differences between the two faunal assemblages at Lubbub Creek, Scott examined several patterns thought to indicate environmental disturbance associated with agriculture. First, Scott maintained that the ratio of gray squirrel (*Sciurus carolinensis*) to fox squirrel (*Sciurus niger*) in a faunal collection can provide information on forest composition. Gray squirrels prefer climax deciduous forests; as agricultural fields and subsequent secondary forest growth replace these forests, fox squirrels that are more tolerant of such conditions replace gray squirrels. For the pre-agricultural Woodland period, Scott identified a ratio of 12 gray squirrels to every fox squirrel, based on the NISP, indicating the prevalence of climax deciduous forests. In contrast, for the agricultural Mississippian period, the ratio was 1.8 gray squirrels to every fox squirrel. This observed decrease in the frequency of gray squirrels relative to fox squirrels was interpreted as evidence for deforestation of the area with an increase in secondary forest growth (Scott 1983:362).

Another small-mammal species useful for documenting habitat disturbance is the eastern cottontail (*Sylvilagus floridanus*). The eastern cottontail is found in relatively low frequency in deciduous forest habitats but is highly adaptable to disturbed areas, reaching population climax between 5 and 12 years after forest clearing. Escape is a high priority for the cottontail: thickets, high grass, and weeds provided in the early successive stages of fields and forests offer necessary cover (Smith 1975:92). Considering cottontail frequency at the Lubbub Creek site, Scott observed an increase in bone elements in the Mississippian agricultural sample compared with the earlier pre-agricultural assemblage. When the two assemblages were compared, the cottontail made up at least 10 percent of the identified mammalian specimens in the agricultural sample, up from 4.3 percent in the pre-agricultural sample (Scott 1983:362).

Finally, Scott recognized that certain rodent species prefer disturbed and cleared habitats (Scott 1983:363). Two rat species, hispid cotton rat (*Sigmodon hispidus*) and marsh rice rat (*Oryzomys palustris*), are highly adaptable to cleared areas and old fields. These two rodent species are associated with the Mississippian (agricultural-period) features at Lubbub Creek (Scott 1983:363), but neither species was identified in the pre-agricultural assemblage. The harvest mouse, indigenous to the area, also prefers old fields, grassy areas, and scrubby, bush environs (Choate et al. 1994), but it was not identified in the Lubbub Creek faunal assemblage. The three mouse species identified from the Mississippian component at Lubbub Creek were the white-footed mouse (*Peromyscus leucopus*), cotton mouse (*Peromyscus gossypinus*), and woodland vole (*Microtus pinetorium*). The white-footed mouse will occupy only a hardwood forest environment, while the other two species are more adaptable and are found in primary forests as well as disturbed and cleared areas. The presence of the white-footed mouse in the Mississippian faunal sample indicates that some mature hardwoods were maintained in the area during this agricultural period in prehistory (Scott 1983:363).

Using Scott's model (1983) as a basis for this study, I completed a literature search to identify the small-mammal habitats common to the research area. Only those habitats associated with or affected by land clearance are discussed here. These include the undisturbed hardwood deciduous forest and six other habitats representing different stages in secondary growth following deforestation: pine-oak forests, forest edges, cleared fields, old fields, grassy areas, and shrub/bush thickets. Twenty-seven small terrestrial mammal species show a preference for one or more of these habitats (Table 4.1). Small mammals generally are found in deciduous forest habitats, specifically in tropical regions (Hayward and Phillipson 1979:139–142). A similar pattern pertains in this study, where 67 percent (18 of 27) of the local small-mammal species are associated with the hardwood forest habitat. With the exception of the short-tailed shrew (*Blarina carolinensis*), the white-footed mouse, and possibly the gray squirrel (Choate et al. 1994:146), all other species common to hardwood forests are also found in one or more of the disturbed habitats. The small-mammal fauna basic to identifying land clearance and successive stages of regrowth are the nine species that prefer habitats other than deciduous forests. These are the flying squirrel (*Glaucomys volans*), red fox (*Vulpes vulpes*), least shrew (*Cryptotis parva*), nine-banded armadillo (*Dasypus novemcinetus*), woodchuck (*Marmota monax*), marsh rice rat (*Oryzomys palustris*), harvest mouse (*Reithrodontomys humulis*), hispid cotton rat (*Sigmodon hispidus*), and striped skunk (*Mephitis mephitis*). The model in its simplest form dictates that the presence of one or more of these species in an archaeological faunal assemblage could provide evidence for secondary growth associated with land clearance; therefore, the greater the number of these individuals, the greater the area disturbed. Additionally, if comparisons can be made between prehistoric pre-agricultural and agricultural faunal assemblages, the patterns described by Scott should be recognized. Specifically, with land clearance asso-

Table 4.1. Indigenous fauna and certain preferred habitats for the Black Belt in Mississippi

Small Mammal	Preferred Habitat*						
	Hardwood Forest	Pine-Oak	Forest Edge	Cleared Field	Old Field	Grassy	Scrubby/Bush
White-Footed Mouse	X						
Short-Tailed Shrew	X						
Gray Squirrel	X						
Fox Squirrel	X	X					
Golden Mouse	X	X	X	X	X	X	
Eastern Mole	X	X	X	X	X	X	X
Spotted Skunk	X	X	X	X	X	X	X
Raccoon	X		X	X	X		
Eastern Woodrat	X		X	X	X	X	
Opossum	X		X				X
Weasel	X		X				
Bobcat	X		X			X	X
Gray Fox	X		X			X	
Eastern Cottontail	X		X			X	X
Cotton Mouse	X			X	X		
Southeastern Shrew	X					X	
Woodland Vole	X					X	X
Eastern Chipmunk	X						X
Flying Squirrel		X					
Red Fox		X		X	X		
Armadillo			X			X	X
Woodchuck			X				
Cotton Rat			X	X	X		
Striped Skunk			X	X	X	X	X
Least Shrew				X		X	
Harvest Mouse					X	X	X
Marsh Rice Rat					X		

*Derived from Choate et al. 1994 and Smith 1975

ciated with agriculture, an increase in fox squirrels, rabbits, and a variety of rat and mouse species would be expected (Scott 1983).

I would argue that, in addition to increased frequencies of these species in the archaeological faunal assemblage recovered from agricultural sites, there would be a concurrent increase in the representation of carnivores, particularly the smaller ones that feed on rabbits and rodents. These carnivores would include the red fox (*Vulpes vulpes*), gray fox (*Urocyon cinereoargenteus*), striped skunk (*Mephitis mephitis*), long-tailed weasel (*Mustela frenata*), bobcat (*Lynx rufus*) (Choate et al. 1994:224–252), and possibly domestic dog (*Canis familiaris*). The increased representation of carnivores can be demonstrated using the secondary data set from the Lubbub Creek site (Scott 1983:Appendices A and B). When small terrestrial mammals are considered, two carnivore species—bobcat and gray fox—are identified in the pre-agricultural Woodland faunal assemblage. These represent 6.2 percent of the identified specimens and 14 percent of the total small-mammal MNI. In contrast, four carnivore species, striped skunk, dog/wolf, gray fox, and bobcat, are represented in the agricultural Mississippian sample, constituting 11.3 percent of the specimen count and 17.8 percent of the small-mammal MNI. Interestingly, no dogs are associated with the Woodland sample, whereas three are identified in the Mississippian collection. According to MNI data, the ratio of rodent/rabbit to carnivore in the Woodland period is 1.5:1, increasing to 2:1 in the later agricultural period. This increase in rodent/rabbit frequency relative to carnivores may indicate that the prey population was increasing at a faster rate than the predator population, a condition characteristic of rapid adaptation to environmental change. If the predator/prey relationship were in equilibrium, the ratio should be similar for both time periods (Pianka 1988:276–279).

One potential problem with this interpretation is that the increased frequency of carnivores and rodent/rabbits in the later archaeological assemblage may be due to processes other than general hunting for food and skins. Small mammals can enter the archaeological record in a variety of ways (Dincauze 2000; Lyman 1994; Reitz and Wing 1999; Whyte 1991). Dogs, in this instance, may have been domesticated and tolerated for cultural purposes, while rodents occupied human habitats as commensal species or possible competitors. Individual bones or teeth of mammals may have been introduced into feature contexts after serving as decorative or medicinal purposes. Some small mammals probably occupied archaeological sites during and between periods of human habitation. Unfortunately, their remains may not be associated with human occupation debris (Dincauze 2000). In some cases, rodent remains may be deposited in carnivore fecal matter or regurgitated bird pellets (Dincauze 2000; Reitz and Wing 1999; Lyman 1994). Rodents can also be trapped in open pits, increasing the frequency of bone elements in a faunal assemblage (Whyte 1991).

ANALYSIS AND RESULTS

Two sites were chosen in this study to evaluate the application of a small-mammal model in paleoenvironmental analysis: Josey Farm (22OK793) and Yarborough (22CL814) (Figure 4.1). The Josey Farm site (22OK793), located in Oktibbeha County, Mississippi, was chosen because cultural remains were identified from both Middle and Late Mississippian contexts (Rafferty and Hogue 1999). Mississippian populations characteristically engaged in maize agriculture; however, no maize or other cultigens were identified in the botanical remains recovered from this site (Trinkley 1999). This seemed remarkable given that maize or maize use has been documented at other nearby Middle and Late Mississippian sites, including Lyon's Bluff (Hogue 2000) and South Farm (Hogue and Peacock 1995). Because no human burials were recovered from the Josey Farm site, stable carbon isotope analysis could not be used to provide direct evidence for maize consumption. We concluded that either maize was not consumed at the site or that botanical evidence for maize was destroyed by "expansion and contraction of the clay-heavy soils" (Rafferty and Hogue 1999:267). In any case, evidence for maize cultivation is lacking at the Josey Farm site and for this reason the site may represent a "homestead" or "seasonal occupation site" rather than functioning as an "agricultural farmstead" (Rafferty and Hogue 1999). Using a small-mammal model such as the one discussed in this study provides another line of evidence for examining site function when more direct evidence for agriculture is unavailable.

The Josey Farm site is located on a high ridge in a pasture just outside the city of Starkville. It was partially excavated as part of the Six-Sites Project, undertaken by Mississippi State University faculty from 1996 to 1999 in connection with new highway bypass construction. Hand excavation of 43 square meters and subsequent stripping led to the discovery of 15 features, 12 postholes, and debris associated with a prehistoric Mississippian structure, suggesting that the site probably represented a small Mississippian farmstead or other relatively short-term habitation locus consisting of one or two households. All feature fill was either floated or water-screened through 0.16-cm (1/16-inch) mesh.

The second site used in this study, the Yarborough site (22CL814), had ethnobotanical evidence for maize agriculture recovered from flotation samples (Caddell 1982a; cf. Peacock and Reese, this volume). The Yarborough site represents a Late Mississippian farmstead that may have been occupied during the months spanning late winter to early fall (Scott 1982:150). Paleoenvironmental data derived from faunal remains suggest that land clearing did take place at the Yarborough site, presumably for maize agriculture. However, based on faunal evidence, land clearing at Yarborough was determined to be much less extensive than was estimated for the Lubbub Creek agricultural site. The difference in the magnitude of land clearing at the two agricultural sites is due to several factors. First, the Yarborough site, as a farmstead, was considerably smaller than the Lubbub Creek village site and consequently less clearing would have been necessary for housing and fields. Second, the subsistence emphasis at Lubbub Creek was probably on maize agriculture while a more diverse diet of maize and naturally available foods was followed at the Yarborough site (Scott 1982:151).

The Yarborough and Josey Farm sites share certain characteristics that make them ideal for testing the reliability of a small-mammal model to assess paleoenvironmental change. Both sites are located in the Black Prairie physiographic region in Mississippi and therefore share similar overall faunal and floral community types with the Lubbub Creek site locality. Also, maize agriculture was documented at the Yarborough site, so similarities in small-mammal fauna with the Josey Farm site would support interpretation of the latter as a farmstead and would presumably reflect similar landscape alterations created by low-level agriculture. The major problem is that the two collections vary considerably in size, with Yarborough having more than seven times the number of identified small-mammal fragments (NISP) recovered from the Josey Farm site. In addition to size discrepancy, the Yarborough site faunal material was recovered primarily from a midden area (Solis and Walling 1982) whereas the Josey Farm faunal remains were excavated from basin-shaped features and a filled-in gully (Rafferty and Hogue 1999). Midden deposits, built up over time, represent relatively long-term habitation of a locale. In contrast, the fill of subsurface features may represent a single deposit or deposits accumulated over a shorter time span (e.g., Peacock 2000; Peacock and Chapman 2001). Given this discrepancy between the two sites, it is expected that the Yarborough faunal collection would contain more species since the duration of occupation apparently was longer. Another source of bias is the potential microenvironmental variation between the two sites. Although both are located in the Black Prairie, Josey Farm is located on a high ridge in a modern pasture with the nearest large stream, Josey Creek, situated approximately 1 km to the west (Rafferty and Hogue 1999). This stream is shown as intermittent in the Oktibbeha County soil survey (Brent 1973). Analysis of the floral materials recovered from Josey Farm documented the presence of pine, oak, hickory, and maple during site occupation (Trinkley 1999). In contrast, the Yarborough site was situated on a natural levee of Tibbee Creek, immediately upstream from the confluence of Tibbee Creek and Lee Creek. Soils in the floodplain would have supported either grassland prairie or a deciduous forest habitat, the latter being characterized by various combinations of oak and hickory (Solis and Walling 1982). A deciduous forest setting is indicated by a comparative study of different archaeobotanical data sets from Yarborough (Peacock and Reese, this volume). When the faunal assemblages from the two sites are compared, it is important to consider the possibility of biases resulting from differential depositional processes, site locations, and proximity to a permanent water source.

Using the faunal materials recovered from the Mississippian components, one can assess evidence for prehistoric land clearance at the two sites. Thirteen mammal species were identified in the Josey Farm

Table 4.2. Small-mammal species from the Josey Farm and Yarborough sites

Small Mammal	Josey Farm Site	Yarborough Site
Raccoon	X	X
Opossum	X	X
Eastern Cottontail	X	X
Gray Squirrel	X	X
Bobcat	X	X
Woodland Vole	X	X
Marsh Rice Rat	X	X
Peromyscus sp.	X	X
Hispid Cotton Rat	X	X
Eastern Mole	X	
Domestic Dog	X	
Swamp Rabbit		X
Fox Squirrel		X
Eastern Wood Rat		X
Striped Skunk		X
Woodchuck		X
Gray Fox		X

assemblage, including domestic dog (*Canis familiaris*). Of these 13 species, 10 are classified as small mammals (Table 4.2): raccoon (*Procyon lotor*), opossum (*Didelphis virginiana*), eastern cottontail (*Sylvilagus floridanus*), gray squirrel (*Sciurus carolinensis*), woodland vole (*Microtus pinetorium*), eastern mole (*Scalopus aquaticus*), New World mouse (*Peromyscus sp.*), probably white-footed (*Peromyscus leucopus*) or cotton mouse *(Peromyscus gossypinus)*, and hispid cotton (*Sigmodon hispidus*) and marsh rice (*Oryzomys palustris*) rats. The domestic dog is also included in the analysis as a carnivore. These small-mammal species were represented by 133 identified specimens and 21 MNI. Except for eastern mole and domestic dog, the same small mammals were present at the Yarborough site. Six additional small-mammal species were also identified (Table 4.2): swamp rabbit (*Sylvilagus aquaticus*), fox squirrel (*Sciurus niger*), woodchuck (*Marmota monax*), eastern wood rat (*Neotoma floridana*), gray fox (*Urocyon cinereoargenteus*), and striped skunk (*Mephitis mephitis*). The small-mammal species represented at the Yarborough site totaled 872 NISP and 60 MNI.

The first source of evidence for prehistoric land clearance at the Josey Farm and Yarborough sites was the presence of species in the archaeological collections that are not associated with forest habitats. Rodent species indicative of land clearance—the hispid cotton rat and the marsh rice rat—were identified in both faunal assemblages. These species prefer old fields, although the hispid cotton rat can also be found in forest-edge and cleared-field habitats (Table 4.1). Striped skunk

was also identified in the Yarborough faunal assemblage. Like the hispid cotton rat, the striped skunk prefers disturbed habitats, primarily
fields and forest edges (Table 4.1).

Additional support for prehistoric landscape alterations at the Josey
Farm and Yarborough sites can be documented using a variant of
Scott's model for small mammals. For this study, the percentages of
small-mammal specimens (NISP) and species MNI were calculated
for the eastern cottontail, rodent species, and carnivores. Comparative information derived from the Lubbub Creek pre-agricultural (Pre-
agricultural LC) and agricultural (Agricultural LC) collections was used
to assess similarities and differences among the four assemblages (Table
4.3; Figures 4.2 and 4.3). The Lubbub Creek locality yielded two different small-mammal assemblages, one representing a pre-agricultural
landscape with "little or no clearing" and the second representing "major agricultural clearing." These two faunal assemblages, as polar op-
posites, provide patterns for a continuum established for comparative
purposes. Since the Yarborough site functioned as a Mississippian
farmstead, clearing for agricultural purposes was probably less extensive than agricultural clearing at the larger Lubbub Creek village locality. For this reason the frequencies of fauna indicative of clearing
for the smaller farmstead site would be expected to fall somewhere between those established for the two Lubbub Creek small-mammal assemblages. If agricultural activities and land clearing had occurred at
the Josey Farm site, a similar pattern for animal representation would
be expected.

The eastern cottontail is considered first. This species represented
8.1 percent of the identified species and 28.6 percent of the MNI at the
Josey Farm site (Table 4.3; Figures 4.2 and 4.3). At Yarborough, 29 percent of the identified small-mammal species and 20 percent of the MNI
were eastern cottontail. In both cases these percentages are greater
than those calculated for the pre-agricultural Lubbub Creek site. When
MNI is considered, both the Josey Farm and Yarborough sites show
higher frequencies of eastern cottontail than the Lubbub Creek assemblages.

Rodent species also adaptable to secondary growth totaled 19 percent of the identified fragments and 28.6 percent of the MNI at Josey
Farm site and 1.9 percent (NISP) and 8.3 percent (MNI) at the Yarborough site (Table 4.3; Figures 4.2 and 4.3). When the data are compared
across sites, the percentages observed in the Josey Farm collection are
higher than those for the other three sites. Interestingly, fewer rodents
are represented at the Yarborough site than at the Lubbub Creek agricultural locality.

As for carnivores, only one wild species, bobcat, was present at
the Josey Farm site. The other carnivore present in the faunal collec-

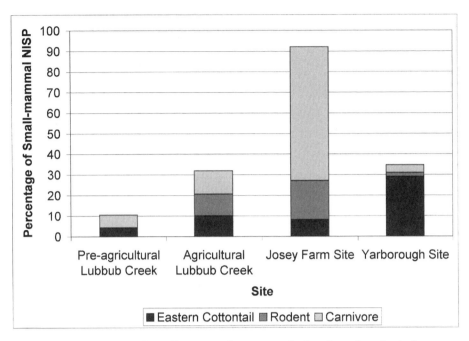

Fig. 4.2. Percentage of small-mammal NISP at Black Belt archaeological sites.

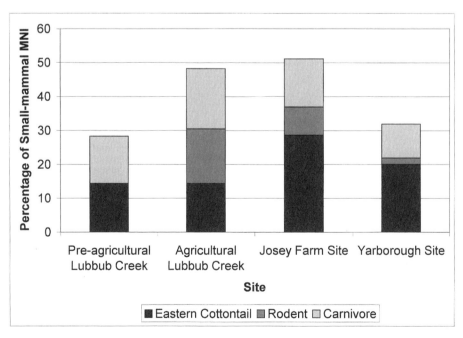

Fig. 4.3. Percentage of small-mammal MNI at Black Belt archaeological sites.

Table 4.3. Percentages of small-mammal NISP and MNI for archaeological sites in the Black Belt

Site	Eastern Cottontail		Rodent Species		Carnivore Species	
	NISP	MNI	NISP	MNI	NISP	MNI
Lubbub Creek Site (pre-agricultural)	4.3	14.3	0	0	6.2	14
Lubbub Creek Site (agricultural)	10	14.3	10.6	16.1	11.3	17.8
Josey Farm Site	8.1	28.6	19	28.6	65	14.2
Yarborough Site	29	20	1.9	8.3	3.8	10

tion was the domestic dog. Two dogs were recovered, one as a burial and the second represented by 69 disarticulated fragments recovered from feature fill. The latter may represent a disturbed dog burial, as there was no evidence of butchering on the bones. If considered small-mammal specimens, the dog specimens would constitute 9.5 percent of the MNI and 63 percent of the bone count. Unfortunately, the large number of elements recovered from this one dog exaggerates its importance when the percentage of identified elements is considered. Together, bobcat and dog constitute 14.5 percent of the MNI and 65 percent of the identified small-mammal bone at Josey Farm (Table 4.3; Figures 4.2 and 4.3). Three carnivore species—bobcat, striped skunk, and gray fox—identified at Yarborough represent 3.8 percent of the identified small-mammal species and 10 percent of the MNI.

When compared across the four Black Belt sites, the percentages of eastern cottontail and rodent species NISP are similar for the Lubbub Creek agricultural site and the Josey Farm site. Unfortunately, the large percentage of domestic dog remains at the latter site skews the results (Figure 4.2). However, when MNI is considered, the Lubbub Creek agricultural site and Josey Farm site appear very similar, especially when rodents are compared. In contrast, the Lubbub Creek pre-agricultural and Yarborough sites are comparable in their low frequency of rodent species. The MNI percentages for carnivores are similar for the four sites.

Finally, the ratio of rodent/rabbit to carnivore indicates an increase in small prey when compared with the pre-agricultural Woodland assemblage at Lubbub Creek. MNI data show the ratio of rodent/rabbit to carnivore to be 3:1 for the Josey Farm site and 3.5:1 for the Yarborough site, double that for the pre-agricultural sample at the Lubbub Creek site (Figure 4.4).

CONCLUSIONS

In conclusion, the frequency of small-mammal fauna, specifically eastern cottontail and rodent species recovered from Mississippian features

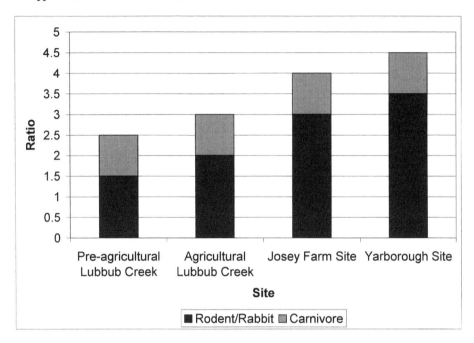

Fig. 4.4. Ratio of rodent/rabbit to carnivore, Black Belt archaeological sites.

at the Josey Farm and Yarborough sites, provides evidence for landscape alterations associated with agriculture. Additional support is given by the presence of small carnivores that feed on rodent and rabbit species and the increased ratio of rodent/rabbit to carnivore in the faunal assemblages associated with agricultural sites. These findings are in agreement with data from plant remains that suggest local land disturbance at the Yarborough site (Peacock and Reese, this volume).

Few distinct patterns emerge when comparisons of small-mammal MNI percentages are made among the four faunal samples (Figure 4.5). One is that the pre-agricultural Lubbub Creek assemblage has no rodents. A second pattern is a higher frequency of eastern cottontail at the Josey Farm and Yarborough sites when compared with the other two sites. This could reflect a different subsistence pattern for farmsteads, where a more generalized diet consisting of maize and naturally available foods was present (Hogue 2000; Hogue and Peacock 1995; Hogue et al. 1995). In contrast, inhabitants of the larger village site may have depended more on maize for their dietary staple, a pattern documented for larger agricultural populations (Buikstra 1992; Hogue 2000; Lynott et al. 1986).

One finding worthy of further investigation is the presence of domestic dog in Mississippian contexts at the Josey Farm site. Tradition-

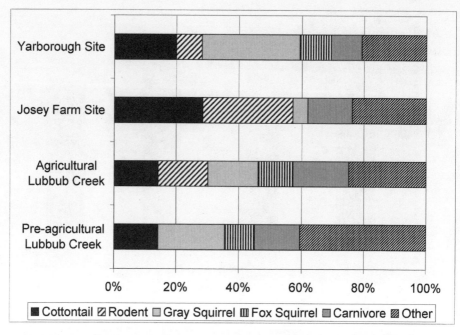

Fig. 4.5. Small-mammal representation, Black Belt archaeological sites.

ally, scholars have explained the presence of dogs in several ways: dogs were used for hunting and guarding; as pets, religious sacrifices, spirit guardians, and afterlife companions; and for food (Kerber 1997:94–95). In addition to these functions, I propose that in agricultural communities dogs may have played a favorable role as ratters, strengthening their symbiotic relationship with prehistoric farmers. Rats and mice would not only have adapted quickly to cleared fields, both new and fallow, but would have found areas used for discarded refuse or corn storage quite attractive. These areas are typically located near the living quarters, or in the case of refuse middens, on the village periphery. Ethnohistorical accounts of corn storage describe corncribs "raised seven or eight feet from the ground on posts that were polished so mice could not climb them" (Hudson 1976:299). The use of such labor-intensive storage facilities by prehistoric groups would suggest a relatively large and annoying mouse population around the camp—a mouse population that could be tempered by the presence of dogs in the living areas.

Application of a small-mammal model such as the one used here can provide independent or collateral evidence for paleoenvironmental change. However, several factors can affect the preservation and recovery of small-mammal bones: soil acidity, burning or other types of cultural alteration, and recovery techniques. In addition, it is imperative that a good comparative collection be available to aid in identifying the small mammals most important for paleoenvironmental reconstruction. Sample size should also be considered a possible source of bias. In this study the small size of the Josey Farm faunal collection clearly led to the overrepresentation of dog when NISP is considered. For this reason, the results of this study are considered a preliminary but important and necessary step in understanding and interpreting past landscape alterations.

5 A Comparison of Three Methods of Paleoenvironmental Analysis at an Archaeological Site on the Mississippi Black Prairie

Evan Peacock and Mary Celeste Reese

INTRODUCTION

Using biotic data from archaeological sites to "reconstruct" environmental settings in locales inhabited by past human beings is one of the standard goals of environmental archaeology (e.g., Walsh 1999). Butzer (1982:6), for example, suggested that the "primary goal of environmental archaeology should be to define the characteristics and processes of the biophysical environment that provide a matrix for and interact with socioeconomic systems." According to Reitz et al. (1996:3), the ultimate goal is "to develop a fuller understanding of the ecology of human communities." More recently, Dincauze (2000:20) defined environmental archaeology as "the study of paleoenvironments as human habitats." However, as Rafferty (1978), O'Brien (2001), and others have pointed out, "reconstruction" is something of a misnomer. In many studies, data derived from one type of biotic remains—pollen, snails, plant macrofossils, and other remains—are presented, and the implications of those data for understanding human adaptations in a particular place and time are made explicit (e.g., Peacock and Melsheimer, this volume). Although tracking changes in a particular data set may reveal patterns useful for scientists interested in human/nature interactions (for example, increases in ragweed pollen, disturbance-favored snail or other animal species, or sedimentation rates providing evidence for human landscape alteration), such single data sets do not allow for wholesale reconstruction of past environments. Even studies using multiple types of biotic data cannot begin to reconstruct the vastly complex ecosystems of any given space/time locus. The best ecological surveys by field biologists do not provide data sufficient for complete characterization of *contemporary* environmental systems. How can they, when enormous components of those ecosystems, such as soil biota, have scarcely been recognized, let alone systematically named, inventoried, and quantified (Wilson 1992)?

What paleoecologists and environmental archaeologists actually engage in is *construction*—the slow assembling, one piece at a time, of a model of past environments as complete as can be obtained given the limitations of the data sources available. These past environments may have no modern analogs, so that our understanding of long-term human relationships to the physical world depends on adding as many buttresses to the construction as possible. We do this by employing data from many different sources (e.g., deFrance et al. 1996; Leveau 1999; Nicholson and O'Conner 2000; Zutter 1999). This process leads to a whole series of very complicated observational problems related to differential preservation, recovery methods and attendant biases, and the different rates at which plant and animal species react to one of two constants: (1) the environment as a whole is never static but constantly changing, and (2) culture, too, is constantly changing, partly in response to environmental factors (Bamforth 1988; Nicholas 1988a).

The problems that attend paleoenvironmental data can be lumped into two main areas of concern: material bias and interpretive scale. The materials with which we work come to us as fragmentary remains, formed by the vagaries of natural and/or cultural deposition; altered by subsequent chemical and mechanical forces; shaped by the methods and techniques of recovery and processing; and subject to the time, efforts, equipment, and skills available for analysis and interpretation. Interpretive scale refers to the wider ecological and cultural context within which paleoenvironmental data are understood. A researcher interested in climatic change, for example, might employ variations in the proportions of different tree species represented by charcoal at archaeological sites to chart changes in forest composition through time. The obvious potential cultural biases aside, we know that forest associations—characteristic floral groupings as denoted via contemporary, essentially synchronic, observation—do not react as a unit in the face of environmental change. Rather, individual species react at different rates to any given change in conditions (Botkin 1990; Colinvaux 1987; P. Delcourt and H. Delcourt 1987; Gaudreau 1988; Joyce 1988). The same is true for any group of organisms, and the effect is a constant ebb and flow of life across the face of the planet. The biosphere can be conceived of as a liquid, thick in some places and thin in others, full of fragile aggregate masses and individual specks of life, through which the current of time constantly runs. To accommodate this flux is to acknowledge that our standard units of analysis—species, archaeological "cultures" or periods—are likewise *constructions*, relevant only insofar as they serve to address whatever questions we choose to ask.

Fortunately for environmental archaeologists, some biological and ecological constructions—for instance, species—are relevant at scales commensurate with at least a functionalist understanding of the whys, whens, and wherefores of the New World archaeological record. Though the boundaries of both biological and archaeological units may be arbitrary from an evolutionary perspective (Mayr 1949, 1987; O'Brien and Lyman 2000), once employed they may at least help us to realize evolutionary questions, especially in those interesting cases where they fail to produce even a satisfactory functionalist explanation for material patterns in time and space. Uniformitarian assumptions regarding habitat requirements are founded on the idea that no significant changes in the ecological preferences of plant or animal species have occurred during the relatively short time spans covered in most New World archaeological studies, except in cases of domestication (whether incidental or purposeful; Smith 1992). We thus consider the use of species as analytic units in Holocene paleoenvironmental studies defensible, even if such studies are evolutionary in nature.

Of the two areas of concern—material bias and interpretive scale— the former, though replete with cautionary tales, is nonetheless easier to deal with in practical and theoretical terms. Through controlled experiment and careful observation, we are able to *know*, to the extent made possible by our observational apparatus, what biases have been in operation and how they have affected our data sets. Accordingly, we can search for ways to compensate for such biases. Studies of bias in shell assemblages (Muckle 1994; Peacock 2000; Peacock and Chapman 2001), the post-depositional movement and degradation of pollen in the soil (Bunting and Tipping 2000; Kelso et al. 2000), and taphonomic processes affecting animal bones (Lyman 1994) are just a few examples. The difficulties of incorporating different kinds of data, which are best interpreted at different scales, into a single study are much more complex, both conceptually and in practice (Stein and Linse 1993; Walsh 1999). Some practitioners of archaeology (Hardesty and Fowler 2001), cultural or human ecology, paleoecology (Gaudreau 1988), and neo-ecology (Zimmerer 1994) have advocated "multi-scalar" or "nested" approaches, but that umbrella soon becomes so wide that the original phenomena of interest may become hidden from view. It is in this arena that standard units of analysis become most strained, and it may be that a truly evolutionary approach—that is, one capable of dealing with change as a continuum rather than as a series of differences in state (Dunnell 1980; O'Brien and Lyman 2000)—may not be achievable in an interdisciplinary vein unless the ways in which we structure our observations and categorize our data are reconceptualized.

In this paper, we do not offer a solution for overcoming such problems. What we offer is yet another cautionary tale, but one that is ap-

Fig. 5.1. Location of the Yarborough (22CL814) and Lyon's Bluff (22OK520) archaeological sites, Mississippi.

propriate to this volume as it deals with the unique environmental and cultural setting of the Mississippi Black Prairie. We demonstrate how three different sets of paleoenvironmental data—pollen, charred plant remains, and plant impressions in daub—yield three different pictures of environmental conditions at a late-fifteenth-century Native American farmstead in Clay County, Mississippi. The material biases related to each of these data sets are discussed, and the implications for ecological and archaeological interpretation at the local scale are given.

SITE DESCRIPTION

The Yarborough site (22CL814) is a small, prehistoric site located on a natural levee adjacent to Tibbee Creek, a tributary of the Tombigbee River (Figure 5.1). The lower Tibbee Creek floodplain lies within the Black Prairie physiographic province of Mississippi. The site was extensively excavated in late 1980 before inundation resulting from the creation of Columbus Lake (Solis and Walling 1982).

Although some earlier artifacts and features were encountered, the primary occupation at Yarborough is represented by a single, Late Mississippian-period domestic structure (Structure 1). Associated with this prehistoric house was a refuse dump on the side of the levee. The site produced excellent assemblages of artifacts and biotic remains (Solis and Walling 1982). An A.D. 1480 average of three radiocarbon dates suggests that the refuse dump "may . . . have been deposited during the latter half of the 15th century" (Solis and Walling 1982:170). Solis and Walling (1982:169) interpret the site as a "Late Mississippian . . . rural farmstead" representing "a basically year-round settlement, agriculturally based but with a well-mixed, broad-spectrum economy exploiting a wide variety of the available resources in this environment" (cf. Hogue, this volume).

MATERIAL CATEGORIES AND ANALYTIC METHODS

Three types of data are used in this paper to describe environmental conditions in the Black Prairie as they existed during the time the Yarborough farmstead was occupied. Two of these—pollen and charred plant remains—were reported in Solis and Walling (1982). The other—plant impressions in daub, or clay plaster—was presented in Reese (2000). For this study, Dr. Gloria Caddell made available to us previously unpublished data on charred seeds from Yarborough.

POLLEN

Sheehan (1982) analyzed pollen from 10 soil samples taken during the excavations at Yarborough. Only one of these samples "contained pollen in meaningful quantity"; the rest contained "traces" (Sheehan 1982:133). The analytical procedure is given by Sheehan (1982:133):

> The Pollen [*sic*] processing technique included the following procedures: (1) removal of clays with sodium pyrophosphate; (2) Removal of coarse mineral and organic particles by screening through 300 micrometre mesh; (3) Removal of carbonates with hydrochloric acid; (4) Removal of silicates with hydrofluoric acid; (5) Removal of "soft" organic matter by acetolysis; (6) Removal of fluorosilicates and fine organic matter by screening through seven micrometre mesh; (7) Dehydration in ethanol; (8) Suspension in tert-butyl alcohol; and (9) Mounting of final suspension in silicone oil (viscosity 12,500 cs.) on glass slides.
>
> Slides were scanned for pollen at magnification of 300X with a Wild M-20 research microscope. Identification of grains was normally made at 600X, occasionally at 1500X.

A total of 192 grains were counted, including fern spores. Of this total, 134 grains (approximately 70 percent) came from Sample No.

Table 5.1. Pollen from the Yarborough site (22CL814) (from Sheehan 1982)

	Number of Grains
Pine (*Pinus* sp.)	69
Sweet Gum (*Liquidambar styraciflua*)	7
Black Gum (*Nyssa sylvatica*) .	1
Alder (*Alnus* sp.)	1
Dogwood (*Cornus* sp.)	1
Sycamore (*Platanus occidentalis*)	1
Oak (*Quercus* sp.)	14
Hickory (*Carya* sp.)	7
Black Walnut (*Juglans nigra*)	2
Basswood (*Tilia* sp.)	3
Tulip Tree (*Liriodendron tulipfera*)	1
Hazel (*Corylus* sp.)	2
Ragweed (*Ambrosia* sp.)	13
Daisy tribe	2
Parsley family	1
Convolvulus (morning glory) type	2
Viburnum sp.	1
Chenopodiaceae/Amaranthaceae	15
Grass	2
Fern Spores	11
Total	156

1003 (Sheehan 1982:Table 32). The report does not give provenience information for the samples, although they apparently were taken from beneath the daub layer during excavation (Solis and Walling 1982:21). The total identifiable pollen grains from the site are listed in Table 5.1.

Charred Plant Remains

Plant remains from Yarborough were analyzed by Caddell (1982a). An impressive amount of soil (1,671 liters) was subjected to flotation: this included samples taken from excavation unit levels, features, and "all soil from excavation units of Structure 1" (Caddell 1982a:134). The soil was immersed in water and agitated, and all floating materials were captured in fine (0.35-mm) screen. Heavier elements were subjected to chemical flotation and likewise retrieved. Nearly 80,000 fragments of plant remains were analyzed (Caddell 1982a:135). These data, along with data on charred seeds not tabulated in the original report, are summarized in Table 5.2.

Daub

Native Americans living in the Black Belt and elsewhere in the Southeast during the Mississippian period (ca. A.D. 1000–1500) constructed houses of wattle and daub, with cane (*Arundinaria* sp.) providing much of the framework (e.g., Connaway 1984). The daub, or clay plaster, was tempered mainly with grasses to provide strength and even drying

Table 5.2. Charred plant remains from Late Mississippian contexts at the Yarborough site (22CL814)*

Nutshell	Number of Specimens
Hickory (*Carya* sp.)	28,273
Black Walnut (*Juglans nigra*)	391
Acorn (*Quercus* sp.)	3,137
Nutmeat	
Acorn	6
Juglandaceae	81
Domesticates	
Sunflower (*Helianthus* sp.)	25
Maize (*Zea mays)*	3,007
Beans (*Phaseolus* sp.)	4
Other	
Liliaceae	1
Grape (*Vitis* sp.)	10
Pine (*Pinus* sp.)	1
Chenopodium sp.	4
Hawthorn (*Crataegus* sp.)	1
Persimmon (*Diospyros virginiana)*	72
Maypop (*Passiflora incarnata)*	2
Plum (*Prunus* sp.)	2
Sumac (*Rhus* sp.)	1
Nightshade (*Solanum* sp.)	1
Total	35,019

Source: Caddell 1982a:Table 45 and unpublished seed data
* excludes galls, buds, and unidentified fruits, seeds, and bark

(Boudreau 1980; Connaway 1984; Solis and Walling 1982:173–175).
Adair (1930:451) provided an account of the construction process witnessed during a mid-eighteenth-century visit to the Chickasaw in northern Mississippi: "Then they weave them [log poles] thick with split saplings, and daub them all over about six or seven inches thick with tough clay, well mixt with withered grass: when this cement is half dried, they thatch the house with the longest sort of dry grass that their land produces."

Not surprisingly, perhaps, these thatched houses often burned, and the inadvertent firing of the plaster provided a record of plant impressions left in the once-wet clay. Southeastern archaeologists have begun to take advantage of this data source. Ruhl (1987) undertook a study of the plant temper in daub in Florida, and Connaway (1984) suggested using leaf impressions in daub for paleoenvironmental analysis. Caddell (1982a:138) noted that, at the Yarborough site, "Impressions and casts of several types of plants were identified in the daub itself. Cane and grass impressions were abundant. Casts of acorns were noted frequently, and some of these were casts of the entire acorn, including the cap. A cast of cocklebur fruit (*Xanthium strumarium*) was identified in one piece of daub."

Moreover, she pointed out, "The numerous impressions of acorns and the impression of a cocklebur in the daub indicate that it was applied to the structure in the early fall" (Caddell 1982a:140). Quantified daub data are not presented in her report, and it is not clear whether the daub from the site was systematically analyzed at that time. Peacock (1993) analyzed daub from two sites in the Mississippi Black Prairie. Site 22OK694 is a small, Mississippian-period site located on the western edge of the Black Prairie: a thermoluminescence date of A.D. 1140 was obtained from a ceramic sherd associated with daub at that site (Peacock 1993:149, 1995). Plant impressions were mostly of oak and unidentified deciduous tree leaves; a few needles of pine also were identified. Daub from various Mississippian contexts at the Lyon's Bluff site (22OK520), a large mound and village complex located in the Black Prairie on a tributary of Tibbee Creek (Figure 5.1), contained numerous plant impressions, again dominated by deciduous hardwoods (Figure 5.2).

A major assumption underlying daub analysis is that, with the exception of grass added for temper and the poles and cane used in house framing, plant impressions represent incidental inclusions, materials that adhered to the wet clay as it was being quarried and prepared for application as plaster (Peacock 1993; Reese 2000). Other than leaves, daub frequently contains impressions of nuts, seeds, and fruits: handprints also are common, as are artifacts (e.g., pieces of pottery, stone flakes, burned bone), snail casts, and other objects that presumably were incidental inclusions. This assumption has major implications for how data from daub are interpreted.

The amount of daub recovered from the site is not given in the original report, but it filled several boxes. Four of these boxes (approximately 0.03 m^3 each) were randomly selected to provide a sample for daub analysis. Individual pieces of daub ranged in size from less than a centimeter to several centimeters across: those weighing more than 30 g were analyzed. The outer surface was visually examined for leaf or seed impressions. Inner surfaces were then carefully exposed using picking tools such as screwdrivers and dental picks. Daub breaks along planes created by leaves, grass, and other inclusions that have burned or leached out of the clay. These planes are often visible in the side of a given piece of daub, making the selection of breaking points fairly easy.

Grass impressions, presumably representing temper, were abundant in most of the daub examined. Impressions of cane (*Arundinaria* sp.)

Fig. 5.2. Impression of persimmon leaf in daub from the
Lyon's Bluff site. From Peacock (1993). Photo by Jimmy Cole.

also were common: these represent the wall wattle to which the wet
clay daub was applied. Abundant leaf, nut, and seed impressions found
on the surface and inside pieces of daub were identified by comparisons
with literature sources (Foster and Duke 1990; Hutchens 1991; Martin
and Barkley 1961; Radford et al. 1968; Timme 1989; Young and Young
1992) and herbarium specimens at Mississippi State University, and
with the assistance of professional biologists. Specific leaf identifications were based on margins, apices, and/or venation patterns in the
impressions. Nuts and seeds were identified from latex molds of cavi-
ties in the daub, following Peacock (1993).

No attempt was made to identify the ubiquitous grass impressions.
Dr. Rubin Shmulsky, then at the Mississippi State University Forest
Products Laboratory, identified a few pieces of *Quercus* sp. charcoal
found in the Yarborough daub. The data resulting from the daub analy-
sis are presented in Table 5.3; the charcoal data have been added in
Table 5.4.

Table 5.3. Plant impressions in daub from the Yarborough site (22CL814) (from Reese 2000)

	Number of Impressions
Quercus phellos (willow oak)	78
Quercus nigra (water oak)	3
Quercus sp.	39
Ulmus rubra (slippery elm)	2
Cornus drummondii (rough-leaf dogwood)	5
Celtis laevigata (hackberry)	1
Gleditsia triacanthos (honey locust)	1
Robinia pseudo-acacia (black locust)	1
Xanthium strumarium (cocklebur)	1
Arundinaria sp.	1,640
Juncus sp. (rush)	1
Carex sp. (sedge)	3
Poaceae (grass)	present
Total	1,775

RESULTS

Pine pollen overwhelmingly dominates in the samples from Yarborough (Table 5.1); oak, hickory, sweetgum, black walnut, hazel, and tulip poplar are also represented in the arboreal pollen. According to Sheehan (1982:133), "The impression given by this pollen assemblage is of a pine-dominated vegetation with oak and hickory as associates." Sheehan also noted the presence of ragweed (*Ambrosia* sp.) and Chenopodiace-Amaranthaceae pollen at the site.

The charred plant remains were dominated by nutshell (Table 5.2), which made up over 43 percent by count and almost 53 percent by weight of the identified floral remains (Caddell 1982a:Table 45). Hickory was the most abundant, followed by acorn and black walnut. Maize was common: more than 3,000 cupules, kernels, glumes, or other fragments were counted. More than 313 g of wood charcoal were recovered but not identified to taxon: Caddell noted only that most of the wood likely associated with Structure 1 "is diffuse-porous, and a few fragments of ring-porous wood are also present" (Caddell 1982a:138). Caddell provided the authors with previously unpublished seed data: taxa represented include *Chenopodium* sp., hawthorn, persimmon, sunflower, maypop, plum, sumac, wild grape, and nightshade (Table 5.2).

The daub contained abundant plant impressions, including many casts of whole acorns (Figure 5.3). A number of *Quercus phellos* or willow oak leaves and acorns were found (Table 5.3). Water oak (*Q. nigra*) also was identified. Many fragmentary impressions were identified as *Quercus* sp., making oak the dominant tree genus recognized in the

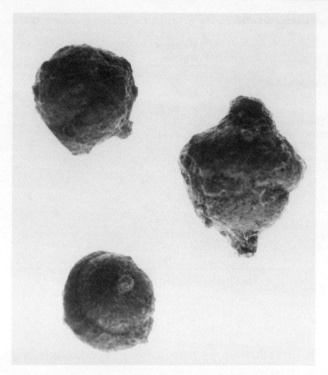

Fig. 5.3. Casts of acorn from daub, the Yarborough site.
Photo by Jimmy Cole.

daub. Slippery elm (*Ulmus rubra*) was present in low numbers. Other
tree species identified were understory trees, such as rough-leaf dogwood
(*Cornus drummondii*), honey locust (*Gleditsia triacanthos*), black locust (*Robinia pseudo-acacia*), and hackberry (*Celtis laevigata*) (Table 5.3).

INTERPRETATIONS AND CONSIDERATIONS
OF BIAS AND SCALE

Table 5.4 lists the taxa identified as present or absent from the three
methods. The picture of environmental conditions presented by each
is markedly different in several important aspects that will be discussed in this section.

Sheehan (1982:133) suggested that the pine-dominated pollen spectrum from Yarborough was "not unlike the pollen assemblage produced by the modern vegetation of the Gulf-South region, but is also
similar to the general pattern there of the last 5,000 years." He further
noted that:

Further analogy of the . . . pollen assemblage with the modern
pollen rain is provided by the high proportion of ragweed pollen

Table 5.4. Presence/absence of taxa revealed by different methods of environmental analysis at the Yarborough site (22CL814)

	Pollen	Charred Plant Remains	Daub
ARBOREAL			
Hickory (*Carya* sp.)	x	x	
Pine (*Pinus* sp.)	x	x	
Quercus phellos			x
Quercus nigra			x
Oak (*Quercus* sp.)	x	x	x
Black Walnut (*Juglans nigra*)	x	x	
Sweetgum (*Liquidambar styraciflua*)	x		
Black Gum	x		
Alder (*Alnus* sp.)	x		
Dogwood (*Cornus drummondii*)			x
Dogwood (*Cornus* sp.)	x		
Slipperyelm (*Ulmus rubra*)			x
Sycamore (*Platanus occidentalis*)	x		
Basswood (*Tilia* sp.)	x		
Tuliptree (*Liriodendron tulipfera*)	x		
Hazel (*Corylus* sp.)	x		
Persimmon (*Dispyros virginiana*)		x	
Plum (*Prunus* sp.)		x	
Hawthorn (*Crataegus* sp.)		x	
Hackberry (*Celtis laevigata*)			x
Honey Locust (*Gleditsia triacanthos*)			x
Black Locust (*Robinia pseudo-acacia*)			x
UNDERSTORY SHRUBS/VINES			
Sumac (*Rhus* sp.)			
Cane (*Arundinaria* sp.)		x	x
Viburnum sp.			
Grape (*Vitis* sp.)		x	
WEEDY/DISTURBANCE FAVORED			
Chenopodiaceae	x	x	
Amaranthaceae	x		
Ragweed (*Ambrosia* sp.)	x		
Cocklebur (*Xanthium strumarium*)			x
Convolvulus (morning glory) sp.	x		
OTHER			
Daisy tribe	x		
Parsley family	x		
Grass	x		x
Sedge			x
Rush (*Juncus* sp.)			x
Fern	x		
Maypop (*Passiflora incarnata*)		x	
Maygrass (*Phalaris caroliniana*)		x	
Nightshade (*Solanum* sp.)		x	
Liliaceae		x	
DOMESTICATES			
Maize (*Zea mays*)		x	
Beans (*Phaseolus vulgaris*)		x	
Sunflower (*Helianthus* sp.)		x	

(12 percent) in the sample. In lacustrine sediments spanning the Holocene, equivalent percentages of ragweed pollen occur only in post-European settlement strata. . . . This suggests that pollen in this sample may be intrusive from later times. Still, the possibility exists that intense local disturbance resulting from human occupation of the Yarborough Site could, at any time, have re-

sulted in strictly local abundance of ragweed pollen (Sheehan 1982:133–134).

Pollen data can suffer from a number of biases. It is well known that pollen grains with bladders (like those of pine) can travel great distances via wind transport. The resulting spectrum from any given locale thus presents a picture of regional, rather than strictly local, conditions. This in itself is not a problem, if the regional picture is what is desired. A more insidious problem is the apparent ease with which pollen grains, once deposited, can move downward through the soil (Kelso et al. 2000). When coupled with the degradation common in biologically active soils (Bunting and Tipping 2000), pollen data from dryland contexts must be considered suspect.

It is difficult to evaluate the Yarborough pollen spectrum via comparison with pollen data from other locales, partly because of the low number of pollen sites reported in the Southeast and partly because of the post-depositional disturbance regime particular to each sampling locale. Whitehead and Sheehan (1985) analyzed pollen from an oxbow lake in eastern Mississippi, noting that "[p]ine increases steadily from 2400 years [B.P.] to the present. The expansion of pine corresponds with decreases in oak, hickory and *Nyssa* in the last 2000 years. Sweetgum remained an important forest constituent. We believe that this pine rise was caused by aboriginal land practices (early agriculture) and an associated increase in fire frequency" (Whitehead and Sheehan 1985: 135). This late-Holocene increase in pine is seen in other pollen spectra from the Southeast (e.g., Watts 1980a; Prentice et al. 1991) and is usually attributed to gradually increasing temperatures in the region since the end of the Pleistocene (e.g., Grimm and Jacobson 1992; Prentice et al. 1991:2047). Two competing hypotheses—climate change vs. anthropogenic disturbance—thus could explain the high proportion of pine and ragweed pollen at Yarborough. However, this line of inquiry becomes moot if the pollen spectrum is essentially a modern, rather than a prehistoric, one.

This question can be addressed to some extent by looking at the other data sets from the site. While the charred plant remains might be biased by the cultural selection of species, it is assumed that, excepting the cane wattle and grass temper, the plant impressions in the daub represent incidental inclusions. It also can be suggested that, owing to the weight of the clay, the quarry for daub material was close to the site. Tree species thus known via the daub analysis to have been in the local area (e.g., honey locust, black locust; Table 5.3) should be represented in the pollen data if the pollen is in fact prehistoric: they are not. Also telling in this regard is the lack of maize pollen, since maize was quite abundant in the charred plant remains (Table 5.2).

This may simply be a sample-size effect, given the small number of grains that were identified. However, if the pollen retrieved from the site is contemporary with the prehistoric occupation, it is curious that it was not present in relatively equivalent amounts in all the samples. While arguing from negative evidence is always risky, we suggest that the pollen from Yarborough is in fact modern, based on the absence of species represented in the other data sets and the fact that 70 percent of the pollen grains came from only one sample, rather than being more generally distributed.

The other data sets suffer from their own biases. The charred plant remains represent species used by the prehistoric inhabitants of the Yarborough site for specific purposes (e.g., fuel wood, construction material, consumables). We do not know how far away from the site any particular plant species was gathered for any of these uses, although it can be assumed that one or more agricultural fields were not too distant. Also, some plants are more likely to be carbonized than others because of processing techniques and consumption patterns (Caddell 1982b:8). In terms of site-specific environmental conditions, it is likely that hickory is overrepresented owing to gathering, storage, and processing (e.g., parching) of nuts (see Gardner 1997). Post-depositional preservation differences also are a concern (cf. Caddell 1982b:8). A major strength of this data set is the presence of domesticates (maize, beans, sunflower) not represented in either the pollen or the daub. The seed data also yield environmental and subsistence data not provided by the other data sets (e.g., the presence of maypop and maygrass). It would be useful to analyze the wood charcoal in detail to see what additional information might be forthcoming from the charred plant remains.

The daub provides a detailed picture of (presumably) site-specific conditions. Two major weaknesses present themselves, however. The first is the absence of plant taxa represented in the other data sets, especially in the charred plant remains. It may be that casts of small seeds are present in the daub but were not recognized in the lab. The second weakness is that the daub may be *too* site-specific to yield a picture of general environmental conditions in the environs of the site. Excluding the cane and grass impressions, the overwhelming predominance of willow oak in the sample suggests that the daub came from one source. It is entirely possible that most of the oak leaves and acorns identified came from *one tree.* This might explain why hickory and pine, both present in varying amounts in the other two data sets, are not represented in the daub. Currently we have no way of investigating this possibility. It would be interesting to conduct similar research at a much larger site with several houses represented, to see if differences existed among them.

The analysis of daub from several structures across a site might also allow for the examination of change through time in local plant cover, and thereby provide a way to look for increasing anthropogenic pressure on the environment. Daub from the first structures would provide a picture of conditions at the time of initial settlement, while daub from later structures would show how the landscape was being altered. Daub falls are detectable via controlled surface collections or shovel testing, or via remote sensing, and thus can be targeted for excavation to pursue this line of research. Also, houses were often rebuilt in place, so a record of change through time at any given site may be obtainable from a few locales. Comparisons of daub from mound and non-mound contexts also would be interesting. Was the clay for a mound-top structure, presumably a locus for elite/ceremonial activities, being obtained from a special source? Were building construction techniques the same in elite vs. non-elite contexts?

A major strength of daub analysis is the precision of the identifications. Where pollen and charred plant remains often can be identified only to the level of family or genus, finding a good leaf impresson or nut cast in daub is almost like picking up that specimen from where it lay on the ground centuries ago. Details of leaf shapes and margins and venation patterns often are remarkably clear in daub impressions (e.g., Figure 5.2). Also, as noted by Caddell (1982a) and Solis and Walling (1982), the seasonality data available from daub are excellent. Different plant species should be represented in construction taking place at different times of the year. If the growth stages of leaves and nuts are considered, it may be that the period of construction of any given wattle-and-daub structure can be ascertained to within a few weeks.

CONCLUSIONS

When combined, the data from three different methods of environmental analysis at the Yarborough site probably provide a generally accurate construction of local environmental conditions during the latter half of the fifteenth century. The site was located in an oak-dominated, bottomland hardwood environment. Local land disturbance is indicated by the presence of abundant cultigens, a suggestion bolstered somewhat by the presence of disturbance-favored species such as persimmon, plum, chenopods, and cocklebur. Caddell (1982b) noted an increase in the seeds of herbaceous annuals from Middle Woodland to Late Woodland contexts in the central Tombigbee River valley in Alabama, and attributed this change to land clearance by prehistoric humans. The same sort of evidence is present at Yarborough in the form of seeds of maypop and nightshade, for example. Faunal evidence from Yarborough (Scott 1982; Hogue, this volume) also indicates local disturbance. Although Sheehan (1982) saw evidence for possible land alteration in the pollen data (e.g., ragweed), a comparison of those data with the other data sets suggests that the pollen from Yarborough was modern, not prehistoric. The major weaknesses with this interpretation are the small sample size and the lack of precise knowledge concerning the pollen sampling points.

Paleoenvironmental data retrieved from archaeological contexts have been received with caution by some scientists because of the "softness" of the data (e.g., Knox 1976; cf. Crumley 1994:4–5; Stahl 1996: 107). Caution is certainly warranted when interpreting biotic data from archaeological sites. Different data sets yield different kinds of information, interpretable at different scales and altered by different kinds of cultural and natural biases. However, rather than being an impediment to understanding, this variability provides information useful for exploring past environmental conditions and how they changed through time. If different data sets disagree, environmental or cultural inferences may be drawn and hypotheses formulated to test those inferences. As we construct more fully informed paleoenvironmental models, our models of past human behavior become more sophisticated as a result. Comparative studies like the one presented here should help us to gain a better undertanding of what the world was like in prehistoric times and how people adapted to and changed that world during the course of their daily lives. Contemporary ecological models should then benefit from the incorporation of historical data at a variety of scales.

Acknowledgments. We are indebted to Dr. Gloria Caddell for providing unpublished seed data from the Yarborough site. Jimmy Cole photographed the daub and acorn casts for Figures 5.2 and 5.3. We would like to thank Sidney McDaniel, B. Serviss, John MacDonald, and Rubin Shmulsky for their technical assistance and Janet Rafferty for editorial comments. We also would like to thank the U.S. Army Corps of Engineers, Mobile District, for making the Yarborough daub available for study.

6 Louisiana Prairies

MICHAEL H. MACROBERTS, BARBARA R.
MACROBERTS, AND LYNN STACEY
JACKSON

INTRODUCTION

Prairies are one of the best-studied plant associations in the world. Thousands of papers and books have been produced on them and entire conferences focus on special aspects of their ecology, management, and restoration (Sims and Risser 2000). Louisiana prairies were documented in the eighteenth and nineteenth centuries by land surveyors, cartographers, and explorers (Darby 1816; Du Pratz 1774; Featherman 1872; Flores 1984; Lockett 1969; D. T. MacRoberts et al. 1997; McDermott 1963; Rowland 1930); however, botanists did not begin to study these prairies until the 1930s (Brown 1941a, 1941b, 1953, 1997). Although prairies have been described in surrounding states (Carr 1993; Collins et al. 1975; Diggs et al. 1999; Foti 1989, 1990; Gordon and Wiseman 1989; Irving et al. 1980; Jordan 1973; Leidolf and McDaniel 1998; Moran et al. 1997; Rostlund 1957; Smeins and Diamond 1988; Wackerman 1929), there is virtually nothing in the literature on prairies in Louisiana (Anderson and Bowles 1999; DeSelm and Murdock 1993).

In this paper we review what is known about Louisiana prairies, concentrating on the smaller, "isolated" prairies of the north and central parts of the state (B. R. MacRoberts and M. H. MacRoberts 1997; M. H. MacRoberts and B. R. MacRoberts 1997a; MacRoberts, MacRoberts, and Moore 1997a). The paper's purpose is to provide basic descriptive coverage to facilitate comparison with prairies in other states. The once-extensive coastal prairies of southwestern Louisiana have been destroyed almost entirely and little is known about them except from historical accounts (Allen and Vidrine 1989; Bridges 1987; Featherman

1872; Smeins et al. 1992). It is hoped that this summary will aid in the study and preservation of Louisiana's remaining prairies.

GENERAL DESCRIPTION

Louisiana prairies are identical in appearance to the prairies in southern Arkansas (Foti 1989, 1990), Mississippi (Moran et al. 1997), and in the Pineywoods and Coastal Plain of eastern Texas (Carr 1993; Jordan 1973; Smeins et al. 1992).

Early descriptions are brief but capture the main features. Lockett (1969:71) described a prairie in northern Louisiana in 1869:

> We came to a beautiful little prairie called Prairie de Cote in which is situated the neat little village of Copenhagen. The prairie is almost exactly circular in shape and about one mile in diameter; its soil is light, yellow loam. Its surface is gently undulating, covered with a luxuriant growth of grass and thousands of bright wild flowers, and is free from trees, except for a few clumps of thick-growing hawthorns. Large herds of cattle and flocks of sheep graze here.

The coastal prairies were apparently spectacular:

> These prairies are all vast, treeless expanses, covered with a luxuriant growth of grass. Generally they are quite level. . . . The green carpet spreads out all around you, bounded by the distant horizon or terminated by the dark lines of forest that project into the prairies like the headlands of a lake. . . . Roaming everywhere are . . . immense herds of cattle and horses (Lockett 1969:94).

In 1871, Americus Featherman made a botanical survey of the southwestern portion of Louisiana. Of the coastal prairies he wrote:

> During the spring season the prairies are beautiful beyond description, especially where the old withered grass has been burnt and a uniform green carpet of vegetation decks the undulating prairie level, as far as the eye can reach, with the softest verdure, variegated with the bright colors of the luxuriant prairie flowers. Here the blue-eyed skullcap vies with the dark purple clusters of the psoralea, and the yellow and white-flowered false indigo intermingles freely with the fringe-flowered blue spiderwort; the narrow leafed evening primrose every where gilds the grass with its golden spangled flowers, contrasted by the rose blossoms of the

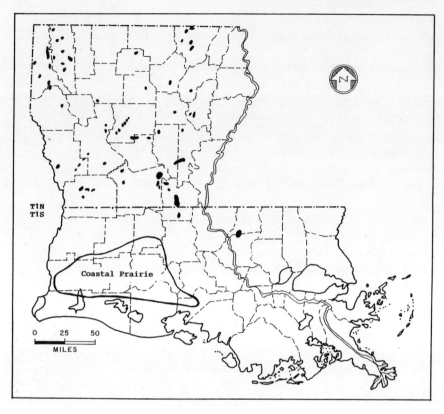

Fig. 6.1. Distribution of Louisiana prairies.

wild onion, whose range of growth is most extensive (Featherman
1872:122).

DISTRIBUTION AND SIZES

Bringing together land surveys, geological surveys, historical records,
maps, and botanical surveys, we mapped the occurrence of Louisiana
prairies at the time of European settlement (M. H. MacRoberts and
B. R. MacRoberts 1997a). The map presented in Figure 6.1 continues
to develop detail as new prairies or records of them are discovered.

Prairies are known to have occurred in most Louisiana parishes west
of the Mississippi River. Except for the coastal prairies, they were generally small, measuring at most only about 13 square km. Although
most were probably smaller than 5 ha, many were much larger, such
as Caddo Prairie north of Shreveport, Anacoco Prairie in Vernon Parish,
Bertram's and Tancock's prairies in northern Grant Parish, and Catahoula Prairie in La Salle Parish (M. H. MacRoberts and B. R. Mac-

Roberts 1997a). It has been estimated that there were about 1 million ha of coastal prairie and 16,000 ha of isolated prairie in Louisiana two centuries ago (Grace 1998; M. H. MacRoberts and B. R. MacRoberts 1997a).

In Historic times, a dramatic loss of prairie has occurred throughout the United States. Less than 1 percent remains (Noss 1997; Whitney 1994). Louisiana is no exception. Virtually all Louisiana prairies have been destroyed in the past two centuries: 99 percent of the isolated prairies and 99.99 percent of the coastal prairies are gone (M. H. Mac-Roberts and B. R. MacRoberts 1997a). This dramatic loss has resulted in the ranking of prairies as endangered throughout their range (Noss 1997), and the Louisiana Natural Heritage Program ranks them as critically imperiled in the state. The causes of destruction are the same in Louisiana as elsewhere: land exploitation largely by agriculture, urban sprawl, and grazing. The coastal prairies were turned into sugarcane and rice fields and the isolated prairies became pasture, cotton fields, and pine plantations (Post 1940).

PRAIRIE CLASSIFICATIONS

Coastal prairies are a type of tallgrass prairie that occurs along the coast of Louisiana and Texas (Smeins et al. 1992). Almost nothing is known about these prairies in Louisiana. They were virtually destroyed before botanists and ecologists came on the scene (Allen and Vidrine 1989; Bridges 1987). Isolated prairies are also a tallgrass prairie type.

Diamond and Smeins (1988; cf. Diggs et al. 1999) have developed a classification of tallgrass prairie from Texas to Canada. They describe six basic types. Differences in data collection methods prevent a direct comparison between Texas and Louisiana prairies. On the basis of incomplete data, however, it would appear that the coastal prairies of Louisiana are most closely related to Texas coastal prairies and that Louisiana isolated prairies are most similar to "True Prairie" and "Central Texas" types in the Diamond and Smeins classification.

There are other classifications. The Louisiana Natural Heritage Program (1998) and the Nature Conservancy (Weakley et al. 1999; but see Turner et al. 1999) recognize several types of isolated prairie using geologic formation and soil type as designators: Morse clay calcareous prairie, Cook Mountain calcareous prairie, Fleming calcareous prairie, and Jackson calcareous prairie. Except for the Cook Mountain type (Smith et al. 1989; B. R. MacRoberts and M. H. MacRoberts 1996a), none has been well studied and consequently their exact status remains unknown (but see McInnis 1997 and Carr 2000 on the Morse clay type). Another type, which is now known only from historical data, is made up of the prairies described by Custis and Freeman (Flores

1984; D. T. MacRoberts et al. 1997) and recorded on early maps as occurring along the Red River north of Natchitoches. These prairies may have been the result of Native American agricultural practices and not entirely due to "natural" factors. Because these prairies no longer exist, little can be determined about them. Early accounts indicate that there were prairie plant species in this region that today are absent and that must have been associated with some natural prairie type.

NATIVE AMERICAN AND EUROPEAN LAND USE

The early land-use history of Louisiana prairies is poorly known. Archaeological records are very incomplete (Early 2000b). Native Americans were in the area for many thousands of years. The presence of Clovis points attests that big-game hunters occupied the area (Neuman 1984) at the end of the Pleistocene, a time when the landscape was much more open and prairie or savanna-like communities occupied much more terrain than they do today (P. A. Delcourt and H. R. Delcourt 1993; Watts 1980a; Webb 1988). Not only was the climate cooler and dryer, but the flora was very unlike that of today: extensive pine forests did not invade the area until about 5,000 years B.P. Tallgrass prairies probably were much more extensive than when European contact occurred. Native Americans had developed complex pre-agricultural sedentary or semi-sedentary societies (Gibson 1999; Saunders et al. 1997); agriculture based on Central American crops eventually followed (Early 2000a, 2000b). Indigenous peoples built mounds on Jefferson Prairie (Forshey 1845; Neuman 1984) and cultivated the surrounding lands (Figure 6.2). Custis and Freeman in 1806 (Flores 1984) found Native Americans cultivating crops on some of the prairies in Caddo and Bossier parishes, but, as we have pointed out above, it is not entirely clear whether Native Americans were simply exploiting prairie openings or actually creating them. It has been suggested that many of the Red River prairies may have been little more than old fields created by Native Americans (Thomas Foti, personal communication 1997). Native American cultures were virtually eliminated from Louisiana in the first half of the nineteenth century before anthropologists made contact with them (Early 2000b; Gregory 1992), and little is therefore known about their ecological relationship with prairies. Even their use of fire in land management and modification remains unknown, although it is implied in the historical records.

European use of the prairies is clear. The Europeans exterminated native grazers such as bison and introduced cattle, horses, hogs, and sheep. Some prairies were cultivated and others were converted to pine plantations, as described in the earlier passages by Lockett and Featherman. Lockett (1969:25), referring to a coastal prairie, said, "The whole

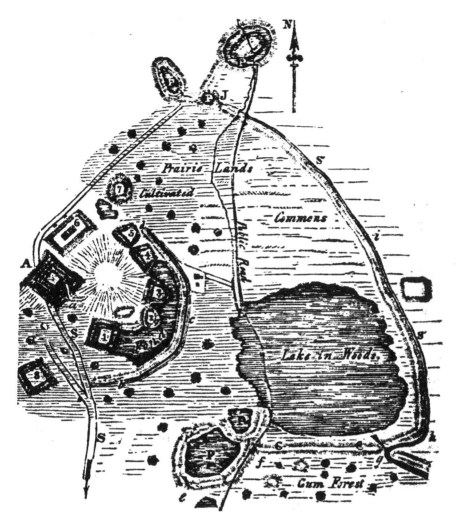

Fig. 6.2. Native American mounds on Jefferson Prairie, Morehouse Parish, Louisiana. From Forshey (1845).

prairie, from one end to the other, was filled with cattle and droves of horses." Later, coastal prairies were plowed and turned into rice and sugarcane fields.

PRAIRIE SOILS

Louisiana prairies occur on a variety of soils, but the better-known and best-preserved ones occur on the newly named Keiffer series (formerly Sumter clay, Cook Mountain) (Guillory et al. 1997). This se-

ries consists of deep, well-drained, slowly permeable soils that formed
in highly calcareous, unconsolidated Tertiary marine deposits. Soils
are on nearly level to moderate (1–12 percent) sloping uplands. Swell-
ing and shrinking cause surface cracks during short droughts. Calcium
carbonate nodules with diameters of more than 2 mm make up as
much as 15 percent by volume of the A horizon. These soils are classified taxonomically as fine-silty, carbonatic, thermic Rendollic Eutro-
chrepts. Other Louisiana prairies (Morse, Jackson, Fleming) occur on
soils similar to those of the Keiffer: calcareous clay marine deposits,
often with limestone aggregations and sometimes with shells. These
soils are alkaline (pH near 8) and have a high shrink-swell ratio. The
Louisiana prairie soils are closely related to the blackland prairies of
Mississippi (Moran et al., this volume), Arkansas, and eastern Texas.
Unfortunately, no one has exhaustively studied Louisiana prairie soils;
comparison among sites remains difficult, confounded as it is by a
plethora of names and descriptions (Moran et al. 1997). A current soil
study on the Keiffer prairies in Winn Parish shows that encroaching
woody vegetation significantly alters the soils toward "forest-like" conditions (Bekele 2001; Bekele and Hudnall 2000).

CLIMATE

Prairies in Louisiana—as in the entire Southeast generally—receive
sufficient rain to support forest (Wackerman 1929). Annual precipitation is more than 100 cm. Short summer droughts occur, but these are
insufficient to explain prairie openings. Summer temperatures regularly rise above 30°C; winters are mild, with few days below freezing.
Annual temperature is about 20°C. The present climate is humid; past
climates were cooler and drier and were undoubtedly more suitable for
prairie flora (P. A. Delcourt and H. R. Delcourt 1993; Watts 1980a;
Webb 1988). The current climate is no more than 5,000 years old.

PRAIRIE FLORA

Floristically, tallgrass prairie is probably the best-known plant commu-
nity in North America (Axelrod 1985; Diamond and Smeins 1988;
Diggs et al. 1999; Kucera 1992; Sims and Risser 2000; Weaver 1968).
Total floristic lists have been developed for four prairies in central Loui-
siana: two in Winn Parish and two in Natchitoches Parish (B. R. Mac-
Roberts and M. H. MacRoberts 1995, 1996a; Smith et al. 1989). Char-
acteristic grasses are *Andropogon gerardii* Vitman, *Panicum virgatum*
L., *Schizachyrium scoparium* (Michx.) Nash, *Sorghastrum nutans* (L.)
Nash, and *Sporobolus compositus* (Poir.) Merr. Poaceae, Asteraceae,
and Fabaceae dominate, accounting for 41 percent of the species. Tables

Table 6.1. Floristic information for four Louisiana prairies

	Prairie	Species	Genera	Families	Size (ha)
Winn Parish	Coldwater	124	99	41	1.6
	Milam	100	82	39	1.2
Natchitoches Parish	K50H	92	71	34	0.4
	Ratibida	76	64	31	0.2

Table 6.2. Longevity information for four central Louisiana prairies

	Number of Species	Percentage of Annuals	Percentage of Perennials
Monocots	46	4	96
Dicots	140	21	79
Asteraceae	34	18	82
Fabaceae	16	6	94
Poaceae	27	7	93
All Species	186	17	83

6.1 and 6.2 summarize information on vascular species occurring in these prairies; additional information, including complete floristic lists, can be found in Smith et al. (1989) and B. R. MacRoberts and M. H. MacRoberts (1995, 1996a).

The total for monocots (plus gymnosperms) in the four prairies was 25 percent (n = 46); for dicots it was 75 percent (n = 140). Ninety-eight percent of the 186 species are native; the three introductions are *Ranunculus sardous* Crantz, *Verbena brasiliensis* Vell., and *Lonicera japonica* Thunb., none of which is a significant component of the flora.

High-quality prairies are identifiable by their diversity, richness in conservative species, and lack of exotic species (Packard and Ross 1997). Although no one has developed a rating system for prairie species for the southeastern United States, such do exist for the midwestern tallgrass prairies (Ladd 1997; Masters 1997; Packard and Ross 1997). Central Louisiana prairies are rich, averaging about 100 species in a 1-ha prairie. A comparison of the four central Louisiana prairies that have total floristic lists with Ladd's (1997) list for midwestern tallgrass prairies shows between 52 and 63 percent similarity in species. This is impressive but underestimates the true similarity, since many species found in the Louisiana prairies, such as *Sporobolus junceus* (Beauv.) Kunth, *Mimosa strigillosa* Torr. and Gray, and *Neptunia lutea* (Leavenworth) Benth., are closely related southern congeners of more northern species.

FLORISTIC SIMILARITY TO OTHER
SOUTHEASTERN PRAIRIES

Few floristic lists of southeastern prairies are complete enough to allow detailed comparisons. However, there are some. Leidolf and McDaniel (1998) documented 152 species from the Black Prairie of Mississippi. Foti (1989) listed 133 species from frequently inventoried blackland prairies in southern Arkansas. We have documented 186 species from four prairies in Natchitoches and Winn parishes in central Louisiana. Approximately 50 percent of the listed species from both the Mississippi and Arkansas prairies occur in the Natchitoches and Winn Parish prairies, even though these prairies are about 402 and 241 km (250 and 150 miles) away, respectively. Undoubtedly, more thorough surveys of these sites would uncover additional species in common. For example, while *Spiranthes magnicamporum* Sheviak is reported from both the Louisiana and Mississippi sites, it has not been reported from Arkansas although it is abundant on some prairies near Arkadelphia (MacRoberts and MacRoberts, personal observation 1997). The similarities among the isolated prairies of eastern Texas and prairies in Louisiana, Mississippi, and Alabama have been suggested but never described in detail (MacRoberts and MacRoberts personal observation 1997 to present; Warner 1926).

PRAIRIE FLORISTIC STABILITY

In 1939, C. A. Brown made several visits to a group of prairies in Winn Parish and made collections and field notes. Those prairies are still intact. Brown left no formal record of this work, but using his notebooks and the Louisiana State University herbarium we were able to reconstruct a list of plants he either collected or reported (B. R. MacRoberts and M. H. MacRoberts 1997). Although the sample is far from complete, Brown collected or reported 86 species, all of which occur today in the prairies or roadsides adjacent to the sites in which he collected. It is clear that Brown neither made total collections nor sampled regularly. However, this information suggests that overall the prairies are floristically the same today as they were 60 years ago and have not lost species. Vavrek (2000) studied the stability of prairie flora (including seed banking) in the Keiffer prairies in Winn Parish.

RARE PLANT SPECIES

The Endangered Species Act and Natural Heritage programs have resulted in state lists for rare, endangered, and threatened plant species. In Louisiana, this list contains many prairie species (Table 6.3). There are no endangered or threatened prairie species (Louisiana Natural

Table 6.3. Rare Louisiana plant species that occur in prairies

---

Asclepias stenophylla Gray
Astragalus crassicarpus Nutt.
Bouteloua curtipendula (Michx.) Torr.
Callirhoe alcaeoides (Michx.) Gray
Camassia scilloides (Raf.) Cory
Carex meadii Dewey
Carex microdonta Torr. and Hook.
Ceanothus herbaceus Raf.
Cirsium engelmannii Rydb.
Cooperia drummondii Herbert
Echinacea purpurea (L.) Moench
Euphorbia bicolor Engelm. and Gray
Eustoma exaltatum ssp. *russellianum* (Hook.) Kartesz
Heliotropium tenellum (Nutt.) Torr.
Houstonia purpurea L. var. *calycosa* Gray
Indigofera miniata Ortega
Koeleria macrantha (Ledeb.) Schultes
Lindheimera texana Gray and Engelm.
Nemastylis geminiflora Nutt.
Panicum flexile (Gatt.) Scribn.
Polytaenia nuttallii DC.
Rudbeckia missouriensis Engelm. *ex* C. L. Boynt and Beadle
Spiranthes magnicamporum Sheviak
Sporobolus ozarkanus Fern.
Zigadenus nuttallii (Gray) S. Wats.

Heritage Program 1999; M. H. MacRoberts and B. R. MacRoberts 1995; Smith et al. 1989); virtually all taxa listed are central tallgrass prairie plants that are rare in Louisiana because most of their habitat in the state has been destroyed. *Eustoma exaltatum* ssp. *russellianum* (Hook.) Kartesz was found in a prairie in either Caddo or Bossier Parish in 1806 but never again in the state (Flores 1984; D. T. MacRoberts et al. 1997).

FAUNA

Almost nothing is known about faunal relationships for Louisiana prairies. To our knowledge, there have been no studies of insects, herpetofauna, or mammals in Louisiana prairies. Ingold (2000) has conducted a study of the avifauna of the Keiffer prairies.

PRAIRIE LOSS

In Historic times there has been a dramatic loss of prairie throughout the United States. As stated earlier, less than 1 percent remains (Noss 1997; Whitney 1994). This holds true for Louisiana as well, where virtually all coastal prairie has vanished (Allen and Vidrine 1989; Bridges 1987) and where 99 percent of the isolated prairies have been lost (M. H.

MacRoberts, B. R. MacRoberts, and Stacey 1997; Thomas 1986). Brown's surveys (1941a, 1941b, 1953, 1997; see also M. H. MacRoberts, B. R. MacRoberts, and Moore 1997) in the 1930s and those of Thomas (1986) in the mid-1980s discovered almost no prairie. The cause of prairie loss is largely anthropogenic, both directly by land conversion and indirectly through such practices as fire suppression.

Using land-survey records and aerial photographs (Figure 6.3), we studied the rate of prairie loss on the Keiffer and Packton prairies (Winn and Grant parishes), which are some of the best-preserved prairies in Louisiana (M. H. MacRoberts, B. R. MacRoberts, and Stacey 1997). Since 1835, overall loss has been 91 percent from conversion to pine plantation and encroachment of woody vegetation resulting from fire suppression. Fifty-one percent of 12 extant prairies has been lost since 1940 owing to encroachment of woody vegetation.

WOODY INVASION OF PRAIRIES

We have made some observations on woody species' invasion of Louisiana prairies (MacRoberts and MacRoberts, unpublished data). Using the earliest (1940) aerial photographs, we selected areas within the Keiffer prairies that were open 60 years ago but that are now closed canopy. In these invaded areas we counted in standardized plots all species more than 1.5 m tall. We found that invaded areas varied considerably in species composition: some were dominated by cedar (*Juniperus virginiana* L.); others had no cedar and were dominated by such species as sweetgum (*Liquidambar styraciflua* L.) and loblolly pine (*Pinus taeda* L.). In another study of prairie edges, we listed all woody species in standardized plots and again found great variation in species present: some plots were dominated by cedar, others by rough-leaved dogwood (*Cornus drummondii* C. A. Mey.) or persimmon (*Diospyros virginiana* L.) and hawthorn (*Crataegus* spp.). Apparently, invading species are those present in the surrounding landscape. This observation supports Hubbell et al. (1999), who found that, if recruitment is local, colonizable areas will reflect the nearby vegetation even if that vegetation is not the best competitor at that site. In other words, whatever gets there first is what takes hold. If cedar is ubiquitous at a site, in the absence of other factors (e.g., fire) it will become dominant; if it is not present, other species will take over.

REMAINING PRAIRIES

Only a few Louisiana prairies remain in any identifiable condition: the Keiffer and Packton prairies in Grant and Winn parishes in the Winn Ranger District of the Kisatchie National Forest (Allen 1993; B. R.

Fig. 6.3. Aerial photograph of Keiffer Prairies, northern Louisiana,
ca. 1940. North is to the left.

MacRoberts and M. H. MacRoberts 1996a, 1996b, 1997; M. H. Mac-
Roberts and B. R. MacRoberts 1997b; M. H. MacRoberts, B. R. Mac-
Roberts, and Stacey 1997; Smith et al. 1989) are undoubtedly the most
intact. There also are a few small prairie remnants in Natchitoches
Parish in the Kisatchie Ranger District of the Kisatchie National Forest
(B. R. MacRoberts and M. H. MacRoberts 1995). These badly damaged
remnants may be more similar to an upland-prairie community associated with sandstone outcrops (M. H. MacRoberts and B. R. MacRoberts 1993). The Copenhagen prairie complex in Caldwell Parish (Norman 1991) has only recently been acquired by the Nature Conservancy
(Landmarks: Louisiana 2001). The prairies on Barksdale Air Force Base
in Bossier Parish (Carr 2000; McInnis 1997) are our best Morse clay
prairies. At least one small prairie remnant at Fort Polk in Vernon Parish needs attention (Hart and Lester 1993). The 20-ha Rector's Prairie

on Udalf-Bussy soils on the Bastrop Ridge north of Handy Brake National Wildlife Refuge is apparently the only prairie remnant remaining in once prairie-rich Morehouse Parish (B. Erwin, personal communication 2000; R. Hopgood, personal communication 2000). This prairie is probably the best-managed prairie in Louisiana; it has been burned four times since 1995 and is regularly bushhogged. Recently, David Moore (personal communication 1999) has discovered prairie remnants on Keiffer soils south of Provencal in Natchitoches Parish. There were once prairies south of Shreveport, in Caddo and DeSoto parishes on either side of Interstate 49; no survey of these has been undertaken, but a few remnants may exist. Undoubtedly other prairie remnants exist, but no concerted effort has been made to find them in recent years (Thomas 1986).

PRAIRIE MANAGEMENT AND RESTORATION

Until the 1980s there was virtually no interest in preserving Louisiana prairies. In that decade, the Louisiana Natural Heritage Program surveyed for prairies and located several in Louisiana (Bridges 1987; Norman 1991; Smith et al. 1989; Thomas 1986); during the same period, local interest in south Louisiana led to an effort to secure a few badly damaged remnants of coastal prairie (Allen and Vidrine 1989). Since the recognition that these prairies are rare, arrangements to secure them have, in several instances, been successful. Some prairie remnants on both public and private land apparently now are secure.

The next step was to initiate management. Prairie management literature is extensive (Collins and Wallace 1990; Packard and Mutel 1997; Samson and Knopf 1996). Local management plans were developed (Hyatt 1999; B. R. MacRoberts and M. H. MacRoberts 1996b; M. H. MacRoberts and B. R. MacRoberts 1997b; Smith et al. 1989) and are currently being implemented on several prairies in the Kisatchie National Forest. Management techniques include bushhogging, woodsgatoring, hand-clearing, burning, frilling, and basal bark treatment.

WHAT NEEDS TO BE DONE?

Because virtually nothing is known about Louisiana prairies, everything needs to be done. Aside from preserving the few known fragments, information is desperately needed on floristics and soils. Complete floristic lists from any of the remaining sites are essential for proper classification, as are studies of vertebrates and invertebrates. Detailed soil analyses from these sites would help us to understand similarities and differences. Since historical use is important to understanding present conditions, historical analysis would be of great assistance, especially in understanding the relationship between Native Americans and prairies. But most important, prairies on private land need to be secured by agencies such as the Nature Conservancy, and prairies on public land need to be properly managed and restored where necessary.

Acknowledgments. Beth Erwin and Rector Hopgood showed us Rector's Prairie. Steve Lynch helped with the figures. The work was supported by various grants and cost-share agreements described in our previous papers and by Challenge Cost-Share Agreements 08-98-06-CCS-002 and 08-99-06-CCS-006.

ADDITIONAL INFORMATION

In addition to the references cited in this paper, the Louisiana Natural Heritage Program has mainly unpublished information, notably site surveys on many prairies. C. A. Brown left notes on his botanical surveys during the 1930s and 1940s. That information is available in the archives at Hill Memorial Library, Louisiana State University. Information on prairies in the Kisatchie National Forest is on file at the forest supervisor's and district offices. Our own information on Louisiana prairies is available from Bog Research, the Louisiana Natural Heritage Program, and the Kisatchie National Forest.

7 Blackland Prairie Landscapes of Southwestern Arkansas

Historical Perspective, Present Status, and Restoration Potential

THOMAS L. FOTI, SCOTT SIMON, DOUGLAS ZOLLNER, AND MERYL HATTENBACH

INTRODUCTION

Southwestern Arkansas, as the term is used here, includes all or parts of seven counties recognized as a distinctive region of the state, the Southwestern Arkansas Section of the West Gulf Coastal Plain Natural Division (Foti 1974). This section is underlain by geological deposits from the Cretaceous period, in contrast to the Tertiary-period deposits that underlie the rest of the West Gulf Coastal Plain of southern Arkansas, with which it nonetheless shares many characteristics. An important difference is that the geological substrate of southwestern Arkansas sometimes includes calcareous materials such as limestone, chalk, and marl. Areas within southwestern Arkansas underlain by these deposits are here referred to as the blackland prairie region. This term does not denote one contiguous area, but rather several discrete areas shown on the General Soil Map of Arkansas as blackland prairie or Oktibbeha-Sumter soil association (USDA Soil Conservation Service 1982; Figure 7.1). Within these areas, calcareous soils supporting blackland prairies and related communities are interspersed with areas of acidic soils covered with pine-hardwood forests like those of the rest of the coastal plain.

Roberts (1979) estimated the total area of the blackland prairie region of southwestern Arkansas at about 130,000 ha. Although the landscape is generally made up of rolling hills, slopes of over 50 percent gradient occur, along with at least one nearly vertical cliff (White Cliffs in Little River County). Severe erosion is common, with gullies up to 10 m deep. Level areas are characterized by black soils with high levels of organic matter that give the region its name, but soils abused by

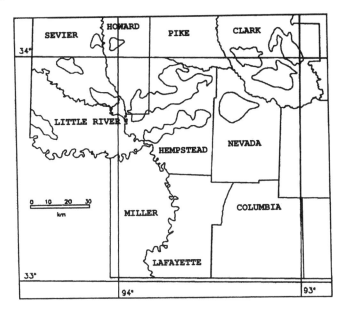

Fig. 7.1. Blackland soil associations of southwestern Arkansas as mapped by NRCS.

poor management practices (such as overgrazing land) and other eroded soils over chalk are olive to white in color. The presence of calcareous geologic materials has had profound effects on the vegetation, soil, and land use of the region. A distinctive landcover type, the blackland prairie, and related savanna, woodland, and forest communities occurred on these calcareous substrates. Owing to a lack of systematic inventories, descriptions, and studies, however, the nature of these communities has been poorly understood. As recently as 1974, no contemporary examples were recognized (Foti 1974).

As used here, a *prairie* is an area dominated by characteristic herbaceous plants (typically over a hundred species). Blackland prairies are those that occur on these distinctive calcareous substrates; they differ in both dominant vegetation and characteristic species from other tallgrass prairies of the Midwest and Midsouth. On calcareous soils within the blackland prairie region of southwestern Arkansas, four prairie communities, six woodland communities, and two forest communities were defined by Hattenbach et al. (2000). The dominant grasses include little bluestem (*Schizachyrium scoparium*) and Indiangrass (*Sorghastrum nutans*), with big bluestem (*Andropogon gerardii*) and gamma grass (*Tripsacum dactyloides*) on moister areas. Compassplant (*Sil-

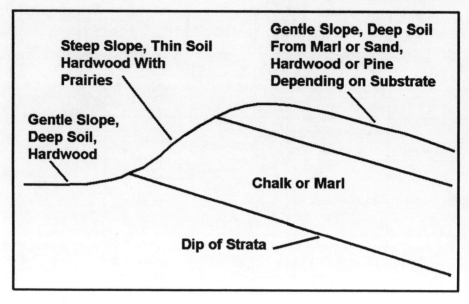

Fig. 7.2. A generalized model of the geology, soil, vegetation, and topography of a cuesta in southwestern Arkansas.

phium laciniatum) and prairie clover (*Dalea purpurea*) are typical forbs. These prairies usually occur on shallow soils over chalk ridges or marl (calcareous clay) slopes, often on the steep faces of asymmetrical ridges known as cuestas, which have a shallow slope and a steep slope. On the steep slopes are chalk or marl outcrops mantled with only a thin layer of soil that may be black but is more commonly olive. According to the original land-survey notes, it appears that the prairies occurred primarily on the steep slopes but extended for a distance onto the gentle slopes at the foot of the ridge. However, they were usually replaced by forest within a short distance of the toes of the slopes (Figure 7.2).

Woodlands have few enough trees that herbaceous prairie vegetation dominates the ground level (typically 25–60 percent tree cover). *Savannas* are mostly prairie but with scattered trees. Trees of savannas and woodlands include chinkquapin oak (*Quercus muhlenbergii*), bois d'arc (*Maclura pomifera*), eastern redcedar (*Juniperus virginiana*), and nutmeg hickory (*Carya myristicaeformis*). Interestingly, field notes from both the first land survey and current research show that pecan (*Carya illinoensis*) makes up about 10 percent of the trees within savannas and woodlands in the blackland prairie region. In other regions it is usually associated with sandy riverfronts along large rivers, in contrast to the calcareous clays of the blackland prairies.

Eroded spots are common; in some places, bedrock exposures become extensive enough to form chalk *glades*. Although similar to a prairie or woodland, a glade occurs on rocky substrates of chalk, limestone, and gravel with thin ground cover and bare rock visible. The thin ground cover of glades includes ground plum (*Astragalus crassicarpus*) and side-oats grama (*Bouteloua curtipendula*). In such areas with very thin soil, the original community developed as woodland dominated by Ashe's juniper (*J. asheii*) and Durand's oak (*Quercus sinuata*).

A major problem in understanding the original character of southwestern Arkansas is that the area has been subjected to extensive and intensive land uses including row-crop agriculture, grazing, forestry, mining, and urbanization for almost two centuries. These changes have so modified the landscape that it is virtually impossible to find undisturbed areas; consequently, it is difficult to reconstruct the original character of the landscape without the use of historical resources such as those cited in this study. Archaeological studies can provide insight into areas of the landscape that were substantially modified well before historical descriptions were written. Moreover, as the area has been the subject of few ecological studies, there is little baseline information on the character and distribution of natural communities. Because of the dearth of ecological information from southwestern Arkansas, the Arkansas Natural Heritage Commission (ANHC) determined in 1985 to increase its efforts within this region. The work began with comprehensive surveys to locate least-disturbed areas. Data on those areas as well as from the scientific literature and historical sources were then used to develop a better understanding of the natural systems of the region, and eventually to preserve representative examples of the region's natural diversity.

The purposes of this paper are to synthesize and update 15 years of inventory and study and to present an overview of the historical distribution and character, as well as the present status, potential, and plans for protection and restoration, of natural landscapes of the blackland prairie region of southwestern Arkansas. Comparisons with other blackland prairie ecosystems in the West Gulf Coastal Plain are also made. Detailed physiognomic/floristic classifications of the natural communities and descriptions of current management and restoration efforts are given elsewhere (Zollner et al., this volume).

HISTORICAL DESCRIPTIONS OF THE BLACKLAND PRAIRIE REGION OF SOUTHWESTERN ARKANSAS

Because unreliable sources can impair understanding, historical sources must be used carefully. Landscape descriptions can be evaluated by comparing historical descriptions with present-day areas that have changed little, and by comparing descriptions of the same area by several authors. The authors quoted here are widely cited, and their descriptions were compared with existing conditions in the field. Special problems associated with interpreting General Land Office (GLO) notes will be discussed later. A different problem involving the use of historical descriptions in southwestern Arkansas is that the region was settled early by Europeans and Americans and was occupied by the Caddo Indians for centuries before that. Therefore, inferences that early-nineteenth-century descriptions represent the natural state in the absence of people must be made carefully if not avoided altogether. Nevertheless, these descriptions certainly reflect landscapes less affected by people than those of today and offer valuable points of reference, not necessarily goals of restoration.

Sargent's map (1884) is the best-known historical map of the region (Figure 7.3). It matches well with remnant vegetation in Arkansas today, even in relatively small areas. The map does not typically show clearings or other changes made by people (except for one area devoid of timber for construction of a railroad), but rather displays general vegetation patterns. Because the map was created before the state's first comprehensive timber cut occurred, it provides a good representation of "original" vegetation.

The map shows southwestern Arkansas as a whole (without distinguishing the blackland prairie region), covered primarily by pine forest. Judging from existing vegetation, these forests were dominated by loblolly pine (*Pinus taeda*) on moister sites and shortleaf pine (*Pinus echinata*) on drier sites. In general, there was more shortleaf pine in this part of the coastal plain than farther east in the Arkansas Coastal Plain, at least partly because the climate of southwestern Arkansas, influenced by southwesterly winds, is drier than it is farther east. The northern part of the region, adjacent to the shortleaf-dominated Ouachita Mountains, has an even greater dominance of this species. Hardwood forest is shown in the Sargent map principally along the rivers. This bottomland hardwood forest was dominated by such species as overcup oak (*Quercus lyrata*), water hickory (*Carya aquatica*), willow oak (*Quercus phellos*), and green ash (*Fraxinus pennsylvanica*).

Sargent and later mappers of regional vegetation have shown an area of uplands in southern Howard and Hempstead counties dominated by hardwood forest (Figure 7.3). Inspection of the original land-survey notes and present vegetation shows this characterization to be fairly accurate. The area overlaps a portion of the blackland prairie region. For example, of 400 bearing or line trees used to mark section lines or corners within Township 11 South, Range 27 West (an area of 36 square

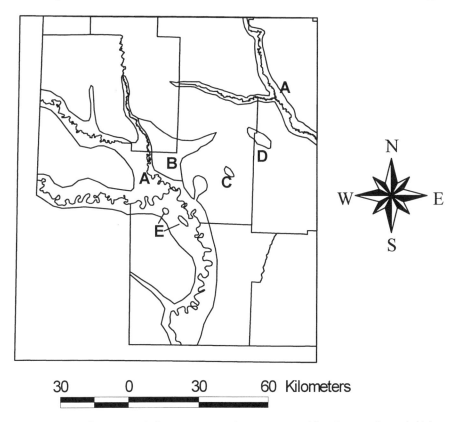

30   0   30   60 Kilometers

Fig. 7.3. Southwestern Arkansas vegetation as mapped by Sargent (1884). (A) bottomland hardwood forest areas mapped as hardwood forest; (B) blackland prairies and associated communities mapped as hardwood forest; (C) "prairie de Roane" mapped as prairie; (D) "prairie de Ann" mapped as prairie; (E) presumed abandoned Indian croplands mapped as prairies.

miles, or 9,216 square ha), no pines were used, only hardwoods. In contrast, pines were often used in some nearby townships. The soil is often clay with a high pH, favoring the growth of hardwoods over pines that do better on sandy, more acidic soils. Such acidic sites are present within this area, but they are relatively limited. Hardwood forests on relatively deep calcareous soils, and woodlands on shallower soils, were often dominated by oaks and hickories, leading Sargent and others to map the area as upland hardwood forest. However, within this area were blackland prairies and related communities that define the blackland prairie region.

Sargent delineated two prairies in the eastern part of the study area and two more along the Red River. These "prairies" were determined by field study to be on geological substrate and soil that is not typical of blackland prairies. With the exception of the most northeasterly of these, Prairie De Anne, they do not have relict prairie flora; therefore, they may not have been prairie. Prairie De Anne and the nearby Prairie De Roane do have soils that are somewhat similar to those of the blackland prairies. However, the "prairies" along the Red River were almost certainly abandoned Caddo Indian cropland because Caddo sites are concentrated within these areas (Ann Early, Arkansas Archeological Survey, personal communication 2001).

Featherstonhaugh (1844:158) described the prairies near present-day Blevins in Hempstead County, near the eastern extremity of the blackland prairie region: "a chain of prairies running westward and parallel with Red River for a great distance, until the whole country becomes one vast prairie, devoid of trees, except those which grow immediately upon the watercourses. Some of these prairies were mere bald spots of half an acre and more, whilst others contained several hundred acres, in every instance surrounded with a belt of timber and plants peculiar to the country." He described the soil as "black as charred wood [with] . . . a much more inky color than the rich vegetable mold usually found in low grounds" (Featherstonhaugh 1844:159).

Owen (1860) described the soils of the blackland prairie region as often rich, black, and fertile; on ridges, however, he noted that the soil was eroded and less fertile. Our inventory shows that these ridges were more likely prairie or woodland, whereas the rich, black soils were more likely to have been covered with forest.

Some historical descriptions also pointed out that plant communities of the blackland region were greatly influenced not only by geological substrate and soil, but also by a combination of lightning-set and human-set fires. Du Pratz (1774) gave an interesting account of the historical occurrence of fire in the landscape of southern Arkansas and northern Louisiana. During his stay at Natchez in the early eighteenth century, he traveled down the Mississippi River to the Red River; then up the Red, Black, and Ouachita Rivers; across the Ouachita Mountains to the Arkansas River; and down to the St. Francis River. He traveled back up the St. Francis River to the lead-mining district of Missouri before crossing the Mississippi and returning (most of this journey, while along the rivers, was overland). He began his trip "early in the month of September, which is the best season of the year for beginning a journey in this country: in the first place, because, during the summer, the grass is too high for traveling; whereas in the month of September, the meadows, the grass of which is then dry, are set on fire, and the ground becomes smooth, and easy to walk on" (Du Pratz 1774: 134). He described the land along the Black and Ouachita Rivers as "one very extensive meadow, diversified with little groves" (Du Pratz

1774:169). One hundred years later, in southwestern Arkansas west of the Ouachita River, the GLO survey documented a landscape that was more open than today but not "one very extensive meadow."

Historical data demonstrate that within this region prairies occurred on calcareous soils and were maintained by a combination of droughty sites, high pH, and fire. Some openings cited in historical descriptions appear to have been former Native American cropland and settlements.

ESTABLISHING PRESENT STATUS: METHODS AND MATERIALS

Historical sources and data from scientific literature, along with field inspection of the known "natural" areas, were used to create an initial description of the vegetation of the region. Known examples of each community were examined on the ground and in aerial photos to determine whether and how the community could be identified, and how well degree of disturbance could be determined using photos. Sometimes topographic, geologic, or soil maps provided valuable ancillary data such as locations of cuestas and of calcareous substrate. This initial description was coupled with aerial photography to locate the least-disturbed areas. Photos were examined in the county offices of the Soil Conservation Service (SCS—now Natural Resources Conservation Service, or NRCS) and Agricultural Stabilization and Conservation Service (ASCS—now Consolidated Farm Services Agency, or CFSA) and in the offices of the Arkansas Highway and Transportation Department in Little Rock.

Land-condition codes, as interpreted from the photographs, were marked on USGS topographic quadrangle maps. Any area that appeared to be relatively undisturbed, as judged from the photographs and using the criteria described above, was outlined on the topographic maps and was briefly described on standard agency forms. The outlined areas were considered potential natural areas (PNAs) to be investigated in the field. Each was categorized as to the general plant community it likely represented and its condition as interpreted photographically. PNAs that were interpreted to be prairies or related herbaceous, woodland, or forest areas are emphasized here.

PNAs were initially inspected between 1985 and 1988, and their actual condition was observed. If an area was highly disturbed, such as by plowing (which could have occurred after the date of the aerial photograph or through misinterpretation of the photo), this fact was noted and the area was given no further attention. If the area appeared little disturbed, its dominant vegetation was described and it was used in determining the natural character and vegetation of the region before massive alteration.

Where questions arose as to the early character of an area, micro-filmed field notes of the Public Land Survey (PLS) of the GLO were examined in the state land surveyor's office at the Arkansas Geological Commission in Little Rock. GLO notes are a valuable source for characterizing landscape appearance in the first half of the nineteenth century. Surveyors quantitatively described the boundaries of each square mile of the Louisiana Purchase, using a basic approach developed by Thomas Jefferson. At each mile and half-mile point, bearing or "witness" trees were identified and located. Surveyors provided qualitative descriptions of each mile, including "land" (the productivity of the soil), "timber" (the forest species), and "undergrowth" (low-growing vegetation). The quality of these notes varied by surveyor. Some conscientiously recorded certain landscape features; others did not (Bourdo 1956).

In some cases the GLO descriptions corresponded well with present vegetation or ecologically inferred past vegetation. In other cases conditions varied, sometimes dramatically, from those recorded in surveyors' notes. It is therefore necessary to evaluate the notes of each surveyor individually. For this study, the notes were used in a general way to determine whether prairies were mapped or mentioned in a given mile of survey. The potential for bias in this case is that a surveyor who ignored or did not recognize prairie would not have noted prairie where it in fact existed. In a few instances, the presence of prairie or woodland was inferred from the statement that no trees were near enough to the corner to be used as bearing trees or that the distance to the tree was great. It is possible that in these cases the land cover consisted of small trees and shrubs, too small to use as witness trees. Their location on prairie soils makes such an error less likely. A simple way to test for basic accuracy of the notes is whether streams and other landmarks are mapped correctly in the plat maps; this was required and its quality demonstrates that the surveyor actually performed the survey. Information from the GLO notes is summarized or quoted here as appropriate.

The Arkansas Field Office of the Nature Conservancy (ARFO-TNC) began its protection planning in the region during the late 1980s, generally concentrating more intensively on fewer and higher-priority sites than did the ANHC inventory. In 1999, ANHC provided funding to ARFO to revisit sites previously identified, to characterize the type and quality of surrounding landscapes and if possible to identify new PNAs. The bulk of this effort was to be concentrated within four to six landscapes of 2,400–25,000 ha that had been shown in previous studies to have high concentrations of blackland prairie remnants and related communities. This new effort would develop a long-term plan for conservation of the ecosystem to meet protection goals of the two entities. It would also support broad-scale ecoregional planning being led by TNC in the Upper West Gulf Coastal Plain Ecoregion of Arkansas, Louisiana, Texas, and Oklahoma.

PRESENT STATUS AND RESTORATION POTENTIAL OF VEGETATION OF THE BLACKLAND REGION OF ARKANSAS

About 295 PNAs were initially identified within the study area in 1985, including 118 blackland prairie PNAs. An additional 49 were rocky glades or other openings in forest. The "prairies" often were woodlands or savannas. Approximately 90 percent of the PNAs have been examined via field inspection; the others are posted against trespass and permission to enter has not yet been obtained. About 60 of the PNAs retain substantial natural character; these have been of greatest value in describing the region and formulating protection plans.

The distribution of blackland prairie remnants located by the inventory, and the original distribution of blackland prairie and related communities as inferred from geology and historical data sources, are shown in Figure 7.4 (updated from Foti 1989). Less than 6,000 ha of blackland prairie and related communities remain in relatively natural condition with more than 600 plant species and 315 animal species recorded (Hattenbach et al. 2000).

Numerous plant species of concern tracked by ANHC have been recorded in the blackland prairie region, including purple beardtongue (*Penstemon cobaea*), the sedge *Carex microdonta,* Carolina larkspur (*Delphinium carolinianum* ssp. *penardii*), celestial lily (*Nemastylis geminiflora*), earleaf foxglove (*Agalinis auriculata*), Durand's oak (*Quercus sinuata*), black-eyed Susan (*Rudbeckia maxima*), lax hornpod (*Cynoctonum mitreola*), compact prairie clover (*Dalea compacta* var. *compacta*), ground plum (*Astragalus crassicarpus* var. *crassicarpus*), stenosiphon (*Stenosiphon linifolius*), puccoon (*Lithospermum tuberosum*), eared goldenrod (*Solidago auriculata*), southern lady's slipper (*Cypripedium kentuckiense*), and big-head evax (*Evax prolifera*), among others. Two tracked animal species, Bachman's Sparrow and Red-shouldered Hawk, also occur.

Foti (1989) reported about 40 relatively high-quality prairie remnants and related woodlands and forests, and approximately 10 have been recorded since. Many more exist in degraded but restorable condition. Most of the prairies are in private ownership and have been grazed by cattle. However, several tracts have been acquired by conservation agencies and organizations. Forest and woodland areas have been affected by timber harvest and conversion, clearing for pasture, fire

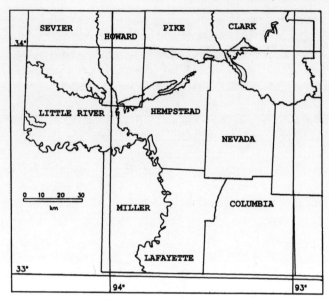

Fig. 7.4. Original distribution of blackland prairies and associated communities in southwestern Arkansas.

suppression, and other changes. High-quality and restorable prairies
and related communities are concentrated in several landscape-scale
areas of the blackland prairie region (Figure 7.5), and it has become
apparent that conservation activities should focus on these.

The Saratoga-Columbus-Washington landscape site was at the time
of Euro-American settlement the largest area dominated by blackland
prairie/woodland/savanna vegetation, and it remains so today. The site
is approximately 15 km east–west by up to 6 km north–south. It is
unique among the landscape sites in having prairie that extended well
out from the base of the cuestas on an elevated "table land" before
dropping still farther to the hardwood-dominated creek bottom. Prairies were more common in this landscape, judging from the GLO
notes. Protected areas include Arkansas Game and Fish Commission's
(AGFC's) 2,000-ha Grandview Prairie Wildlife Management Area, the
U.S. Army Corps of Engineers' (USACE's)/ANHC's/TNC's 74-ha Saratoga Landing Blackland Prairie, and TNC's 62-ha Columbus Prairie.
About half of the area between Saratoga Landing and Grandview is native grassland and woodland restorable to high-quality communities.
Thus there is potential for a restored blackland vegetation complex of
4,000–8,000 ha, with additional acreage east of Grandview.

The Grandview Prairie Wildlife Management Area is probably the
largest area of blackland prairie ecosystem in public ownership. In the

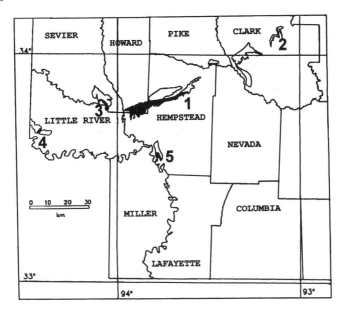

Fig. 7.5. Landscape sites containing concentrations of
blackland communities in southwestern Arkansas today.
1. Saratoga-Columbus-Washington. 2. Terre Noire.
3. White Cliffs. 4. Rocky Comfort. 5. Nacatoch.

first land survey, completed in the 1820s, several "mile notes" within
this area indicated it was "mostly prairie." At several corners no trees
occurred, even though prairie was not formally recorded, suggesting
that this area may have included a prairie/woodland/savanna of several
hundred to several thousand hectares. A similar-sized "prairie" was
mapped just to the east, north of the town of Washington. Therefore,
at the time of the GLO land survey, the bulk of what is now GPWMA
land was blackland prairie and related communities. AGFC, TNC, and
ANHC are cooperatively restoring Grandview to a "natural" complex
of prairie, woodland, and savanna.

Within the Saratoga–Grandview–Washington landscape site is a 74-
ha complex of prairies and woodlands known as Saratoga Landing
Blackland Prairie. This site has been preserved through a management
agreement involving ANHC, TNC, and the owner, the USACE. Today
the largest individual prairie in this complex covers about 16 ha. This
is not the pre-American settlement condition, because the area has
been grazed and fire has been excluded for decades until recently. This
management (or lack of management) has encouraged the establishment of woody plants, and GLO notes indicate that the area is probably

more thickly wooded today than in 1819. The notes on the line that passes north–south through this area (that is, the southern half of the line between Sections 31 and 32, Township 11 South, Range 27 West) call it "broken third-rate prairie land not suited for cultivation." A prairie was mapped nearby on a township plat sheet. There were trees to mark the quarter-section corner, so the area was not treeless. However, the distances to the two bearing trees at this point were 53 feet (16 m) to a 10-inch-diameter (25-cm-diameter) white oak and 63 feet (19 m) to a 10-inch-diameter (25-cm-diameter) black oak in the other direction, suggesting that the country was very open. The two mile-long lines running east–west a half-mile north of this quarter-corner (that is, between Sections 30 and 31 and between Sections 29 and 32) both carry the general comment "mostly prairie." This notation was fairly uncommon in the vicinity, with prairie notes more often taking the form "2 prairies," "two small prairies," or "4 small prairies." Recent prescribed fires and removal of eastern redcedar by TNC and ANHC have begun to restore the appropriate conditions to this natural area.

Information on the historical condition of blackland prairies may be developed through excavation of a Caddo site on Grandview. Although excavation of this site has just begun, it has produced undisturbed blackland soil beneath a mound. It is estimated that this soil was covered, and thus protected, for 500 years (Schambach 2001). This excavation may provide information not only on soil composition and structure but also on vegetative cover at the time.

The Terre Noire landscape site occupies a north–south-trending, west-facing cuesta west of Arkadelphia. It consists of about 4,800 ha of prairies, woodlands, and forests. Within the site today are approximately 320 ha of high-quality or restorable blackland prairie and related communities within a 1,000-ha landscape site. ANHC and TNC own the Terre Noire Blackland Prairie Natural Area comprising 30 ha. In addition, TNC owns 8 ha and TNC, ANHC, and International Paper jointly protect an area of 67 ha.

The White Cliffs landscape site contains not only blackland prairies, woodlands, and forests but also chalk glades, covered with woodlands dominated by Durand's oak and Ashe's juniper. This community is reminiscent of the Edwards Plateau of Texas, 275 km to the southwest. The signature area of this site is a bluff or cliff of chalk towering 30 m above Little River, now impounded as Millwood Lake. The cliff and 150 ha of glades, prairies, and woodlands are protected by ANHC.

The Rocky Comfort landscape site covers 400 ha, including blackland prairies and various woodlands and glades. At present none of this area is in public or conservation ownership.

The Nacatoch landscape site covers 800 ha, including blackland prairies and mesic ravines dominated by Durand's oak or pine-hardwood forests. It also adjoins bottomland forests of hardwood and pine, and cypress swamps with large rookeries of herons, egrets, and other wading and water birds, some found nowhere else in Arkansas. ANHC and TNC own the 83-ha Nacatoch Ravines Natural Area and TNC, International Paper, and ANHC jointly protect the 175-ha International Paper Blackland Ravines Unique Area.

COMPARISON WITH OTHER BLACKLAND PRAIRIES OF THE WEST GULF COASTAL PLAIN

The blackland prairie community in Texas has been described as a belt of prairie extending in a northeast-to-southwest direction through the eastern part of that state (Collins et al. 1975; Dyksterhuis 1946; Hill 1901; Kuchler 1964). It is generally dominated by big bluestem, little bluestem, Indiangrass, and gamma grass. Virtually all of the Texas blackland prairie has been converted to cropland and pasture.

Because of their geographical proximity and alkaline soils, the Arkansas and Texas blackland prairies share many species. Species such as ground plum, yellow star grass (*Hypoxis hirsuta*), yellow-puff (*Neptunia lutea*), purple prairie clover (*Dalea purpurea*), blue sage (*Salvia azurea*), and Indian plantain *(Cacalia plantaginea)*, along with the dominant grasses, are typical of both areas. However, the prairies are quite different in overall character. The Texas prairies are (or were) expanses of prairie over deep fertile soil. The relatively high rainfall (76–114 cm per year) and the high water-retention capability of the soil, relative to other Texas prairies, give the prairie a "lowland grassland appearance even on upland, well-drained situations" (Collins et al. 1975). The Arkansas blackland prairie region receives more precipitation than the Texas region (75–125 cm per year); therefore the deep, fertile soils of Arkansas are forested and the prairies are limited to thinner soils. These prairies are notably drier and smaller than other prairies in Arkansas and certainly do not have a lowland grassland appearance. It is probable that communities similar to those described here occur on comparable sites in Texas, particularly in the northeastern end. Further study should be devoted to finding, describing, and relating these communities.

Cretaceous deposits similar to those of Texas occur along the interior boundary of the West Gulf Coastal Plain in southwestern Arkansas as well as in a belt from eastern Mississippi to Georgia. The best-known area is in Mississippi and Alabama, where blacklands (the Black Belt) have been delineated (Kuchler 1964; Shantz and Zon 1924). These have been recognized and mapped based on distinctive vegetation. However, the vegetation of the Black Belt has been a topic of controversy. Shantz and Zon showed the area on their map as "tallgrass prairie." Rostlund

(1957) disputed this, contending that "a natural prairie belt" in the Mississippi/Alabama Black Belt was a "myth." Jones and Patton (1966), in a response to Rostlund, presented evidence that within the Black Belt, grassland was the characteristic vegetation on calcareous clay soil.

There may be more similarity between the vegetation of the blackland prairie region of Arkansas and the Black Belt of Mississippi and Alabama, even though the regions are geographically more separated than those of Arkansas and Texas. The prairies in Mississippi and Alabama are small, are located on thin soils over chalk on cuestas, and occur on the same soil series (or very similar soils) as those in Arkansas. The distribution of the Black Belt prairies in relation to previously cited soils is very similar to the pattern encountered in Arkansas. This study of the Arkansas distribution pattern supports the conclusion of Jones and Patton (1966) as opposed to that of Rostlund (1957).

Schauwecker (1996) recorded 103 species in the blackland prairie regions of Arkansas and Mississippi. Of the species recorded, 99 occurred in Mississippi and 56 in Arkansas. Species that occurred in greater than 10 percent of quadrats in both Mississippi and Arkansas were little bluestem, rattan (*Berchemia scandens*), the sedge *Carex cherokeensis*, partridge pea (*Cassia chamaecrista*), purple prairie clover, Illinois bundleflower (*Desmanthus illinoiensis*), milk pea (*Galactia volubilis*), eastern redcedar, wild petunia (*Ruellia humilis*), blue-eyed grass (*Sisirynchium albidum*), and old field goldenrod (*Solidago nemoralis*). In Arkansas, black-eyed Susan (*Rudbeckia hirta*) and Indiangrass were abundant, but they were very infrequent or absent in Mississippi. In contrast, three-awn grass (*Aristida dichotoma*), white prairie clover (*Dalea candida*), blazing star (*Liatris squarrosa*), and gray-headed coneflower (*Ratibida pinnata*) were common in Mississippi but were absent from his Arkansas study sites.

CONCLUSIONS

The blackland prairie region of southwestern Arkansas originally had a high diversity of calcareous prairie, woodland, and forest communities, along with acidic pine and hardwood forests. These generally have been destroyed or degraded by development during the last 150 years. However, there are a substantial number of remnants, degraded to varying degrees. Many of these remnants are concentrated in several landscape-scale areas where some protection and restoration have already taken place. In all probability, the most efficient strategy for restoration of this ecosystem is concentration of efforts within these landscape sites. It appears that most communities and species can be protected within these sites, and the landscape context will ensure greater viability of the individual elements. Given the perspective presented here, restoration of communities and species in a landscape context seems possible in the blackland prairie region of southwestern Arkansas. This will require acquisition, management, and restoration of lands by state and federal agencies, along with private conservation organizations. Private landowners must be involved through easements and voluntary management agreements. Objective criteria for location, spatial arrangement, and total area will have to be developed to achieve diversity, representativeness, and viability within this region.

8 A Plant Community Classification for Arkansas's Blackland Prairie Ecosystem

Douglas Zollner, Scott Simon, and Thomas L. Foti

INTRODUCTION

The primary purpose for developing a plant community classification is to provide information on plant communities useful to conservation planning and ecological management (Grossman et al. 1994). Plant community classifications define groups of plants that share biotic similarities and abiotic, system process, and structural characteristics. This is done by grouping plants by species composition and community structure, overlain on physical features and ecosystem parameters.

In Arkansas, the blackland ecosystem includes prairie-savanna, woodland, and forest types (Foti et al., this volume). These plant communities are being classified using the system developed by the Nature Conservancy (Grossman et al. 1998) in cooperation with state, federal, and academic partners (Foti et al. 1994). The Nature Conservancy classification is a modified version of the UNESCO vegetation classification system (UNESCO 1973). This national classification has been developed to present a consistent framework for conserving and stewarding biodiversity. An objective of the Nature Conservancy and many state-based natural heritage programs is identification and conservation of representative examples of all natural plant community types (TNC 1996). Plant communities can also be used as a coarse filter approach in planning the conservation of biological diversity. Plant community descriptions with ecosystem information can be useful in developing management regimes that maintain biodiversity across the landscape by incorporating relatively large-scale ecosystem process models during the planning process. Ecosystem transition models can be used in the restoration of degraded natural communities. The spatial arrangement of plant communities on the landscape can be used to interpret gaps in the landscape picture where plant communities are no longer extant. With this information it may be possible to conserve much of the natural diversity of an area through strategic conservation planning and ecological management.

As part of a conservation initiative for Arkansas's blackland ecosystem that includes land acquisition, ecological restoration, and stewardship, plant community descriptions were developed across the range of abiotic variation. The plant community descriptions include spatial models of community relationship to other plant communities, soil, moisture, topography, and fire regimes. A model of ecosystem dynamics was also developed.

METHODS

The national classification has seven levels of hierarchy: class, subclass, group, subgroup, formation, alliance, and association. These levels are described below. The first five levels are broad physiognomic classes and the final two are based on plant species composition (Grossman et al. 1998).

At the highest level there are seven *classes:* (1) forest areas dominated by trees over 5 m tall with overlapping crowns; (2) woodland areas dominated by open stands of trees over 5 m tall with a shrub and/or herbaceous understory usually present; (3) shrubland areas dominated by shrubs over 0.5 m tall; (4) dwarf-shrubland areas dominated by low growing shrubs; (5) herbaceous vegetation areas dominated by herbs and grasses; (6) nonvascular vegetation areas dominated by lichens, bryophytes, or algae; and (7) sparse vegetation areas where the vegetative cover is nearly absent.

Subclasses are divisions within each class based on predominant leaf phenology: evergreen, deciduous, and mixed for wooded areas and perennial gramminoid, perennial forb, hydromorphic rooted vegetation, and annual gramminiod or forb for herbaceous vegetation.

The *group* level of the hierarchy is defined by a combination of climate, leaf morphology, and leaf phenology. Categories within each subclass may be based on climate (tropical, temperate, subpolar). For wooded types categories may be based on leaf type (broad-leaved, sclerophylous, needle-leaved). For herbaceous types categories may be based on the presence or absence of tree, shrub, or dwarf shrub canopy coverage of less than 25 percent.

Subgroups divide natural or near-natural (mildly altered) vegetation from converted or cultivated vegetation.

Formations within each subgroup are based on crown shape (rounded, cylindrical, conical), crown height (tall, medium-tall, and so forth), elevational zone (alpine, montane, lowland), and hydrologic regime (after Cowardin et al. 1979).

An *alliance* is a group of plant communities having the same primary dominant species and similar physiognomy. It is an aggregation of plant community types. The alliance can be considered equivalent to the cover type used in most USGS Gap Analysis Programs (GAPs) to standardize mapping. Descriptions of alliances for the southeastern United States are available from Weakley et al. (1999).

An *association* is an assemblage of plant species with a defined species composition and physiognomy that repeats across landscapes as plant species interact with the environment. Associations are named using dominant and characteristic species.

Association-level plant communities for Arkansas's blackland ecosystem are described in this paper. These descriptions are included within the hierarchy of the national classification. The plant communities describe actual vegetation with an emphasis on natural and near-natural types. The community types were developed by combining a qualitative survey of known blackland sites concentrating on natural areas with quantitative data collected while instituting a monitoring program at several managed areas.

Plant species nomenclature follows *Keys to the Flora of Arkansas* (Smith 1994) with exceptions. Species separated by a dash (—) are found in the same strata and species separated by (/) are found in different strata. Species listed in parentheses are typical of most sites but are not found at every site. Soil information is from county soil surveys of the Natural Resource Conservation Service (USDA 1982). Geological information is from the Geological Map of Arkansas (USGS 1993).

EXPLANATION OF HERITAGE ELEMENT RANKING

Each species and natural community is given two ranks, a global (G) rank reflecting its rarity throughout the world and a state (S) rank reflecting its rarity at the state level. Global rank is indicated by the following designations:

G1—Critically imperiled globally because of extreme rarity (five or fewer occurrences or very few remaining individuals or hectares) or because of some factor of its biology making it especially vulnerable to extinction.

G2—Imperiled globally because of rarity (6–20 occurrences or few remaining individuals or hectares) or because of other factors demonstrably making it very vulnerable to extinction throughout its range.

G3—Either very rare and local throughout its range, or found locally (even abundantly at some of its locations) in a restricted range, or because of other factors making it vulnerable to extinction throughout its range; in the range of 21–100 occurrences.

G4—Apparently secure globally, though it may be quite rare in parts of its range, especially at the periphery.

G5—Demonstrably secure globally, though it may be quite rare in parts of its range, especially at the periphery.

GH—Historically known, with the expectation that it may be rediscovered.

GX—Believed to be extinct.

GU—Not yet ranked.

?—There is a question about the given rank.

Q—There are taxonomic questions concerning a species.

T—Associated with global rank, indicating a global rarity for a particular subspecific taxon.

MODELS

Two types of models have been developed. The first is a soil moisture-soil depth model that assists in locating the blackland community types spatially on the landscape. This model also seeks to determine placement of hypothetical types and create a search image that can lead to a concentrated survey for actual communities. The second model is a process model that attempts to explain plant community dynamics and transition pathways between some associations. This predictive model could be used to design management alternatives given various current conditions.

RESULTS AND DISCUSSION

Eighteen association-level plant communities have been described. These plant communities include several that are widespread on the Upper West Gulf Coastal Plain of Arkansas outside the blackland ecosystem. These community descriptions include seven prairie-savanna, one glade-outcrop, three woodland, three riparian woodland, one forest, and one riparian forest type on blackland soils, and two woodlands and one forest type that are also common outside the blackland ecosystem. It seems likely that many of these plant communities are also found in neighboring states with suitable substrates but would be endemic to the blackland region in general. The heritage rankings (G—ranks) are explained above.

RANGEWIDE BLACKLAND COMMUNITY DESCRIPTIONS

∽

Schizachyrium scoparium—Sporobolus compositus—Rudbeckia hirta—(Fimbristylis puberula var. *puberula)* Dry Blackland Prairie Herbaceous Vegetation (CEGL007768)—G2.

Little Bluestem—Tall Dropseed—Black-eyed Susan—(Hairy Fimbry) Dry Blackland Prairie Herbaceous Vegetation.

DESCRIPTION: This dry blackland prairie community typically occurs on dry ridges and chalk outcrops on the Upper West Gulf Coastal Plain of Arkansas. Examples also occur on recovering eroded areas. Vegetation is typically short (.60–1 m [2–3 feet]) and somewhat sparse, with bare ground present. It can become shrubby with fire suppression but woody species are held in check by drought. Little fuel accumulates at the end of one growing season (vegetation does not burn completely after one growing season). Dominant species include *Schizachyrium scoparium, Sporobolus compositus (=asper), Rudbeckia hirta* (in places large colonies covering 2–3 square meters, perhaps the result of heavy grazing in the past), and *Fimbristylis puberula* var. *puberula* (not present at Grandview Prairie). Other herbaceous species include *Acacia angustissima, Agalinis skinneriana, Asclepias viridiflora, A. viridis, Aster ericoides, Carex meadii, Chamaecrista fasciculata, Coreopsis lanceolata, Croton capitatus, C. monothagynus, Dalea purpurea* var. *purpurea, Delphinium carolinianum, Echinacea pallida, Euphorbia bicolor, E. corollata, Evax prolifera* (rare), *Grindelia lanceolata, Hedyotis longifolia* var. *longifolia, Liatris squarrosa, Neptunia lutea, Oenothera speciosa, Pycnanthemum tenuifolium, Ruellia humilis, Setaria geniculata, Sporobolus clandestinus, S. vaginiflorus, Tridens flavus,* and *Verbena simplex*. Bare soil is often covered with blue-green algae (*Nostoc* sp.). *Quercus muehlenbergii* and/or *Sideroxylon* (=*Bumelia*) *lanuginosa* can form small copses of dwarfed, gnarly trees on chalk outcrops or low-density savannas within the dry blackland prairie. Occasional woody species may include *Berchemia scandens, Cornus drummondii, Diospyros virginiana, Fraxinus americana, Ilex decidua, Juniperus virginiana, Smilax bona-nox,* and *Ulmus alata* occurring locally during periods of fire suppression or between severe droughts. Fire and edaphic factors (drought) limit woody vegetation distribution in this community. Woody vegetation succession is not as rapid as in the other blackland prairie community types. Soils are shallow, alkaline clays with the high shrink-swell character of the Sumter and Demopolis series over thick, calcareous substrates such as Annona and Saratoga chalks, which give the soils a light or even white appearance and with broken limestone of the Dierks and DeQueen formation. Fossils are common. This community typically grades into *Sorghastrum nutans—Schizachyrium scoparium—Echinacea pallida—Dalea purpurea* var. *purpurea* dry-mesic blackland prairie. High-quality examples of this community type are known from Grandview Prairie, the Saratoga Landing Natural Area, Stone Road Glade, and the Terre Noire Natural Area complex. Additional examples of varying quality are known from private lands and the White Cliffs Natural Area. The type location occurs in Clark County, Arkansas. Other examples are known from Hempstead, Howard, and Little River counties, Arkansas, and are likely found in Nevada and Sevier counties, Arkansas.

DISTRIBUTION: AR, TX? OK? LA?

TNC ECOREGION: 40:C; Bailey subsection: 231Eb.

FEDERAL LANDS: Corps of Engineers (Lake Millwood).

COMMENTS: The fimbristylis can be dominant in the spring, with tall dropseed or little bluestem dominant later in the year. We have speculated that the fimbristylis dominance is a result of disturbance in the form of heavy grazing earlier in the century, but we have no evidence of this. In general, little bluestem is dominant but tall dropseed dominates in many prairie openings. Most blackland prairies in Arkansas do not contain much of this dry type. Usually dry-mesic occurs on the ridgetops. It is possible that this rare community has expanded its normal range off the shallow soil chalk outcrops because of soil erosion. We have included the previous dry limestone glade community within this community owing to the similarities of the two groups.

⌐

Sorghastrum nutans—Schizachyrium scoparium—Echinacea pallida—Dalea purpurea var. *purpurea* Dry-mesic Blackland Prairie Herbaceous Vegetation (CEGL007769)—G2G3.

Yellow Indiangrass—Little Bluestem—Pale Purple Coneflower—Purple Prairie Clover Dry-mesic Blackland Prairie Herbaceous Vegetation.

DESCRIPTION: This dry-mesic blackland prairie community typically occurs on upper and middle slopes, frequently to ridgetops on the Upper West Gulf Coastal Plain of Arkansas. Vegetation is tall (1.2–1.8 m [4–6 feet]) and dense; bare soil is not present. Eroded areas with dry prairie are extant and succeed to dry-mesic prairie. This community becomes shrubby with fire suppression. Fuel accumulation is rapid (complete burn after one growing season). Dominant species include *Schizachyrium scoparium, Sorghastrum nutans, Echinacea pallida,* and *Dalea purpurea* var. *purpurea.* Other herbaceous species include *Acacia angustissima, Agave virginica, Aster ericoides, Aster prealtus, Asclepias tuberosa, Brickellia eupatorioides, Cacalia tuberosa, Carex chero-*

keensis, C. meadii, Centrosema virginiana, Chamaecrista fasciculata, Delphinium carolinianum, Desmanthus illinoensis, Echinacea purpurea, Eryngium yuccifolium, Euphorbia bicolor, E. corollata, Eupatorium altissimum, Grindelia lanceolata, Gaura longifolia, Hedyotis longifolia var. longifolia, Helenium autumnale, H. flexuosum, Hypericum sphaerocarpum, Liatris aspera, L. ligulistylis, L. squarrosa, Mimosa quadrivalis var. nuttallii (=Schrankia nuttallii), Neptunia lutea, Onosmodium molle, Penstemon cobaea, P. digitalis, Rhynchosia latifolia, Ratibida pinnata, Rosa setigera, Rubus trivialis, Rudbeckia hirta, Ruellia humilis, Salvia lyrata, Silphium laciniatum, Solidago canadensis, S. nemoralis, S. rigida, Sporobolus compositus (=asper), Stenosiphon linifolius, Tomanthera auriculata, Tragia urticifolia, Tridens flavus, Tripsacum dactyloides, Vernonia baldwinii, and V. missurica. The non-natives Lespedeza cuneata, Melilotus alba, and Melilotus officinalis can be abundant in disturbed areas. Quercus muehlenbergii and Ulmus crassifolia, infrequently Q. shumardii and Carya myristiciformis, form savannas within the dry-mesic blackland prairie. These savanna trees are medium-tall (to 11 m [35 feet]) and density is low (about 10 trees per half-hectare). In this gently rolling landscape, trees seem to favor north- and east-facing slopes. Other woody species may include Berchemia scandens, Cercis canadensis, Cornus drummondii, C. florida, Diospyros virginiana, Fraxinus americana, Ilex decidua, Juniperus virginiana, Sideroxylon (=Bumelia) lanuginosa, Smilax bonanox, S. rotundifolia, and Ulmus alata occurring locally during periods of fire suppression. Fire and edaphic factors (drought) play a role in limiting woody vegetation distribution in this community. Woody vegetation succession can be rapid, shading out herbaceous prairie species. Soils are relatively shallow alkaline clays with the high shrink-swell character of the Sumter and Demopolis series over thick, calcareous substrates such as Annona and Saratoga chalks, which may give the soils a light or even white appearance. This community typically grades into Sorghastrum nutans—Andropogon glomeratus—Lythrum alatum—Aster prealtus—Tripsacum dactyloides mesic blackland prairie and Quercus shumardii—Carya myristiciformis—(Cercis canadensis)—Carex cherokeensis—Scleria oligantha—Sorghastrum nutans dry-mesic calcareous upland woodland. High-quality examples of this community type are known from Columbus Prairie Preserve, Grandview Prairie, the Saratoga Landing Natural Area, and the Terre Noire Natural Area complex. Additional examples of varying quality are known from private lands and from the White Cliffs Natural Area. The type location is in Clark County, Arkansas. Other examples can be found in Hempstead, Howard, Little River, Nevada, and Sevier counties, Arkansas.

DISTRIBUTION: AR, LA? TX? OK?

TNC ECOREGION: 40:C; Bailey subsection: 231Eb.

FEDERAL LANDS: Corps of Engineers (Lake Millwood).

COMMENTS: This community is the matrix blackland prairie type in Arkansas. High-quality examples are rare but recoverable in present circumstances (grazed, hayed, fire suppressed). The Arkansas version does not contain big bluestem. This community has responded well to fire management and cedar/sweet clover removal. Large acreages are being restored in Arkansas. Coneflowers are being heavily exploited in places.

↩

Sorghastrum nutans—Andropogon glomeratus—Lythrum alatum—Aster prealtus—Tripsacum dactyloides Mesic Blackland Prairie Herbaceous Vegetation (CEGL007774)—G1?

Yellow Indiangrass—Bushy Bluestem—Winged Loosestrife—Willow-leaved Aster—Eastern Gamma Grass Mesic Blackland Prairie Herbaceous Vegetation.

DESCRIPTION: This mesic blackland prairie community occurs along the lower slopes, flat tabletops, and areas of relatively high soil moisture on the Upper West Gulf Coastal Plain of Arkansas. Seepage is common along the lower slopes during periods of high rainfall, when the community could be described as temporarily saturated. Vegetation is typically thick, 1.8 m (6 feet) tall or above. Fuel accumulation is rapid. This community becomes shrubby with fire suppression. Animals create bare areas for use as mineral licks. Dominant species include *Sorghastrum nutans, Andropogon glomeratus, Helianthus grossiserratus, Lythrum alatum,* and *Tripsacum dactyloides.* Other herbaceous species include *Acacia angustissima, Ambrosia trifida, Apocynum cannabinum, Campsis radicans, Carex cherokeensis, C. meadii, Centrosema virginiana, Chamaecrista fasciculata, Dalea purpurea* var. *purpurea, Desmanthus illinoensis, Eryngium yuccifolium, Eupatorium altissimum, E. coelestinum, Gaura longifolia, Helenium flexuosum, Lobelia spicata, L. siphilitica, Panicum anceps, Penstemon digitalis, Rosa carolina, Rubus trivialis, Ruellia humilis, Schizachyrium scoparium, Scirpus pendulus, Silphium integrifolium, S. laciniatum* (can dominate), *Solidago canadensis, S. rigida, Tomanthera auriculata, Tragia urticifolia, Vernonia baldwinii,* and *V. missurica.* Woody species including *Berchemia scandens, Cercis canadensis, Cornus drummondii, C. florida,*

*Fraxinus pennsylvanica, Juniperus virginiana, Quercus muehlen-
bergii, Rhus glabra, Smilax bona-nox, S. rotundifolia, Ulmus
alata, U. americana,* and *Viburnum rifidulum* occur locally during periods of fire suppression, colonizing and growing faster than
in the drier blackland prairie communities. Fire and edaphic factors (xero-hydric soil conditions) play a role in limiting woody
vegetation distribution in this community. Woody vegetation can
become dense, shading out herbaceous prairie species. Soils are
alkaline clays with the high shrink-swell character of the Houston
and Sumter series. No high-quality examples of this community
are known. It typically grades into *Lythrum alatum—Panicum
anceps—Aster lanceolatus* wet-mesic blackland prairie or *Quercus pagoda—(Carya illinoensis)/Ilex decidua/Carex cherokeensis
—Leersia virginica* mesic woodland. Examples at Columbus Prairie Preserve, Grandview Prairie, and the Terre Noire Natural Area
complex are being restored. The type location is in Clark County,
Arkansas. Other examples can be found in Howard and Hempstead counties and should be found in Little River, Nevada, and
Sevier counties, Arkansas.

DISTRIBUTION: AR.

TNC ECOREGION: 40:C; Bailey subsection: 231Eb.

FEDERAL LANDS: None known.

COMMENTS: This is a very rare community type with limited distribution. High-quality examples are unknown. It seems likely
that this community used to cover the flatter topographic positions on the landscape, where it transitions into a wet-mesic version. These flatter topographic areas of the landscape have been
largely converted to fescue pasture or been covered by dense stands
of young *Fraxinus pennsylvanica.*

↩

Lythrum alatum—Panicum anceps—Aster lanceolatus Wet-mesic
Blackland Prairie Temporarily Flooded Herbaceous Vegetation—G1?

*Winged Loosestrife—Beaked Panicum—Swamp Aster Wet-
mesic Blackland Prairie Temporarily Flooded Herbaceous Vegetation.*

DESCRIPTION: This wet-mesic blackland prairie community occurs in shallow draws and depressions and on level areas where
soils have a high capacity for holding water on the Upper West
Gulf Coastal Plain of Arkansas. This community is occasionally
to seasonally saturated. Water may "pond" briefly in localized depressions because of the tight soils. Vegetation is typically thick,
1.8 m (6 feet) tall or higher. This community becomes shrubby

very quickly with fire suppression. Fuel accumulation is rapid. Dominant species include *Lythrum alatum, Panicum anceps, Andropogon glomeratus,* and *Aster* spp. *Tripsacum dactyloides* could have been dominant in the community historically. Other herbaceous species include *Aster lanceolatus, A. novae-angliae, Carex annectans, C. cherokeensis, C. frankii, Desmanthus illinoensis, Eupatorium coelestinum, E. perfoliatum, Festuca pratensis, Glyceria striata, Helianthus grossiserratus, Juncus effusus, Lycopus* sp., *Phyla lanceolata, Scirpus pendulus, Sporobolus* sp. *Trepocarpus aethusae, Tripsacum dactyloides,* and *Vernonia baldwinii.* Woody species including *Berchemia scandens, Carya illinoensis, Celtis laevigata, Cercis canadensis, Cornus florida, Diospyros virginiana, Fraxinus pennsylvanica, Juniperus virginiana, Quercus macrocarpa, Q. muehlenbergii, Smilax bona-nox,* and *S. rotundifolia* occur locally during periods of fire suppression, colonizing and growing faster than in the drier blackland prairie communities. Woody vegetation can become dense, shading out herbaceous prairie species. Soils are alkaline clays with the high shrink-swell character of the Houston clay and Terouge silty clay series. This community has a limited distribution and high-quality examples are unknown. The community used to cover the lower flats and upper swales that become riparian woodlands lower on the landscape. These areas have been largely converted to fescue pasture or dense young stands of *Fraxinus pennsylvanica* on the flats and in the swales and small drains. We hypothesize that much of the wet-mesic blackland prairie has succeeded to low-quality riparian blackland woodland. Examples are known from Columbus Prairie Preserve, Grandview Prairie, and the Terre Noire Natural Area complex. The type location is in Hempstead County, Arkansas. Other, small and degraded, examples are known from Clark and Howard counties, Arkansas.

DISTRIBUTION: AR.

TNC ECOREGION: 40:C; Bailey subsection 231Eb.

FEDERAL LANDS: None known.

COMMENTS: This community description is somewhat speculative. It is based on a series of degraded (grazed, fire-suppressed, planted or improved pasture) sites now being restored. The description will likely change over the next few years with increased prescribed burning.

↬

Quercus muehlenbergii—Quercus sinuata/Rhus aromatica/Liatris aspera—Allium canadense var. *mobilense—Schizachyrium scoparium* Dry Chalk Savanna—G2.

Chinquapin Oak—Durand's Oak/Fragrant Sumac/Rough Blazing Star—Purple Prairie Onion—Little Bluestem Dry Chalk Savanna.

DESCRIPTION: This dry, calcareous savanna community occurs on ridgetops and knobs within blackland prairie on the Upper West Gulf Coastal Plain of Arkansas. Overstory trees are short (to 6 m [20 feet]), gnarly, and widely spaced. In a fire-maintained condition, the overstory is open and the understory consists of prairie vegetation. The herbaceous layer is predominately forb and grass in composition and moderately dense. Bare soil may be present and is covered with *Nostoc commune.* Fire plays a role in maintaining the savanna structure, and fire-suppressed savannas can have a dense midstory and suppressed herbaceous layer. The dominant tree species in the sparse overstory is overwhelmingly *Quercus muehlenbergii* to the northeast and *Quercus sinuata* to the southwest. Other overstory trees may include *Carya myristiciformis, Cercis canadensis, Fraxinus americana, Quercus shumardii, Ulmus crassifolia,* and *U. alata. Juniperus virginiana* and *Juniperus ashei* (to the west) become prominent with fire suppression. *Rhus aromatica* is often a dominant woody shrub. Other shrubs may be present, including *Cornus drummondii, Diospyros virginiana, Frangula caroliniana, Ilex decidua, Juniperus virginiana, Rosa carolina, Sideroxylon lanuginosa, Symphoricarpos orbiculatus,* and *Viburnum rifidulum.* Woody vines include *Berchemia scandens, Parthenocissus quinquefolia, Smilax rotundifolia,* and *Toxicodendron radicans,* but these are not particularly important to the structure of the community. The herbaceous layer is dominated by forbs and grasses (sedges). Dominant herbaceous species include *Allium canadense* var. *mobilense, Bouteloua curtipendula, Carex cherokeensis* (in fire-suppressed state), *Echinacea purpurea, Helianthus hirsutus, Liatris aspera,* and *Schizachyrium scoparium.* Other herbaceous species may include *Agrimonia parviflora, Asclepias tuberosa, Aster cordifolius, A. patens, Astragalus canadensis, Chasmanthium sessilifolium, Dalea purpurea* var. *purpurea, Delphinium carolinianum, Desmodium dillenii, Echinacea pallida, Euphorbia bicolor, E. corollata, Galium pilosum, Glandularia canadensis, Lespedeza* spp., *Liatris aspera, Lonicera sempervirens, Onosmodium molle, Opuntia humifusa, Panicum* sp., *Penstemon cobaea, P. digitalis, Phlox pilosa, Physalis* sp., *Rudbeckia hirta, Ruellia humulis, Salvia azurea, Scleria oligantha, Seymeria cassioides, Silphium laciniatum, Smilax herbacea* var. *lasioneuron, Sorghastrum nutans, Spigelia marilandica, Stenosiphon linifolius, Verbena bipinna-*

tifida, Verbesina helianthoides, and *Vernonia baldwinii.* Historically, fires sweeping through the blackland ecosystem would have maintained the savanna/woodland structure of this community. This community has responded well to fire management, cedar removal, and the suspension of grazing. Soils are shallow, eroded, well-drained, low-permeability, low-water-holding-capacity, alkaline Demopolis silty clays over chalk. Chalk outcrops frequently and is usually within 30 cm (12 inches) of the surface. This community is typically surrounded by *Schizachyrium scoparium—Sporobolus compositus—Rudbeckia hirta—Fimbristylis puberula* var. *puberula* dry blackland prairie but may grade into *Sorghastrum nutans—Schizachyrium scoparium—Echinacea pallida—Dalea purpurea* var. *purpurea* dry-mesic blackland prairie on deeper soils on more exposed slopes. The highest-quality remnant is found on Saratoga Landing Blackland Prairie and on adjacent grazed lands. The type locality is in Hempstead County, Arkansas. This community type also can be found in Clark, Howard, and Little River counties in Arkansas. Other examples are known from the International Paper Blackland Ravines Unique Area, Grandview Prairie Wildlife Management Area, and White Cliffs Natural Area.

DISTRIBUTION: AR.

TNC ECOREGION: 40:C; Bailey subsection 231Eb.

FEDERAL LANDS: Millwood Lake (COE).

COMMENTS: This community has changed significantly since cedar removal and fire restoration. Refinement in the description should be expected after a few additional burns. Additional examples of this community may occur on adjacent lands currently being surveyed as part of a blackland ecosystem assessment.

⌐

Quercus muehlenbergii/Andropogon gerardii—Dalea compacta —Seymeria cassioides Dry-mesic Chalk Savanna—G1?

Chinquapin Oak/Big Bluestem—Showy Prairie Clover—Yellow False Foxglove Dry-mesic Chalk Savanna.

DESCRIPTION: This dry-mesic calcareous savanna community occurs on flattened ridgelines within blackland prairie on the Upper West Gulf Coastal Plain of Arkansas. Overstory trees are short (to 8 m [25 feet]), gnarly, and widely spaced. In a fire-maintained condition, the overstory is open and the understory consists of prairie vegetation. The herbaceous layer is predominately grass and forb in composition and moderately dense. Fire plays a role in maintaining the savanna structure, and fire-suppressed savannas can have a dense midstory and suppressed herbaceous layer. The dominant tree species is overwhelmingly *Quercus muehlenbergii*. Other occasional midstory woody vegetation may include *Cornus drummondii, Diospyros virginiana, Ilex decidua, Juniperus virginiana*, and *Sideroxylon lanuginosa*. Dominant herbaceous vegetation includes *Andropogon gerardii, Dalea compacta*, and *Seymeria cassioides*. Other herbaceous species include *Acacia angustissima, Asclepias tuberosa, Asclepias viridiflora, Aster patens, Brickellia eupatorioides, Cacalia tuberosa, Carex cherokeensis, C. microdonta/meadii, Dalea candida, Delphinium carolinianum, Desmanthus illinoensis, Desmodium dillenii, Dracopis amplexicaulis, Echinacea pallida, E. purpurea, Gaura longifolia, Glandularia canadensis, Grindelia lanceolata, Hedyotis nigricans, Helianthus hirsutus, Hypericum sphaerocarpum, Liatris aspera, Mimosa quadrivalis* var. *nuttallii* (=*Schrankia nuttallii*), *Neptunia lutea, Penstemon cobaea, P. digitalis, Rudbeckia hirta, Ruellia humilis, Salvia azurea, S. lyrata, Schizachyrium scoparium, Silphium laciniatum, Sorghastrum nutans, Stenosiphon linifolius*, and *Verbena bipinnatifida*. Historically, fires sweeping through the blackland ecosystem would have maintained the savanna structure of this community. This community has responded well to fire management, suspension of grazing, and cedar removal. Soils are shallow, eroded, well-drained, low-permeability, low-water-holding-capacity, alkaline Demopolis silty clays over chalk. Chalk outcrops frequently and is usually within 30 cm (12 inches) of the surface. Currently the community is known only from this one location and covers approximately 12 ha (30 acres). This community typically grades into *Sorghastrum nutans—Schizachyrium scoparium—Echinacea pallida—Dalea purpurea* var. *purpurea* dry-mesic blackland prairie. It may grade into *Quercus shumardii—Carya myristiciformis/ (Cercis canadensis)/Carex cherokeensis—Scleria oligantha— Sorghastrum nutans* dry-mesic calcareous upland woodland on deeper soils and north-facing slopes. The highest-quality remnant is found at Saratoga Landing Blackland Prairie. The type locality is in Hempstead County, Arkansas.

DISTRIBUTION: AR.

TNC ECOREGION: 40:C; Bailey subsection 231Eb.

FEDERAL LANDS: Millwood Lake (COE).

COMMENTS: This community has changed significantly since cedar removal and fire restoration. Refinement in the description should be expected after a few additional burns. Additional examples of this community may occur on adjacent lands currently being surveyed as part of a blackland ecosystem assessment.

〜

Quercus falcata—Carya illinoensis/Silphium integrifolium—
Panicum anceps (Carex cherokeensis—Festuca arundinacea)
Mesic Blackland Savanna—G1.
  Southern Red Oak—Pecan/Rosinweed—Beaked Panic Grass
  —(Cherokee Sedge—Tall Fescue) Mesic Blackland Savanna.

DESCRIPTION: This mesic blackland savanna community occurs in areas of deep, moist soil, usually on nearly level or gentle terrain on the Upper West Gulf Coastal Plain of Arkansas. The trees are medium-tall to 14 m (45 feet), with large spreading crowns. Basal area averages about 2.5 m per half-hectare (25 square feet per acre) with 25 stems over 5 cm (2 inches) in diameter at breast height (dbh) per 0.4 ha. The herbaceous vegetation is tall (1.8 m [6 feet] or higher) and dense. Fuel accumulation is rapid except under the trees, where it is relatively sparse. Fire plays a role in the formation and maintenance of the community, as young woody vegetation readily invades and suppresses the herbaceous vegetation. Fire coverage in this savanna has been complete except under the overstory trees, which were not affected because the herbaceous layer was suppressed. Dominant tree species include *Quercus falcata* and *Carya illinoensis.* Other woody species include *Cornus drummondii, Carya myristiciformis, Celtis laevigata, Cercis canadensis, Crataegus marshallii, C. spathulata, Diospyros virginiana, Fraxinus americana, Gleditsia triacanthos, Juniperus virginiana, Maclura pomifera, Quercus macrocarpa, Q. muehlenbergii, Q. nigra, Q. shumardii, Q. stellata, Pinus echinata, P. taeda, Rhus copallina, Smilax bona-nox, Toxicodendron radicans, Ulmus alata, U. americana,* and *U. crassifolia* occurring as occasional sapling, shrub, and woody vines. The dominant herbaceous species include *Carex cherokeensis, Festuca arundinacea,* and *Panicum anceps.* Other herbaceous species include *Acacia angustissima* var. *hirta, Allium canadense* var. *canadense, Ambrosia trifida, Apocynum cannabinum, Asclepias viridis, Aster prealtus, Aster novae-angliae, Cacalia tuberosa, Campsis radicans, Chamaecrista fasciculata, Dactylis glomerata, Daucus carota, Desmanthus illinoensis, Desmodium paniculatum, Echinacea purpurea, Elymus virginicus, Eupatorium altissimum, Euphorbia bicolor, Euthamia leptocephala, Helenium flexuosum, Helianthus grossiserratus, Liatris aspera, Lythrum alatum, Medicago lupulina., Passiflora incarnata, Penstemon digitalis, Poa* sp., *Polypodium polypodioides, Prunella vulgaris, Pteridium aquilinum, Rosa carolina, R. setigera, Rubus trivialis, Ruellia strepens, Rumex crispus, R. hastatulus, Salvia lyrata, Schizachyrium scoparium, Setaria glauca, S. geniculata, Solidago canadensis, Sorghastrum nutans, Sorghum halepense, Sporobolus compositus, Stachys* sp., *Symphoricarpos orbiculatus, Teucrium* sp., *Tragia* sp., *Trifolium pratense, Tridens flavus, Tripsacum dactyloides, Vernonia missurica, Viola sororia,* and *Xanthium strumarium* occurring as *occasionals.* Soils are deep (114 cm [45 inches] or more), alkaline clays with the high shrink-swell character of the Houston clay series. Unlike in adjacent blackland prairie communities, deep chalk formations are not near the surface and the soils are not eroded, probably owing to the relative lack of topography. A high- or medium-quality example of this savanna does not exist. Typical herbaceous vegetation would likely be similar to the adjacent *Sorghastrum nutans—Schizachyrium scoparium—Echinacea pallida—Dalea purpurea* var. *purpurea* dry-mesic and *Sorghastrum nutans—Andropogon glomeratus—Lythrum alatum—Aster prealtus—Tripsacum dactyloides* mesic blackland prairie herbaceous vegetation into which it grades. A large example is known from Grandview Prairie. The type location is in Hempstead County, Arkansas. Other examples likely occur in Howard County, Arkansas.

DISTRIBUTION: AR.

TNC ECOREGION: 40:C; Bailey subsection: 231Eb.

FEDERAL LANDS: None known.

COMMENTS: This community description is somewhat speculative because of the degraded nature of the remaining examples. The deep soil and the absence of a massive chalk layer allow for the savanna formation. The relatively flat topography and tight soils permit the formation of mesic prairie. The mesic blackland prairie described previously is on the lower slopes and swales, whereas the savanna forms on the tabletops above the dry-mesic prairie. There is a problem identifying *Quercus pagoda* and *Quercus falcata* in the blackland ecosystem, as they appear to integrade. The *Quercus falcata* on dry-mesic, slightly acid soils is typical and keys out well; the *Quercus pagoda* in the temporarily flooded, calcareous riparian areas also keys out well. On the tabletops, where deep soil mesic conditions exist, the species is difficult to distinguish; so we left it as *Q. falcata* although it has *pagoda* characteristics.

᠅

Quercus shumardii—Carya myristiciformis—(Quercus muehlenbergii)/Cercis canadensis/Carex cherokeensis—Scleria oligantha—Sorghastrum nutans Dry-mesic Calcareous Woodland (CEGL007775)—G1G2.

Shumard's Oak—Nutmeg Hickory—(Chinquapin Oak)/Red-bud/Cherokee Sedge—Nut Rush—Yellow Indiangrass Dry-mesic Calcareous Woodland.

DESCRIPTION: This dry-mesic calcareous upland woodland community occurs in areas of deep, moist soil, usually on nearly level terrain or possibly in topographically protected areas on the Upper West Gulf Coastal Plain of Arkansas. The trees are medium in height (to 14 m [45 feet]). The herbaceous layer can be moderately tall (to 1.2 m [4 feet]) and dense or, where fire suppressed, short (.60 m [2 feet] or less) and sparse. Fire plays a role in the formation and maintenance of the community, as *Juniperus virginiana* readily invades and suppresses the herbaceous vegetation. Dominant tree species include *Quercus shumardii* and *Carya myristiciformis; Quercus muehlenbergii* is commonly present. Other woody species include *Cercis canadensis, Cornus drummondii, Frangula caroliniana, Fraxinus americana, Ilex decidua, Juglans nigra, Juniperus virginiana, Liquidambar styraciflua, Quercus pagoda, Q. stellata, Rhamnus caroliniana, Ulmus crassifolia,* and *Viburnum rufidulum* occurring as occasional trees, saplings, and shrubs. Dominant woody vines include *Berchemia scandens, Parthenocissus quinquefolia, Smilax bona-nox, S. rotundifolia,* and *Toxicodendron radicans.* Dominant herbaceous species include *Carex cherokeensis, Scleria oligantha,* and *Sorghastrum nutans* (in fire-maintained woodlands). Other herbaceous species include *Arisaema dracontium, Asclepias purpurea, Asplenium platyneuron, Aster cordifolius, A. patens, Carex cherokeensis, C. glaucodea, Desmodium paniculatum* var. *dillenii, Echinacea purpurea, Elymus virginicus, Festuca obtusa, Galium circaezans, Helianthus hirsutus, Leersia virginica, Liatris aspera, Panicum anceps, Penstemon digitalis, Ruellia humulis, R. strepens, Salvia lyrata, Solidago auriculata, Spigelia marilandica, Sanicula canadensis, Verbesina helianthoides,* and *Viola triloba.* During periods of prolonged fire suppression, the woodlands become denser and herbaceous vegetation abundance and diversity decrease. In high-graded woodlands, *Carya myristiciformis* becomes dominant. Soils are relatively deep, alkaline clays, with the high shrink-swell character of the Sumter series. The absence of chalk near the surface allows for woodland development. These communities are typically bordered by *Sorghastrum nutans—Schizachyrium scoparium—Echinacea pallida—Dalea purpurea* var. *purpurea* dry-mesic blackland prairie and *Quercus stellata/Chasmanthium sessiliflorum—Schizachyrium scoparium* in dry woodland that is slightly higher topographically. The highest-quality remnants of this community occur at Grandview Prairie, the Saratoga Landing Natural Area, and the Terre Noire Natural Area complex. This community has responded well to fire management, with reduced woody-vegetation density and increased herbaceous-layer diversity. Disturbed examples typically include *Callicarpa americana, Gleditsia triacanthos, Liquidambar styraciflua,* and *Maclura pomifera.* The type location is in Clark County, Arkansas. Other examples are known from Howard and Hempstead counties, Arkansas. It is likely extant in Little River, Nevada, and Sevier counties, Arkansas.

DISTRIBUTION: AR, LA? OK? TX?

TNC ECOREGION: 40:C; Bailey subsection: 231Eb.

FEDERAL LANDS: Corps of Engineers (Lake Millwood).

COMMENTS: The distribution of disturbed (fire-suppressed, cutover, grazed) sites parallels that of the blackland prairie sites of southwestern Arkansas. Complete fire suppression pushes this woodland to forest. *Carex cherokeensis* appears to play an important role in reducing fire intensity in these woodlands owing to its evergreen nature in southern Arkansas.

↝

Quercus pagoda—(Carya illinoensis)/Ilex decidua/Carex cherokeensis—Leersia virginica Mesic Blackland Woodland—G1?

Cherrybark oak—(Pecan)/Deciduous Holly/Cherokee Sedge—Whitegrass Mesic Blackland Woodland.

DESCRIPTION: This mesic blackland woodland community forms on rich, mesic sites on the Upper West Gulf Coastal Plain of Arkansas. The community occurs in areas bordering ephemeral streams and flats that are often saturated in the late winter and early spring. The trees are medium-tall (to 21 m [70 feet] or higher) and the canopy open to closed. The herbaceous layer can be sparse with heavy leaf litter under fire suppression, or moderately dense and about .60 m (2 feet) tall. Frequent fire in the surrounding prairie-woodland matrix pushes the community to an open woodland structure; fire suppression allows rapid densification. A rich herbaceous understory is present in high-quality sites. The dominant tree is *Quercus pagoda.* Other overstory trees may include *Carya cordiformis, C. illinoensis, C. myristiciformis, C. ovata, Fraxinus americana, F. pennsylvanica, Morus alba, Quercus muehlenbergii, Q. phellos, Q. shumardii, Q. stellata, Pinus taeda, Ulmus alata, U. americana,* and *U. crassifolia.* The understory includes saplings of overstory trees and scattered *Crataegus marshallii, C. spathulata, Frangula caroliniana, Ilex decidua, Juniperus virginiana,* and *Viburnum rufidulum.* Woody vines include *Berchemia scandens, Parthenocissus quinquefolia, Smilax bona-nox,* and *Toxicodendron radicans.* The dominant herbs in medium- and low-quality sites are *Carex cherokeensis* and *Scleria oligantha.* Occasional herbaceous species include *Carex flaccosperma, Chasmanthium latifolium, C. sessiliflorum, Elymus glabiflorus, Leersia virginica, Ruellia strepens, Sanicula canadensis, Spigelia marilandica, Symphoricarpos orbiculatus, Trachelospermum difforme,* and *Trepocarpus aethusae.* In high-graded woodlands *Carya* sp. become dominant. The soils are nearly level to gently sloping, deep (to 15 m [50 feet] or more), fertile, and mildly acidic Kipling series loams and silty clay loams. These soils are slowly permeable and shrink and crack upon drying. The water table is within 46 cm (18 inches) of the surface, and these soils are usually associated with ephemeral and semipermanent creeks and flats intermingled with blackland prairies and woodlands. Abundant *Maclura pomifera* and *Callicarpa americana* are evidence of grazing or other disturbance. These communities are typically adjacent to, grade into, or form a mosaic with *Quercus shumardii—Carya myristiciformis— (Quercus muehlenbergii)/Cercis canadensis/Carex cherokeensis —Scleria oligantha—Sorghastrum nutans* dry-mesic calcareous woodland, *Quercus falcata—Quercus stellata—(Pinus echinata —Pinus taeda)/Chasmanthium sessiliflorum—Danthonia spicata* dry-mesic woodland, and *Sorghastrum nutans—Andropogon glomeratus—Lythrum alatum—Aster prealtus—Tripsacum dactyloides* mesic blackland prairie. Because of the richness of the sites this community often has components of the drier calcareous woodland. Fingers of cherrybark oak are similarly often found in dry-mesic calcareous woodlands. *Quercus pagoda* woodlands have pockets of standing water; the dry-mesic calcareous blackland woodlands do not. Examples of this community are known only from Grandview Prairie. The type location is in Hempstead County, Arkansas. The community is likely also found in Clark, Howard, Little River, and Sevier counties, Arkansas.

DISTRIBUTION: AR, OK?

TNC ECOREGION: 40:C; Bailey subsection 231Eb.

FEDERAL LANDS: None known.

COMMENTS: We retained the woodland designation because of its close association with fire-maintained blackland prairies. This is a very rare community type. Few examples are known because these rich sites were cleared for cotton in the early 1900s and later converted to pasture. There is a wetter, temporarily flooded variant with cherrybark and willow oak not yet described.

~

Quercus stellata/Vaccinium arboreum/Chasmanthium sessiliflo-
rum—Danthonia spicata—Schizachyrium scoparium Dry Blackland Woodland (CEGL007777)—G2?
   Post Oak/High bush blueberry/Spanglegrass—Poverty Oats—
Little Bluestem Dry Blackland Woodland.

DESCRIPTION: This dry upland woodland community typically occurs as small patches of 8 ha (20 acres) or less or linear transitions
within the blackland ecosystem on the Upper West Gulf Coastal
Plain of Arkansas. The community occurs on acidic soils adjacent
to or on top of alkaline prairie and woodland soils. The location
and size of the community is dependent on the steepness of the
transition between soil types. The larger versions occur on shallower transitions and may also be a function of the fire regime.
The trees are short (to 12 m [40 feet]) with spreading crowns. The
herbaceous layers can be moderately dense and tall (to 1 m [3
feet]) or sparse, when suppressed, with a thick litter layer. With
fire suppression *Juniperus virginiana* invades both the interior
and edges of this community. The dominant tree species is *Quer-*
cus stellata often with *Carya* sp., *Pinus echinata, Quercus fal-*
cata, and *Q. marilandica.* Other overstory trees may include
Carya alba, C. myristiciformis, C. ovata (rare), *C. texana, Frax-*
inus americana, Pinus taeda (rare), *Quercus laurifolia* (rare),
Q. muehlenbergii, Q. shumardii, Q. velutina, and *Ulmus alata.*
The understory comprises saplings of overstory trees with *Cornus*
florida, Crataegus marshallii, C. spathulata, Ostrya virginiana,
and *Vaccinium arboreum.* Woody vines include *Berchemia scan-*
dens, Parthenocissus quinquefolia, Smilax bona-nox, S. rotundi-
folia, and *Vitis rotundifolia.* Dominant herbaceous species are
Chasmanthium sessiliflorum, Danthonia spicata, and *Schizachy-*
rium scoparium with *Andropogon gerardii* (rare), *Aster paludosus*
subsp. *hemisphericus, A. patens, Baptisia nuttalliana, Carex*
blanda, Centrosema virginiana, Chamaecrista fasciculata, Del-
phinium caroliniana, Desmodium paniculatum var. *dillenii,*
Erechtites hieraciifolia, Euphorbia corollata, Helianthus hirsu-
tus, Liatris asper, L. squarrosa, Panicum linearifolium, Phlox
pilosa, Ruellia humilis, R. strepens, Mimosa quadrivalis var. *nut-*
tallii (=*Schrankia nuttallii*), *Scleria oligantha, Solidago odora,*
S. ulmifolia, Sorghastrum nutans, Tephrosia virginiana, Trios-
teum perfoliatum, and *Verbesina helianthoides.* The soils are
deep (to 76 cm [30 inches]), Oktibbeha series silty clay loams on
flat hilltops or gentle slopes. These acidic soils usually overlie alkaline marls and chalks. Woody vegetation succession is rapid

during periods of fire suppression. Almost impenetrable thickets are formed at the edges and within this community, completely shading out the herbaceous vegetation. This dry woodland forms a mosaic with *Quercus falcata* var. *falcata—Quercus stellata— (Pinus echinata—Pinus taeda)—Chasmanthium sessiliflorum— Danthonia spicata* dry-mesic woodland and *Quercus shumardii —Carya myristiciformis—(Quercus muehlenbergii)/Cercis canadensis/Carex cherokeensis—Scleria oligantha—Sorghastrum nutans* dry-mesic calcareous woodland. A greater understanding of this community type should result with fire management. Medium- to low-quality examples of this community are known from Grandview Prairie, the Saratoga Landing Natural Area, and the Terre Noire Natural Area complex. The type location is in Clark County, Arkansas. Other examples are known from Howard and Hempstead counties. The community type also should be found in Little River, Nevada, and Sevier counties, Arkansas.

DISTRIBUTION: AR.

TNC ECOREGION: 40:C; Bailey subsection 231Eb.

FEDERAL LANDS: Corps of Engineers (Lake Millwood).

COMMENTS: Good response to fire management.

⌐

Quercus falcata var. *falcata—Quercus stellata—(Pinus echinata —Pinus taeda)/Chasmanthium sessiliflorum—Danthonia spicata* Dry-mesic Woodland (GECL007776)—G2?

Southern Red Oak—Post Oak—(Shortleaf Pine—Loblolly Pine)/Spanglegrass—Poverty Oats Dry-mesic Woodland.

DESCRIPTION: This dry-mesic mixed oak (or oak-pine) upland woodland community generally occurs on rolling terrain, usually in areas that transition from calcareous blackland soils to acidic sands on the Upper West Gulf Coastal Plain of Arkansas. The trees are medium-tall (to 20 m [65 feet] or more) with spreading crowns. The herbaceous layer is moderately dense but usually less than 1 m (3 feet) tall. Fire plays a role in the formation and composition of this community. Dominant tree species include *Quercus falcata* var. *falcata*, *Q. stellata*, and *Ulmus alata*. *Quercus alba* may be present but is replaced by *Q. stellata* in western Arkansas. *Pinus* sp. density appears to depend on disturbance frequency and can be missing or dominant. Large *Pinus echinata* appear almost relictual and with non-fire disturbance patterns, *Pinus taeda* replaces this species. Other tree species may include *Carya alba*, *C. myristiciformis*, *C. texana*, *Quercus marilandica*, *Q. velutina*, and *Ulmus americana*. Other woody species include occasional *Asimina triloba, Callicarpa americana, Crataegus spathulata, C. marshallii, Diospyros virginiana, Ilex decidua, Ostrya virginiana,* and *Vaccinium arboreum.* Fire-suppressed examples have abundant saplings of overstory trees. Woody vines include *Berchemia scandens, Campsis radicans, Parthenocissus quinquefolia, Smilax bona-nox, S. rotundifolia, Toxicodendron radicans,* and *Vitis rotundifolia.* The dominant herb is *Chasmanthium sessiliflorum.* Other common herbaceous species include *Carex cherokeensis, Danthonia spicata, Rudbeckia hirta,* and *Scleria oligantha* with *Andropogon gerardii* (rare), *A. virginicus, Asclepias variegata, Aster ericoides, A. patens, Baptisia alba, Botrychium virginianum, Carex flaccosperma, C. debilis, C. complanata, C. meadii, Camassia scilloides, Coreopsis lanceolata, Echinacea pallida, Elephantopus carolinianus, Elymus virginicus, Erechtites hieraciifolia, Gnaphalium purpureum, Helianthus hirsutus, Leersia virginica, Penstemon digitalis, Phlox pilosa, Polystichum acrostichoides, Rubus flagellaris, Ruellia strepens, Salvia lyrata, Sanicula canadensis, Schizachyrium scoparium, Solidago canadensis, S. odora, S. petiolaris, Sorghastrum nutans, Sporobolus* sp., *Tradescantia ohiensis, Tripsacum dactyloides, Vernonia baldwinii,* and *Viola palmata* occurring as occasionals. This community occurs adjacent to blackland prairie and woodland (blackland ecosystem), usually at a higher topographic location on mixed calcareous blackland and acidic sands. Fires traveling off the prairie into these woodlands maintain the woodland structure and species composition. These communities quickly succeed to dense forest with fire suppression. During periods of prolonged fire suppression, the woodlands become denser and the herbaceous vegetation is suppressed. The amount of pine within these communities seems to be a result of fire history and canopy-opening disturbance events. The dominance of *Chasmanthium sessiliflorum* may also be caused by fire suppression and densification, as *Schizachyrium scoparium* becomes dominant with fire management. Restoration of natural processes and recovery from past disturbances may change species dominance patterns. Soils are nearly level (Oktibbeha series) to sloping hillside (Sacul and Kirvin series), fine sandy loams. Sacul and Kirvin soils are deep, acidic, well-drained, fine sandy loams. Oktibbeha soils have acidic surface layers over calcareous marls with a high shrink-swell character and could be described as xerohydric. Small ravines or eroded areas that cut through the Oktibbeha soils create habitat for calciphiles such as *Carya myristiciformis* and *Quercus muehlenbergii.* Oktibbeha soils are most commonly found within the blackland ecosystem; Sacul and Kirvin are usually found adjacent. The mixed nature of the soils allows *Quercus falcata* and *Q. pagoda* to interdigitate. This community grades into and forms a mosaic with *Quercus alba—Quercus falcata* var. *falcata—Quercus stellata—Nyssa sylvatica—(Pinus echinata—Pinus taeda)/Chasmanthium sessiliflorum* dry-mesic forest, *Quercus stellata/Vaccinium arboreum/Chasmanthium sessiliflorum/Danthonia spicata—Schizachyrium scoparium* dry blackland woodland, *Quercus shumardii—Carya myristiciformis—(Quercus muehlenbergii)/Cercis canadensis/Carex cherokeensis/Scleria oligantha—Sorghastrum nutans* dry-mesic calcareous woodland, and *Sorghastrum nutans—Schizachyrium scoparium—Echinacea pallida—Dalea purpurea* var. *purpurea* dry-mesic blackland prairie. Examples are known from Grandview Prairie and the Terre Noire Natural Area complex. The type location is in Hempstead County, Arkansas. This community type is also known from Clark County, Arkansas, in a small, degraded remnant form.

DISTRIBUTION: AR.

TNC ECOREGION: 40:C; Bailey subsection 231Eb.

COMMENTS: These communities are rare because of conversion to pine plantation and fire suppression.

⤳

Quercus alba—Quercus falcata var. *falcata—Quercus stellata—Nyssa sylvatica—(Pinus echinata—Pinus taeda)/Chasmanthium sessiliflorum* Dry-mesic Forest (CEGL004727)—G3G4.

White Oak—Southern Red Oak—Post Oak—Black Gum—(Shortleaf Pine—Loblolly Pine)/Spanglegrass Dry-mesic Forest.

DESCRIPTION: This dry-mesic mixed oak (or oak-pine) upland forest community generally occurs on nearly level terrain, usually in higher topographic positions on the landscape. The soils are moderately deep with high moisture-holding capacities. The trees are tall (to 26 m [85 feet] or more) with a relatively open to closed canopy. The herbaceous vegetation is often sparse and suppressed, with a thick litter layer, although with fire management a grassy understory develops. Fire plays a role in the formation and composition of this community. Dominant tree species include *Quercus alba, Q. falcata* var. *falcata, Q. stellata* (sometimes replacing *Q. alba* to the west), and *Nyssa sylvatica. Pinus* sp. density appears to depend on disturbance frequency and can be missing or dominant. Large *Pinus echinata* appear almost relictual, and with non-fire disturbance patterns *Pinus taeda* replaces this species. Other tree species include *Carya alba, C. myristiciformis, Carya texana, Quercus marilandica,* and *Q. muehlenbergii.* Other saplings, shrubs, and woody vines include *Asimina triloba, Berchemia scandens, Callicarpa americana, Campsis radicans, Ostrya virginiana, Parthenocissus quinquefolia, Rubus flagellaris, Smilax bona-nox, S. rotundifolia,* and *Toxicodendron radicans.* The dominant herbaceous species is *Chasmanthium sessiliflorum* with *Andropogon gerardii* (rare), *A. virginicus, Asclepias variegata, Baptisia alba, Botrychium virginianum, Carex cherokeensis, Camassia scilloides, Coreopsis lanceolata, Echinacea pallida, Elephantopus carolinianus, Gnaphalium purpureum, Penstemon digitalis, Phlox pilosa, Polystichum acrostichoides, Ruellia strepens, Schizachyrium scoparium, Scleria oligantha, Solidago odora, S. petiolaris, Sorghastrum nutans, Tripsacum dactyloides, Vernonia baldwinii,* and *Viola palmata.* During periods of prolonged fire suppression, the forests become denser and the herbaceous vegetation is suppressed. Soils are nearly level, fine sandy loams of the Oktibbeha, Sacul, and Kirvin series. Sacul and Kirvin soils are deep, acidic, well-drained fine sandy loams. Oktibbeha soils have acidic surface layers over calcareous marls with a high shrink-swell character and could be described as xerohydric. Small ravines or eroded areas that cut through the Oktibbeha soils create habitat for calciphiles such as *Carya myristiciformis* and *Quercus muehlenbergii.* No high-quality remnants of this community are known. This matrix community for the Upper West Gulf Coastal Plain often occurs adjacent to the blackland ecosystem as well as in other upland locations. Examples are known from Grandview Prairie and the Terre Noire Natural Area complex. The type location is in Sevier County, Arkansas. This community type is also known from Clark and Hempstead counties, Arkansas. The community is likely extant throughout southern Arkansas.

DISTRIBUTION: AR, OK.

TNC ECOREGION: 40:C; Bailey subsection 231Eb, M231Ad, and probably others.

FEDERAL LANDS: USFWS—Pond Creek NWR.

COMMENTS: Most sites have been converted to pine plantation or have become very low-quality forest communities. The amount of pine within these communities seems to be a result of fire history and canopy-opening disturbance events. Recent logging and fire suppression have greatly expanded the frequency of *Pinus taeda* (and perhaps *Nyssa sylvatica*) while decreasing both *Pinus echinata* and *Quercus* spp. The dominance of *Chasmanthium sessiliflorum* may be a result of fire suppression and densification.

〜

Ulmus americana—Fraxinus pennsylvanica—Carya illinoensis/ Glyceria striata—Elymus canadensis—(Carex cherokeensis) Mesic Riparian Blackland Woodland (CEGL007778)—G2?

American Elm—Green Ash—Pecan/Fowl Manna Grass— Canada Wild Rye (Cherokee sedge) Mesic Riparian Blackland Woodland.

DESCRIPTION: This riparian mesic blackland woodland community occurs on deep, moist to temporarily saturated soils on gently sloping hillsides (although in places deeply eroded ravines are extant) to relatively level terrain, typically as linear communities bordering ephemeral streams and flats on the Upper West Gulf Coastal Plain of Arkansas. The trees are medium-tall (to 18 m [60 feet]) and the canopy is very open to closed. Old-growth remnants form gallery woodlands over a moderately dense herbaceous layer. Degraded examples form dense thickets with a sparse herbaceous layer. Fire plays a role in the formation and maintenance of this community. Dominant tree species include *Carya illinoensis, Ulmus americana,* and *Fraxinus pennsylvanica.* Other overstory trees may include *Carya cordiformis, C. myristiciformis, C. ovata, Celtis laevigata, Platanus occidentalis, Populus deltoides, Quercus macrocarpa, Q. muehlenbergii, Q. nigra, Q. shumardii,* and *Ulmus crassifolia.* Other woody vegetation may include *Acer negundo, Cercis canadensis, Cornus drummondii, Diospyros virginiana, Ilex decidua, Liquidambar styraciflua, Maclura pomifera* (locally dominant in disturbed areas), *Morus rubra, Ostrya virginiana, Prunus serotina, Ulmus alata,* and *Viburnum rufidulum.* Woody vines are common and may include *Ampelopsis arborea, Bignonia capreolata, Berchemia scandens, Campsis radicans, Parthenocissus quinquefolia, Smilax bonanox, S. glauca, S. rotundifolia, Toxicodendron radicans,* and *Vitis cinerea.* Dominant herbaceous species include *Glyceria striata* (and/or *Carex cherokeensis* with increasing disturbance), and *Trepocarpus aethusae* with *Andrachne phyllanthoides, Arisaema dracontium, Arundinaria gigantea, Aster lateriflorus, A. lanceolatus, Boehmeria cylindrica, Carex meadii, C. tribuloides, Campanula americana, Cryptotaenia canadensis, Desmodium illinoensis, D. paniculatum* var. *dillenii, Echinacea purpurea, Elymus canadensis, E. virginicus, Eupatorium coelestinum, Galium aparine, Geum canadensis, Helianthus grossiserratus, Iva annua, Juncus effusus, Leersia oryzoides, L. virginicus, Passiflora incarnata, Podophyllum peltatum, Ranunculus hispidus, R. sardous,*

Rudbeckia triloba, Ruellia humilis, R. strepens, Salvia lyrata, Sanicula canadensis, Scleria oligantha, Senecio glabellus, S. obovatus, Silene stellata, Silphium integrifolium, S. laciniatum, Solidago canadensis, Sorghastrum nutans, Spigelia marilandica, Tradescantia ohiensis, Tripsacum dactyloides, Verbesina helianthoides, and *Vernonia baldwinii.* Temporarily high water tables strongly influence the herbaceous community and moderately influence woody species composition. Fingers of this community dominated by *Carya illinoensis* often occur far upslope in swales well into dry-mesic blackland prairie forming an open savanna. With fire suppression woody vegetation succession is rapid, and almost-impenetrable thickets of vine-covered *Fraxinus pennsylvanica, Ulmus* sp., *Celtis laevigata,* and many shrubs colonize moist prairie habitats. *Carex cherokeensis* dominates the herbaceous vegetation in these more-disturbed communities. The soils are deep, poorly drained, silty clays of the Terouge and Tuscumbia series, somewhat altered by recent erosion and deposition in most areas. These soils are fertile, neutral to alkaline, occasionally flooded, and usually saturated in winter and spring. This community occurs adjacent to *Sorghastrum nutans—Schizachyrium scoparium—Echinacea pallida—Dalea purpurea* var. *purpurea* dry-mesic blackland prairie, *Sorghastrum nutans—Andropogon glomeratus—Lythrum alatum—Aster prealtus—Tripsacum dactyloides* mesic blackland prairie, and *Lythrum alatum—Panicum anceps—Aster lanceolatus* wet-mesic blackland prairie. No high-quality examples of this community are known. A greater understanding of this community type should result with fire management. This community is known from Columbus Prairie Preserve, Grandview Prairie, and the Terre Noire Natural Area complex. The type location is in Clark County, Arkansas. Other examples occur in Hempstead and Howard counties, and the community type should be found in Little River, Nevada, and Sevier counties, Arkansas.

DISTRIBUTION: AR.

TNC ECOREGION: 40:C; Bailey subsection 231Eb.

FEDERAL LANDS: Corps of Engineers (Lake Millwood).

COMMENTS: Past alteration and disturbance are extensive. *Carex cherokeensis*-dominated herbaceous vegetation can make these communities virtually fireproof.

⌒

Maclura pomifera—Diospyros virginiana/Glyceria striata—(Carex cherokeensis) Mesic Riparian Woodland (CEGL007779)—G2?

Bois d'Arc—Persimmon/Manna Grass—(Cherokee Sedge) Mesic Riparian Woodland.

DESCRIPTION: This bois d'arc-dominated riparian mesic blackland community occurs in deep soils on level terrain, typically as relatively narrow communities bordering ephemeral streams. The community is very similar to the *Ulmus americana—Fraxinus pennsylvanica—Carya illinoensis/Glyceria striata—Elymus canadensis—(Carex cherokeensis)* mesic riparian blackland woodland community. Native Americans used *Maclura pomifera* extensively and may have planted it in many of the lowlands of the blackland prairie region. These communities may be remnants of that historical practice. Dominant tree species include *Maclura pomifera* and *Diospyros virginiana* with *Acer negundo, Ampelopsis arborea, Berchemia scandens, Campsis radicans, Celtis laevigata, Cercis canadensis, Fraxinus pennsylvanica, Liquidambar styraciflua, Lonicera japonica, Parthenocissus quinquefolia, Toxicodendron radicans, Ulmus americana,* and *Vitis cinerea,* occurring as occasional woody vegetation during periods of fire *suppression*. The dominant herbaceous species is *Glyceria striata* or *Carex cherokeensis* with *Arundinaria gigantea, Carex debilis, Carex tribuloides, Helianthus grossiserratus, Juncus effusus,* and *Leersia oryzoides.* Occasional herbs include *Boehmeria cylindrica, Carex tribuloides, Juncus effusus, Ranunculus hispidus, Senecio glabellus, Sisyrinchium angustifolium, Smilax glauca, Spigelia marilandica,* and *Tradescantia ohiensis.* Temporarily high water tables probably strongly influence the herbaceous community and moderately influence woody species composition. Woody vegetation succession is rapid during periods of fire suppression, when woody types form almost impenetrable thickets of vines and shrubs. No high-quality examples of this community are known. Fire management should yield a better understanding of this community type. Fire-suppressed remnants of this community type occur at the International Paper Blackland Prairie and Woods tract. The type location is Clark County, Arkansas. Other examples are known from Howard and Hempstead counties, and the community type should be found in Little River, Nevada, and Sevier counties, Arkansas.

DISTRIBUTION: AR, TX?

TNC ECOREGION: 40:C; Bailey subsection 231Eb.

FEDERAL LANDS: Corps of Engineers (Lake Millwood).

COMMENTS: This community may have an anthropogenic origin. *Carex cherokeensis* dominance in the herbaceous layer denotes fire suppression, grazing, and crown closure.

~

Quercus muehlenbergii—Liquidambar styraciflua/(Arundinaria gigantea)/Carex cherokeensis—Chasmanthium latifolium Mesic Riparian Forest (CEGL007780)—G3?

Chinkapin Oak—Sugarberry—Sweetgum/Giant Cane/Cherokee Sedge—River-oats Mesic Riparian Forest.

DESCRIPTION: This mesic blackland forest community occurs on deep soils in relatively level, wide bottoms along ephemeral streams in Arkansas's Upper West Gulf Coastal Plain. Overstory trees are tall (to 30 m [100 feet]) with a closed canopy. In mature forest (rare) a gallery effect is present. Fire plays a role in forest composition and structure because of the forest's placement in the midst of blackland prairie. Dominant tree species include *Quercus muehlenbergii, Celtis laevigata,* and *Liquidambar styraciflua.* Other overstory trees often include all or some of the following: *Carya cordiformis, C. illinoensis, Fraxinus pennsylvanica, Juglans nigra, Platanus occidentalis* (common in the streambed), *Quercus michauxii, Q. shumardii, Q. macrocarpa* (rare), and *Ulmus americana.* The midstory can be well developed with *Acer rubrum, Asimina triloba, Carpinus caroliniana, Cercis canadensis,* and saplings of overstory trees. The shrub layer is dominated by *Arundinaria gigantea,* which can occur sparsely or in dense patches, except in areas of recent heavy grazing. Vine tangles are common, especially in recently disturbed areas. Woody vines include *Ampelopsis arborea, Berchemia scandens, Campsis radicans, Parthenocissus quinquefolia, Toxicodendron radicans,* and *Vitis cinerea.* The herbaceous layer is well developed and dense, especially in the spring. Dominant herbaceous species include *Carex cherokeensis* and *Chasmanthium latifolium.* Other herbs include *Allium canadense, Arisaema dracontium, Aster cordifolius, A. lanceolatus, Carex* sp., *Cryptotaenia canadensis, Geum canadense, Glyceria striata, Mitchella repens, Panicum* sp., *Ruellia strepens, Sanicula canadensis, Solidago auriculata,* and *Trepocarpus aethusae.* Upland tree species are uncommon because of the seasonally high water table. Soils are deep, recently deposited blackland alluvium (topsoil from surrounding hills) or calcareous sands. No high-quality examples of this community are known. Because fire may play a role in the formation and maintenance of this community type, fire management should promote a better understanding of it. Disturbed remnants of this community type occur at the Terre Noire Natural Area complex, Grandview Prairie Wildlife Management Area, and Nacatoch Ravines Natural Area. The type location is in Clark County, Arkansas. Other examples are known from Howard and Hempstead counties. The community type also should be found in Little River, Nevada, and Sevier counties, Arkansas.

DISTRIBUTION: AR, OK? LA? TX?

TNC ECOREGION: 40:C; Bailey subsection 231Eb.

FEDERAL LANDS: Corps of Engineers (Lake Millwood).

COMMENTS: This community type has been heavily disturbed. The small streams are somewhat to greatly entrenched. Woody vegetation succession is rapid during periods of fire suppression. The stream channels are narrow (but mesic) and abut dry-mesic and mesic prairie as well as wet-mesic ravine forest farther down the hydrologic gradient. Seasonally higher water tables and greater herbaceous vegetation may be more common in areas of lower tree densities.

∿

Quercus sinuata/Solidago auriculata/Zigadenus nuttallii Mixed Herb Dry-mesic Blackland Ravine Woodland—G1?

   Durand's Oak/Eared Goldenrod—Death Camas Mixed Herb Dry-mesic Blackland Ravine Woodland.

DESCRIPTION: This dry-mesic, calcareous, woodland community occurs on slopes and ravines adjacent to blackland prairie on the Upper West Gulf Coastal Plain of Arkansas. Overstory trees are relatively short (to 11 m [35 feet]) and widely spaced. In fire-maintained woodlands the overstory is not closed and the midstory is sparse. The herbaceous layer is predominately forb in composition and moderately dense with little litter buildup. Fire plays a role in maintaining the woodland structure, and fire-suppressed woodlands can have dense midstories and suppressed herbaceous layers. The dominant tree species is overwhelmingly *Quercus sinuata*. Other overstory trees may include *Carya myristiciformis, Fraxinus americana, F. quadrangulata* (very rare), *Juglans nigra, Quercus x mcnabiana, Q. muehlenbergii, Q. shumardii, Tilia caroliniana* (rare), and *Ulmus crassifolia*. The midstory may include *Acer barbatum* (rare*), Carpinus caroliniana, Celtis laevigata, Cercis canadensis, Crataegus marshallii, Diospyros virginiana, Maclura pomifera, Ostrya virginiana,* and *Viburnum rifidulum*. The shrub layer is also usually sparse and may include *Aesculus pavia, Aralia spinosa, Arundinaria gigantea* (may occur in dense patches), *Frangula caroliniana,* and *Sabal minor* (rare). Woody vines include *Berchemia scandens, Smilax glauca,*

Toxicodendron radicans, and *Vitis rotundifolia,* which are not particularly important to the structure of the woodlands. Forbs and sedges dominate the herbaceous layer. Dominant herbaceous species include *Aster cordifolius, Carex cherokeensis, Desmodium paniculatum* var. *dillenii, Geum canadense, Helianthus hirsutus, Leersia virginica,* and *Solidago auriculata.* Other herbaceous species include *Arisaema dracontium, Asclepias purpurea, Asplenium platyneuron, A. patens, Aureolaria grandiflora, Cacalia tuberosa, Camassia scilloides, Carex annectans, C. crawei, C. glaucodea, Centrosema virginiana, Chaerophyllum tainturieri, Delphinium carolinianum* var. *penardii, Dentaria laciniatum, Echinacea purpurea, Elymus virginicus, Erythronium albidum, Festuca obtusa, Galium circaezans, Lactuca floridana, Liatris aspera, Lonicera flava, Maianthemum paniculatum, Penstemon digitalis, Phlox pilosa, Polypodium polypodioides* var. *michauxianum, Polystichum acrostichoides, Ruellia humulis, Salvia lyrata, Schizachyrium scoparium, Senecio glabellus, Sisyrinchium* sp., *Solidago ulmifolia, Spigelia marilandica, Thalictrum thalictroides, Trepocarpus aethusae, Verbena bipinnatifida, Verbesina helianthoides, Viola triloba,* and *Zigadenus nuttallii.* Historically, fires sweeping through the adjacent blackland prairies would have maintained the woodland structure of this slope community. This community has responded well to the suspension of grazing and fire management. Soils are deep but eroded (in places deeply) alkaline clays, with the high shrink-swell characteristics of the Sumter series. This community is located at the southern end of the Woodbine escarpment above the Little River overflow bottoms. Chalk is absent near the surface, and Sumter soils overlie calcareous Nacatoch sands at this locality. Currently the community is known only from this one location and covers approximately 81 ha (200 acres). This community grades into *Quercus stellata—Vaccinium arboreum—Chasmanthium sessiliflorum—Danthonia spicata—Schizachyrium scoparium* dry blackland woodland and *Quercus falcata—Quercus stellata— (Pinus echinata—Pinus taeda)/Chasmanthium sessiliflorum— Danthonia spicata* dry-mesic woodland on higher ridgelines and adjacent Oktibbeha soils. The community grades into *Quercus alba—Quercus rubra—Fraxinus americana/Ostrya virginiana/ Arundinaria gigantea/Cynoglossum virginianum—Arisaema dracontium—Cypripedium kentuckiensis* mesic ravine forest north along the Woodbine escarpment, where the blackland soils play out. Historically, the *Quercus sinuata* woodland would also have been adjacent to *Sorghastrum nutans—Schizachyrium sco-*

parium—Echinacea pallida—Dalea purpurea var. *purpurea* dry-mesic blackland prairie herbaceous vegetation, but the community has been extirpated in this locality. The highest-quality remnant is found in the Blackland Ravines Unique Area and on adjacent grazed lands. The type locality is in Hempstead County, Arkansas. No other examples are known.

DISTRIBUTION: AR.

TNC ECOREGION: 40:C; Bailey subsection 231Eb.

FEDERAL LANDS: None.

COMMENTS: *Quercus x mcnabiana* Sudw. is the supposed hybrid between Durand's oak and post oak previously recorded from this locality. In any case two forms of Durand's oak are present. Var. *austrina* may also be present. This community is likely to be found in Little River County along the escarpments above the Red River terraces and overflow bottoms where Cretaceous-period calcareous features are found.

‿

Quercus alba—Quercus rubra—Fraxinus americana/Ostrya virginiana/Arundinaria gigantea/Cynoglossum virginianum—Arisaema dracontium—Cypripedium kentuckiense Mesic Calcareous Slope Forest (CEGL007971)—G2G3.

White Oak/Northern Red Oak/White Ash/Hop Hornbeam/ Giant Cane/Hound's Tongue—Green Dragon—Southern Yellow Lady's Slipper Mesic Calcareous Slope Forest.

DESCRIPTION: This mesic forest community occurs on rich, mildly calcareous, mesic slopes and ravines on the Upper West Gulf Coastal Plain of Arkansas. Overstory trees are tall (over 30 m [100 feet]) with many more than 1 m (3 feet) in diameter. The canopy is closed. All forest layers are well developed with diverse midstory, shrub, and herbaceous strata. The diverse overstory is dominated by *Quercus alba,* especially on upper and mid slopes, with *Quercus rubra* and *Fraxinus americana* sharing dominance on lower slopes. Other overstory trees include *Acer barbatum* (rare), *Carya alba, C. cordiformis, Juglans nigra, Liquidambar styraciflua, Nyssa sylvatica, Quercus falcata, Q. michauxii, Q. muehlenbergii, Q. velutina,* and *Tilia carolina.* The midstory is diverse with abundant, large (to 38 cm [15 inches] dbh) *Ostrya virginiana* and *Cornus florida* usually dominant. Other understory species include *Acer rubrum* var. *rubrum, Aralia spinosa, Asimina triloba, Carpinus caroliniana, Cercis canadensis, Frangula caroliniana, Prunus serotina, Sassafras albidum,* and saplings of overstory trees. The shrub layer is diverse with open to dense, continuous stands of *Arundinaria gigantea* dominating with *Aesculus pavia, Castanea pumila* var. *pumila, Hamamelis virginiana, Lindera benzoin, Sabal minor* (rare), *Sambucus canadensis, Styrax grandifolia,* and *Xanthoxylum americanum.* Woody vines include large *Vitis palmata* and *V. rotundifolia* with *Berchemia scandens, Bignonia capreolata, Parthenocissus quinquefolia, Smilax rotundifolia, S. smallii,* and *Toxicodendron radicans.* The herbaceous layer is most diverse in the spring and is dominated by forbs that include *Arisaema dracontium, Aristolochia serpentaria, Aster cordifolius, Cynoglossum virginianum, Desmodium paniculatum* var. *dillenii, Heliopsis helianthoides, Podophyllum peltatum, Polystichum acrostichoides,* and *Sanicula canadensis.* Other herbaceous species include *Arisaema triphyllum, Aristolochia reticulata, Asplenium platyneuron, Athyrium filix-femina, Cypripedium kentuckiense, Carex* ssp., *Chamaelirium luteum, Chasmanthium latifolium, Desmodium sessilifolium, Elephantopus carolinianus, E. tomentosus, Geranium maculatum, Lithospermum tuberosum, Onoclea sensibilis, Osmunda cinnamomea* (ravine seep), *O. regalis* (ravine seep), *Oxalis stricta, O. violacea, Panicum* sp., *Passiflora lutea, Phlox pilosa, Polypodium polypodioides* var. *michauxianum, Sanguinaria canadensis, Solidago auriculata, Tipularia discolor, Trillium recurvatum,* and *Uvularia sessilifolia.* Fire sweeping off the pine-dominated uplands likely played a role in this community's structure and composition. More important are the steep slopes and soils that cause the ravines to remain moist throughout the year. Large treefall gaps are common. The soils are formed of carbonate fine sandy loams over Arkadelphia marl. This community is typically bordered at higher elevations by dry-mesic pine and pine-oak-dominated woodlands typical of the Upper Gulf Coastal Plain. At the base of the slopes where the ravines widen and flatten, it grades into *Liquidambar styraciflua—Platanus occidentalis/Acer negundo/Saururus cernuus—Senecio glabellus—Carex tribuloides* wet mesic ravine forest. The highest-quality example is at the Nacatoch Ravines Natural Area and on adjacent hunt club lands. The type locality is in Hempstead County, Arkansas. Other examples may occur in Howard, Little River, and Sevier counties, Arkansas.

DISTRIBUTION: AR, LA?

TNC ECOREGION: 40:C; Bailey subsection: 231 Eb.

FEDERAL LANDS: USFWS, possibly at Pond Creek NWR.

COMMENTS: This community has fewer caciphilic plants than do the alkaline soils of the blacklands.

⌒

Liquidambar styraciflua—Platanus occidentalis/Acer negundo/ Saururus cernuus—Senecio glabellus—Carex tribuloides Wet-mesic Ravine Forest—G3?

Sweetgum/American Sycamore/Box Elder/Lizard's tail/Butter-weed/Blunt-broom Sedge Wet-mesic Ravine Forest.

DESCRIPTION: This wet-mesic forest community occurs along the flat, rich, lower ravines and at the bases of slopes on the Upper West Gulf Coastal Plain of Arkansas. The soils are rich, calcareous, and usually nearly saturated and seepy. The forest canopy is tall (over 30 m [100 feet]) with many trees over 1 m (3 feet) in diameter. The canopy is closed but treefall gaps are common, likely because of the nearly saturated soils. All forest layers are well developed with diverse midstory, shrub, and herbaceous strata. The overstory is dominated by *Liquidambar styraciflua* with *Platanus occidentalis*. Other overstory species may include *Quercus michauxii, Q. nigra, Q. pagoda, Q. phellos,* and *Ulmus americana.* The midstory is dominated by *Acer negundo* and *Acer rubrum* with *Carpinus caroliniana, Celtis laevigata, Ilex opaca, Salix nigra,* and saplings of overstory trees. Shrub species include *Arundinaria gigantea, Lindera benzoin, Rhododendron canescens, Sabal minor,* and *Sambucus canadensis.* Woody vines include *Berchemia scandens, Parthenocissus quinquefolia, Smilax bona-nox,* and *Toxicodendron radicans.* The herbaceous layer is dense and dominance changes with slight alterations in topography. Common herbaceous species include *Arisaema triphyllum, Carex crinita, C. tribuloides, Chasmanthium latifolium, Juncus effusus Leersia oryzoides, L. virginica, Salvia lyrata, Sanicula canadensis, Saururus cernuus, Senecio glabellus,* and *S. obovatus.* Other herbaceous species may include *Arisaema dracontium, Aster lanceolatus, Bignonia capreolata, Boehmeria cylindrica, Campsis radicans, Carex blanda, C. intumescens, C. glaucodea, C. grayi, Geum canadense, Clematis* sp., *Cypripedium kentuckiense, Dicliptera brachiata, Euonymus americanus, Eupatorium perfoliatum, Lobelia cardinalis, Panicum* sp., *Passiflora lutea, Phegopteris hexagonoptera, Pluchea camphorata, Polygonum* sp., *Polypodium polypodioides* var. *michauxianum, Polystichum acrostichoides,* and *Ranunculus abortivus.* The soils are alluvial clays and fine sandy loams created from erosion off the upland blackland ecosystem. The soils are moist to wet throughout the year and large treefall gaps are a regular occurrence. Fire will creep through this community in dry years. In non-ravine areas much of this plant community has been converted to agriculture or was

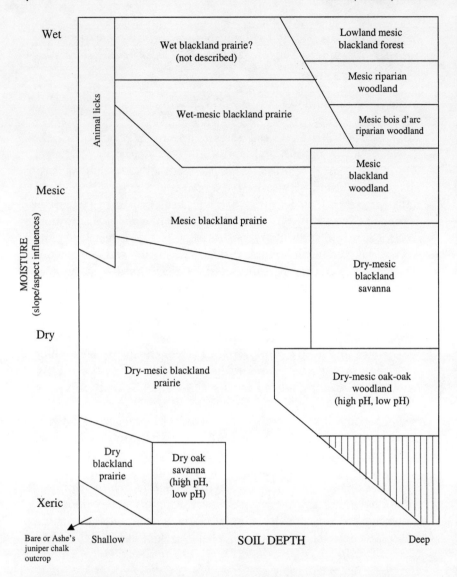

Fig. 8.1. Hypothesized blackland community distribution along soil-moisture and soil-depth gradients.

previously farmed for cotton and is now abandoned. This community is typically bordered by *Quercus muehlenbergii—Liquidambar styraciflua/(Arundinaria gigantea)/Carex cherokeensis—Chasmanthium latifolium* mesic riparian forest (CEGL007780) upstream and/or *Quercus alba—Quercus rubra—Fraxinus americana/Ostrya virginiana/Arundinaria gigantea/Cynoglossum vir-*

ginianum—Arisaema dracontium—Cypripedium kentuckiensis mesic calcareous slope forest. The highest-quality example is at the Nacatoch Ravines Natural Area and on adjacent hunt club lands. The type locality is in Hempstead County, Arkansas. Other examples may occur in Clark, Howard, Little River, and Sevier counties, Arkansas.

DISTRIBUTION: AR, LA?

TNC ECOREGION: 40:C, Bailey subsection: 231 Eb.

FEDERAL LANDS: None known.

MODELS

Most of the blackland ecosystem has been severely altered through conversion to agriculture and pasture as well as by haying, grazing, and long-term fire suppression. The communities described are relatively small remnants and degraded fragments of the original ecosystem that are extant on the landscape in blocks ranging from a few to perhaps 1,214 ha (3,000 acres).

Figure 8.1 illustrates how blackland ecosystem plant communities relate to each other on the landscape using soil-moisture and soil-depth gradients.

Figure 8.2 illustrates two models of blackland community states and ecological processes. These models are being developed to aid land managers in restoration of degraded blackland sites. Heavy grazing and fire suppression lead all communities toward an increase in woody stems of fire-sensitive species. Fire, with periodic drought, creates conditions more favorable to prairie and open woodlands.

In some cases severe erosion has altered the historical plant community distribution. For example, dry prairie was found on shallow soils where chalk was close to the surface historically. Owing to severe erosion over the last 100 years, slopes that would have been dry-mesic prairie historically do not have enough soil to maintain the community and species have shifted to dry prairie.

CONCLUSIONS

In this paper we have described 18 association-level plant communities. We have also discussed models explaining spatial and ecosystemic relationships among the plant community types across the blackland ecosystem of Arkansas. Because much of Arkansas's blackland ecosystem has been significantly altered by agriculture, forestry, and urbanization, several communities that probably occurred historically within the ecosystem have been extirpated.

The plant community classification offered here should serve as

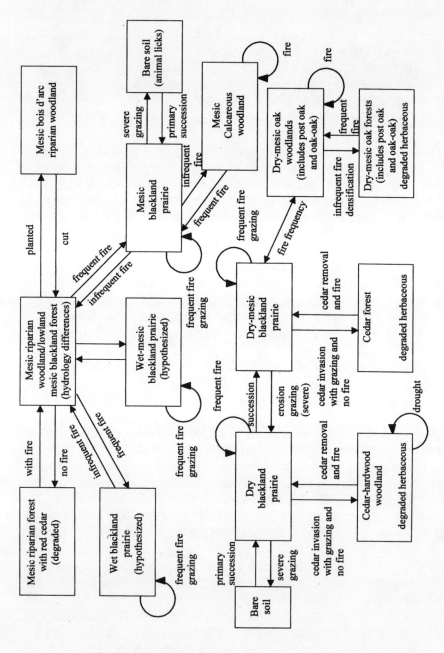

Fig. 8.2. Hypothesized model of blackland plant community states and ecological processes.

an aid in conservation planning, ecological restoration, and land management. In addition, the integration of information on plants, soils, physiography, understory, and other physical and biological characteristics should provide a useful framework for archaeologists, historians, cultural geographers, and other scientists interested in understanding past and present human/nature interactions in blackland prairie ecosystems. The role of humans as modifiers of the landscape, through fire, agriculture, and other actions, is evident in the classification. Our role as managers of these fragile ecosystems is still being determined.

9 Plant and Soil Interactions in Prairie Remnants of the Jackson Prairie Region, Mississippi

L. P. MORAN, D. E. PETTRY, AND R. E. SWITZER

INTRODUCTION

Historical accounts by travelers and explorers locate and describe prairie areas in Mississippi dating back to Hernando de Soto's expedition in the sixteenth century (Rostlund 1957). The Mississippi Natural Heritage Program has identified and described more than 54 current prairie remnants in the Jackson Prairie region of Mississippi (Figure 9.1). They define the prairies as natural grasslands with predominantly native perennial grasses and some herbaceous plants (Gordon and Wiseman 1989). Prairies are considered closed communities with common ecological features such as the dominance of grasses, scarcity of shrubs and trees, presence of typical drought-enduring and largely disease-free vegetation, prevalence of vegetative reproduction, and rapid renewal of vegetative growth with plant longevity (Weaver 1968). Prairie soils are usually fine-textured, productive, and fertile with high cation exchange capacity clays and weatherable minerals that serve as plant nutrient reserves.

According to Hutchison (1994), early travelers in the Midwest characterized areas that were neither good prairie nor good forest as barrens. Barren vegetation was characterized as a mixture of both stunted trees and herbaceous species with the grasses occurring as clumps. Dead trees or trees with dead limbs were common and shrubby species typically formed thickets. The occurrence of barrens was often related to thin, bare soils with bedrock at or near the surface, and slopes facing south-southwest that provided more heat and less available moisture, conditions conducive to the development of dry forbs and grasses rather than trees.

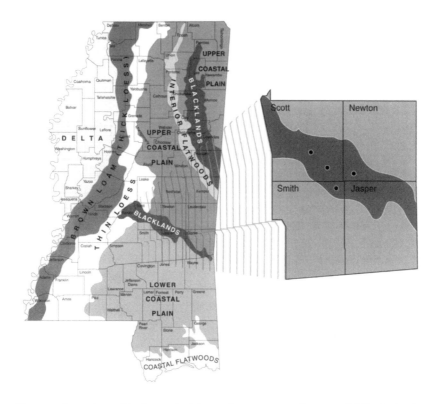

Fig. 9.1. Location of Jackson Prairie study areas, south-central Mississippi. From Moran et al. (1997; Figure 1)

The Jackson Prairie region in Mississippi consists of gently rolling uplands underlain by the Yazoo clay of the Jackson group. The Yazoo clay is a green to gray calcareous clay of Eocene age, high in montmorillonite and reflective of near-shore marine deposition (Merrill et al. 1985). The prairie soils are commonly thick, alkaline, montmorillonitic Vertisols of high natural fertility. The prairies are calcareous islands surrounded by mixed acidic pine and hardwood forests on level to gently sloping upland positions (Moran 1995).

The Jackson Prairie region has undergone intense settlement and cultivation that has greatly affected soil and vegetative conditions for the past 200 years. A large portion of this region is forested and contains more introduced species than in the past, reflecting the extensive erosion after European settlement (cf. Peacock 1992, 1993 for the Mississippi Black Prairie). Characterizing and understanding present-day soil and vegetative interactions of the remaining remnants are crucial for successful management and conservation. Following a brief review of vegetative characteristics and current management practices, we will discuss typical soil and plant relationships in prairie remnants in the Jackson Prairie region.

NATURAL CHARACTERISTICS AND MANAGEMENT PRACTICE

Graminoids (15 percent), composites (21 percent), and legumes (12 percent) comprise the majority of plant species in the prairie remnants of the Jackson Prairie region (Wieland et al. 1991). The vegetation is similar to that of prairie species in the midwestern United States (Wieland 1991). Table 9.1 lists common species found in the Bienville National Forest in the Jackson Prairie region. Historical sources indicate that eastern prairies had low tree densities. Low tree-density areas (fewer than 25 trees ha⁻¹) occurred on alkaline upland fine-textured soils. High tree densities (more than 295 trees ha⁻¹), on the other hand, occurred on acidic areas lying outside the low tree-density areas in the Mississippi Black Prairie (Jones and Patton 1966; Rankin and Davis 1971). Wieland and Weeks (1990) conducted a study of the soils and vegetation in the Jackson prairies, finding pine trees on gentle, acidic slopes and tall grasses on sloping, alkaline sites.

Burning is one of the most significant ecological management tools for prairie openings. Fire reduces tree and shrub competition. Fire also increases aboveground plant production in prairie ecosystems by releasing available nitrogen and phosphorus, increasing nitrogen mineralization rates, enhancing nitrogen fixation, and altering microclimatic soil and plant conditions. Short-term effects of fire include increased soil temperature and light exposure and decreased soil moisture (Ojima et al. 1990; Old 1969). Long-term effects include decreasing soil organic matter, modifying vegetative composition, and maintaining productivity despite the loss of labile organic matter (Ojima et al. 1990). Frost et al. (1986) cited fire frequency and depth of the water table as environmental gradients that determine the nature of grassland vegetation on lower coastal plain terraces. In the Jackson Prairie and elsewhere, prairie species frequently are maintained by the application of a management program, including controlled burning.

Different artificial burning treatments have been investigated in prairie and barren remnants (e.g., Schauwecker and MacDonald, this volume) with mixed results. Hutchison (1994) stated that fire was a critical factor in maintaining and expanding barrens in the Midwest and Southeast. He noted that barrens did not have to burn often, suggesting no more than once every 50 years for perpetual effects. Robertson and Heikens (1994) reported that fire reduction has contributed to increases in woody species coverage and subsequent reduction in her-

Table 9.1. Common species in prairie openings in the Bienville National Forest of the Jackson Prairie region, Mississippi (adapted from Wieland et al. 1991)

Herbaceous

Schizachyrium scoparium	*Andropogon gerardi*
Sorghastrum nutans	*Panicum virgatum*
Sporobolus asper	*Carex cherokeensis*
Aster dumosus	*Helenium autumnale*
Ratibida pinnata	*Scleria oligantha*
Dalea purpurea	*Dalea candida*
Crotolaria sagittalis	*Erigeron strigosus*
Desmanthus illinoensis	*Rudbeckia hirta*

Trees and Shrubs

Cercis canadensis	*Juniperus virginiana*
Ulmus alata	*Berchemia scandens*
Prunus americana	*Fraxinus americana*
Vitis sp.	*Smilax* sp.
Liquidambar styraciflua	*Crataegus gali*
Cornus drummondii	*Quercus* sp.

baceous components in southern Illinois barrens. Tyndall (1994) studied the effects of clear-only and clear-and-burn treatments: the latter significantly affected more species and increased bare soil coverage. He concluded that these restoration treatments could lead to communities with different vegetative structures. Heikens et al. (1994) studied the short-term responses of southwestern Illinois barrens to fire, finding that fire neither significantly reduced the arboreal component nor increased the herbaceous component during the growing season. Collins (1987) reported that burning significantly reduced species diversity on ungrazed prairies, although grazing increased diversity on burned prairies in Oklahoma. This emphasized the importance of interaction among natural disturbances on plant community structures in grasslands.

Most prairie preserves are small and occur as patches (Riser 1986). The openings in the Jackson Prairie region range in size from less than 1 to 65 ha and total about 325 ha (Wieland et al. 1991). The remaining prairies currently undergo certain management practices for successful conservation. Fundamental ecological principles, including spatial heterogeneity, prairie size, landscape position, wildlife habitat, integrated pest management, degree of flooding, fire frequency, and soil and water conservation (Riser 1986) are considered for successful conservation, long-term integrity, and maximum biological diversity. Soil properties such as the nature of soil structure, pedogenic development, and topography also should be considered (Frost et al. 1986). Proximal openings enhance biological diversity, including those animals that depend on heterogeneous vegetation. Large patches also enhance plant diversity by sustaining the dispersal of native prairie species: extinction of prairie species increases as the distance between openings increases. At the landscape scale, prairie remnants play an important ecological role as temporary habitats for species that depend on other ecosystems in the surrounding landscapes. Invasion of exotic species is an increasing problem for the management of these remaining prairies.

MATERIALS AND METHODS

STUDY SITES

Four prairie remnants in the Jackson Prairie region were selected to study soil and plant interactions (Table 9.2). The four sites were Durand Oak Prairie and Harrell Prairie Hill in Scott County, Five Acre Prairie in Smith County, and Eureka Church Prairie in Newton County (Figure 9.1). The area of the sites ranged from 0.4 to about 20 ha. Durand Oak and Harrell Prairie Hill are gently sloping prairie remnants with slopes of 5 to 7 percent. Five Acre and Eureka Church Prairies are level prairie remnants with slopes of less than 2 percent. Selection of the study sites was based on prairie remnant size, degree of disturbance, and proximity to other prairie remnants. The climate in the region is temperate and continental: winters are mild, with short cold spells, and summers are hot (Murphree 1957). The summer and fall seasons contain short, recurrent dry periods, but severe droughts are uncommon. The mean annual temperature (1960–1990) in the region is 18°C, and the mean annual precipitation averages about 145 cm (U.S. Department of Commerce 1992).

VEGETATIVE ANALYSIS

Indigenous species in each prairie site were collected and identified to develop a prairie plant inventory. Collections were made during the spring and fall seasons from March 1994 to May 1995. Plant specimens were identified using the taxonomic nomenclature in Radford et al. (1968) and Timme (1989). Species were dried and pressed for storage in the Mississippi State University Herbarium. Midseason live, aboveground biomass production in the prairie remnants was determined in August 1995 for comparison with midwestern prairies. Live, aboveground biomass was collected in 1-square-meter plots and separated into graminoid and forb components that were dried and weighed. Shoots of common prairie species in Harrell Prairie Hill were analyzed for nutrient content. Tissue analysis was performed to measure calcium, magnesium, sodium, and potassium contents in each prairie spe-

Table 9.2 Study sites in the Jackson Prairie region of Mississippi

Prairie Remnant	County	Slope (percentage)	Size (ha)	Soil Classification	Location
Harrell Prairie Hill	Scott	5–7	19.2	Chromic Hapludert	Sec. 25–26, T6N, R8E
Durand Oak Prairie	Scott	5–7	4.1	Chromic Hapludert	Sec. 8–9, T5N, R9E
Five Acre Prairie	Smith	0–2	4.7	Chromic Hapludert	Sec. 10–11, 14–15, T4N, R8E
Eureka Church Prairie	Newton	0–2	0.4	Chromic Hapludert	Sec. 22, T5N, R10E

cies. Three native prairie species at Harrell Prairie Hill were excavated to characterize their root systems. Soil was meticulously removed by continual washing with water, and root length was measured. Plants were clipped at the base and dried to determine root:shoot ratios.

Soil from depths of 0 to 5, 5 to 10, and 10 to 20 cm was carefully excavated from three random 1-square-meter plots at Harrell Prairie Hill to determine the major seed reservoir. Soils were passed through a 0.63-cm screen mesh and placed in trays (37 × 52 cm) over 10 cm of sand. Trays were periodically watered, and emerged plants were counted and identified from May 1994 to June 1995 to calculate the distribution of forbs and graminoids by depth and site. Trays within the greenhouse were randomly interchanged to prevent distribution of seeds to other trays. Mature seeds were removed from each plant to minimize secondary seed emergence. Soil from each depth was analyzed for pH, calcium carbonate equivalent (CCE), organic matter, and extractable cations.

SOIL ANALYSIS

Positional transects along each remnant were made for the analysis of selected soil properties. Undisturbed cores were taken for saturated hydraulic conductivity, bulk density, and moisture retention. Hydraulic conductivity was determined by the constant head method (Klute 1965). Moisture retention was determined using the pressure membrane technique (Richards 1949). Bulk density was determined by the core technique (Blake 1965). Soil collected for chemical analyses was air-dried, pulverized, and passed through a No. 10 (2-mm) sieve to remove coarse fragments. Extractable bases were determined by ammonium acetate extraction and atomic absorption spectrophotometry (Chapman 1965a). Extractable aluminum was determined by the method of Yuan (1959). Extractable hydrogen was determined by the barium chloride-triethanolamine method (Peech 1965b). Cation exchange capacity (CEC) was calculated by the summation method (Chapman 1965b). Calcium carbonate equivalent was determined by a titrimetric hydrochloric acid treatment method (Richards 1954). Acid dichromate digestion was used to determine organic matter content (Peech et al. 1947). Soil pH was determined in 1:1 soil:water suspension (Peech 1965a).

RESULTS AND DISCUSSION

More than 60 prairie species were identified and collected in the prairie remnants (Table 9.3). Twenty families of dicots, four families of monocots, and one family of ferns were collected. The number of species collected, though not making up the complete list for the Jackson Prairie, nonetheless demonstrates the high natural diversity in these remnants and their similarity to the midwestern prairies. The dominant families of dicots were Asteraceae (Compositae) with 17 species, Leguminoseae with eight species, and Labiatae with three species. The dominant family of monocots was the Graminae family with 14 species.

Pteridium aquilinum (bracken fern) was conspicuous in the transition zone at Harrell Prairie Hill. This transition zone of bracken fern reflects the current impact of cultural disturbance on ecological conditions and soil. Moran (1995) reported that erosion had truncated the A horizon (mollic epipedon) in the upper slopes of Harrell Prairie Hill, moving organic matter, coarse clay, silt, and sand downslope. Subsequent weathering and leaching of carbonates produced acidic conditions suitable for the invasion of *Pteridium aquilinum* downslope.

Two species identified, *Setaria geniculata* and *Paspalum urvillei,* are not native prairie species but have been introduced (Sidney McDaniel, personal communication). McDaniel and Carraway (1995) stated that Mississippi prairies might once have had different vegetational composition. They reported that prairie indicators such as *Bouteloua curtipendula* and *Silphium laciniatum* did not occur in prairie remnants in the Tallahalla Wildlife Management Area. These indicator plants were also not found in our prairie study areas.

Aboveground biomass production in the four remnants is presented in Table 9.4. Total aboveground biomass was high at Harrell Prairie Hill, Durand Oak Prairie, and Five Acre Prairie, exceeding 5,000 kg ha^{-1}. The aboveground biomass in these remnants is similar to that of the midwestern prairies, which typically average 5,220 kg ha^{-1} y^{-1} (Barbour et al. 1987). Biomass was lower at Eureka Church Prairie (2,698 kg ha^{-1}). The lower total biomass values at Eureka Church Prairie reflect the lower moisture content and higher bulk density due to the extensive occurrence of carbonates at the surface. Abrams et al. (1986) measured

Table 9.3. Common flora in the Jackson Prairie remnants

Scientific Name	Family Name	Common Name
	Acanthaceae	
Ruellia caroliensis (Gmel.) Steud		Wild Petunia
Ruellia humilis Nuttall		Wild Petunia
	Apiaceae	
Eryngium yuccifolium Michx		Rattlesnake Master
	Asteraceae (Compositae)	
Aster novae-angliae L.		New England Aster
Aster patens Ait.		Purple Daisy
Aster pilosus Willd.		White Heath Aster
Echinacea purpurea (L.) Moench		Purple Coneflower
Eupatorium altissimum L.		Boneset
Eupatorium coelestinum L.		Mistflower
Eupatorium incarnatum Walter		Boneset
Helenium autumnale L.		Sneezeweed
Helianthus divaricatus L.		Sunflower
Helianthus silphioides		Sunflower
Liatris aspera Michx.		Blazing Star
Ratibida pinnata (Vent.) Barnh.		Yellow Coneflower
Rudbeckia hirta L.		Black-eyed Susan
Rudbeckia triloba L.		Coneflower
Solidago odora Ait.		Goldenrod
Verbesina virginica L.		White Crown-Beard
Vernonia gigantea (Walt.) Trel.		Ironweed
	Asclepiadaceae	
Asclepias tuberosa L.		Butterfly Milkweed
Asclepias viridis Walter		Green Milkweed
	Campanulaceae	
Lobelia puberula Michx.		Blue Lobelia
	Euphorbiaceae	
Euphorbia corollata L.		Flowering Spurge
	Gentianaceae	
Sabatia angularis (L.) Pursh		Prairie Pink
	Labiatae	
Physostegia virginiana (L.) Benth		Obediant Plant
Salvia azurea Lam		Blue Sage
Salvia lyrata L.		Lyre-Leaved Sage

Table 9.3. Common flora in the Jackson Prairie remnants

Scientific Name	Family Name	Common Name
	Leguminosae	
Cassia chamaecrista L.		Partridge Pea
Centrosema virginanum (L.) Benth.		Butterfly Pea
Crotolaria sagittalis L.		Rattlebox
Dalea candida Michx.		White Prairie Clover
Dalea purpurea Vent.		Purple Prairie Clover
Desmanthus illinoensis (Michx.) MacM		Yellow Sensitive
Neptunia lutea (Leavenw.) Benth.		Prairie Mimosa
Trifolium pratense L.		Red Clover
	Lythraceae	
Lythrum lanceolatum Ell.		Loosestrife
	Onagraceae	
Gaura biennis L.		Honeysuckle
Oenothera speciosa Nutt.		Evening Primrose
	Passofloraceae	
Passiflora incarnata L.		Passionflower
	Polemoniaceae	
Phlox pilosa L.		Prairie Phlox
	Ranunculaceae	
Ranunculus fascicularis Muhl. ex Bigel		Early Buttercup
	Rhamnaceae	
Ceanothus americanus L.		New Jersey Tea
	Rosaceae	
Rubus trivialis Michx.		Dewberry
	Rubiaceae	
Hedyotis purpurea var. *calycosa*		Bluets
	Scrophulariaceae	
Agalinis tenuifolia (Vahl) Raf.		Gerardoa
	Valerianaceae	
Valerianella radiata (L.) Dufr.		Corn Salad
	Verbenaceae	
Verbena brasiliensis Vell.		Brazilian Vervain
	Cyperaceae	
Carex cherokeensis Schweinitz		
Carex microdonta Torr. and Hook.		

Table 9.3. Common flora in the Jackson Prairie remnants

Scientific Name	Family Name	Common Name
	Graminae	
Andropogon gerardii Vitman		Big Bluestem
Andropogon glomeratus (Walter) BSP.		Broomsedge
Erianthus contortus Baldwin ex Ell.		Beardgrass
Panicum anceps Michaux		
Panicum flexilis (Gattinger) Scribner		
Panicum virgatum L.		Switchgrass
Paspalum floridanum Michaux		
Paspalum urvillei Steudel		
Setaria geniculata (Lam.) Beauvoís		
Schizachyrium scoparium Michaux		Little Bluestem
Sorghastrum nutans (L.) Nash		Foxtail
Tridens flavus (L.) Hitchcock		Indiangrass
Tridens strictus (Nuttall) Nash		Purple Top
	Iridaceae	
Sisyrinchium albidum Raf.		Blue-eyed Grass
	Liliaceae	
Allium canadense L.		Wild Onion

midseason, live and dead aboveground biomass for a 10-year period in a Kansas tallgrass prairie on shallow, rocky upland and deep, non-rocky lowland soils. They reported that midseason, live biomass was 4,220 kg ha^{-1} on annually burned and 3,640 kg ha^{-1} on unburned sites for the 10-year period.

Aboveground biomass production in each prairie was divided into different components. Typically, graminoids comprised 40 to 50 percent of the total production, whereas forbs constituted 20 to 40 percent of the total. Total production in the transition zone of bracken fern at Harrell Prairie Hill was also analogous to that of the Mississippi and midwestern prairies. Nonetheless, graminoid and forb production decreased in this zone. Graminoids comprised approximately 30 percent of the total production, and forbs constituted nearly 10 percent of the total production in the transition zone, reflecting the decrease in diversity after the invasion of bracken fern. Abrams et al. (1986) reported that graminoids comprised the majority of the total live biomass in burned and unburned prairie sites in Kansas.

Factors such as fire, grazing, moisture, temperature, soil type, and soil depth influence aboveground biomass production (Abrams et al. 1986; Barbour et al. 1987; Old 1969). Table 9.5 presents selected soil surficial properties in the prairie sites. The lower bulk densities and higher moisture content at Durand Oak, Harrell Prairie Hill, and Five Acre Prairies reflect the high montmorillonitic clay and organic matter contents. The higher hydraulic conductivity (Ks) in the gently sloping

Table 9.4. Midseason aboveground biomass production of the Jackson Prairie study sites

Study Site	Location	Aboveground Component (percentage)	Biomass[H] (kg ha⁻¹)
Harrell Prairie Hill	Prairie	Graminoids	2,449
		Forbs	3,052
		Remains[I]	767
		Twigs	83
		Total	6,351
	Bracken Fern	Bracken Fern	3,139
		Graminoids	1,849
		Forbs	572
		Remains	85
		Twigs	54
		Total	5,699
Durand Oak Prairie	Prairie	Graminoids	2,076
		Forbs	1,472
		Remains	1,443
		Twigs	441
		Pine Needles	5
		Total	5,437
Five Acre Prairie	Prairie	Graminoids	2,255
		Forbs	1,848
		Remains	1,225
		Total	5,328
Eureka Church Prairie	Prairie	Graminoids	1,249
		Forbs	646
		Remains	803
		Total	2,698

H = Biomass was collected in August 1995.
I = Mixture of unrecognizable graminoid and forbs biomass.

remnants reflects the granular structures and the extensive root distribution in the surface. The higher bulk density and conductivity in the soil surface at Eureka Church Prairie were due to the presence of quartz fragments and extensive calcium carbonate fragments and concretions. The quartz fragments indicate a higher energy depositional environment or reworking of sediments in this site. The surfaces in all sites were neutral to slightly alkaline, calcareous, and high in organic matter.

Table 9.5. Selected surface-soil properties in the Jackson Prairie study sites

Site	N	BD (g cm⁻³)	Kₛ (µm s⁻¹)	FC %	PWP %	PAW %	CCE %	OM %	pH_w
Durand Oak Prairie	13	0.95	59.1	55.5	46.8	8.7	12.9	7.4	7.6
Harrell Prairie Hill	12	0.99	41.6	47.6	38.9	8.5	6.3	5.9	6.5
Five Acre Prairie	10	1.01	26.8	44.8	39.4	5.4	13.4	5.6	7.6
Eureka Church Prairie	10	1.10	26.8	30.7	25.0	5.7	30.7	4.6	7.7

N = number of replications; BD = bulk density; K_s = saturated hydraulic conductivity; FC = water at field capacity; PWP = permanent wilting point; PAW = plant available water; CCE = $CaCO_3$ equivalency; OM = organic matter; pH_w = pH in water.

The lower total biomass and low moisture contents at Eureka Church Prairie classify this site as a barren rather than a prairie community (Tables 9.4 and 9.5). Homoya (1994) defined Indiana barrens as terrestrial ecosystems with prevailing edaphic drought and infertility. He stated that factors leading to dryness are excessive drainage owing to particle size, southern or western aspects, steep slopes, and the presence of a hardpan or bedrock at or near the surface. DeSelm (1994) described the barrens of Tennessee as small openings in the forest dominated by perennial grasses of the same taxa that dominate the midwestern tallgrass prairies. He stated that the barrens appear to be successional and to have been maintained by human action and periodic drought, especially on shallow soils, and grazing/trampling/browsing, and fire. Baskin et al. (1994) reported that the Big Barrens region of Kentucky and Tennessee supports a diversity of native plant communities. The barrens in these regions were characterized as culturally derived and maintained grasslands dominated by native perennial grasses. The prairies were characterized as xeric limestone communities of anthropogenic origin dominated by native perennial grasses and/or forbs. Heikens et al. (1994) defined the barrens in southern Illinois as natural forest openings on rocky, shallow soils with xeric trees, shrubs, and herbaceous species typical of prairie communities.

The roots of three common species were excavated and characterized at Harrell Prairie Hill (Table 9.6). The species were *Andropogon glomeratus* (graminoid), *Dalea purpurea* (forb), and *Pteridium aquilinum* (introduced species). Each plant had a different root system type. The root system in the graminoid was characterized as a clump of extensive fibrous fine roots. The forb was characterized by a thick taproot system. The root system in the bracken fern was rhizomatous, with the rhizomes underlain by 3 to 5 cm of topsoil and numerous fine roots extending to the deeper depths. The root:shoot ratios varied with each species. The graminoid had the lowest ratio (0.5:1), the fern the highest (6.1:1). Barbour et al. (1987) stated that plants of resource-limited conditions have larger root:shoot ratios but lower productivity than

Table 9.6. Root features of common prairie species at Harrell Prairie Hill

Scientific Name	Common Name	Root System Type	Root:Shoot Ratio
Schizachyrium scoparium	Broomsedge	Fibrous	0.5
Dalea purpurea	Purple Prairie Clover	taproot	1.9
Pteridium aquilinum	Bracken Fern	rhizomatous	6.1

Table 9.7. Nutrient contents of diagnostic prairie species at Harrell Prairie Hill (all values in mg per kg^{-1})

Plant Species	Ca	Mg	K	Na
Forbs				
Ratibida pinnata	18,540	3,380	13,190	639
Cassia chamaecrista	10,430	1,810	8,390	557
Dalea purpurea	15,490	2,110 ·	7,170	492
Echinacea purpurea	18,320	4,540	23,700	1,850
Graminoids				
Schizachyrium scoparium	1,574	502	4,720	409
Sorghastrum nutans	2,904	1,100	10,320	816
Transition Zone				
Pteridium aquilinum	4,673	3,340	7,870	503

plants of resource-rich habitats owing to the rapid fine-root turnovers in plants of resource-rich habitats. This relationship may explain why graminoid biomass production is high and forb production is low in the prairies.

Aboveground nutrient flux in representative native prairie species is presented in Table 9.7. The flora in Mississippi prairies are calcium- and potassium-rich species. Calcium was the highest nutrient in the forbs, whereas potassium was higher in the graminoids and fern. Calcium contents ranged from 10,430 to 18,540 mg kg^{-1} in the forbs and from 1,574 to 2,904 mg kg^{-1} in the graminoids; the bracken fern had 4,673 mg kg^{-1}. Potassium contents ranged from 7,170 to 23,700 mg kg^{-1} in the forbs and from 4,720 to 10,320 mg kg^{-1} in the graminoids; the bracken fern had 7,870 mg kg^{-1}. Magnesium and sodium contents were relatively low in all the species, reflecting the low contents of these nutrients in the soil. Higher aboveground nutrient flux in the forbs reflects the importance of the forbs to the soil-nutrient pool in these prairies.

SEED BANK

Twelve families of dicots (29 species) and two families of monocots (10 species) were identified in the Harrell Prairie Hill seed bank (Tables 9.8

Table 9.8. Family distributions in the Harrell Prairie Hill seed bank (all values are percentages)

Family	Soil Depth (cm)			Average
	0–5	5–10	10–20	
Dicots				
Asteracea	29.5	22.9	—	17.4
Euphorbiaceae	6.1	16.4	15.2	12.6
Oxalidaceae	14.4	8.4	9.1	10.6
Leguminosae	20.1	5.1	2.1	9.1
Onagraceae	1.4	2.3	—	1.2
Malvaceae	1.1	1.4	—	0.8
Apiaceae	1.1	—	0.6	0.6
Labiatae	—	1.4	—	0.5
Anacardiaceae	—	0.9	—	0.3
Rubiaceae	0.4	—	—	0.1
Scrophulariaceae	—	0.5	—	0.2
Vitaceae	—	0.5	—	0.2
Total	74.1	59.8	27.0	53.6
Monocots				
Gramineae	22.3	31.8	72.4	42.2
Liliaceae	3.6	8.4	0.6	4.2
Total	25.9	40.2	73.0	46.4

and 9.9). The soil at each site contained distinct chemical properties (Table 9.10). Lower extractable calcium, CEC, base saturation, calcium carbonate equivalent, pH, and organic matter in the lower slopes reflect the truncation of the A horizon in the upper slopes, the movement and accumulation of organic particles downslope, and subsequent acid weathering and leaching of carbonates. A total of 824 seedlings emerged from soil depths of 0 to 5 cm, 5 to 10 cm, and 10 to 20 cm. The overall seedling density was 476 seedlings/square meter. Total seedling density varied with depth. Dicot (forb) density decreased and monocot (graminoid) density increased with depth, indicating the susceptibility of the forb population to accelerated erosion. Dicot emergence was positively correlated with soil organic matter and extractable potassium (Table 9.11). Monocot emergence was negatively correlated with these properties, and no significant correlation was found between seedling emergence and the other soil properties.

The dominant asters were *Eupatorium serotinum, Rudbeckia hirta,* and *Ambrosia artemisifolia.* The major legumes in the seed bank were *Cassia chamaecrista, Dalea purpurea,* and *Desmanthus illinoensis. Euphorbia maculata* and *Acalypha gracilescens* of the Euphorbiaceae

Table 9.9. Emerged flora in the Harrell Prairie Hill seed bank

Family	Species	Depth (cm) 0-5	5-10	10-20	Total
		Number of seedlings			
Asteraceae (Compositae)	Eupatorium serotinum	52	36	–	88
	Rudbeckia hirta	18	5	–	23
	Ambrosia artensifolia	3	8	–	11
	Helenium autumnale	3	–	–	3
	Eupatorium capillifolium	2	–	–	2
	Krigia cespitosa	2	–	–	2
	Erechtites hieracifolia	1	–	–	1
	Echinacea purpurea	1	–	–	1
Leguminosae	Cassia chamaecrista	23	3	–	26
	Dalea purpurea	19	2	1	22
	Desmanthus illinoensis	1	6	5	12
	Crotolaria sagittalis	5	–	–	5
	Neptunia lutea	2	–	–	2
	Stylosanthes biflora	2	–	–	2
	Centrosema virginianum	1	–	–	1
	Strophostyles helvola	1	–	1	2
	Lespedeza sp.	1	–	–	1
	Lespedeza repens	1	–	–	1
Euphorbiaceae	Acalypha gracilescens	12	17	1	30
	Euphorbia maculata	5	18	49	72
Oxalidaceae	Oxalis dillenii	40	18	30	88
Ongraceae	Oenothera biennis	4	5	–	9
Anacardiaceae	Rhus radicans	–	1	–	1
	Rhus copallina	–	1	–	1
Malvaceae	Sida spinosa	3	3	–	6
Apiaceae	Eryngium yuccifolium	3	–	2	5
Labiatae	Blephilia ciliata	–	3	1	4
Rubiaceae	Diodia teres	1	–	–	1
Scrophulariaceae	Veronica arvensis	–	1	–	1
Gramineae	Digitaria ciliaris	4	7	128	139
	Digitaria ischaetum	–	–	20	20
	Panicum lindheimeri	15	56	78	149
	Panicum flexilis	2	2	5	9
	Panicum laxiflorum	–	–	3	3
	Panicum dichotomum	36	–	–	36
	Panicum depauperatum	2	–	–	2
	Setaria geniculata	3	1	5	9
	Andropogon sp.	–	2	2	4
Lillaceae	Allium canadense	10	18	2	30

family and *Oxalis dillenii* of the Oxalidaceae were also common in the soil. The major graminoids in the seed bank were *Digitaria ciliaris* and *Panicum lindheimeri*. The exotic species, such as *Digitaria ciliaris*, *Digitaria ischaetum* (crabgrass), and *Setaria geniculata* (foxtails), were dominant at 5 to 10 and 10 to 20 cm depths, and the native monocots commonly emerged at 0 to 5 and 5 to 10 cm depths. The Asteraceae

Table 9.10. Selected soil properties of seed-bank soils at Harrell Prairie Hill

Depth (cm)	Ca	Mg	K	Na	H	Al	CEC	BS (percentage)	CCE (percentage)	pH$_w$	OM (percentage)
	Extractable Cations (cmol$_c$ kg^{-1})										
Site 1 (toeslope)											
0–5	15.81	4.41	0.63	0.08	15.68	0.04	36.61	57.17	1.07	5.30	8.49
5–10	12.77	3.70	0.34	0.10	15.79	0.93	32.71	51.71	1.04	4.90	5.01
10–20	9.47	3.19	0.16	0.11	15.18	6.89	28.11	46.00	0.54	4.57	1.16
Site 2 (shoulder)											
0–5	48.73	3.81	0.81	0.09	8.14	0.00	61.58	86.78	2.80	6.80	7.07
5–10	44.74	3.80	0.58	0.08	9.12	0.00	58.32	84.36	2.55	6.56	5.78
10–20	43.28	4.33	0.44	0.10	8.01	0.00	56.16	85.74	2.24	6.68	2.45
Site 3 (summit)											
0–5	56.24	2.17	0.67	0.07	4.89	0.01	64.04	92.36	14.31	7.45	5.96
5–10	50.72	1.86	0.56	0.08	6.21	0.01	59.43	89.55	15.76	7.50	4.68
10–20	50.77	1.82	0.37	0.09	5.26	0.04	58.31	90.98	22.24	7.65	2.40

CEC = cation exchange capacity; BS = base saturation; CCE = CaCO$_3$ equivalency; pH$_w$ = pH in water; OM = organic matter

Table 9.11. Correlation analysis between flora emergence and selected soil properties

Soil Property	N	Monocots	Dicots
pH$_w$	9	-0.22	0.22
CEC (cmol$_c$ kg^{-1})	9	-0.41	0.41
CCE (percent)	9	0.19	-0.19
BS (percent)	9	-0.29	0.29
Extractable CA (cmol$_c$ kg^{-1})	9	-0.32	0.32
Extractable Mg (cmol$_c$ kg^{-1})	9	-0.23	0.23
Extractable K (cmol$_c$ kg^{-1})	9	-0.85*	0.85*
Extractable Na (cmol$_c$ kg^{-1})	9	0.66	-0.66
OM (percent)	9	-0.84*	0.84*
Extractable Al (cmol$_c$ kg^{-1})	9	0.53	-0.53
Extractable H (cmol$_c$ kg^{-1})	9	0.15	-0.15

pH$_w$ = pH in water; CEC = cation exchange capacity; CCE = CaCO3 equivalency; BS = base saturation; OM = organic matter. * = significantly differs from zero at the 0.01 level.

(17.4 percent), Euphorbiaceae (12.6 percent), Oxalidaceae (10.6 percent), and Leguminosae (9.1 percent) families dominated the overall distribution of dicots in the seed bank. The Gramineae family (42.2 percent) dominated the total distribution of monocots. The majority of emerged species are quite similar to those in midwestern prairies. The tall growing species of forbs were notably abundant in the upper 10 cm, and the lower-growing or prostrate species, such as *Euphorbia maculata* and *Oxalis dillenii,* dominated at 10 to 20 cm depths, indicating that accelerated erosion could reduce the biodiversity of dicots in these prairies. Other workers have studied seed banks in grassland communities. Rabinowitz (1981) found a seedling density of 6,470 seedlings m^{-2} in a Missouri tallgrass prairie. Lippert and Hopkins (1950) found densities from 300 to 800 seedlings m^{-2} in undisturbed short and mixgrass prairies, and 3,638 seedlings m^{-2} in disturbed sites. Johnson and Anderson (1986) reported seedling densities of 2,019 seedlings m^{-2} in an Illinois tallgrass prairie.

SUMMARY

Soil and plant interactions were studied in four prairie remnants in the Jackson Prairie region of Mississippi. The remnants are considered natural grasslands with vegetation of predominantly native perennial grasses and herbaceous plants. More than 60 species were identified and collected, demonstrating high natural diversity and similarity to midwestern prairies. The dominant families of dicots are the Asteraceae, Compositae, Leguminosae, and Labiatae. Graminae comprise the dominant family of monocots. Aboveground biomass production was high (more than 5,000 kg ha^{-1}) in Durand Oak Prairie, Harrell Prairie Hill, and Five Acre Prairie, similar to contents reported in midwestern prairies. Because of lower aboveground biomass production and soil moisture parameters, Eureka Church Prairie is classified as a barren rather than as a true prairie community. The lower total biomass values in this remnant reflect lower moisture contents resulting from the extensive occurrence of carbonates at the surface.

Graminoids comprised 40 to 50 percent and forbs approximately 20 to 40 percent of the total biomass production, reflecting the predominance of perennial grasses in the prairie system. The graminoid root system consisted of clumps of extensive fibrous fine roots. The forb root system was characterized as a thick taproot system. The graminoids had lower root:shoot ratios than the forbs, explaining their higher aboveground biomass production. The flora are rich in calcium and potassium. Calcium levels tended to be highest in the forbs, whereas potassium was higher in the graminoids. Magnesium and sodium were relatively low in all species analyzed. The higher nutrient contents in the forbs reflect their importance to the soil-nutrient pool and biocycling in these areas.

A transition zone of *Pteridium aquilinum* (bracken fern) occurred downslope at Harrell Prairie Hill. The transition zone reflects an acidic prairie and the current impact of cultural disturbance. Biomass production was high and similar to that of the adjacent native prairie. Graminoids comprised approximately 30 percent and forbs 10 percent of the total production, reflecting the decrease in diversity after the invasion of fern. The root system was rhizomatous; rhizomes were underlain by 3 to 5 cm of topsoil and numerous fine roots extending to deeper depths. The root:shoot ratio was much higher than in the native prairie species. The fern had calcium and potassium contents similar to those of the native graminoids. Tall growing species of forbs were abundant in the upper 10 cm of the seed bank at Harrell Prairie Hill. Graminoids and lower-growing or prostrate forbs dominated the 10 to 20 cm soil depth, indicating that accelerated erosion could reduce the biodiversity of dicots and affect the soil-nutrient pool.

CONCLUSIONS

This study illustrates complex soil and vegetative relationships existing in prairie remnants in the Jackson Prairie of Mississippi and the need for interdisciplinary research to characterize them. Clayey Vertisols with low bulk densities, high moisture retention, and high cation exchange capacities provide suitable habitat for the diverse prairie species. Well-developed surface soil structure enhances water infiltration and promotes extensive root distribution of prairie vegetation. Nutrient-rich epipedons with abundant calcium and neutral-to-alkaline pH levels provide a critical environment for the natural seed bank supporting native grasses and herbaceous plants. Cultural activities resulting in accelerated soil erosion and deterioriation of soil quality adversely affect the vestigial prairie vegetation. Recognizing and documenting remaining prairie remnants and characterizing the soils, flora, and fauna will be pivotal to understanding and maintaining these unique areas.

Acknowledgments. Special thanks are expressed to Sidney T. McDaniel and Ronald Wieland for their cooperative support and encouragement of this research.

II   CULTURE

10 Prehistoric Settlement Patterning on the Mississippi Black Prairie

JANET RAFFERTY

INTRODUCTION

The Black Prairie of Mississippi and Alabama sometimes has been treated as an area where, because little archaeological knowledge exists, there was little activity in prehistoric times. In Mississippi, such an assumption may be accurate for large expanses of low-relief interior uplands, where surface water is at a premium (Macrander and Telle 1989:17) and where year-round habitation would be difficult without water catchment devices. Two parts of the Black Prairie in Mississippi are well-documented exceptions to this pattern, however. One is along the Tombigbee River and the lower reaches of its major western tributaries, Town Creek, Tibbee Creek, and the Noxubee River, which cut through or border on the Black Prairie (Figure 10.1). There, numerous deep, large archaeological sites dating from the Early Archaic through Mississippian periods, a span of 7,000–8,000 years (6000 B.C.–A.D. 1550), have been recorded and excavated, especially along the main river in connection with construction of the Tennessee-Tombigbee Waterway (Futato 1989:185–190, 193). The other exception is on the ridges around and south of Tupelo. Archaeological work began there in the 1930s with planning for the Natchez Trace Parkway; since that time, many Protohistoric and Historic-period aboriginal occupations, which are conventionally assigned a Chickasaw tribal identification (Jennings 1941; Johnson 1997, 2000), have been investigated.

A third area, where many sites have been found but from which much less has been published, is the portion of the Black Prairie in eastern Oktibbeha and Clay counties (Figure 10.1). Intermittent archaeological work since the mid-1970s has resulted in an impressive number of sites (ca. 1,000) being recorded in these counties and a few

Fig. 10.1. Clay and Oktibbeha counties, in the Black Prairie of northeastern Mississippi.

being more intensively investigated (Baca and Peacock 1997; Blakeman 1985; Giliberti 1999; Gray 1993; Gray et al. 1997; Hogue and Peacock 1995; Johnson et al. 1984; Johnson et al. 1991; Lolley 1992; Marshall 1986; Peacock 1995; Poole 1990; Rafferty and Hogue 1999). Many of these sites, like those around Tupelo, are located on ridges underlain by the Prairie Bluff or Demopolis chalk formations (Bergquist 1943; Logan 1903; Moore 1969) and thus are elevated well above permanent watercourses. Occupations at these sites range over 2,500 years, from the Gulf Formational (beginning ca. 800 B.C.) through Protohistoric (ending ca. A.D. 1650) periods.

Explaining the pattern of prehistoric human habitation in this part of the Black Prairie is a problem facing archaeologists. Characteristics of the prairie environment, including soils, vegetation, and availability of water, must be taken into account as limiting and enabling factors, particularly in considering the practice of maize agriculture and sedentary (i.e., year-round) occupation of the ridges. A related task is showing how and explaining why prehistoric settlement changed through time. Determining whether there were long periods of abandonment, establishing occupation densities, and examining changes in landscape-use patterns are involved in addressing these questions. The evolution of year-round site use, which can be regarded as a density-dependent phenomenon triggered by packing of ranges occupied by mobile hunter-gatherers (Kelly 1998; Rosenberg 1998), may be one element that explains such changes. Sedentary settlement patterns, once established, may affect selective pressures and allow further population growth (Rafferty 1985). Agricultural subsistence adds further growth potential, and such activities as earthwork and mound building may be selected to buffer resource variability (Dunnell 1989:49). Demographic and social factors thus are active elements, along with environmental parameters, in an evolutionary account of human landscape use.

Gaining chronological control of the archaeological data is essential to understanding variability in both space and time. The basic chronology for the central Tombigbee River valley has been established (Table 10.1), mostly using diagnostic pottery styles and radiocarbon dates (Jenkins and Krause 1986), but details of its application to sites in the uplands west of the river continue to be worked out (cf. Peacock 1997; Rafferty 1994, 1995).

Existing settlement pattern hypotheses have focused on archaeological assemblages containing pottery to which crushed mussel shell was added as a tempering agent. Those from upland settings have been assigned to the Late Mississippian/Protohistoric period by Jay Johnson (Johnson 1996; Johnson et al. 1984, 1991), with Mississippian people seen as expanding into the interior only in the late fifteenth and early sixteenth centuries, abandoning the habitation sites and mounds they had established in the major river drainages. Other researchers (Peacock and Rafferty 1996; Rafferty 1996) have questioned this hypothesis, arguing that it results in a too-simplistic settlement pattern model based on faulty chronological assumptions. Instead, these researchers have proposed that there are important continuities in upland settlement patterning from the Woodland period through Mississippian and Protohistoric times (Rafferty 1996) and that better temporal control allows identification of an earlier and more gradual Mississippian settlement expansion (Rafferty 1998) onto the Black Prairie ridges. In his more recent work (Johnson 2000), Johnson acknowledged that the shift in settlement may have been more gradual than he previously thought.

The current study looks in considerable detail at sites on the chalk formations and in associated stream and river valleys in Oktibbeha and Clay counties in eastern Mississippi. It is assumed that most of the sites considered, occupations at which cover the time from ca. 800 B.C. to A.D. 1650 (Table 10.1), represent sedentary habitation. The assumption is warranted by a few excavated examples from each period, from which large quantities of pottery; postholes and/or daub as evidence of

Table 10.1. Ceramic chronology for the central Tombigbee River valley

Dates	Cultural Period	Diagnostic Pottery Styles
A.D. 1550–1650	Protohistoric	fossil shell-tempered
A.D. 1100–1550	Mississippian	mussel shell-tempered
A.D. 550–1100	Woodland: Miller III phase	grog-tempered cordmarked
A.D. 200–550	Woodland: Miller II phase	sand-tempered cordmarked
200 B.C.–A.D. 200	Woodland: Miller I phase	sand-tempered fabric-marked
800–200 B.C.	Gulf Formational	fiber-tempered
		sand-tempered pinched
		sand-tempered punctate

houses; human burials; and other features such as large and small pits, large hearths, and dog burials were recovered (Baca and Peacock 1997; Galloway 2000; Giliberti 1999; Hogue and Peacock 1995; Johnson et al. 1991; Kaplan 1998; Marshall 1986; Peacock 1995; Rafferty and Hogue 1998, 1999). Such a range of activities argues that the sites were used for general habitation, while the quantity of pottery and diversity of floral and faunal remains argue that they were used year-round (Rafferty 1985).

DATA STRUCTURE

About 1,165 square km within the Black Prairie, in the eastern half of Oktibbeha County and the eastern three-quarters of Clay County (Brent 1973; Murphree and Miller 1976), are included in the study area (Figure 10.1). Although considerable archaeological survey has occurred there, only a small percentage of the landscape has been subjected to intensive survey. The 155 assemblages used in this study were recorded in the course of such systematic surveys (Atkinson and Elliott 1978; Blakeman 1975, 1985; Gray 1993; Gray et al. 1997; Johnson et al. 1984, 1991; Poole 1990; Rucker 1974), including sites collected during the 1994, 1996, 1997, and 1999 Mississippi State University archaeology field schools. In examining the figures showing site distributions below, it is important to remember that the entire area has not been subject to archaeological survey. This means that differences in the distributions of various kinds of assemblages are meaningful, but that large areas of vacant space may not mean lack of habitation but merely lack of survey.

The sites considered do not make up the entire inventory of known sites, which includes ones occupied in pre-ceramic Paleo-Indian and Archaic times (ca. 9000–800 B.C.) as well as a number of sites occupied in periods when pottery was made but which produced assemblages lacking appropriate diagnostic pottery styles. Taken together, the assemblages that were excluded from this analysis undoubtedly represent a great diversity of sedentary, non-sedentary, and special-purpose occupations. Many of these latter two kinds of sites are located along perennial streams, not on the chalk uplands that are of primary concern in this work.

The study may be biased by failure to include sites that were used for sedentary habitation but which have not produced diagnostic pottery styles. Many sites have yielded small pottery assemblages, attributable to vegetation cover and/or to small site size. Woodland occupations are the most probable ones to be underrepresented. This is because the diagnostic styles for Woodland comprise non-plain surface finishes (Table 10.2), less likely to be found or identified in small or eroded sherd samples. Mississippian- and Protohistoric-period occupations are recognized by temper modes, which usually can be identified for even the smallest potsherds. About 16 percent of pottery-bearing collections in Oktibbeha County (19 out of 120) and 33 percent of those in Clay County (33 out of 99) could not be assigned to the specific cultural periods discussed below.

The archaeological occupations that are included are treated using long chronological periods. Although finer chronological distinctions are possible, they break the available sample of assemblages into groups too small for simultaneous examination of spatial patterning and temporal change. The assemblages have been divided into those representing shorter and longer duration habitation. Shorter-duration assemblages include those containing one pottery type or mode, each treated as diagnostic of one cultural period (Table 10.1): fiber temper of the Gulf Formational period, sand-tempered fabric-marked pottery of the Early Middle Woodland period (Miller I phase), sand-tempered cordmarked pottery of the rest of the Middle Woodland period (Miller II phase), grog-tempered cordmarked pottery of the Late Woodland period (Miller III phase), mussel shell temper of the Mississippian period, and fossil shell temper of the Protohistoric period (Jenkins 1981; Jenkins and Krause 1986; Jennings 1941). If two sequent types co-occurred in an assemblage (for example, sand-tempered fabric-marked and cordmarked), the assemblage also was considered to represent shorter-duration habitation and was assigned to the later of the two culture-historical units (in this example, to the Miller II phase). This method was a substitute for treating such two-type assemblages as intermediate in time between the two periods, as this would double the number of periods. In fact these assemblages likely are intermediate, as the sequent pottery types are known to have overlapped with one another through time (Jenkins 1982; Peacock 1997; Rafferty 1994, 1995, 1996).

A total of 138 assemblages were determined by this method to represent shorter-duration site use. Each of the periods to which assemblages were assigned covers a span of several hundred years, but it is believed on good evidence (e.g., Hogue and Peacock 1995; Peacock 1995; Rafferty 2001; Rafferty and Hogue 1999) that most shorter-duration sites were occupied for decades within these time spans, not for the entire span. Each shorter-duration assemblage appears only once in each of the data displays below.

Longer-duration sites often have anthropic soil development, high artifact content, and thick cultural deposits (Rafferty 1994), though they are not necessarily particularly large in area. Their assemblages were identified by the presence of artifacts diagnostic of three or more of the cultural periods mentioned above. Diagnostic styles were chosen so that no more than two could overlap in time. For example, fiber-tempered and sand-tempered pinched/punctate pottery may have been made at the same time, but use of fiber tempering had been discontinued by the time sand-tempered fabric-marked pottery began to be made. Thus, the presence of three or more of these diagnostic styles in the same assemblage is taken to indicate that the sites from which the artifacts came were used over long time spans, minimally encompassing several hundred years. It is not supposed that the sites were occupied continuously over these spans, although that is not precluded, but merely that they were occupied often enough for a continuous set of diagnostics to be represented in the collections. There were 17 such longer-duration assemblages. In each data display, a particular assemblage was counted once for each period for which it contained a diagnostic. In addition to longer- and shorter-duration assemblages, 19 others contained diagnostics from non-sequent periods, perhaps representing reoccupation after long abandonment or perhaps as a result of sampling error; these were not used in the analysis.

Obviously, it is possible that any given shorter-duration assemblage might in actuality derive from a relatively long continuous occupation, all within one cultural period, whereas a longer-duration assemblage might derive from many short-term uses of a site across several cultural periods. Evidence for this kind of variability may well be preserved at particular sites in the form of artifact distribution data. For example, artifacts from one use might not coincide spatially with those from an earlier use, allowing the two occupations of the site to be separated analytically (Rafferty 2001). Given that the vast majority of the collections used for this study were obtained by general surface collection, in which all the artifacts recovered from a site were treated as having the same location, it is not possible to determine the exact occupation history of each site using these data.

It is the case that many of the longer-duration sites are fairly small, leaving little room for major spatial discontinuities in which settlement might have been reestablished in the same site area but not at the exact location occupied earlier. Sizes of the 17 longer-duration sites vary from 900 to 16,000 square meters (Figure 10.2), with an average of 4,900 square meters (about 1.2 acres). The two largest sites are Brogan village (22CL501b) and the Herman site (22OK762), both terrace habitation sites that are associated with Middle Woodland mounds. If they are excluded, the average longer-duration site size drops by about a third, to 3,500 square meters (0.9 acre), with sizes ranging from 900 to 6,000 square meters. Size distribution data for all longer- and shorter-duration sites are shown in Figure 10.2. Average sizes vary little: 3,500 square meters for Woodland, 4,800 square meters for Mississippian (excluding the 17-ha mound site, Lyon's Bluff), and 4,000 square meters for Protohistoric shorter-duration sites. The similarity of these sizes to the average for longer-duration sites strengthens the argument made above that repeated abandonment and reoccupation of longer-duration sites were not necessarily common occurrences. Figure 10.2 shows that the very small site sizes (less than 900 square meters) created by some shorter-duration occupations do not occur at all in the longer-duration sites.

Further, the 17 longer-duration sites show no obvious characteristics of topography, soil type, or water availability that would constrain settlement to these particular spots. One group is on terraces near major drainages, whereas the other main set is located on upland ridges. If it were postulated that it was common to abandon and reoccupy the same small places within the confines of sedentary settlement, it would be necessary to show why these particular spots were so attractive. Conversely, it is possible that some of the sites designated here as longer-duration sites were occupied continuously over the course of several hundred years or more. They arguably represent small settlements at favorable, though not tightly spatially constrained, locales. If so, they might well have survived over a long span. At this point, these questions must remain unresolved.

The Gulf Formational and Woodland periods have been combined for most purposes in this study because only seven sites were occupied during Gulf Formational times. The combined period, referred to below as Gulf Formational/Woodland, maximally extends from ca. 800 B.C. to A.D. 1100, a period of nearly 2,000 years (Table 10.1).

ANALYSIS AND RESULTS

The distribution of longer-duration sites in Clay and Oktibbeha counties is shown in Figure 10.3. As a result of the way longer-duration assemblages were defined, all 17 longer-duration sites used in this

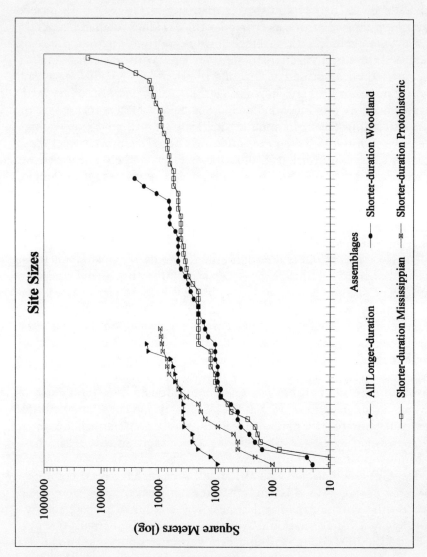

Fig. 10.2. Site sizes for archaeological sites in the Mississippi Black Prairie.

analysis were occupied during Gulf Formational/Woodland times. However, much continuity, not only within the Gulf Formational/ Woodland period but also between Woodland and Mississippian times, is represented in these data. Twelve of the 17 sites were occupied from Gulf Formational/Woodland times into the Mississippian and/or Proto-historic periods: two beginning in Gulf Formational, three beginning in Miller I, five beginning in Miller II, and two beginning in Miller III (Table 10.1); these represent as much as 2,300, 1,700, 1,300, and 800 years of occupation, respectively. Such sites are located primarily near the Tombigbee River and its major tributaries, while the four occupied in Woodland but not Mississippian times are near smaller water-courses well upstream from the major creeks and rivers (Figure 10.3). Three longer-duration sites are on upland ridges, some distance from any perennial stream (Figure 10.3). These are the only ones where occupation continued into Protohistoric times, after A.D. 1550 (Table 10.2).

The approach used here masks smaller-scale variability, especially the difference between the peak period of a site's use and the entire possible occupation span of that site. This is because one component has been assigned for each cultural period represented in an assemblage, regardless of whether few or many diagnostic sherds are present. Differences do exist among sites in peak occupation period, as is indicated by an examination of the percentages of various diagnostic pottery types making up each assemblage (Figure 10.4). For instance, the three longer-duration sites on upland ridges have produced only a few diagnostic Woodland potsherds but much larger numbers of Mississippian or Protohistoric sherds, indicating that they were mostly used in the latter periods (Table 10.2, Figure 10.6).

The shorter-duration sites (Table 10.3) are distributed temporally and spatially quite differently than the longer-duration ones (Figures 10.4 and 10.5). Of the 43 Gulf Formational/Woodland shorter-duration sites, only seven show evidence of being occupied in the 1,000 years preceding A.D. 200 (Figure 10.4). The other 36 were used in the second half of the Woodland period (in either Miller II or Miller III times), from ca. A.D. 200 to 1100. The places in use are located along major tributary streams, along small streams, and in the upland areas well away from creeks (Figure 10.5). The locations generally are scattered, rather than being close to or patterned with some particular reference to longer-duration sites. This suggests that longer-duration sites were merely particularly favorable locations, not central places with different functions in a site hierarchy than the shorter-duration locations. The two Woodland mound/village sites (22CL501/22CL501b, Brogan mound and village, and 22OK762, Herman mound and village) that were included in the analysis both have assemblages classified as representing longer-duration occupation (Figure 10.3). Intensive survey

Table 10.2 Pottery in assemblages from longer-duration sites

SITES	Total sherds	Fiber-tempered	Sand-tempered pinched/puncate*	Sand-tempered fabric marked	Sand-tempered cordmarked	Sand-tempered other	Bone-tempered	Limestone-tempered	Grog-tempered cordmarked	Grog-tempered other	Mussel shell-tempered#	Fossil shell-tempered#
22CL501b	617			194	128	75	5	4	57	76	78	
22CL510	143	16			6	10			49	75	3	
22CL527	1,296		2	1	23	28			251	844	131	
22CL533	109			5	13	86			2	3		
22CL814	11,712	26	504	48	285	4,266	12	7	20	81	6,463	
22CL841	29		1	1	5	22						
22CL904	56		1	2	1	33			5	14	1	
22CL968	54			1	8	22			11	11	1	
22CL980	31				7	18			2	3		
22OK637	400				2	296			1	89	1	11
22OK698	281		9			170			1	34	53	14
22OK746	1,515		17	249	91	1,099	18		3	34	4	
22OK762	222				5	54	2		46	97	18	
22OK893	140			1	3	85			8	43		
22OK905+	159				2	3			1	1	71	81
22OK912	145					65			2	20	41	17
22OK942	1,904			4		178			2	38	1,682	

* not counted as Gulf Formational diagnostic if mussel shell- or fossil shell-tempered sherds were present in assemblage

+ pottery from Features 2 and 3 only

includes mixed grog- and mussel shell- or fossil-shell temper

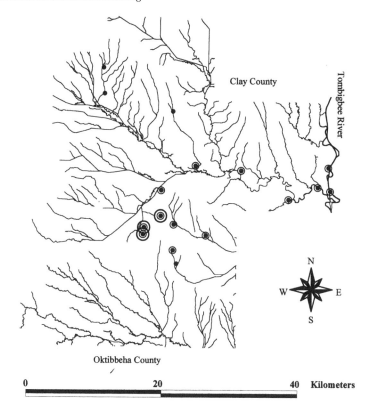

Longer-duration Sites

- **Woodland Components**

○ **Mississippian Components**

○ **Protohistoric Components**

Fig. 10.3. Distribution of longer-duration archaeological sites in Oktibbeha and Clay counties, Mississippi.

has not been done in either vicinity, so the status of Woodland mounds as central places is untested. Such mound sites clearly have different functions than other sites, but that does not necessarily imply that they formed part of a hierarchy of sites, as central places do by definition (Hodder and Orton 1976). The Brogan mound seems to be Miller I in age (Baca and Peacock 1997) and thus was in use as a burial mound at a time when most of the relatively few sites then occupied were located on major rivers.

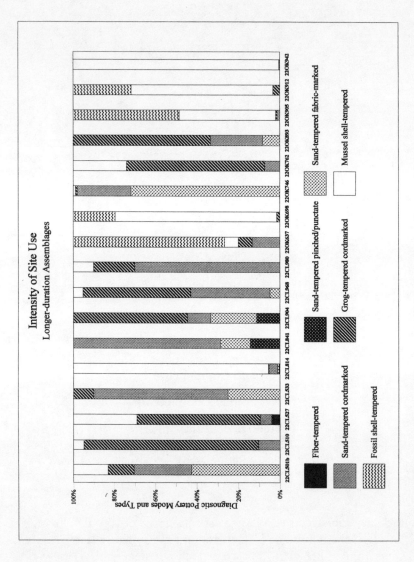

Fig. 10.4. Intensity of site use as measured by frequency of ceramic diagnostics.

Table 10.3 Pottery in assemblages from shorter-duration sites

	Total sherds	Fiber-tempered	Sand-tempered pinched/punctate*	Sand-tempered fabric-marked	Sand-tempered cordmarked	Sand-tempered other	Bone-tempered	Limestone-tempered	Grog-tempered cordmarked	Grog-tempered other	Mussel shell-tempered#	Fossil shell-tempered
WOODLAND												
22Cl551	13				2	6			1	4		
22Cl552	1				1							
22Cl558	41								28	13		
22Cl596	37				2	35			1	9		
22Cl829	10					13						
22Cl830	24				11	13			1			
22Cl831	2				1	1						
22Cl855	14			1		11				2		
22Cl856	20					11			2	7		
22Cl857	12				3	9						
22Cl862	11				3	8						
22Cl865	17		1			12				4		
22Cl867	2				1	1						
22Cl875	74				11	62				1		
22Cl882	39				3	34				2		
22Cl892	49				2	47						
22Cl902	5				1	4						
22Cl915	6	1				5						
22Cl917	815	4	188			522						
22Cl967	10				3	7						
22Cl972	4				1	3						
22Cl974	61				9	49			1	2		
22Cl979	4				2	2						
22Cl982	41				2	24			2	15		
22Ok548	17				2					15		

Table 10.3 (cont'd)

	Total sherds	Fiber-tempered	Sand-tempered pinched/punctate*	Sand-tempered fabric-marked	Sand-tempered cordmarked	Sand-tempered other	Bone-tempered	Limestone-tempered	Grog-tempered cordmarked	Grog-tempered other	Mussel shell-tempered#	Fossil shell-tempered
22Ok552	6					2			2	2		
22Ok555	4					1			2	1		
22Ok582	75				3	9			12	68		
22Ok600	47					3			3	41		
22Ok601	92	1			1	20			2	68		
22Ok605	43				2	9			1	2		
22Ok610	31			3						28		
22Ok623	39				1	30			2	6		
22Ok628	63				1	36			2	24		
22Ok697	1								1			
22Ok718	11				5	6				11		
22Ok724	410				4	395				11		
22Ok745	66				9	54	1		1	1		
22Ok888	103			3	4	95				1		
22Ok894	62				8	53						
22Ok908	1,402			255	4	1,143						
22Ok909	509				5	178	4		70	252		
22Ok972	8				1	2			1	4		
MISSISSIPPIAN												
22Cl525	28										28	
22Cl526	32										32	
22Cl535	122								42	61	19	
22Cl764	1127					13					1,114	
22Cl870	107										107	
22Cl871	60					5					55	
22Cl877	28					5					23	

Table 10.3 (cont'd)

	Total sherds	Fiber-tempered	Sand-tempered pinched/punctate*	Sand-tempered fabric-marked	Sand-tempered cordmarked	Sand-tempered other	Bone-tempered	Limestone-tempered	Grog-tempered cordmarked	Grog-tempered other	Mussel shell-tempered#	Fossil shell-tempered
22Cl878	27										27	
22Cl886	49										49	
22Cl887	59					1					58	
22Cl888	47										47	
22Cl889	110										110	
22Cl894	30										30	
22Cl895	295										295	
22Cl896	58										58	
22Cl929	28					3					25	
22Cl933	252					1					251	
22Cl943	49					1					48	
22Cl944	147					12					135	
22Cl945	176					1					175	
22Cl948	132										132	
22Cl953	86					24				2	60	
22Cl954	104					19					85	
22Cl961	126					6					120	
22Ok520@											x	
22Ok529	40					36				33	7	
22Ok531	55					20				15	4	
22Ok532	58									15	23	
22Ok533	7								2		5	
22Ok534	33					2			3	5	23	
22Ok536	29										29	
22Ok538	100					30			1		69	
22Ok539	40									14	26	
22Ok540	29									25	4	

Table 10.3 (cont'd)

	Total sherds	Fiber-tempered	Sand-tempered pinched/punctate*	Sand-tempered fabric-marked	Sand-tempered cordmarked	Sand-tempered other	Bone-tempered	Limestone-tempered	Grog-tempered cordmarked	Grog-tempered other	Mussel shell-tempered#	Fossil shell-tempered
22Ok541	6									3	3	
22Ok542	12									4	8	
22Ok543	26					1				6	19	
22Ok544	27									2	25	
22Ok545	48					1				16	31	
22Ok546	73										73	
22Ok547	28					2				14	12	
22Ok554	7									4	3	
22Ok559	2									1	1	
22Ok560	2									1	1	
22Ok565	15									10	5	
22Ok566	40									10	30	
22Ok567	104					33					71	
22Ok568	78					21				6	51	
22Ok569	31										31	
22Ok570	56					1				27	28	
22Ok571	14									10	4	
22Ok574	16					3				7	6	
22Ok576	4									1	3	
22Ok578	7										7	
22Ok581	18					2			1	12	3	
22Ok584	6									3	3	
22Ok672	47					2					45	
22Ok673	29										29	
22Ok691	45										45	
22Ok701	137					50					87	
22Ok703	25					4					21	

Table 10.3 (cont'd)

	Total sherds	Fiber-tempered	Sand-tempered pinched/punctate*	Sand-tempered fabric-marked	Sand-tempered cordmarked	Sand-tempered other	Bone-tempered	Limestone-tempered	Grog-tempered cordmarked	Grog-tempered other	Mussel shell-tempered#	Fossil shell-tempered
22Ok713	2										2	
22Ok716	7									2	5	
22Ok720	11					3			2	2	4	
22Ok775	36										36	
22Ok800	22										22	
22Ok949	5									1	4	
22Ok955	5										5	
22Ok956	4					2				1	1	
22Ok958	6					2					4	
22Ok959	1										1	
22Ok964	1										1	
22Ok965	4										4	
22Ok999	1										1	
PROTOHISTORIC												
22Ok583	120					10				23	73	14
22Ok595	1,147					118	2				831	196
22Ok700	64										63	1
22Ok705	36					19					11	6
22Ok719	332					36				13	116	167
22Ok769	42										15	17
22Ok779	56										31	11
22Ok787	56					18					34	4
22Ok793	698					232				11	416	39
22Ok819	52									2		50
22Ok904	673					93				15	272	293
22Ok907	127										105	22

Table 10.3 (cont'd)

	Total sherds	Fiber-tempered	Sand-tempered pinched/punctate*	Sand-tempered fabric-marked	Sand-tempered cordmarked	Sand-tempered other	Bone-tempered	Limestone-tempered	Grog-tempered cordmarked	Grog-tempered other	Mussel shell-tempered#	Fossil shell-tempered
22Ok911	14					2					11	1
22Ok921	7					5						2
22Ok929	7										5	2
22Ok931	44					2					24	16
22Ok932	32					21					9	2
22Ok933	17					7					7	3
22Ok988	21					10					8	3
22Ok990	21										18	3

* not counted as Gulf Formational diagnostic if mussel shell- or fossil shell-tempered sherds were present in assemblage

+ pottery from Features 2 and 3 only

includes mixed grog- and mussel shell-temper

@ no ceramic tabulation available

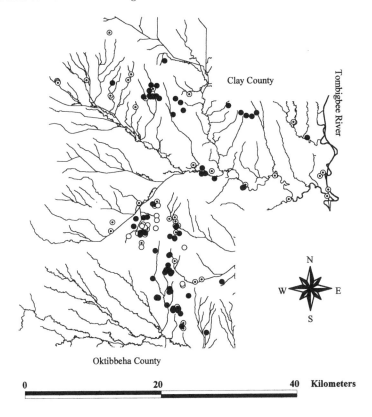

Shorter-duration Sites

- ⊙ **Woodland Occupations**

- ● **Mississippian Occupations**

- ○ **Protohistoric Occupations**

Fig. 10.5. Distribution of shorter-duration archaeological sites in Oktibbeha and Clay counties, Mississippi.

Shorter-duration sites used during Mississippian times differ some-what from places used for shorter-duration occupation during Woodland times (Figure 10.5). One difference is that virtually all are located in upland areas, at a considerable remove from perennial streams. It should be remembered, though, that there are Mississippian components on major streams, at the longer-duration sites. The other, most striking, feature of the shorter-duration Mississippian sites is their large number. There are 75 such sites in the sample (Table 10.3, Fig-

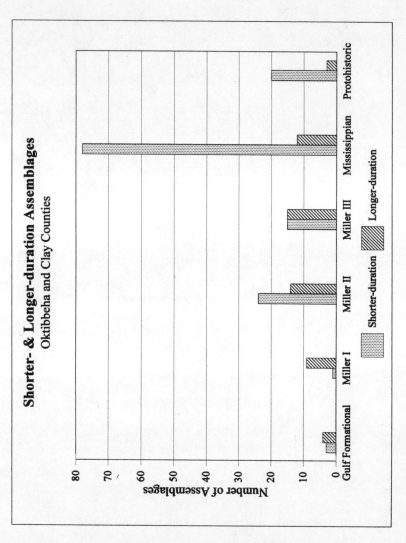

Fig. 10.6. Number of shorter- and longer-duration assemblages by cultural period.

ure 10.5), maximally spanning the 450-year length of the Mississippian period: from A.D. 1100 to 1550. This is many times the rate of site production in Woodland times—about 17 sites per hundred years compared with Woodland rates as low as 0.7 sites per hundred years (Gulf Formational and Miller I) and as high as 4 sites per hundred years (Miller II and III).

The one Mississippian mound and village site included, Lyon's Bluff (22OK520), is represented in the shorter-duration assemblages because the only diagnostic pottery style that is documented from there is mussel shell temper. It is unusual compared with other shorter-duration Mississippian sites in its large size (ca. 17 ha) and location near a major stream, Line Creek, as well as having a rectangular flat-topped mound (Galloway 2000; Marshall 1986). Unlike the other shorter-duration Mississippian sites, Lyon's Bluff apparently was occupied throughout the Mississippian period, as indicated by radiocarbon dates that span the period A.D. 1100–1550 (Hogue 2000; Marshall 1977). The other Mississippian site with a mound is 22OK578 (Blakeman 1985), also treated here as a shorter-duration site; as it produced only seven sherds from the surface, it is doubtful that a village is present there. Mississippian mound sites usually are assumed to have served as central places, as they may contain many houses, public structures, plazas, palisades for defense, and elite cemeteries (Jenkins and Krause 1986: 95–98); aside from a mound, with as many as five structure floors encountered in a 1934 excavation (Galloway 2000:44), numerous houses, and a possible palisade (Peacock and Reynolds 2001) at Lyon's Bluff and a mound at 22OK578, most of these functions have not yet been confirmed for these two sites.

Finally, all 20 shorter-duration Protohistoric sites are located in the uplands, along with the three longer-duration sites occupied then (Figures 10.3 and 10.5). The most identifiable change from Mississippian times is that most Protohistoric habitation occurred in a relatively small area in the north-central part of Oktibbeha County, with none identified so far in Clay County. This striking clustering of sites is not characteristic of any earlier period. The number of sites occupied during the ca. 100-year span of the Protohistoric period is similar to the Mississippian-period rate.

DISCUSSION

Explanations for settlement pattern continuities and discontinuities can be suggested, but no decisive answers can be given at this point. Continuity in use of the longer-duration sites is identifiable across the entire time span. This is likely referable to the inferred presence of sedentary settlement systems throughout this 2,500-year span. Within this basic continuity a variety of changes may be seen. One is a temporal change in the location of occupied sites, with the number of inhabited longer-duration sites near the Tombigbee River remaining stable through Woodland and Mississippian times and then decreasing, while the number occupied in major tributaries and, finally, the uplands increased (Figure 10.3). A concomitant increase in the amount of shorter-duration site use in the uplands is evident (Figure 10.5). These patterns serve to further confirm earlier observations (Peacock and Rafferty 1996; Rafferty 1996), which suggested that the undoubted settlement shift from areas near the Tombigbee River and its major tributaries to upland areas of the Black Prairie was gradual, rather than occurring abruptly in Late Mississippian times. Other changes that occurred in some periods are the formation of villages, existing alongside numerous small dispersed habitation sites, and changes in the extent and function of mound building (Jenkins and Krause 1986).

These issues aside, the Gulf Formational/Woodland settlement pattern can be characterized as one in which occupied sites increased in number through time, slowly at first and then more rapidly. This is hypothesized to represent a spread of population out from the major riverine areas after the advent of sedentary settlement patterns in Gulf Formational times. Gulf Formational site locations are more strongly correlated with large streams than those of later periods (four of seven sites with Gulf Formational components included in the study are located on such streams, compared with six of 60 Woodland sites, six of 88 Mississippian sites, and none of 20 Protohistoric sites); they also are strongly correlated with longer-duration use. Such results would be expected if these locations represented the first ones inhabited by sedentary peoples, with the most favorable places taken first and occupied longest. Increased population growth, often an effect of settling down (Rafferty 1985; Rosenberg 1998), would be primarily responsible for expansion of settlement into smaller river valleys and upland areas. This pattern is very similar to that seen in a previous study of sites located farther north in Mississippi, in Lee, Union, and Pontotoc counties (Rafferty 1994). Extensive Woodland-period settlement is also seen in the uplands west of the study area (Peacock 1997). The Oktibbeha and Clay County area displays in detail part of an extensive Woodland-period settlement expansion into the upland regions of northern Mississippi (Peacock 1996, 1997; Rafferty 2002).

River-valley occupation continued during Mississippian times, but upland site density dramatically increased in the study area. Three possible explanations come to mind. One is that population grew much faster in Mississippian times, so that more sites were created as small habitation sites proliferated. The second possibility is that sites were occupied for shorter spans, so that more sites resulted. A third possibility is that population consolidated in some areas, creating more sites there. A combination of these three factors also is possible.

Population growth might be argued to have occurred during Mississippian times as a result of increasing dependence on maize agriculture, which has been demonstrated for the study area through carbon isotope analysis done on human skeletal material (Hogue and Erwin 1993; Hogue 2000), through increased presence of maize at Mississippian sites (Hogue and Peacock 1995), and by inference based on environmental indicators (Hogue, this volume). Compared with hunting and gathering, agricultural subsistence allows faster population growth and higher population density (Cohen 1977; Rindos 1984).

That shortened site duration may be important in explaining the large number of Mississippian sites is indicated by five excavated upland Mississippian sites in the area, including 22CL764 (Johnson et al. 1991), 22OK534 (Hogue and Peacock 1995), 22OK942 (Kaplan 1998), 22OK694 (Peacock 1995), and 22OK793 (Rafferty and Hogue 1999). The five sites all were small, with at most one to two houses uncovered in the ones extensively excavated. Pottery styles, the lack of house rebuilding, few or no burials, and the relative paucity of storage pits indicate that the sites were occupied for several, rather than tens, of decades. The Lyon's Bluff mound site demonstrates that at least some places were inhabited over most of the Mississippian period (Hogue 2000; Marshall 1986) and served as population centers throughout their occupation span.

If more frequent relocation of households occurred in the Mississippian period than in Woodland times, it might be expected that short-duration Woodland sites would be larger, denser, or deeper than the even shorter-duration Mississippian sites. Current evidence does not allow this idea to be tested, although Woodland and Mississippian site sizes track one another fairly closely (Figure 10.4). One reason it is difficult to test is that, during survey, one site number may be assigned to a place that later, in the course of more intensive work, is found to represent several spatially and chronologically distinct occupations (Rafferty 2001; Rafferty and Hogue 1999). This situation has affected both Woodland and Mississippian sites, making it difficult to project the detailed structure of site occupation from survey data alone. Why more frequent moves might have occurred in Mississippian times is unknown. Again, that this period saw the advent of dependence on maize agriculture may be significant, as rapid depletion of nutrients in upland soils under maize cultivation may have been a factor in selecting for frequent household moves.

Population consolidation also may have occurred, as there is evidence of widespread abandonment of the upland areas west and north of the study area during Early Mississippian times (Peacock 1997; Rafferty 1998). These populations presumably congregated in other areas, possibly including the prairie portions of Clay and Oktibbeha counties. Concentration of Mississippian populations in the main river valleys has been taken for granted in many areas of the Southeast, following Smith's (1978) model that Mississippian peoples were adapted to broad river-valley environments that contained a mixture of fertile agricultural land, forests where deer and turkey were hunted, and aquatic resources in oxbow lakes and rivers. The large number of Mississippian sites in the western Black Prairie uplands, ca. 40 km from the Tombigbee River, belies the applicability of that model here.

It is plain from examining a larger geographic area that the patterns observed in this study are part of a regionwide series of settlement pattern changes. Two other parts of the Black Prairie where similar concentrations of Mississippian and Protohistoric sites have been documented are in Chickasaw and Lee counties, Mississippi (Jennings 1941; Johnson 1997, 2000; Rafferty 1996), and in Marengo County, Alabama (Patterson 1990). As in Clay and Oktibbeha counties, sites inhabited during these periods are concentrated in uplands underlain by chalk formations and far from major creeks. Another congruity is that the sites have produced primarily mussel shell–tempered and fossil shell–tempered pottery (Jennings 1941; Patterson 1990:91; Rafferty 1995), indicating similar chronological placement to the collections from Clay and Oktibbeha counties. Finally, sites in these areas apparently are found in clusters, with many small short-duration sites represented (Johnson 1997, 2000; Johnson et al. 1989; Patterson 1990:94). Although detailed spatial analysis comparing these site locations with those producing Woodland-period pottery has not been done, the similarities are suggestive of similar evolutionary processes at work in all three Black Prairie regions: the study area, the Black Prairie of Alabama, and the Lee-Chickasaw County area.

The parts of Oktibbeha and Clay counties where Mississippian and Protohistoric shorter-duration sites are concentrated are likely to have been in or near patches of tallgrass prairie. As noted by Wilson (1981), Rankin (1974), and Peacock (Hogue and Peacock 1995), the historic locations of prairie vegetation are well predicted by alkaline soils. If the distribution of these soils is compared with site distributions (Figure 10.7), it can be seen that most sites fall along their edges but with some sites located in areas where alkaline soils currently are exposed. If it is assumed that prairie patches are caused by alkaline soils, it might be argued that these areas were attractive to prehistoric agricultural peoples because they were not heavily forested. Another possibility is related to the fact that the areas mapped as alkaline soils are those that have suffered extensive erosion, exposing the chalk. Prehistoric and Protohistoric occupations thus may have been preferentially

Distribution of Shorter-duration Sites in Eastern Oktibbeha County

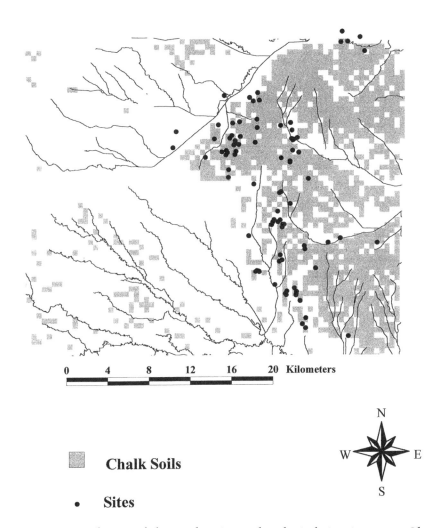

Fig. 10.7. Distribution of shorter-duration archaeological sites in eastern Oktibbeha County, Mississippi, in relation to chalk soils.

located on acid caps that overlay less-eroded areas. Such acidic soils probably were covered with oak-hickory forest (Peacock 1992) and were better drained than areas of exposed chalk. More survey is needed in alkaline soil areas to test these distributional hypotheses.

From the data on settlement continuity at longer-duration sites that

have been presented, it is argued that Mississippian populations evolved
locally from Woodland-period peoples and that the high upland site
density was caused partly by local factors, including short duration of
site use. However, the large increment in occupation in Mississippian
times also might be partly attributable to an influx of population from
the area immediately to the west, as a consequence of abandonment of
the North Central Hills and Flatwoods by people making mussel shell–
tempered pottery. More archaeological survey in areas farther west,
in the Big Black River drainage, and south, along the Noxubee River,
will help solve this problem by providing information on whether there
also were rapid increases in Mississippian-period populations in those
areas.

The possible role of springs in enabling upland settlement is also
worth discussion (see Schmitz et al., this volume). Without such a
source of water, sedentary habitation sites would have been difficult to
maintain in any period. It should be fruitful to investigate the location
and history of springs in light of the apparent ability of Mississippian-
period peoples to live almost anywhere on the ridges of the Prairie Bluff
formation, with some sites on the Demopolis formation also (Figure
10.7). Historic and geological accounts (Carroll 1931:24; Logan 1903:9;
Schmitz et al., this volume) indicate that a number of springs or seeps,
most of which are now dry, flowed from the sides of ridges where the
Prairie Bluff formation is overlain by small patches of what Logan
(1903) called the Lafayette formation, now identified as the sand/chalky
clay Clayton formation of the Midway group (Bergquist 1943:43; Moore
1969; Stephenson and Monroe 1940:216). Logan (1903) showed isolated
occurrences of this sandy formation in east-central Oktibbeha County
and Bergquist (1943) mapped small areas in western Clay County. The
Ripley formation of the Selma group, which generally lies west of and
overlying the Demopolis formation and east of and underlying the Prairie Bluff formation, also is composed of sand, clay, and sandy limestone
(Moore 1969). Logan (1903:9) mentioned that springs flowed from it in
the northern part of Oktibbeha County. The formation has not been
completely mapped, as shown by exposures noted in cuts made recently for the Highway 82 bypass north of Starkville (D. W. Schmitz,
personal communication 2000). The extent to which late prehistoric
through Protohistoric settlements are associated with the Clayton and
Ripley formations is unknown, but this can be tested by further geologic mapping and archaeological survey. The acidic capping soils mentioned above are developed in these sandy formations.

Mapping these formations in more detail and thus hypothesizing the
location of potential seep springs (Schmitz et al., this volume) may be
crucial to helping explain how upland sites were inhabited in increasing numbers through Woodland and Mississippian times. Whether

the concentration of sites in north-central Oktibbeha County in Proto-historic times might be due to a change in spring water availability is also a question to be investigated. Such changes might be attributed to lessened rainfall or to erosion allowing faster runoff. While these thoughts are purely speculative, the definitive and changing patterns identified in prehistoric site locations do encourage hope that explanations are in sight.

11 Water-resource Controls on Human Habitation in the Black Prairie of North-Central Mississippi

DARREL W. SCHMITZ, CHARLES L. WAX, AND EVAN PEACOCK

Fresh water is the blood of the land. Religions bathe their children and their saved with water. Greek philosophers described water as one of the four elements that made up the earth. Where is no water, there is no life. Humans can live a month without food, but die in a week without water. We live by the grace of water.

Parfit 1993

INTRODUCTION

The importance of water as a factor influencing culture cannot be overstated. The development of water resources has always challenged human ingenuity as people have attempted to meet this basic need for survival. Nearly 4,000 years ago the king of Babylon boasted of making the desert bloom after bringing water to it. On the other side of the world, the Hohokam made a different desert bloom with the construction of intricate systems of irrigation canals between about 700 and 1450 A.D.. Long before the birth of Christ, Egyptians, Greeks, and Romans all had well-developed water-supply systems that allowed these great civilizations to rise to world prominence (Owen 1980). Indeed, a classic theory regarding the very birth of civilization centered on the control of this critical resource (Wittfogel 1957). Water is at once the great enabler and the great limiting factor of human settlement.

The type of water source available to support life is strongly connected to human use of the landscape. Settlement patterns and densities are related to the accessibility of a stable and potable water resource to support domestic use. As technologies for providing more stable and higher-quality water sources have emerged through time, populations and settlement distributions have grown and changed. All early settlements initially used primarily surface water; wells generally did not become commonplace until the late 1800s. With the exception of springs, the use of groundwater was unusual throughout most of the nineteenth century until pollution and disease in surface waters forced people to develop subsurface access (Kazmann 1972).

The Black Prairie physiographic province of Mississippi (Figure 11.1) is developed on an outcrop of Cretaceous chalk. An investigation into the water resources of this province in Mississippi, where it is commonly referred to as the Black Prairie, shows that geology exerts a stronger control on the presence of sources of water for human use than in other areas of the state not underlain by chalk. Figure 11.2 shows the relationship between the controlling geology and surface-water features on the Black Prairie. Perennial streams do not normally exist unless their sources are outside the province, and almost all streams that do originate on the Black Prairie are ephemeral and depend on rainfall only to provide runoff. The chalk's control over the course of the Tombigbee River on the eastern edge of the Black Prairie is also evident.

The development of water resources in the Black Prairie appears to fall into several discrete time categories, each associated with identifiable technological innovations that affected the constraints or opportunities for settlement in the region. Each progressively higher level of technology allowed greater opportunity for a less limiting arrangement of house sites and settlement distribution. The purpose of this study is to document the different levels of water-resource technology that were used to support humans as they occupied the Black Prairie from prehistoric times to the present.

CULTURAL BACKGROUND AND TECHNOLOGICAL STAGES

From the earliest historical times, one of the most frequently cited characteristics of the Black Belt physiographic province has been the general lack of surface water (Bienville 1736, as quoted in Rowland and Sanders 1927:304; Adair 1930 [originally published in 1775]; Hawkins 1799, quoted in Rostlund 1957:401; Nutt 1805, in Jennings 1947; Darby 1818; Roberts 1818, in Rankin 1974; Long 1824, in Jennings 1947; Nance 1832; Gavin 1843; Lyell 1849, quoted in Rankin 1974). During the summer months evaporation is rapid and the smaller-order streams tend to dry up completely (Nutt 1805, in Jennings 1947:41; Burgess et al. 1960; Nance 1832; Rankin 1974; Rostlund 1957; Wailes 1854), a factor that influenced Historic settlement (Tower 1961) and undoubtedly prehistoric settlement as well. The lack of water available

Fig. 11.1. The Black Belt of Mississippi and Alabama.

to the earliest Historic-period settlers in the Black Prairie region is indicated by a virtual lack of water-derived place names. Though absent
in the Black Prairie itself, names such as Clear Springs, Double Springs,
and Poplar Springs west of the region, and Bay Springs, Kolola Springs,
Morman Springs, and Military Springs east of the region, are suggestive of a greater relative availability of water for human use on the periphery of the Black Prairie. Locations of these and other water-related
sites are shown in Figure 11.3, an 1860 map of the area (Davis et al.
1983).

Technological advancements for water-supply development allowed
for expansion of populations over time. Four main stages of development are noted. First was the use of the few perennial streams and peripheral natural springs. This was followed by the construction of impoundments and dug cisterns as a second stage. The availability of
equipment to access greater depths than dug wells provided the third
major stage of development—hand-bored wells that developed groundwater beneath the chalk. The fourth stage identified is that of rotary-
(mechanical-) drilled wells. Drilling technology and changes in demands for water resulted in different types of bored and drilled wells.

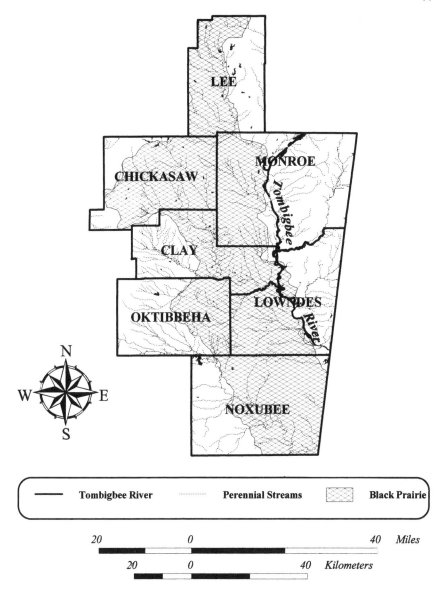

Fig. 11.2. Surface-water features of the Black Prairie region.

When the groundwater was first developed, it flowed under artesian conditions. Later, when artesian flow conditions no longer prevailed, various methods of lift were employed to bring the water to the surface. Each of the newer technologies increasingly removed constraints on settlement location, resulting in greater choice of home sites not limited by water sources.

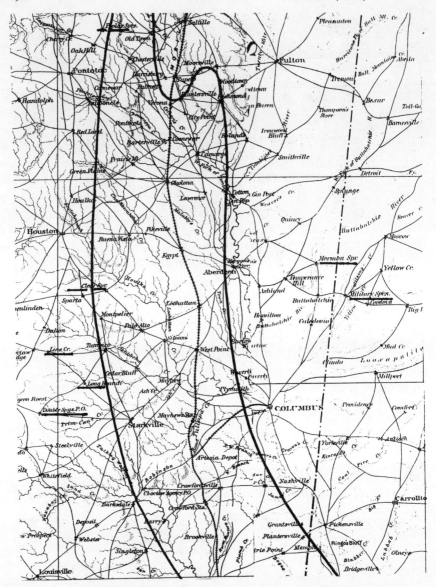

Fig. 11.3. 1860 map showing place-names mentioning springs on the periphery of the Black Prairie.

Springs and Collection Pits

Native Americans in the Black Prairie had very limited water sources, and their settlements were thus often geographically restricted. Longterm prehistoric settlement sites found in the Black Prairie occur primarily along perennial streams that originate outside of and flow

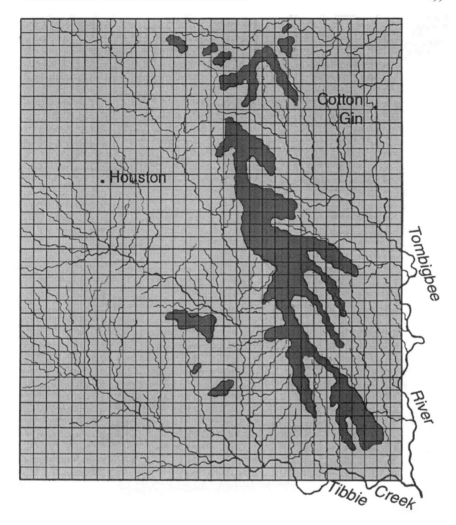

Fig. 11.4. Terrace deposits on the Black Prairie (after Harper 1857). Each square is one land section.

across the region, such as Tibbee Creek and the Noxubee River (Rafferty 2001, this volume). Short-term sites, on the other hand, tend to be located on upland ridges during the late prehistoric and early Historic periods (Atkinson 1979; Rafferty, this volume). A greater number of such sites are found on the periphery of the region where the geologic setting produces springs or seeps. Other sites are found near terrace deposits on top of the chalk, which may have provided water seeps. These terrace deposits are abandoned alluvium capable of holding groundwater. Figure 11.4 shows the location of terrace deposits on the Black Prairie.

At Chickasaw sites near present-day Tupelo, Mississippi, pits dug into the chalk at the surface apparently were used to collect rainwater. Sieur Claude Drouet de Richarville (1739), a captive of the Chickasaw in the 1730s, reported: "There are no rivers in any of the villages. They have only some springs where they dig wells that furnish them water." In 1771 Bernard Romans observed, "They [the Chickasaw] live nearly in the center of a very large and somewhat uneven savannah, of a diameter of above three miles; this savannah at all times has but a barren look, the earth is very Nitrous, and the savages get their water out of holes or wells dug near the town" (Romans 1999:124). The size of these excavations at the time may be judged by a further observation that the Chickasaw were "all good swimmers, notwithstanding they live so far from waters, but they learn their children to swim in clay holes, that are filled in wet seasons by rain" (ibid.:125). In 1805 Rush Nutt, also describing Chickasaw settlements in northern Mississippi, stated, "The country around Big Town for many miles affords good farming land, many prairies, no running water near the town, those who live in town use stagnant water, & are unhealthy" (Jennings 1947:43). He continued:

> The fortifications I have before spoken of with the sink holes near them seems [sic] now, from what I can learn, to have been wells for obtaining water; as we can see now in the towns where they sink holes in moist places, convenient to town. This water answered them to use in drinking, washing &c. they will soak their skins in it, wash themselves also the hogs &c. all take water out of the same hole. We should not wonder at these people being sick, when viewing their water. But the fact is that they were more healthy than now (Nutt 1805 [in Jennings 1947:54).

Jennings considered it "more likely these pits were merely borrow pits whence the earth . . . was removed [for use as daub—see Peacock and Reese, this volume]. Their use as water holes is considered to be incidental" (Jennings 1947:54).

Figure 11.5 shows an example of such a pit, which is estimated by its geometry to have held a maximum of approximately 300–400 gallons (114–151 decaliters). Based on the limited area from which runoff could be collected, such pits would have dried up during extended periods without rainfall or manual replenishment. This course of action may be suggested in a letter by Diron d'Artaguette concerning the Chickasaw, dated October 24, 1737, which states: "Water is the only thing that worries them because they have none in the drought, so they are obliged to go far to get any. The nearest place where there is any is

Fig. 11.5. Possible Chickasaw water-collection pit at Tupelo, Mississippi. Photo courtesy of John O'Hear.

an eighth of a league distant. The women go to fetch it in jugs that
they put in baskets" (Rowland et al. 1984:151).

Historic-period settlement in the Black Belt began in the early 1800s
and increased rapidly following land surveys in the early 1830s (Burgess et al. 1960; Jones and Patton 1966; Peacock 1992). When Europeans began to settle the area they also initially used springs along the
Black Prairie's edge as their water source, and apparently they also
made use of collection pits. Gavin's 1843 account of prairie in Noxubee
and Lowndes counties is informative:

There are wells called prarie [sic] or seep wells which sometimes
serve for drinking and culinary purposes but they are uncertain
and often fail. They are dug through the soil to the rock which
I think underlays all this prairie country, and the water soaks
through the soil and collects in basins of the rock. And if the well
happens to be dug in a large basin that holds a quantity of water
it lasts a longer time. If not it soon fails. This rock [the Cretaceous chalk] sometimes comes above the soil and sometimes de-
scends as low as 10 to 12 feet. (Gavin 1843:68)

Springs and seeps along the periphery of the Black Prairie today have
only limited flow. Some of these features no longer exist, such as the
springs recorded to have existed at Starkville, Mississippi (Carroll

1931:24). Flow rates found in springs and seeps today in the area near Starkville, along the western edge of the Black Prairie, are only about 1 gallon (0.38 decaliters) per minute, and these features cease to flow during drought periods. By comparison, springs only a short distance from the Black Prairie were a much more reliable water source. Such a spring just west of the Black Prairie region in Choctaw County has a modern flow rate of about 25 gallons (9.5 decaliters) per minute (Schmitz et al. 1999). Land-use change resulting from European settlement and cultural practices (see Peacock 1992) likely caused small springs and seeps to disappear. Since these features had such low flow, even small alterations in the local water balance (change in vegetative cover, increase in demand from both population increase and crop need) could have caused their disappearance.

CONSTRUCTED IMPOUNDMENTS AND DUG CISTERNS

Springs provided a finite water supply and geographically restricted settlement to the periphery of the region, so additional growth in population from European settlement required a different method of obtaining fresh water. The first new methods were constructed impoundments and dug cisterns. Simple levees were constructed to impound surface runoff, creating small pools. Peacock (1998b:19) reported such a levee in the North Central Hills some 48 km west of the Black Prairie. Although its precise age is unknown, it is certainly a Historic-period feature that must predate government acquisition of the land in the 1930s. During recent highway bypass construction, another levee, associated with an early–nineteenth-century house site, was recorded on the western edge of the Black Prairie in Oktibbeha County (Janet Rafferty, personal communication 2001). Figure 11.6 shows one such levee still in existence today in the Mississippi Black Prairie. Measurements made in this impoundment show a potential maximum holding capacity of approximately 9,000 gallons (3,409 decaliters). Even an impoundment of this size would dry up during extended periods of drought.

Additionally, cisterns were dug into the chalk to catch and hold water. As Gavin (1843:68) noted, "Some of the planters dig cisterns in the rock and catch rain water in the winter for drinking and culinary purposes in the summer and dry seasons." Figure 11.7 is a sketch showing construction details of these dug cisterns, called "bottle" cisterns. Note that the neck of the cistern from the surface down to the top of the chalk is lined with brick, allowing water to seep through the soil into the cistern. The remainder of the cistern is a hand-dug cavity in the chalk. The relatively impervious chalk would hold any water in the cavity. The geometry of one such cistern still in existence suggests a maximum holding capacity of about 4,000 gallons (1,515 decaliters).

Fig. 11.6. Levee for a constructed impoundment.

Based on the water level at the time it was visited in 2000, the cistern was holding about 1,000 gallons (379 decaliters).

HAND-BORED WELLS

Hand-bored wells were found in the region beginning in the 1840s (Gavin 1843) and were still being constructed as late as the turn of the century. Initially these wells were found at the edges of the Black Prairie or in terrace deposits on the Black Prairie itself. These terraces are associated only with the major streams of the region, such as Tibbee Creek and Noxubee River. Stephenson et al. (1928:357) reported that "deep wells were sunk to the water-bearing sands of the Eutaw formation in Noxubee County as early as 1852," even though Wailes, in 1854, reported no wells drilled through the chalk and no wells out on the Black Prairie. However, Wailes mapped more than 30 wells east of the Tombigbee River in Lowndes County (Wailes 1854). Three years later, Harper (1857) reported artesian wells bored through the chalk of up to 300 feet (91 m) in depth at some locations, and borings of up to 600 feet (183 m) in depth at other locations that did not penetrate the chalk. He stated that "the country where the limestone group crops out is generally not well-watered; and in summer there is a want of water, which is, in many places, supplied by artesian wells; but such wells can only be bored, with perfect success, in Lowndes County and a Part of Oktibbeha County; only there the Cretaceous rocks are not

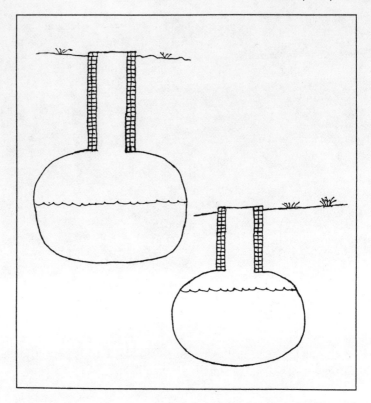

Fig. 11.7. Examples of Black Prairie "bottle cisterns." (From Atkinson 1992; used by permission of the National Park Service, Southeastern Archeological Center.)

too thick, and the water has fall enough to rise above the surface" (Harper 1857:118).

Hilgard (1860:76) reported "borings of 700' to 1000' being no uncommon occurrence in S. Chickasaw. E. Oktibbeha, Noxubee, and N.E. Kemper [counties]." He further noted "the vast importance which the boring of deep, and partly artesian, wells has acquired in this region. Where these have not been obtained, cisterns are in general use" (Hilgard 1860:81). Figure 11.8 depicts equipment and techniques for hand-boring wells through the chalk on the Black Prairie and elsewhere. It is notable that deep, bored wells were being developed in this region nearly 100 years earlier than outside the Black Prairie (Schmitz et al. 1999). Figure 11.9 shows the distribution of numerous deep artesian wells on the Black Prairie, which developed water resources from beneath the chalk.

These hand-bored wells initially exhibited flowing artesian conditions. However, with continued development of the resource, artesian

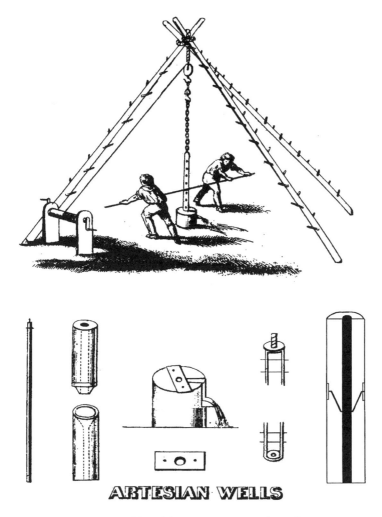

Fig. 11.8. Depiction of hand-boring process and implements (from Wailes 1854).

pressure was not always sufficient to produce flowing wells. Initially this was because of increasing depths of wells; later it was because increased use resulted in lower artesian pressure in the aquifer. Various methods of lift then had to be employed to bring the water to the surface from beneath the chalk. Hand pumps were first used, followed by mechanical methods such as windmills and air- and gas-lift techniques (Stephenson et al. 1928). Figure 11.10 shows one of the hand pumps actually used on the Black Prairie. Logan (1903:11) commented that "the cost of furnishing a pasture with well, pump, and windmill can not greatly exceed the cost of building and keeping in repair the ponds

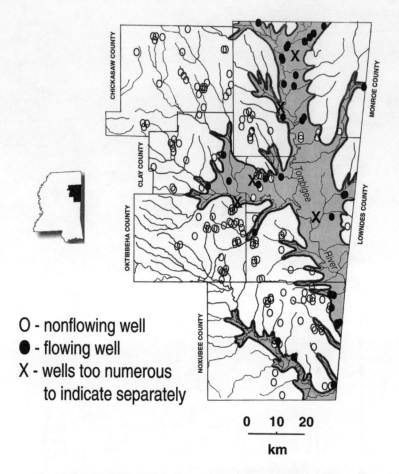

Fig. 11.9. Distribution of deep artesian wells on the Black Prairie in 1928. Shaded area represents the Eutaw and Tuscaloosa formations (after Stephenson et al. 1928).

or pools necessary to supply the required water." Figure 11.11 shows a windmill providing lift for a well on the Black Prairie. Stephenson et al. (1928) reported windmills in use on the Black Prairie with wells completed in 1901 and 1903, but undependable winds precluded the widespread use of windmills in this region. At about this time, around the turn of the century, mechanical rotary drilling methods came into use, leading to the fourth and final stage of technology for obtaining water.

ROTARY-DRILLED WELLS

The final technological advancement, which occurred early in the 1900s, allowed for easier and more cost-effective access to water by

Fig. 11.10. Hand pump
used on the Black Prairie.

drilling through the chalk with a mechanized rotary system. Whereas
earlier and more costly bored wells were constructed primarily in
municipalities and on large plantations, rotary-drilled wells were being constructed at private residences as early as the 1920s (Mike Echols, Echols Drilling, Starkville, Mississippi, personal communication
2000). Figure 11.12 shows a mobile, rotary-drilling system such as was
in use from the 1940s. The number of wells being drilled for private
residences increased particularly after World War II, proliferating in the
late 1950s and into the 1960s. These wells for the first time used electricity to power a rod-type, aboveground pump (Figure 11.13). Because
of this new technology, essentially any location on the Black Prairie
could now have its own water source as long as electricity was available. Initial high costs and the inconvenience of continuously maintaining private wells at residences led to early development of water
associations on the Black Prairie.

Rural water associations were created in an attempt to provide almost everyone with dependable, good-quality water via a water line.
Individual well maintenance and water treatment were no longer necessary. Among the first water associations in the region was what is
today known as Herman Echols Memorial Water Association, the first

Fig. 11.11. Windmill at
West Point, Mississippi,
manufactured in the late
1850s.

Fig. 11.12. Rotary
drilling rig
mounted on a
1940s Studebaker
truck.

Fig. 11.13. Electrically powered, aboveground, rod-type pump.

Fig. 11.14. Water association storage tank.

well for which was drilled in 1959 (Figure 11.14). Most water associations on the Black Prairie were in place by the late 1970s, nearly 20 years before such development occurred in surrounding areas, where water was more readily available to support the expansion of settlement (Schmitz et al. 1999). These associations are the primary source for nearly all water used in the region today, replacing all other sources because of their convenience, dependability, and capacity for delivering healthful water. The associations' water lines cover nearly all parts of the Black Prairie, allowing unlimited expansion of house sites and settlement distribution.

CONCLUSIONS

It is apparent that the unique geologic setting of the Black Prairie has been a controlling influence on settlement in the region because of its effects on water availability. Long-term prehistoric settlements on the Black Prairie were confined to major streams. Smaller, short-term sites may well have been located so as to take advantage of seeps and springs. The early–Historic-period Chickasaw dug pits in the northern portions of the region, and these served primarily or incidentally as water-collection features. Early European settlements (1830s) made use of constructed impoundments and cisterns dug into the chalk for water sources. The first bored wells (1840s) were in the terraces and along the periphery of the Black Prairie; the first bored wells actually penetrating the chalk were reported in the 1850s. Mechanized-lift methods and rotary-drilling techniques were in use by the turn of the century. Cisterns and impoundments, while still in common use in areas adjacent to the Black Prairie, were in limited use on the Black Prairie by the 1920s, when wells drilled through the chalk had become common. As electricity became more readily available, private wells drilled through the chalk proliferated in the 1950s and 1960s, increasing settlement opportunities. Water associations began on the Black Prairie as early as 1959 and were supplying essentially all water needed for human use by the late 1970s, making a cost-effective and dependable water supply available and allowing settlement almost anywhere on the Black Prairie.

The influence of geology and hydrology on culture makes the Black Prairie distinct from surrounding physiographic zones. Prehistoric settlement patterns on the prairie are radically different from those in other physiographic provinces, such as the North Central Hills of Mississippi (Rafferty 2001, this volume; Peacock 1997). Deep bored wells were constructed on the Black Prairie about 100 years earlier than in surrounding areas; and water associations began operating to supply water on the Black Prairie about 20 years earlier than in other parts of

Mississippi. With the increased pressure on water supplies, this vital resource may again become a limiting factor for future settlement on the Black Prairie.

It is evident that the influence of environment on culture, and vice versa, cannot be understood without resort to cross-disciplinary study. Geology, hydrology, archaeology, and history all contribute to a much fuller understanding of changing human settlement patterns in the Black Prairie than would be achievable by any one of those disciplines alone. The results may then feed back into each contributing specialty area, providing impetus for further study and suggesting avenues of research that may not have been considered previously (e.g., Rafferty, this volume). Our models can be still further refined by the incorporation of other types of data, as reported in this volume. It would be fruitful to conduct similar studies on blackland prairie settings in other states and compare the results with our findings from the Mississippi Black Prairie, to see if similar patterns of human settlement emerged in relation to similar environmental conditions.

Acknowledgments. We would like to thank Cliff Jenkins for providing reference material and Pat Galloway for her translation of the de Richarville narrative.

12 Osage Orange Bows, Indian Horses, and the Blackland Prairie of Northeastern Texas

FRANK F. SCHAMBACH

When a biologist tries to answer a question about a unique occurrence such as "Why are there no hummingbirds in the Old World?" or "Where did *Homo sapiens* originate?" he cannot rely on universal laws. The biologist has to study all the known facts relating to a particular problem, infer all sorts of consequences from the reconstructed constellations of factors, and then attempt to construct a scenario that would explain the observed facts of this particular case. In other words, he constructs a historical narrative. . . . It is, of course, never possible to prove categorically, that a historical narrative is "true." . . . Yet every narrative is open to falsification and can be tested again and again.

Ernst Mayr 1998

THE MISSISSIPPIAN WORLD

By about 1,100 years ago most of the Indian tribes of southeastern North America were interrelated through trade, diplomacy, warfare, and perhaps religious proselytizing (Brown 1975:29; Galloway 1992: 179; Griffin 1985:62; Williams 1981:11). Archaeologists refer to such networks of social and economic relationships as *interaction spheres*. This one is called the Mississippian interaction sphere because the most important tribes participating in it seem to have been those living in or near the Mississippi Valley, from northeastern Arkansas north to Illinois. The territory it subsumed (Figure 12.1) is sometimes called the Mississippian world (Payne and Scarry 1998:Figure 2.1). The most important places in that world are represented by the spectacular ar-

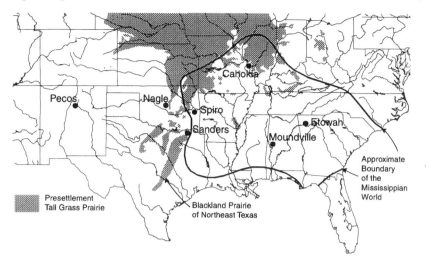

Fig. 12.1. The Mississippian world (after Payne and Scarry 1998, Figure 2.1).

chaeological sites called Cahokia (Fowler 1997; Milner 1998), Etowah (Larson 1971; Moorehead 1932), Moundville (Knight and Steponaitis 1998; Welch 1991), and Spiro (Brown 1996). The people whose world this was are generally referred to as the Mississippians (Griffin 1985; Muller 1997; Peregrine 1992; Smith 1990; Williams 1981), although their cultures varied appreciably from region to region and they probably spoke many different languages. This is not unlike referring to the culturally and linguistically diverse peoples of Europe as Europeans, and to their collective homeland as Europe, or the European world. It would not be amiss to refer to the complex network of social and economic relationships between these countries as the European interaction sphere. Nor would it be amiss to think of Cahokia, Etowah, Moundville, and Spiro as the "central places" in the Mississippian world, just as London, Paris, Berlin, and Rome have long been central places in the European world.

The Mississippians were hoe-horticulturalists who tilled the floodplains of all the major river systems of the Southeast. They grew corn, squashes, and, eventually, beans, all originally domesticated in Mexico. They also grew sunflowers, at least one species of squash, and various other native eastern North American plants that had all been domesticated locally by their ancestors (Fritz 1990; Smith 1992). Innovative though it certainly was in terms of food plants, the Mississippian domestic economy was critically flawed by the absence of domesticated animals that could supply significant quantities of animal protein, fat, and hides suitable for clothing and footwear. The lack of a renewable and expandable source of animal hides, or of wool, from domestic animals was exacerbated by the absence of any plant, such as cotton, that could supply fine fiber for clothing. Thus, as their population increased, like most human populations that achieve a reliable cereal-based diet (Hrdy 1999:187, 196), the Mississippians must have found themselves outstripping the capacity of local wild animals to supply skins for clothing and footwear (Gramly 1977), and probably animal protein and fat as well. Bioanthropological evidence, particularly evidence of severe iron deficiency anemia and high infection rates, suggests that the Mississippians of the central Mississippi Valley were dangerously overdependent on corn, a grain notoriously deficient in lysine, iron, zinc, and niacin (Rose et al. 1991:21). So the Mississippian world had some serious built-in shortages (Schambach 1993a:200). Perhaps more than most, the Mississippians were a people in thrall to Liebig's "law of the minimum" (West 1998:91).

Seeking to cope with these shortages, the Mississippians—like the Pueblo peoples of the Southwest, who had similar problems (Baugh 1991; Riley 1978; Riley 1987; Speth 1991; Spielmann 1991; Spielmann et al. 1990)—turned to the bison herds of the southern Plains, a biomass probably capable of supporting up to 60,000 people on a sustained basis at that time (Flores 1991:480). The evidence that they did so could hardly be better. The major route between their largest population centers in the central Mississippi Valley and the food and fiber resources represented by the bison was the Arkansas Valley (Brown 1975:4). Lying athwart this route was the territory of the westernmost population of Mississippians, a people archaeologists call the Spiroans (Phillips and Brown 1978:9-10). The Spiroans were recognized by one of the first archaeologists to excavate in their territory as "highly efficient aboriginal traders" (Finklestein 1940:15) and so they are regarded still (Brown 1975:26, 1983:135; Phillips and Brown 1978:22; Rogers 1996: 64; Wyckoff 1980:516).

The most important place in their territory, and clearly one of the four most important places in the Mississippian world as well, was a cluster of smallish burial mounds in eastern Oklahoma known to us as the Spiro site because it is near an old railroad town of that name (Figure 12.1). This site occupies a conspicuous bottleneck in the Arkansas Valley a short distance west of the Arkansas–Oklahoma state line. There—with the rugged country of the Ozark Highlands immediately to the north and the Ouachita Mountains nearby to the south— it was perfectly, and probably not accidentally, placed to serve as a gateway community (Brown 1975:4, 1983:145; Drooker 1997:528; Hirth 1978:197; Kelly 1991:442; Riley 1975:630; Tiffany 1991:443) between the Mississippian world and the Plains. Anyone traveling east or west

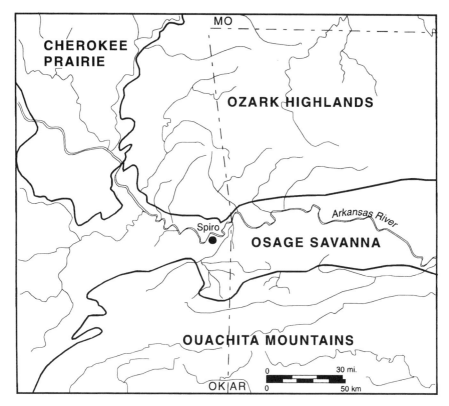

Fig. 12.2. The gateway location of the Spiro site.

via the Arkansas Valley or the Arkansas River would have had to pass close by Spiro (Figure 12.2).

There is good archaeological and historical evidence that bison products (hides, and probably dried meat and tallow as well) were moving from west to east through the Spiroan gateway between ca. A.D. 900 and A.D. 1541 (Schambach 1993a:196–200, 1999c:180–182). Even better —extraordinary, in fact—is the evidence that the Spiroans were well compensated for moving these products and, probably, other goods. They managed to accumulate and bury about three times as much wealth in "prestige goods," as archaeologists call them (Brown et al. 1990:255), as has been found in *all* other Mississippian sites excavated thus far (Muller 1987:18; Peterson 1989:115). Most were from one fabulously rich hoard in the famous Craig Mound at the Spiro site (Brown 1996). Cahokia, Moundville, and Etowah are recognized as having been important places in the Mississippian world on the basis of their great size and monumental earthworks. Spiro, a relatively small site with earthworks of modest dimensions, is recognized as such on the basis

of its wealth. It has been called, with pardonable hyperbole, "an Oklahoma burial mound as rich in artifacts as King Tut's tomb" (Brain
1988:16).

This wealth consisted of goods obtained, literally, from across the
continent. Shell beads of *Olivella biplicata,* a Pacific coast species (Dr.
Laura Kozuch, personal communication, April 3, 2000) and cotton textiles from Arizona or New Mexico (Brown 1983:149) were found side
by side with drinking cups made of large whelk shells, probably from
the Florida Gulf Coast, tools and ornaments of copper obtained from
the southern Appalachians, and pottery from the Tennessee Valley.
Mostly, though, this wealth consisted of goods from the Mississippian
world to the east of Spiro. There were only a few shell beads from Pacific waters but an "enormous" quantity (probably well over a thousand pounds—Brown 1975:14–15) of beads fashioned from Gulf Coast
shell. There were 3,000 to 4,000 (Brown 1975:29) large whelk shell
cups, mostly of the genus *Busycon,* most of them probably obtained
somewhere along the Florida Gulf Coast (Brain 1988:25; Brown 1983:
148), possibly as far south as Sanibel Island. Most had been modified
to serve as drinking cups for the consumption of the ritual drink of
the Mississippians, the so-called black drink, made of leaves of the
yaupon holly (*Ilex vomitoria Ait.*) (Hudson 1976:226–229, 1979). This
shellwork may have been done at workshops near the Gulf Coast. Or,
possibly, it was done at workshops farther north, in the area between
central Tennessee and southern Illinois where, more certainly, "well
over one thousand" (Brown 1975:29) cups were painstakingly and skill-
fully engraved with figures and symbols from Mississippian life and
religion. Shells of *Busycon* and other marine species were also cut into
large gorgets and then engraved with figures and symbols similar to
those on the cups. Possibly such work was done at sites in the vicinity
of the confluence between the Tennessee, Ohio, and Mississippi Rivers
(Muller 1984:669). Scores of these gorgets made their way to Spiro
(Brown 1996:593–618), in many cases possibly after long use by their
original owners elsewhere. Taken together, the engraved shell cups and
gorgets from Spiro comprise ["t]he largest find of finished engraved
shell" from eastern North America (Muller 1987:18) and "the largest single corpus of figural art ever found in the Southeast" (Brain
1988:21). The published descriptions and illustrations of this material
fill six folio volumes (Phillips and Brown 1978).

Besides the shell there were hundreds of objects made of native
copper, a material apparently as valuable in the Mississippian world
as gold is in ours. There were at least 268 thin sheets of this metal
embossed with figures and motifs similar to those on the shell cups
and gorgets. There were also copper axe heads, copper beads, and copper ornaments of many kinds (Brown 1975:14–15, 1996:Figures 2-107

through 2-112). There was also galena, valued by the Spiroans to the extent that more than 227 kg (500 pounds) of it were carried to Spiro, mostly from deposits in southeast Missouri (Walthall 1981:17). There were "piles of still brilliantly colored textiles" (Williams 1981:11), probably in far greater quantities than the surviving fragments would indicate. These textiles were probably far more costly than the casual observer would imagine, in terms of both the labor needed to make them (Muller 1997:352) and the labor for transporting them from distant places of manufacture. Judging from the raw materials used, which include cotton fiber and bison hair, those places ranged from the Southeast to the Southwest (Brown 1983:149–150; King and Gardner 1981; Kuttruff 1993). There were baskets, most of split cane commonly seen in the Southeast, but some of coiled fibers, a southwestern style of manufacture. There was pottery, some locally made, but much of it imported from the Red River valley to the south and from the Mississippi drainage to the east. There were bowls carved of stone, and of wood, and carved cedar masks. There were polished stone axes, chipped stone daggers and swords, and many hundreds of arrow points (Brown 1996).

Besides these bulk goods, exquisite, one-of-a-kind art objects were found, such as the so-called "Big Boy" statuette/pipe (Brown 1996: Figure 2-99)—the kneeling figure of a Mississippian priest, it would seem—made of Missouri flint clay from the St. Louis region and probably carved at Cahokia during the twelfth century (Emerson and Hughes 2000:90). This sculpture could have been one of the most valuable preciosities in the Mississippian world, the equivalent of the most valuable of the famous copper shields of Northwest Coast culture. Nor was it alone; there were other statuettes of comparable quality and workmanship, some of flint clay, others of clay, still others of wood (Brown 1996:513–526, 531–532).

THE SPIROANS AND THE PLAINS

Getting this wealth was no simple or easy matter. Bison products and other commodities did not flow southward and eastward from the southern Plains to Spiro of their own accord. Nor did the wealth of the Mississippians move westward to Spiro on its own. Someone had to carry or canoe these goods both east and west over hundreds of kilometers. Some scholars (Brain and Phillips 1996:399–400; Flores 1991; Kelly 1991:78; Riley 1971:303–304, 1978:54; Spielmann 1983:269; Wedel 1982; Wilcox 1991:154) share (more or less) my opinion that the goods were transported mainly by parties of specialized long-distance traders similar to those observed by members of the Coronado expedition in the Southwest in 1540 (Riley 1978:54) and, in the summer of 1541, by members of the expedition of Hernando de Soto in what they called the "province" of Capaha located in the Mississippi Valley in northeastern Arkansas (Clayton et al. 1993:407; Varner and Varner 1951:449).

The traders seen by Coronado were, according to Riley (1978:54), a party of 20 men from Pecos pueblo whom the Spaniards encountered at the old Zuni pueblo of Hawikuh about 170 miles (274 km) southwest of Pecos. This party, which Riley suggests was "more or less typical" (1978:54) for that time and place, seems to have had a leader, an important man in the opinion of the Spaniards. Apparently the party also included an interpreter. These men had brought "what were likely to have been standard trade items from the Pecos area—dressed [bison] skins, shields [of bison hide], and head pieces [made from bison heads]—and they received various things including pearl beads, glassware, and the small 'jingle' bells that were much used as trade goods by various European parties in this period" (Riley 1978:54).

The party described by members of the de Soto expedition consisted of "eight Indians in the hands of the Spaniards who had been captured the day they entered that Pueblo [Capaha], and were not natives of it, but strangers and merchants who had traversed many provinces with their goods; among other things, they were accustomed to bring salt to sell" (Clayton et al. 1993:407). The place where the Spaniards caught them, the "Pueblo" of Capaha or Pacaha, was somewhere within the Nodena-phase territory of northeastern Arkansas (Fisher-Carroll 1997:153; Hudson 1997:295). But where the Indians were from we are not told. Nor, apart from salt, do we know what they traded. However, various chroniclers of the de Soto expedition reported that the Spaniards saw, in the contiguous northeastern Arkansas "provinces" of Pacaha, Casqui, and Coligua, an array of bison products strikingly similar to those the Pecos traders had carried from Pecos, the southwestern gateway to the Plains (Riley 1978:54), to Hawikuh. Rangel noted that there were "many heads of very fierce bulls" over the door of the house of the "Lord" of Casqui (Quinn 1979:180). Biedma reported a "large quantity of dressed cows [hides] and other already cured" at Coligua (Quinn 1979:184), where Elvas also saw "two cowhides" (Quinn 1979:133). Especially telling are the many "shields made of raw cowhide" that Elvas mentioned seeing in a town near Pacaha (Quinn 1979:130). Certainly all of these goods were imported. The Spaniards saw no bison anywhere in Arkansas, nor is there ecological reason to believe they should have seen any. The state contains no good bison habitat and no substantial archaeological evidence exists to suggest that bison were ever hunted there in prehistoric times (Neuman 1983). The importers of these bison products were probably traders like those captured by the Spaniards at Pacaha, and they were probably from Spiro, the southeastern gateway to the southern Plains, nearly 300 miles (483 km) west of Pacaha.

Several months later, "on or about" September 30, 1541 (Hudson 1997:320), the Spaniards finally made their way to that gateway, a "province" they called Tula. Modern scholarship on the de Soto route places Tula in the Fort Smith/Spiro area (Early 1993:74–75; Hudson 1993:146–147, 1997:Map 7). There they saw bison products in quantities sufficient to suggest that they had come upon a distribution center. Garcilaso reported that in the town of Tula "our men found serving as bed covers a great number of cowhides which had been softened and dressed without removing the hair; and there were in addition many others waiting to be dressed. Moreover there was beef" (Varner and Varner 1951:457). Elvas stated that after the Spaniards fought their way into Tula, despite determined and skillful resistance, and after de Soto had sent to the Tulan cacique six captured Tulans "with their right hands and their noses cut off," the Tulans began to come to the Spaniards bearing gifts of cowhides: "After three days came an Indian whom the cacique sent laden with cowhides." The next day, "three Indians came laden with cowhides, and three days after that twenty Indians came." Presumably, they too brought cowhides. Then the cacique himself came, bringing "many cowhides as a gift, which were useful because it was a cold land" (Quinn 1979:135).

The Spaniards realized that the hides and "beef" were imported. Garcilaso wrote that "no cows were to be seen in the fields, and it could never be learned from whence the hides had been brought" (Varner and Varner 1951:457). Elvas recorded that "[n]earby to the north there were many cattle" although the "Christians did not see them or enter their land, for the land was poorly settled where they were and had little corn" (Quinn 1979:135). That land was the southern Plains to the west and northwest of Spiro. But to have seen cattle in any numbers to speak of, the Spaniards would have had to travel 150 to 180 miles (240 to 290 km) northwest or west along the Arkansas or Canadian river systems to the eastern edge of the shortgrass or bluestem and bluestem-gramma prairie (Figure 12.3). That would have put them on the eastern edge of the territory where, in Historic times at least, bison first appeared en masse as one traveled west (Schambach 1995:19–20 n.31, 2000b:26; Shaw and Lee 1997; Voget 1974:250, 252). The bison were concentrated thus because only the shortgrasses, not the tallgrasses that dominate the eastern prairie system, provide adequate nutrition for bison year-round (Isenberg 2000:22; Johnson 1951:330; Shaw and Lee 1997:169–170).

One might assume that the nomadic hunters who were exploiting these herds brought the hides, meat, and other bison products to the settled, horticultural Mississippians at Spiro. Undoubtedly that was the prevailing pattern in relationships between Plains bison hunters and village farmers along the eastern edge of the Plains during the Historic period (Blakeslee 1975; Ewers 1954). However, archaeological,

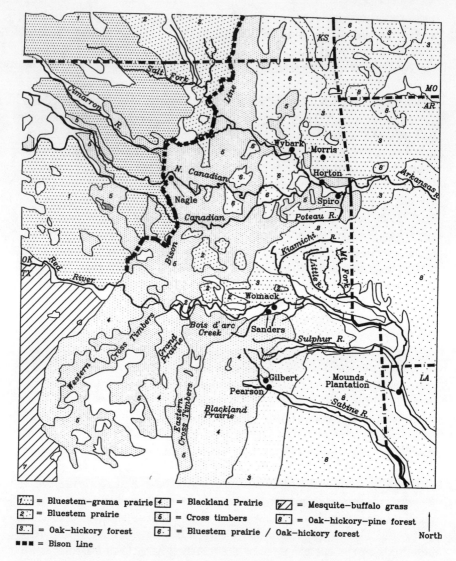

Fig. 12.3. Biogeography of the Spiro, Nagle, and Sanders sites.

bioanthropological, and biogeographical evidence indicates that things were different in prehistoric times. In those pre-horse days, Plains hunters seem to have stayed close to their hunting grounds; the Spiroans, in contrast, traveled far into the southern Plains to obtain bison products from them. The traders of Pecos probably did the same in the mid-sixteenth century. The Jumanos of the early contact period in the Southwest and southern Plains (Anderson 1999:5; Baugh 1998:150–152; Griffith 1954:120–122; Hickerson 1994) clearly did so. Further, we have evidence that the Spiroans dealt with the Plains hunters and other trading partners in a way unique to them and heretofore unsuspected of North American Indians before European contact. They maintained a network of more or less permanent entrepôts, or trading posts, at locations convenient to concentrations of bison and bison hunters, as well as to concentrations of other important resources. I have identified two of these Spiroan entrepôts so far: the Nagle site in central Oklahoma and the Sanders site in northeastern Texas. I expect that others will be identified, particularly at key locations along the eastern edge of the shortgrass prairie west of Spiro (Schambach 1993a:203–208, 1993b, 2000b:27).

The Nagle site is known from the hastily salvaged contents of at least 20 human graves accidentally uncovered during construction of a pipeline along the North Canadian River in central Oklahoma (Schaeffer 1954). The site is practically on the border between the tallgrass and shortgrass prairie systems, a location that—I hypothesize—was its raison d'etre (Figure 12.3). Archaeologists have long suspected, on the evidence of the Nagle-site grave goods alone, that the people buried there were closely connected to Spiro, more than 170 miles (274 km) to the east, and to the greater Mississippian world as well. The inventory of offerings includes pottery, "marine conch shell" beads, copper-covered sandstone "ear spools," and locally exotic arrow points that must have come from Spiro or locations as far east as Cahokia (Griffin 1961:30; Schaeffer 1954:93–97).

This apparent Spiroan connection has been confirmed by several lines of recently developed bioanthropological evidence indicating that many, if not all, of the 20 people buried at Nagle were not only foreigners to the southern Plains but foreigners *from Spiro*. For one thing, these people represent a population with "a totally different series of health problems" from those of the local Plains people. Osteological data reveal "a severe mortality profile associated with pronounced evidence of bone disease," one of which was "syphilis-like" (Owsley and Jantz 1989:140). The closest population with a similar array of health problems was that of the Arkansas Valley in the Spiro locality. There, an identical "syphilis-like" disease (Brues 1957:103), which resembles endemic syphilis in its osteological effects, was "of an epidemic nature" (Brues 1958:31, 1959:67–68). Indeed, the Spiro area was a hotbed of infection during the Mississippian period, most likely because it was a center for long-distance trade that linked, for the first time, populations from coast to coast in North America (Dobyns 1992).

Second, scurvy—always a danger to travelers trying to live on unfamiliar diets in strange lands—was probably one of the disorders that afflicted the people buried at the Nagle site, according to Alice Brues (1957:103–104). It was brought on, she thought, not by starvation, but by some "apparently minor" dietary error by people who probably thought they were eating adequately on a diet of meat, corn, and beans. Yet they might have made the mistake of "eating liver cooked rather than raw" or of "eliminating squash from the roster of cultivated plants" they consumed. One can imagine an immigrant population of Spiroan traders making precisely those errors.

Third, almost conclusive osteological evidence that the four adult males represented by crania and, in one case, cranial fragments, from Nagle were Spiroans has long been available (Brues 1957:104–106) but its significance did not become apparent until quite recently (Schambach 1997:31–32, 2000b:25–26). All of these men had markedly deformed crania, one more indication that they were strangers to the area. Cranial deformation, common though it was in the Southeast during the Mississippian period, was not practiced by the indigenous people of central Oklahoma at the time that the Nagle site was in use (Bell 1984:309). Nor was it practiced by any other known population of the southern, central, or northern Plains (Bell 1984:309, 323; Brooks 1989:78; Brues 1962:75; Owsley 1989:130–133, 137; Owsley and Bruwelheide 1996:201–202; Stewart 1941:349). Moreover, the skulls of the adult males from Nagle exhibit a particular style of cranial deformation, the so-called circular or annular style (Derrick and Wilson 1997; Stewart 1941) that was exceedingly rare in the Southeast, where the very different "tabular or fronto-occipital" style prevailed. The center of distribution for the annular style was the Spiro locality in the Arkansas Valley, where the style is strongly represented by numerous crania from the Horton, Morris, and Spiro sites (Brown 1984; Brues 1958, 1959). The only site besides Nagle where it is significantly represented outside the Spiro locality during the Mississippian period is another Spiroan entrepôt, the Sanders site, discussed below. Aside from this, the only other place in North America where the annular style was used was one small area of the Northwest Coast (Rogers 1975:Figure 4).

As luck would have it, Spaniards of the de Soto expedition observed the annular form of cranial deformation among the Tulans of the Spiro locality in the fall of 1541, and they saw how it was accomplished. According to Garcilaso:

> The people in this province of Tula differ from all those our Spaniards encountered previously; for, as we have said, the others are fine and handsome, whereas these, both male and female, have loathsome countenances. Even though naturally well featured, they render themselves hideous with devices wrought upon their persons. Their heads are incredibly long and taper off towards the top having been made this way by artifice; from the moment they

are born their heads are bound and left thus until they are from nine to ten years of age (Varner and Varner 1951:457–458).

This passage rings true in all important respects, despite Garcilaso's poor reputation as a historian. It is a good description of annular deformation, which makes the head very long, seen from the front or side, and does indeed make it seem to "taper off towards the top," when viewed from the front. Tabular deformation also makes the head look long from the front or side. But because pressure is applied from the front and back only, it causes the head to bulge above the ears so that, viewed from the front, the person looks hyperbrachycephalic— broadheaded or "flat headed" (Lewis 1995:Figure 11.7) as opposed to "narrow headed." Garcilaso's description of how the Tulans produced annular deformation is ethnographically accurate (Comas 1960:392– 395; Derrick and Wilson 1997:140). So is his report that the people of Tula differed "from all those our Spaniards had encountered previously," provided cranial deformation was one of the differences he (or, rather, his informants) had in mind, as seems to be the case. The archaeological and ethnographic data are clear on the point that Tula would have been the first and only place along their route through the Southeast (Hudson 1997:Maps 5–8) where the Spaniards could have encountered a population of people practicing and exhibiting annular cranial deformation.

Apparently the Tulans, or rather their Spiroan forebears, had hit upon a solution to the problem of how to conduct long-distance trade throughout the Southeast, the southern Plains, and perhaps even the Southwest, a vast area inhabited by tribal (Sahlins 1968) peoples. Thus it was an area without overarching political authority, where a stranger trying to move from the territory of one tribe to another "becomes trespasser no matter what his purpose may be" and "the security of the trader becomes the paramount rule of the game" (Ford 1972:32). So their "incredibly long," "tapered," or narrow-looking heads could have served to identify the Tulans/Spiroans as traders in a world in which, as the old English proverb informs us, "The stranger, if he be not a trader, is an enemy" (Chatwin 1987:218). In any case, this uniquely Spiroan custom makes it easy to identify the remains of Spiroans who died far from home at their entrepôts, or along the trails to them.

THE SPIROANS AND THE BLACKLAND PRAIRIE OF NORTHEASTERN TEXAS

Hence the Sanders site (Jackson et al. 2000; Krieger 1946), located 150 miles (241 km) southwest of Spiro on the northeastern tip of the Blackland Prairie physiographic subprovince, in the Red River valley of northeastern Texas (Figures 12.1 and 12.3), is easily identified as a Spiroan entrepôt, and a major one at that (Schambach 1993a, 1995, 1999a, 2000a, 2000b). Except for scurvy (which would not have been a problem for Spiroans wintering on the edge of the Eastern Woodlands in an environment practically identical to that of Spiro itself), the people buried there exhibit the same locally distinctive osteological, epidemiological, and cultural characteristics as do the people buried at the Nagle site. If anything, the differences between them and the locals, and the evidences of their biological and cultural ties with Spiro and points farther east, are more pronounced.

Most notably, the crania of 26 of the 27 adults buried in the 21 shallow graves at Sanders, males and females alike, exhibit the annular deformation characteristic of the Spiroans. Thus these people would have stood out among the Caddo, the local people of the Red River valley, who characteristically practiced fronto-occipital deformation (Derrick and Wilson 1997), as an enclave of "narrow-headed" people amongst a population of "flat-headed" people. Further, their skeletons, exceptionally well preserved by the highly calcareous soils of the Blackland Prairie, provide a key piece of osteological evidence pertaining to the lives of the Spiroans that is not preserved in the osteological remains from the more acidic soils of the Nagle site and the sites in the Spiro locality. The skeletons evince, according to Diane Wilson, an unusually high frequency of degenerative joint disease of a type indicating that the Spiroans regularly carried heavy loads on their backs or heads and did "a great deal of traveling" on foot (Wilson 1993:11). Of course, one might expect to see such disease in the skeletons of people who spent much of their lives carrying goods over the 150-mile-long (241-km) overland route between Spiro and Sanders. However, Wilson's diagnosis was made before the announcement and publication of my hypothesis that Sanders was a Spiroan entrepôt. Therefore Wilson did not simply find what she expected to find in a group of skeletons thought to be those of long-distance overland traders. Rather she perceived an unusual and puzzling characteristic in a cemetery population generally considered representative of a local population of Red River Caddos adapted to the ecotone between the Eastern Woodlands and the Plains (Bruseth et al. 1995; Krieger 1946:172–218). Finally, the skeletons from Sanders, much like those from Nagle, are indicative of a population with an infection rate considered "dramatically" high compared with that of the local population and attributable to the same suite of diseases, including a syphilis-like disease that afflicted the Nagle- and Spiro-area populations (Burnett 1990:393–398; Schambach 1993a:204–205).

The grave goods from Sanders are far more abundant, and provide much stronger evidence of a Spiroan connection, than those from Nagle.

Part of the reason, of course, is that most of the graves at Nagle were destroyed by machinery before archaeologists investigated the site, whereas those at Sanders were professionally excavated. But that is probably not the whole of the matter. The graves at Sanders contained one of the two richest hoards of Mississippian prestige goods yet found west of the Mississippi, a hoard second only to that found at Spiro itself. Counting specimens that the landowner plowed out of these and, probably, additional graves during the 10 years the site was under cultivation before its excavation in 1931, there were four whelk-shell cups, one engraved and three plain; 21 whelk-shell gorgets, some decorated and some plain, the latter linking Sanders stylistically to Spiro (Brown 1983:150) and probably the work of artisans in northeastern Arkansas, eastern Missouri, and Illinois (Brain and Phillips 1996:16, 17, 29, 60); six whelk-shell pendants; six whelk-shell discs; about 5,000 whelk-shell beads; 230 beads of *Olivella* shells; and 25 pearl beads. One grave yielded a spectacularly large 8-gallon (30-liter), shell-tempered Bell Plain olla with an appliqué "carrying cord" decoration identifying it as a Walls-phase specimen imported from northwestern Mississippi or northeastern Arkansas (Griffin 1952:236, Figure 27i; Krieger 1946:Figure 17). From another grave came a Nashville Negative Painted composite bottle consisting of a strap-handled bowl combined with the shoulders and neck of a bottle (Jackson et al. 2000:81). It probably originated somewhere in northeastern Arkansas or possibly east of the Mississippi in central Tennessee. A spatulate celt or "spud" of slate, two stone elbow pipes, and a pair of copper-stained stone ear spools were certainly imports as well.

Archaeologists generally assume that the quantity and quality of the goods that were placed in a Mississippian person's grave are indicative of his or her social and economic status in life. If so, the people who were buried in the most lavishly endowed graves at the Sanders site must have been almost as important, or as wealthy, as most of the Mississippian elite buried (albeit often with lesser wealth) in imposing surroundings in mounds at ceremonial centers throughout the Southeast. What brought these important people and their wealth of exotic Mississippian goods to a seemingly out-of-the-way place on the far southwestern edge of the Mississippian world?

It was not bison. The tallgrasses of the Blackland Prairie would not have supported bison in significant numbers, if at all (Isenberg 2000:22; Johnson 1951:330). Accordingly, archaeological evidence of bison is conspicuously absent from sites in and around the Blackland Prairie (Dillehay 1974:182; Lynott 1980), and ethnohistorical evidence indicates that the local Caddo people did their bison hunting well to the west of it (Griffith 1954:113). Even if the prairie had supported bison, the Spiroans could not have profited from transporting heavy, bulky bison products up the Kiamichi by canoe and then carrying them on their backs, or possibly packing them on the backs of dogs, over the western end of the Ouachita Mountain range to the Arkansas River drainage. Dried, wet-scraped bison hides weighed more than 6 kg (about 14 pounds) apiece (Boszhardt and McCarthy 1999:192).

The resource that brought the Spiroans to the Blackland Prairie of northeastern Texas was lighter and more transportable than bison products. It was a resource of great importance to the Mississippians, one that probably could be found only on the prairie. The Sanders site occupies a low bluff overlooking the broad bottomlands of the 80-mile-long (129-km) Bois d'Arc Creek, which winds its way through the northern end of the Blackland Prairie (Figure 12.3). The Spiroans established themselves on that particular bluff overlooking that particular creek because the Bois d'Arc Creek bottoms supported a major stand of the Osage orange tree (*Maclura pomifera*), also called bois d'arc, bodark, hedge, hedge apple, Osage apple, horse apple, mock orange, bow wood, and yellow wood (Burton 1973:4). There French trappers ranging up the Red River during the latter decades of the first half of the eighteenth century saw the Caddo cutting bow staves from a long, dense, 3- to 6-mile-wide (5- to 10-km) stand of this wood. The reference to this creek is specific. Sibley (1832:729), reporting the recollections of Francois Grappe (who was born and grew up at La Harpe's post on the Red River near present Texarkana), wrote:

> After passing the Kiomitchie, both banks of the [Red] river are covered with thick cane for twenty-five miles, then, left side a high pine bluff appears again to the river for about half a mile, after which nothing but cane again on either side for about forty miles, which brings you to the mouth of a handsome bayou, left side, called by the Indians Nahaucha, which, in English, means the Kick; the French call it Bois d'arc or Bow-wood creek, from the large quantity of the wood that grows upon it. On this bayou, trappers have been more successful in catching beaver than on any other water of Red river. . . . It is believed that this bayou is boatable, at high water, for twenty or thirty leagues, from what I have been informed by some trappers with whom I have conversed, who have been upon it. The low grounds are from three to six miles wide, very rich; the principal growth upon it is the bois d'arc. The great prairies approach pretty near the low ground on each side of this creek; leaving which is cane both sides for about eight miles, when we arrive at the mouth of the Vazzures, or Boggy, River. . . . From the Boggy River to the Blue River is about 50 miles, which comes in on the right side.

Hence the original European name for this species, *bois d'arc*, as well as the name for this 80-mile-long (129-km) "creek" (Flores 1984: 330 n. 14). There are many creeks and bayous with variations of the name Bois d'Arc, but this is the original.

By establishing themselves near the mouth of Bois d'Arc Creek the Spiroans gained access to, and perhaps some control over, a major stand of the superb bow wood for which the Caddo territory in the Red River valley was famous during the Historic period (Swanton 1942:138). Osage orange, known to modern bowyers and archers as one of the two best bow woods in the world, was the best available to North American Indian archers outside the Pacific Northwest, where its only rival, yew, could be found (Atwill 1992; Hamm 1989:22, 1992; Hardcastle 1992:132; Laubin and Laubin 1980:59; Peattie 1953:480). Not surprisingly, abundant documentary evidence exists that Osage orange bows were widely traded and highly valued. Between 1680 and 1880 peoples as distant from the Red River valley as the Yaqui, Tewa, Osage, Omaha, Pawnee, and Blackfoot, and as close to it as the Hasinai of eastern Texas, were using traded bows of this distinctive yellow or reddish-yellow wood (Bell and Weddle 1987:255, 265; Catlin 1973:32; Hamm 1989:17; Mason 1972:10; Pope 1962:14–15; Robbins et al. 1916:68, 68n; Swanton 1942:37, 41).

The Sanders site is evidence that the well-documented Historic-period trade in Osage orange bows had a 400- to 600-year history, beginning around A.D. 1000 when long-distance traders from Spiro began transporting them to bison hunters on the southern Plains and probably to Mississippi Valley peoples as well (Lafferty 1994:201; Schambach 1995). Certainly the Red River Caddo were making sophisticated, powerful, Osage orange bows during the Early Mississippian period. A well-preserved whole bow and fragments of others from the Mounds Plantation site in northwestern Louisiana (Figure 12.3) attest that the Caddo were using Osage orange bows with recurved tips and draw weights in the 70-pound range by around A.D. 1050, according to radiocarbon dates on associated logs (Webb and McKinney 1975:54–63, 72, 104–107). Further, high-status early Caddo mound burials of the type and age of the Mounds Plantation graves that contained the bows characteristically contain imported Mississippian prestige goods of shell, copper, stone, bone, and clay comparable to those found in the hoards at Spiro and in the high-status graves at the Sanders site (Brown 1996; Krieger 1946; Schambach 1995:10). These are evidence that peoples of the Arkansas Valley and probably the Central Mississippi Valley as well were interested in something the Red River Caddo had to offer— arguably, Osage orange bows. I suspect that most of the Mississippian prestige goods found at early Caddo sites in the Red River valley and adjacent areas of northeastern Texas were transported from Spiro to the Sanders entrepôt, where they were exchanged for Caddo-made Osage orange bows and several other kinds of Caddo goods, particularly fine ware pottery and pipes (Schambach 1995:10, n.5).

But why did traders from Spiro establish their bow or bow wood collecting entrepôt at a site overlooking the Bois d'Arc Creek stand of this wood? Were there not, as some of the older literature on Osage orange seems to suggest (e.g., Smith and Perino 1981:Figure 2), stands of Osage orange closer to Spiro, or at least closer to the mouth of the Kiamichi River, the southern end of the natural riverine-overland route from Spiro to the Red River valley? Probably not. Osage orange was rapidly spread throughout much of the continental United States and to various places around the world soon after European contact (Brown 1986:53; Burton 1973:5; Smith and Perino 1981:29–30; Weniger 1996: 237–238; Winberry 1979). But during the last millennium or so before contact it seems to have been confined to an extraordinarily small area in the Red River valley in northeastern Texas, southeastern Oklahoma, and possibly southwestern Arkansas (Burton 1973:3, Figure 1; Flores 1984:260–261, 1985:14; Jurney 1994:11; Leopold et al. 1998:220; Smith and Perino 1981:29, Figure 2; Weniger 1996:239, Figure 2).

The explanation for this small range is that Osage orange is an evolutionary anachronism, one of a small group of North American tree species (others are the persimmon, the pawpaw, the honey locust, and the Kentucky coffee bean) that barely survived the cold weather and the large-animal extinctions of the Pleistocene (Barlow 2000, 2001; Delcourt and Delcourt 1991:27; Janzen and Martin 1982:27). Because Osage orange does not tolerate extreme cold (Burton 1973:3; Smith and Perino 1981:30), the onset of cold weather probably extirpated it throughout all but the southernmost part of its pre-Pleistocene range, which, on fossil evidence, extended to Ontario (Peattie 1953:479). Probably its range was also diminished, and the possibility of reclaiming any of it upon the return of warmer weather during the Holocene was eliminated by the extinction of the Pleistocene megafauna. Because Osage orange seedlings are intolerant of shade from other trees, including parent trees (Burton 1973:4 n.2; Smith and Perino 1981:29–30), the species was dependent on large, frugivorous animals for propagation (Barlow 2000, 2001; Janzen and Martin 1982:27). These would have been animals of various species (probably including horses) that were large enough to consume the sticky, softball-sized fruits of the Osage orange and pass the 8- to 12-mm-long seeds through their digestive systems intact so as to deposit them in dung piles in sunny locations away from the parent trees and other trees. As the large mammals disappeared, the Osage orange's range diminished drastically.

Most likely the main (if not the only) places it survived were the bottomlands of Bois d'Arc Creek and perhaps other streams that traverse the Blackland Prairie, and possibly the Grand Prairie, of northeastern Texas (Figures 12.3 and 12.4). The Osage orange hung on there for a variety of reasons. These streams were bordered by prairie rather than forest, thus meeting its critical ecological requirement for sunshine during the seedling stage of growth. Worth considering, too, is the fact that Bois d'Arc Creek, at least, probably supported a large beaver population in prehistoric times. As Sibley (1832:729) reported, "On this bayou, trappers have been more successful in catching beaver than any other water of Red river." So in the Bois d'Arc Creek bottoms, because the Osage orange's fruits float when dry and the species "is not injured by dormant-season flooding" (Burton 1973:4), the rising and falling waters of frequently relocated beaver ponds may have taken the place of large animals in moving its seeds to sunny locations (Jurney 1994:11). Its ability to reproduce vegetatively, as well as from seeds, would certainly have helped Osage orange endure in these creek bottoms for millennia after its "dispersal mutualists" (Barlow 2000:135) among the Pleistocene megafauna disappeared, and to survive what must have been increasingly heavy human exploitation in its Blackland Prairie refuge after A.D. 500, when the bow and arrow became popular in North America. Like various other tree species, it "produces shoots from lateral roots that may venture many meters from the elder stem" (Barlow 2000:135). Hence the extensive, all-but-impenetrable "bodark swamps," that is, "pure, natural stands" of Osage orange, described in historical accounts of northeastern Texas (Burton 1973). Also, Osage orange is "adept at resprouting multiple stems after the main stem has been injured" (Barlow 2000:135). In fact, Osage orange stumps so readily grow sprouts to fencepost size 15 to 20 years after cutting that old Osage orange hedges can supply fenceposts continuously (Smith and Perino 1981:32). The math on the productivity of these old hedges is interesting. A straight, fencepost-sized log would yield no less than two good bow staves, possibly three or four, and, we are told, "prairie farmers customarily clearcut hedges on a 10- to 16-year cycle, obtaining 1000 fence posts per quarter mile of single-row hedge" (Burton 1973:4; Smith and Perino 1981:32). Hence the 3- to 6-mile-wide (5- to 10-km) thicket of Osage orange that French trappers saw growing in the 80-mile-long (129-km) bottomlands of Bois d'Arc Creek in the early to middle 1700s would have been a practically inexhaustible resource.

Thus, the stand of Osage orange that the Sanders site overlooked was probably not just a first-rate stand. It was probably the northeasternmost significant stand during the Mississippian period, if not the only significant one. So there the Spiroans maintained an entrepôt where they exchanged Mississippian prestige goods with the hierarchically

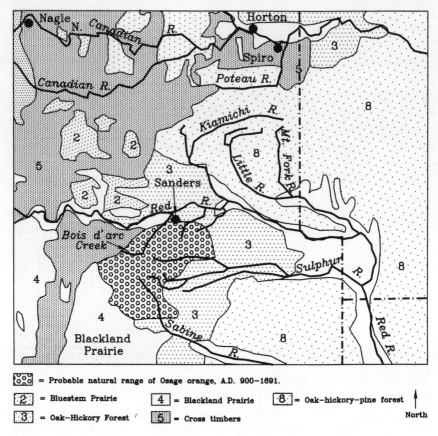

Fig. 12.4. The probable range of Osage orange (*Maclura pomifera*) at the time of European contact.

organized, basically southeastern, Red River Caddo, who could appreciate and use them, for expertly made, powerful, fast-shooting Osage orange bows that only the Caddo could provide (Figure 12.5). The Spiro-ans transported these bows (30 would make a 40-pound [18-kg] bundle) north to the Arkansas Valley via a natural route up the Kiamichi to the headwaters of the Poteau, then down the Poteau to Spiro. From there they canoed or carried some of the bows west and northwest along the Canadian and Arkansas River systems to the eastern edge of the bluestem and bluestem-gramma prairie. There, at entrepôts like the one represented by the Nagle site, they delivered the bows to southern Plains bison hunters, who, though they probably had little use for most Mississippian prestige goods, would have been willing to exchange bison hides, meat, and tallow for Osage orange bows that could

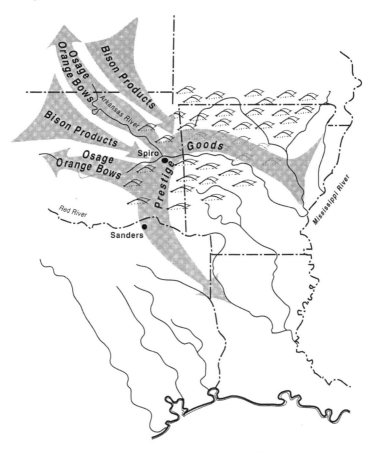

Fig. 12.5. The western part of the Spiroan trade network.

"with great ease throw the Arrow entirely through a Buffalo" (Flores 1984:165–170).

The Spiroans transported the hides and other bison products they received for the bows downriver to the Spiro locality. There, at numerous sites like the Wybark site (Figure 12.3), where tools considered characteristic of the Plains hide trade (Creel 1991:43), particularly end-scrapers and beveled knives, are abundant (Schambach 1993a:198–200), the hides were processed into robes. From Spiro, bison products (robes, dried meat, and tallow), Osage orange bows, and, possibly, goods such as cotton cloth and coiled baskets from the Southwest were canoed down the Arkansas River to the Mississippi Valley where Middle Mississippians of the elite classes were eager to exchange prestige goods for them. Upon entering the Mississippi Valley, bison products, particularly bison robes, probably became prestige goods themselves and, as such, would have been circulated widely via the Mississippian prestige-goods network. The Osage orange bows, which are to bows of most other woods as rifles are to muskets, probably had profound effects on patterns of interaction between various Mississippi Valley societies (Lafferty 1994).

Documentary and archaeological evidence suggests that some of the Osage orange bows that passed through the Sanders site entrepôt went west rather than north. In the late summer of 1542, when the Spaniards of the de Soto expedition (by then led by Moscoso) invaded the Hasinai Caddo country of northeastern Texas (Schambach 1999b:96–98), they found "turquoises and cotton blankets, which the Indians gave them to understand by signs, were brought from the west" (Swanton 1942: 192). Following the passage from the narrative of the Gentleman of El-vas just cited, Swanton noted, "We are not informed what the Hasinai paid in exchange for these things but may suspect that wood of the bois d'arc, or Osage orange, was one of the commodities since the Tewa Indians are known to have obtained this material from the east, and in 1687 Joutel informs us that the Kadohadacho country was famous for it" (Swanton 1942:192). The remarkably numerous archaeological finds of turquoise in northeastern Texas, which seem to be concentrated at Sanders and nearby sites in the Red River valley (Jurney and Young 1995), indicate that Osage orange bows from the stand on the northern end of the Blackland Prairie were the commodity that attracted turquoises and cotton blankets to northeastern Texas, and ultimately to Spiro (Brown 1984:254; Riley 1978:62; Rohrbaugh 1982: 547). Spiroan traders may have transported Osage orange bows to the Southwest in exchange for turquoise, cotton textiles, coiled baskets, and other southwestern goods. However, it seems more likely that this was the work of trading parties out of Pecos, such as the one observed by Coronado (Riley 1978:54). Or it may have been the work of the Ju-manos, whose trafficking between the Southwest and the Caddo of eastern Texas during the early Historic period is well documented (An-derson 1999:5; Baugh 1998:150–152; Griffith 1954:120–122; Hickerson 1994).

The Spiroans seem to have maintained their trade network, circulating Osage orange bows and other goods far and wide, until about 1650 (Schambach 1999c:180–183). Shortly thereafter the network was disrupted by the introduction of European horses from Mexico and the Southwest and of European guns from the East Coast. Then—as I have argued at length elsewhere (Schambach 1999c)—the Spiroans, who had entered history briefly in 1541 as the Tulans, fled down the Arkansas Valley to the Yazoo Basin where they reentered history, courtesy of the French invaders of the Mississippi Valley, as the Tunica.

The introduction of horses opened an important new chapter in the ecological history of the Blackland Prairie of eastern Texas. Horses probably began to reach the Caddo of northeastern Texas around 1650. These animals were stolen from Spanish settlements south of the Rio Grande, then moved northeast to the Caddo country by the Jumanos, along with various goods of Spanish origin (Sauer 1980:243; Swanton 1942:35–36). The Blackland Prairie provided a natural route for the movement of horses and goods from the Rio Grande, via the locus of modern San Antonio, to the Red River valley (Figure 12.1). But it was more than just a route. It was also a highway of fodder eminently suited, as we will see shortly, to the nutritional needs of horses. Hence, by 1690, horses, some of them geldings, some bearing Spanish brands (Foster 1998:243), were common among the Hasinai Caddo of east-central Texas. According to Tonti, who visited them in that year, "there is not a cabin which has not four or five"; he also reported that the Kadohadacho Caddo of the Red River valley in northeastern Texas had about 30 horses (Ewers 1955:2–4). By 1680 horses reportedly from the Kadohadacho country in the Red River valley had reached the Pawnee (Boszhardt 2000:365; Sauer 1980:242) and, probably, several other tribes of the prairie/woodland edge regions of Kansas, Missouri, Nebraska, and Illinois such as the Wichita and the Osage (Blakeslee 1975:62; Ewers 1954:440; Wedel 1981:37).

Still, it is doubtful whether the efforts of the Jumanos as horse traders, and of the Caddo as horse breeders (the latter undocumented in any case), could have made northeastern Texas the significant source of horses for the prairie/eastern Plains tribes that it is thought to have been during the first half of the eighteenth century (Sauer 1980:242–243). In fact, there seems to have been another, much more productive, source, namely the Blackland Prairie itself. This source was created by accident. In the summer, fall, and early winter of 1691 Domingo Teran de Los Rios traveled from Mexico to northeastern Texas, via the future site of San Antonio and, hence, the Blackland Prairie, under orders to reestablish the mission system among the Caddo (Chipman 1992:94–98). He brought with him on this ill-fated expedition "more than 1000 horses and mules . . . at least 200 of which were lost" (Chipman 1992:98; Flores 1985:102, n.8). This was a portentous event because these animals were lost in an ideal habitat for horses. Horses and the tallgrasses that dominated the Blackland Prairie, and indeed the entire eastern prairie system (Farney 1980), seem to have been (and, in an evolutionary sense, apparently were) made for each other. While ruminants, such as bison, do as well as horses on tallgrasses when the plants are young and short, only horses continue to do well and, in fact, thrive on them as the grasses mature into tall, dense herbage (Janis 1975:766). Hence, Teran's lost horses and mules found themselves in an environment empty of large herbivores yet tailor-made to their dietary requirements. The result seems to have been the development of a large herd of feral horses whose existence remained unknown to Europeans until American "mustangers" discovered it around 1800. The herd then became an important source for the feral horses they brought into the Southeast. In 1802 alone, according to Flores (1985: 102, n.9), "an estimated 7,300 Texas horses," most of them apparently from the Blackland Prairie herd, "passed through Louisiana to eastern markets."

Despite what must have been heavy pressure from the mustangers, this herd survived until about 1820 at least. When the trader Anthony Glass ascended the Sulphur River en route from Natchitoches in 1808, he began to see feral horses immediately upon entering the Blackland Prairie. Seven days later, on Bois d'Arc Creek about "75 miles from its mouth," he "saw great numbers of Wild horses" (Flores 1985:38, 43–44). When Thomas Nuttall visited the Red River valley in 1819 he found what he believed to be the first "native stands" of Osage orange growing on "the Horse-prairie 15 miles above the mouth of the Kiamesha" and directly across the Red River from the Womack and Sanders sites. This prairie, Nuttall explained, "derives its name from the herds of wild horses, which till lately frequented it, and of which we saw a small gang" (Nuttall 1980:173).

Elsewhere (Schambach 1999c:209–210) I have argued that this feral horse herd could have grown rapidly enough to have been of economic and historical significance to the Indians by around 1700. Considering the affinity of horses for the grasses of the Blackland Prairie, and the exponential growth characteristic of the introduction of horses and cattle—or, in the case of horses, reintroduction—into New World grasslands empty of large herbivores (Crosby 1972:82–84), an initial 50 to 100 animals could have increased to several thousand in the first 20 years. Such a herd could have numbered between 20,000 and 50,000 in the next 20 years and reached the maximum carrying capacity of the Blackland Prairie within the next, possibly running to hundreds of thousands. I have also argued that during the eighteenth century this herd probably attracted northern people such as the Osage and the Wichita to the Blackland Prairie, where either they or the Tunica maintained horse-hunting/horse-trading entrepôts represented by at least two sites, Womack and Gilbert, located, like the Sanders site, along the northeastern edge of the Blackland Prairie (Figure 12.3).

The introduction of horses into the Blackland Prairie and the development of a feral horse herd of these proportions would have affected the prairie's ecology in many ways. By constantly cropping the tallgrasses, horses may have made the Blackland Prairie more habitable for bison, which were present there in small numbers as of 1808 (Flores 1985:38, 43, 113 n.26, 114 n.31), despite their apparent absence in earlier times. Of particular interest is the possibility that horses may have quickly increased the range of Osage orange. Horses relish the fruit of the Osage orange and possibly were one of its original large-mammal propagators. In any case, horses are—judging from the numerous Osage orange trees now growing in horse pastures in northeastern Texas— capable of propagating the species in the normal way, by passing its large seeds through their digestive systems intact. Thus, when horses were reintroduced into the small territory in which the last native stands of Osage orange were growing, they may have begun the process of spreading the species beyond the extraordinarily limited ecological niche I think it had before European contact—the bottomlands of one or more creeks traversing the Blackland Prairie.

This process would have begun more than 100 years before Meriwether Lewis brought Osage orange to the attention of science in 1804 (Jackson 1962:170–171) and long before trees of this species were seen by the first English-speaking recorders of its distribution in the Red River valley—Anthony Glass in 1808 (Flores 1985:43–44) and Thomas Nuttall in 1819 (Nuttall 1980:170, 175). Nuttall found what he believed were the northernmost "native stands" of Osage orange on the northern side of the Red River, just west of the mouth of the Kiamichi River and some 15 to 20 miles (24 to 32 km) east of the Sanders site and the mouth of Bois d'Arc Creek.

Considering that this extremely anachronistic species almost certainly had no surviving animal vectors capable of assisting in its propagation and dispersal before the reintroduction of horses into North America (Barlow 2000), it is doubtful that these were native stands, particularly as they were growing on a prairie called "the Horse-prairie" where feral horses were still present (Nuttall 1980:173). The strands were more likely the result of the (re)introduction of horses into the Blackland Prairie 128 years earlier.

CONCLUSIONS

Following the extinction of the Pleistocene megafauna, the bottomlands of Bois d'Arc Creek, located within the Blackland Prairie of northeastern Texas, became a refuge for Osage orange (*Maclura pomifera*, aka bois d'arc). This species, originally propagated by large herbivores, happens to be one of the two best bow woods in the world. By A.D. 1000 the Red River valley Caddo were making powerful bows of this very rare wood and long-distance traders based at Spiro had begun transporting the bows to the Plains and the Mississippi Valley. By 1542, southwestern turquoises and cotton blankets were being traded to Indians in northeastern Texas, probably in exchange for Osage orange bows. In 1691 Spanish horses were accidentally introduced into the

Blackland Prairie, creating a rapidly expanding herd of horses that be-
gan to propagate and disperse Osage orange the way its extinct animal
vectors, probably including North American horses, had originally. The
Blackland Prairie then became a generator of two resources vital to the
Indians of the Plains during the eighteenth and nineteenth centuries:
Osage orange and horses.

Acknowledgments. My thanks to Darrell Creel, curator of the Texas
Archeological Research Laboratory in Austin, for permission to exam-
ine the collections from the Sanders and Womack sites; to Mary Lynn
Kennedy of the Arkansas Archeological Survey, for technical assistance in creating Figures 12.1–12.4; and to Donna McCloy, reference
librarian at Southern Arkansas University's Magale Library, for processing multitudes of interlibrary loan requests.

III   SUSTAINABILITY

13 Rediscovery and Management of Prairie Remnants of the Bienville National Forest, East-Central Mississippi

Dean Elsen and Ronald Wieland

INTRODUCTION

According to the U.S. Geological Survey (USGS) geologic map of Mississippi, the Jackson group formation covers approximately 1.4 million acres (566,572 ha), or about 5 percent of the state. The formation is composed of Eocene-age sediments, mostly of green and gray calcareous Yazoo clay containing some sand and marl. Within its western portion (in Yazoo, Madison, Hinds, and Rankin counties), representing 61 percent of the formation, the characteristic marly, often calcareous sediments are mostly buried by Pleistocene loessal soils. Because of these loessal deposits, the surface soils of this western portion are mostly silty in texture. The eastern portion, consisting of a narrow band running diagonally to the southeast across Scott, Newton, Smith, Jasper, Clarke, and Wayne counties, is generally exposed at ground level and has weathered in place. Several distinctive soil series, such as the Vaiden, Okolona, Kipling, Louin, and Sumter, are representative of these exposed, weathered strata. Almost 90 percent of the eastern portion exhibits heavier soil textures of silty clay, silty clay loam, or clay. The Jackson group formation underlies almost two-thirds of the Bienville National Forest lands (Figure 13.1).

Monette (1851), Hilgard (1860), and Lowe (1921) first described the geological formations, soils, and associated vegetation of the Jackson Prairie. Early European settlers preferred prairie soils because of their fertility and conveniently sparse tree cover.

"Rediscovery" began in the early 1970s when Jones (1971) reported on a prairie in Scott County. The impetus of his paper and a report by Watson in 1974 that confirmed Jones's work led to a recommendation that the area be designated as a national natural landmark by the Na-

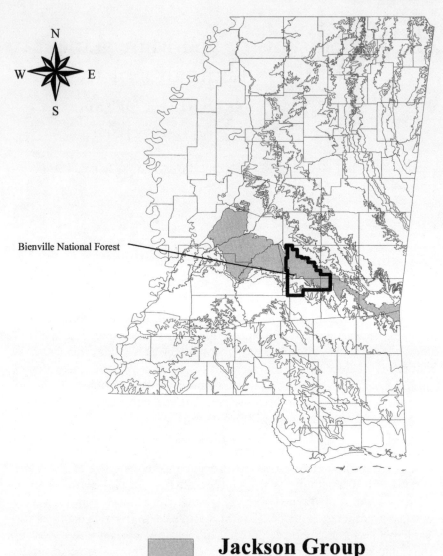

Jackson Group

Fig. 13.1. Location of Bienville National Forest, south-central Mississippi, and the Jackson geological group.

tional Park Service (Waggoner 1975) and later to the establishment of the Harrell Prairie Hill as a botanical area by the U.S. Forest Service (1980). In 1988, with the help of a Forest Service cost-share program, Gordon and Wiseman (1989) completed a survey of the Bienville National Forest to identify additional prairie remnants. Indicator-plant species were used to identify the presence of prairies. Based on the indicator vegetation and the amount of disturbance observed, prairies were ranked to help identify the best representatives of the original ecosystem. About 60 prairie remnants were documented in this study. McDaniel and Carraway (1995) completed additional vegetation sampling on the Tallahala Wildlife Management Area, also on national forest lands. Moran et al. (1997) investigated soils in four prairie openings. Quantitative vegetation composition and environmental analysis was conducted on a select group of 15 prairies in the Bienville National Forest (Wieland 2000). These studies have helped to define the distinctive qualities of the Jackson Prairie remnants. After identification and characterization of these remnants, management was begun by the U.S. Forest Service at some areas to restore and enhance biodiversity. The Mississippi Division of Forestry also has begun restoration on some prairie remnants on county-owned 16th Section prairie lands, and one private landowner has worked to restore a prairie remnant.

HISTORICAL BACKGROUND

The history of the Bienville National Forest lands provides a perspective on how land use influenced prairie remnants during the 1800s and 1900s. Brown (1894) provided anecdotes about the prairies in Newton County: "Much open land and wide-spreading open prairies in the southwestern part of the county [pp. 4] . . . [were] covered with a growth of very rich grass and a very parterre of flowers [pp. 31] . . . these lands in many instances had a large accumulation of small shells in the soil [pp. 31] . . . and were productive of corn and other grain [pp. 32]."

Widespread logging by large timber companies across central Mississippi from 1910 through the 1930s left the lands deforested and vulnerable to erosion. The companies defaulted on tax payments, and livestock were subsequently allowed to range freely on the land. Cattlemen used burning to stimulate grasses and forbs and to initiate earlier springtime green-up, enhancing the quantity and quality of forage in the cutover forests.

After purchase by the federal government in 1934 and 1935, livestock were brought under grazing allotments and eventually eliminated from the Bienville National Forest. Federal land managers instituted fire-exclusion practices to protect young pine plantations, a campaign that persisted for approximately 40 years. Despite such efforts, attempts at planting loblolly pine on the high-pH soils of the prairie remnants usually resulted in poorly formed, slow-growing trees with a low survival rate. As a result of fire exclusion, many prairie remnants in the Bienville National Forest today are "grown up" in trees such as sweetgum (*Liquidambar styraciflua*), white ash (*Fraxinus amerciana*), eastern redcedar (*Juniperus virginiana*), or poor-quality loblolly pine

(*Pinus taeda*). The Alabama supplejack vine (*Berchemia scandens*) grows vigorously on the alkaline prairie soils and, in the absence of fire, can cover most of a prairie remnant.

PRESCRIBED FIRE AS A MANAGEMENT TOOL

The prairies of central Mississippi were due not only to the calcareous soils but also to wildfire, which in pre-European times could burn for many miles across wide pathways in the coastal plains. Historically, fires were caused by lightning and by Native Americans. In the 1970s, controlled burning was introduced in the Bienville National Forest as a way to reduce the buildup of forest fuels and to control unwanted tree species. Research, especially from the Tall Timbers Fire Ecology Lab in Tallahassee, Florida, revealed additional benefits from burning such as enhancement of wildlife habitat (Komarek 1964, 1965, 1968, 1974). Reports from ecologists indicated that prairie lands could be restored and maintained by burning. Fire thus became a useful tool in enhancing forest resources, including prairie remnants.

With the establishment of the Harrell Prairie Hill Botanical Area came a need to apply fire to help maintain the herbaceous plants and to prevent encroachment from trees, shrubs, and vines. The botanical area became a focus point for applying prescribed fire in the Bienville Forest and enabled Forest Service administrators to become comfortable with fire as a management tool. Prescribed burning became more frequent in the 1980s and 1990s as part of multiple-use management of forests and as a restoration tool for prairie remnants. Over the past decade, an average of 10,117 ha (25,000 acres) have been burned each year in the Bienville Forest. The frequency of prescribed burning on the prairie remnants increased from none in the 1960s, to about every eight years in the 1970s, to every five or six years in the 1990s.

Prescribed fires were found to behave differently in prairie remnant areas than in woodlands. The type, amount, and moisture content of fuel on prairie remnants are different from those in shaded woodlands. The heavy dews on the grasses in prairie remnants prevent prescribed fire events from commencing until midday. The higher fine-fuel loads and flammability of the prairie remnants cause greater volatility during prescribed burns. Fires on prairie remnants can create a wind vortex that carries fire high into the air. Smoke management is critical in the Bienville National Forest, as Interstate 20 and other highways intersect the forest. Winds have to be forecast with at least a 1,000-m mixing height and a 4- to 5-m/second transport wind speed for prescribed burning to proceed. These parameters reduce the window of opportunity for prescribed fire and consequently the total area that can be burned across the national forest each year. Experience has shown that one prescribed burn does not suddenly restore a prairie remnant in desirable grasses and forbs; rather, each fire restores a little more than the previous burn, and it takes several prescribed burns over several years to fully return prairie remnants to the desired vegetation community state and degree of openness.

The season of burning is an issue that arises in fire management. Research in Missouri (McCarty et al. 1999) has shown that fall-season burns are advantageous to forbs and promote seed production and plant vigor, whereas summer-season burns tend to improve herbaceous vitality. Late-winter or early-spring burns improve grass productivity. A spring burn stimulates grasses because their reserves are stored in the roots. The burning also turns litter into reusable nutrients. In the Bienville National Forest, fall-season burns are difficult to apply because parameters of the burn protocol often fall outside the zone of safety prescribed by the Keech-Byrum Drought Index. Growing-season burns are often difficult to initiate owing to the high moisture content of the green foliage. Pine straw or fine flashy fuels such as dead grass are often needed to carry fire in the Bienville National Forest.

OTHER MANAGEMENT ISSUES

Another aspect of prairie remnant management is incorporating shrubby edges and adjacent woodlands. Managing for some upland hardwoods on lands surrounding the prairie remnants provides wildlife habitat as well as increased diversity of vegetation. Several less common woody plants, such as Oglethorpe oak (*Quercus oglethorpensis*) and lanceleaf buckthorn (*Rhamnus lanceolata*), are associated with the prairie edge. Some edge-favored plants are listed as species of concern in Mississippi. In many cases, herbicides must be used to control undesirable trees such as sweetgum (*Liquidambar styraciflua*), white ash (*Fraxinus americana*), eastern redcedar (*Juniperus virginiana*), and redbud (*Cercis candensis)* on prairie remnants. The exotic shrubby lespedeza (*Lespedeza bicolor*), planted as a food source for quail in the 1960s, has proven to be a nuisance plant on prairie remnants. *Festuca pratensis* (meadow fescue), an introduced grass, is established on at least 12 prairie remnants.

Management practices recommended by Gordon and Wiseman (1989) are generally carried out by the U.S. Forest Service to protect and enhance the biodiversity of these prairie remnants. Initially early, vintage (1936) photos are inspected to determine the extent of the prairies preceding the fire-suppression phase of forest management. Prairies are then documented on the compartment management maps. Foresters place flagging around prairies to mark boundaries before entering adjacent forest stands to log or carry out other management prescriptions.

To prevent compaction, nonessential trails have been removed and off-road-vehicle use has been prohibited. Other activities detrimental to the ecological integrity of the areas are discouraged: use of the prairies for log landings, plowing and disking for construction of wildlife food plots, and building fire lanes through prairie openings. A Memorandum of Understanding between the U.S. Forest Service and the U.S. Fish and Wildlife Service directs the agencies to work cooperatively to protect and preserve the prairie ecosystem for the benefit of the Jackson Prairie crayfish, *Procambarus barbiger,* a candidate species of the Endangered Species Act of 1973 as amended. The agreement recommends that local erosion be controlled, prairies be maintained by fire to control woody species and enhance native herbs, and unofficial vehicles be prohibited except on designated roads (U.S. Forest Service 1989).

Response from the public is providing additional impetus to find ways to improve prairie management. The Bienville National Forest staff has received very few complaints and a strong positive response to efforts designed to conserve the prairie openings. Prairie field trips have provided interesting venues for student ecology classes from neighboring colleges and high schools. Scientists in geology, pedology, ecology, botany, entomology, mammology, and ornithology have visited the sites on tours or to conduct research. Outdoor writers and members of the local chamber of commerce have expressed a strong interest in the prairies during their visits. Local residents bring family visitors to Harrell Prairie Hill on sightseeing tours. Most hunters value the prairie habitat as beneficial for wildlife and are supportive of prairie restoration efforts; however, some are sensitive to the use of prescribed fire during turkey-nesting season.

Recently, additional rare plant species have been found to be associated with the Jackson Prairie openings. Several rare hawthorns— *Crataegus ashei* (Ashe's hawthorn), *C. triflora* (three-flowered hawthorn), and *C. meridianalis* (hawthorn)—have been discovered in the Bienville National Forest. One of the largest populations of Ashe's hawthorn is found within the Bienville National Forest purchase boundary (Lance 2000). The rarity of these hawthorn species is partly due to the encroachment of pines, hardwoods, and other shrubs. Hawthorns usually prefer partially open areas and do not prosper in heavy shade. Eastern redcedar, prolific under the absence of fire, serves as host to a fungus that attacks hawthorns. Grazing has been noted to improve the success of hawthorns, as cattle help to keep an area open and do not prefer hawthorns (Lance 2000).

CONCLUSIONS

Management of prairie remnants in the Bienville National Forest is currently in the restoration phase. Continued application of prescribed burning can help restore and maintain these areas. Additional management practices, including targeted grazing and herbicide application, may have future use in particular circumstances. Unfortunately, funding to do the necessary habitat work and monitoring has not been reaching the ranger district. Public support is a key factor in resource management, and public response to prairie-remnant management seems to be very positive. There is something about a prairie that captures the imagination of people. The new Museum of Natural Science of the Mississippi Department of Wildlife, Fisheries and Parks, at Jackson, Mississippi, features a recently completed diorama depicting Harrell Prairie Hill. It is hoped that such investments in public education ultimately will result in increased funding for and enhanced appreciation of the unique prairie ecosystems of the state. Increased monitoring, further research on rare species, additional public outreach, and lots of intensive work will be required to restore and maintain the prairie community in the Bienville National Forest.

14 Plant Assemblage Response to Disturbance at a Blackland Prairie Restoration Site in Northeastern Mississippi

TIMOTHY SCHAUWECKER AND
JOHN MACDONALD

INTRODUCTION

Grasslands constitute the most imperiled and least protected biome in North America, and the area of native prairie has declined rapidly in the late nineteenth and twentieth centuries because of agricultural pressure (Weaver and Fitzpatrick 1934). As a result, much recent scientific research has dealt with reestablishing and maintaining prairie remnants (Miller 1998; Anderson and Roberts 1993). Individual or combined effects of fire, grazing, mowing, and fertilization on prairie structure and function (Collins 1992; Collins et al. 1998; Howe 1994, 1995; Turner et al. 1997; Wilson and Shay 1990) are very important issues to conservation managers of prairies. Fire and herbivory are primarily responsible for the origin and maintenance of North American tallgrass prairie ecosystems (Knapp and Seastedt 1998), and some type of disturbance is required to halt succession and keep woody vegetation from encroaching on grasslands. The type and frequency of disturbance, whether by fire, mowing, or grazing, are key factors in determining prairie community composition (Collins 1992; Hartnett et al. 1996). Disturbance regimes also affect competitive interactions and therefore species composition (Wilson and Shay 1990).

Managers of southeastern prairie ecosystems benefit from research into the responses of plant guilds and species to disturbance regimes by using that research in their decision-making processes. In concert with their knowledge of natural history, hard data reveal patterns of guild and species response to form management regimes. Short-term ecological studies are only snapshots of the larger scheme, but they document and remind conservation biologists of past events and patterns. This study is one such snapshot, intended to compare two disturbance regimes (mowing and burning) in a small prairie undergoing restoration. The patterns that emerged from two years of study add to the resources that prairie managers currently draw upon in the decision-making process.

STUDY AREA

The Osborn Prairie is located in northeastern Oktibbeha County, Mississippi (Township 19 North, Range 15 East, Section 16) (Figure 14.1). The 25-ha tract is held in lease by the Starkville Public High School as a teaching aid for general science and biogeography classes and for the purpose of restoring and maintaining one of the best blackland prairie relics in the state of Mississippi (Wiygul et al., this volume). The site consists of gently rolling swales and uplands, dominated by unstable soils underlain by the Demopolis chalk formation of the Upper Cretaceous Selma group. The soils are high in montmorillonite clay particles and calcium carbonate and are moderately to highly alkaline. Soil series found on site are eroded Kipling silty clay loams of 2–5 percent slope, eroded Sumter and Binnsville silty clay loams of 2–5 percent and 5–8 percent slopes, respectively, and gullied Sumter-complex soils of 5–20 percent slope (Brent 1973). The five distinct plant assemblages found at the site include (1) swales dominated by green ash, Osage orange, and hackberry; (2) cedar woodland; (3) native grassland on uplands dominated by little bluestem and juvenile eastern red-cedar; (4) *Schizachyrium scoparium/Sporobolus vaginiflorus*–dominated prairie on eroded, alluvial soils that have been redeposited; and (5) pine/calciphile hardwood on ridgetops with the deepest soils.

The upland prairie and alluvial prairie grasslands and cleared cedar woodland (assemblages 2–4 from above) were chosen for study to assess burning and mowing as restoration techniques. The upland prairie type is open, "good" prairie found on hilltops both in a power line right-of-way and scattered throughout the site, mostly where soils are thin and rates of succession are slow. Alluvial prairie is found where eroded chalk and upland soils have been redeposited in the swales downhill from the erosion. Soils in this habitat are very high in carbonate clay; they are very dry and prone to cracking during the growing season. Cleared cedar woodland occurs anywhere that mature cedars were removed in the spring of 1998 as a first step toward expanding the prairie habitat. In the absence of disturbance, all grassland areas would eventually succeed to cedar woodland and/or pine/hardwood communities (Schauwecker, unpublished report).

Fig. 14.1. Location of Osborn Prairie, Oktibbeha County, Mississippi.

FIELD METHODS

Species presence was recorded in five 0.25-square-meter quadrats per treatment plot for a total of 360 quadrats (five quadrats plot^{-1} × six plots block^{-1} × four blocks habitat^{-1} × three habitats). Species abundance was measured via a nondestructive pin-frame method (Kent and Coker 1992). This method was chosen as a way to estimate aboveground production without removing actual biomass from the sampling plots. Collection of live biomass is a common method of estimating vegetative productivity, but it was unacceptable for this experiment because resampling of the same area in successive years was required. For this reason an alternative means of estimating aboveground biomass was sought. Clipped biomass samples were collected in areas outside the test plots to test the accuracy of the nondestructive methods.

Sampling occurred in September and October of 1998 (pre-treatment) and 1999 (post-treatment). The pin frame consisted of 18 pins of 0.5-cm diameter distributed evenly in a 0.25-square-meter area, with six offset rows of three pins spaced 10 cm apart. The frame was placed over the subplots and the identities of all species touching pins were recorded.

A species present in a subplot but not touching a pin was given credit for one touch. Ephemeral species noted via monitoring but not present at the time of pin-frame sampling were also given credit for one touch.

Sites for treatment blocks were chosen in the spring of 1998. Subplot locations were monitored throughout the growing season for the presence of ephemeral species. The biomass of six plant guilds and species with significant changes in response to the two disturbance types was also calculated to better describe which types of plants were responsible for any treatment effects. The six guilds were C_4 graminoid, C_3 graminoid, legume, woody perennial, herbaceous annual, and herbaceous perennial. These guilds were defined on the basis of plants that differ in physiological and phenological characteristics.

STATISTICAL METHODS

Pin-frame counts for each species were compared with clipped biomass counts from 0.25-square-meter areas outside the experimental plots by linear regression. This test was performed to determine whether pin-frame touches are an accurate estimate of aboveground biomass. Comparison of treatments was by t-test in SYSTAT 9.0 (SPSS 1999). For guild data, whole treatment plots, which were characterized by the five subplots, were analyzed. For species, pre-treatment and post-treatment data were compared only for species that had a greater than 1 percent occurrence of the total pin-frame touches.

RESULTS AND DISCUSSION

The nondestructive pin-frame method was used to estimate biomass. This estimate was significantly correlated to actual biomass measurement in test plots that were sampled to evaluate this method (Figure 14.2). Regression analysis of pin-frame touches and aboveground biomass showed a highly significant relationship between the two estimates of productivity. This method is fairly labor-intensive, but it proved to be very effective at estimating species biomass.

There was a significant reduction of biomass from Year 1 to Year 2 in C_4 graminoids in control, burned, and mowed plots (Table 14.1). This response can probably be attributed to an extended drought in the area over the course of the experiment (Table 14.2). There was a corresponding increase in perennial forbs from Year 1 to Year 2 in mowed and burned plots, but not in control plots (Table 14.1). This suggests a give-and-take relationship between the two dominating guilds in this plant community. In general, graminoids are superior competitors compared with perennial forbs, and they dominate the battle for

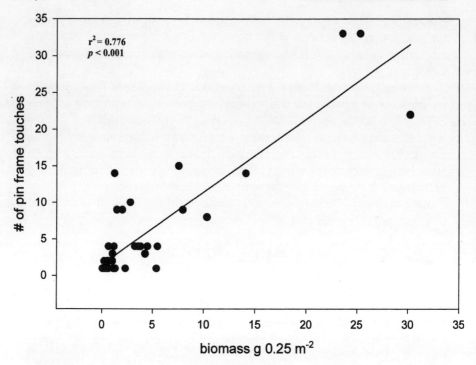

Fig. 14.2. Number of pin-frame touches plotted as a function of actual biomass.

resources. Evidence was given by their higher ratio of productivity compared with that of perennial forbs in control plots (Table 14.1). However, drought and disturbance seem to create opportunities for perennial forbs and allow them to increase their productivity and presumably help to sustain the high diversity that is attributed to grasslands. Annuals, C3 graminoids, legumes, and woody species showed no significant responses at the Bonferroni-corrected significance level of α = 0.0083. Bonferroni correction is necessary when multiple tests of subgroups are performed. In this case the six guilds (a priori comparisons) are subgroups of the data set, so the typical significance level of α = 0.05 must be divided by six, giving a significance level of α = 0.0083.

There were some notable statistically insignificant trends. A marginal decrease of annuals in control plots was contrasted by increases in burned and mowed plots. Perhaps annuals are responding favorably to disturbance and the resulting decrease in competition for light. C3 graminoids increased in control plots but decreased in burned and mowed plots. It is possible that this guild is responding negatively to disturbance in this case. Woody perennials increased in control plots,

Table 14.1. A comparison of pre-treatment and post-treatment mean number of pin-frame touches via paired t-test. Bold values indicate significance at the Bonferroni-corrected level of alpha = 0.0083 (alpha = 0.05/6).

Guild	Control Year 1	Year 2	P	Burn Year 1	Year 2	P	Mow Year 1	Year 2	P
Annual	12.000	11.250	0.741	7.417	11.417	0.145	8.417	12.167	0.128
C3	33.333	50.500	0.166	25.083	18.000	0.146	21.167	16.917	0.114
C4	257.250	208.917	0.005	245.167	174.667	<0.001	259.333	196.417	0.005
Legume	6.750	8.667	0.130	6.000	8.583	0.116	7.167	7.250	0.949
Perennial	34.083	44.667	0.031	40.750	68.333	0.001	38.083	55.167	<0.001
Woody	20.250	27.500	0.051	15.583	1.917	0.084	9.833	7.750	0.696

changed very little in mowed plots, and decreased in burned plots. The results indicate that burning suppressed woody vegetation and encouraged annuals, but the total number of quadrats that contained woody species or annuals before or after treatment was low, so statistical power was also low. The result of burning was a decrease in mean pin-frame touches for woody species from 15.583 to 1.917 (p = 0.084), with control plots increasing in woody biomass from 20.250 to 27.500 pin-frame touches. Statistical significance is a double-edged sword. A given level of significance is required to prove that results are repeatable, yet this is an arbitrary level that may lead some to conclude that results are not biologically meaningful. The trends noted here make biological sense, closely approach the generally accepted arbitrary levels of significance, and could be of use in designing future experiments or making management decisions.

Individual species that responded significantly to the burning and/or mowing treatments included the annuals *Agalinis pseudaphylla*, *Ambrosia psilostachya*, and *Linum medium* (Table 14.3). Perennial forbs that had a significant increase after treatment were *Aster laevis*, *Dalea candida*, *Hedyotis nigricans*, *Hedyotis purpureus*, *Liatris squarrosa*, and *Prunella vulgaris* (Table 14.3). The C3 graminoid *Carex cherokeensis* responded negatively to burning (Table 14.3). The C4 graminoids *Schizachyrium scoparium* and *Eragrostis spectabilis* responded negatively to burning, and *Schizachyrium scoparium* also responded negatively to mowing (Table 14.3). A significant positive or negative response indicated a change in estimated aboveground biomass in the same quadrat from Year 1 to Year 2.

Among the annual species sampled, *Agalinis pseudaphylla* (Scrophulariaciae) and *Linum medium* (Linaceae) were the only species to re-

Table 14.2. Sixty-year average, monthly precipitation, and departure from average for Mississippi State University weather station

Month	Precipitation (cm)			Departure from Average	
	1930–1998 Average	1998	1999	1998	1999
January	13.23	20.12	20.55	6.88	7.32
February	12.57	18.72	6.65	6.15	-5.92
March	14.66	10.80	11.30	-3.86	-3.35
April	12.40	11.91	11.40	-0.48	-0.99
May	10.69	6.43	7.65	-4.27	-3.05
June	9.02	5.23	9.14	-3.78	0.13
July	12.37	14.35	10.26	1.98	-2.11
August	8.61	8.26	2.21	-0.36	-6.40
September	8.03	1.27	9.07	-6.76	1.04
October	7.70	2.39	3.45	-5.31	-4.24
November	10.31	5.66	6.40	-4.65	-3.91
December	13.28	16.61	7.49	3.33	-5.79
Average	132.87	121.74	105.59	-11.13	-27.28

Table 14.3. Species with significant response to burning and mowing (only species with greater than 1 percent of total pin-frame touches considered, via paired t-test)

BURNING

Species	Guild	Response	p
Agalinis pseudaphylla	annual	(+)	0.003
Ambrosia psilostachya	annual	(+)	0.023
Aster laevis	perennial	(+)	0.050
Carex cherokeensis	C3 graminoid	(-)	0.031
Eragrostis spectabilis	C4 graminoid	(-)	0.039
Hedyotis nigricans	perennial	(+)	0.008
Hedyotis purpureus	perennial	(+)	0.044
Liatris squarrosa	perennial	(+)	0.032
Linum medium	annual	(+)	0.007
Schizachyrium scoparium	C4 graminoid	(-)	0.008

MOWING

Species	Guild	Response	p
Agalinis pseudaphylla	annual	(+)	0.009
Aster laevis	perennial	(+)	0.023
Dalea candida	perennial	(+)	0.026
Hedyotis nigricans	perennial	(+)	0.032
Hedyotis purpureus	perennial	(+)	0.002
Linum medium	annual	(+)	0.018
Prunella vulgaris	perennial	(+)	0.046
Schizachyrium scoparium	C4 graminoid	(-)	0.002

spond favorably to both burning and mowing. *Ambrosia psilostachya* (Asteraceae) showed a positive increase in burned plots. *Ambrosia psilostachya* is a more ruderal species than *Agalinis pseudaphylla* or *Linum medium* and took full advantage of disturbed soils in the cedar-removed habitat type, but it was not as prevalent in the upland and alluvial habitats as *Agalinis* and *Linum.*

CONCLUSIONS

Data-gathering techniques that can accurately estimate productivity while allowing measurement in multiple years will be beneficial to long-term studies. Long-term research should be the cornerstone of trend analysis in plant communities. This two-year study is just a snapshot, and as such it should not be construed as a documentation of long-term trends. As discussed above, drought probably affected the results of this investigation. Without long-term data, we can only speculate about the actual effects that climate had on the results. The results can, however, be used to formulate testable hypotheses about the assembly of plant communities (*sensu* Weiher and Keddy 1999) and the relationships between disturbance, productivity, and diversity (*sensu* Huston 1979).

According to Huston's dynamic equilibrium model, diversity should peak at intermediate levels of productivity and disturbance. Other results from this experiment (Schauwecker and Weiher, in press) support one portion of this hypothesis, that diversity is highest at intermediate levels of productivity. Another study in northeastern Mississippi (Forbes 1999) found that shade stress was correlated with a decrease in diversity. These contentions have implications for managers of conservation areas in blackland prairies. Consider the following hypothetical situation. A large tract of land is set aside as a refuge for prairie plants and animals that are threatened by habitat destruction and/or fragmentation. Priorities must be derived to make efficient use of the minimal labor available for on-the-ground management. Studies show that diversity patterns in grasslands follow Huston's hypotheses, where competition among grasses in high-productivity areas of the refuge and a paucity of resources in low-productivity areas preclude the recruitment of new species in restoration efforts. Studies also show that too frequent or infrequent burning decreases diversity. These types of studies allow land managers to make informed decisions about where to concentrate restoration efforts and when and how often to burn to maximize diversity. Managers themselves should conduct experiments to test and verify their decisions and to add to the base of knowledge drawn upon by others responsible for prairie restoration and management.

15 Restoration of a Prairie Remnant in the Black Belt of Mississippi

SHERRILL WIYGUL, KAY KRANS,
RICHARD BROWN, AND VICTOR MADDOX

INTRODUCTION

Many individuals and groups have become involved in preserving and restoring native prairies and other habitats in recent years. The terms *preservation* and *restoration* have been used broadly, and sometimes interchangeably, to cover a variety of conservation activities. In general, preservation involves more restricted management for conservation of pristine natural areas, whereas restoration has been associated with reconstructing a prairie on plowed ground or a former prairie site by planting seeds and performing more intensive management, including the use of mowing, burning, and other methods. Conservationists are aware that pristine natural areas will degrade with time without some level of management and that restoration of low-quality land adjacent to natural areas aids survivorship of species needing larger territories. In this paper, we employ the term *restoration* as broadly defined by the Ecological Society of Restoration and discussed by Packard and Mutel (1997). Thus, restoration includes natural-area management for preserving pristine remnants as well as both reconstruction (planting prairie) and rehabilitation (nursing a degraded prairie back to a more natural condition).

Restoration activities have concentrated on tallgrass prairie of the Great Plains and have involved groups of concerned individuals as well as county, state, and federal agencies. The Grand Prairie Friends in Illinois, for example, has been successful in acquiring and managing prairie remnants, conducting prescribed burns, and propagating and planting indigenous prairie species in 13 preserves (http://www.prairienet.org/gpf/intro.html). The Illinois Prairie Index (http://www.prairiepages.com/Prairie_Indes.html#A) documents the diversity of groups involved in conserving prairie sites. Of 88 prairie sites listed, 24 sites are owned by state agencies (principally the Illinois Department of Natural Resources), 19 are owned by county agencies, and 10 are owned by cities. The Nature Conservancy, federal agencies, cemetery associations, private individuals, foundations, and school districts own another 32 prairie sites.

In contrast to conservation efforts in midwestern states, very little has been done to preserve remaining prairie remnants or to restore previous prairie sites in the Black Belt of Mississippi and Alabama. This lack of conservation effort may be due in part to the misconception that prairie is a midwestern habitat and not a natural habitat in Mississippi and Alabama, a view promulgated by Rostlund (1957). Thus, most individuals who are unaware of the biological uniqueness of this habitat probably perceive an unplowed prairie remnant as a fallow field. Most of the prairie habitat was converted to agricultural use, especially for cotton, during the 1800s (Aiken 1961). Agricultural production in the Black Belt changed from cotton to sod and forage crops, soybeans, and pastureland during the 1900s (Lowe 1911; Garber 1973). Only small remnants of the prairie habitat now remain, and these often are associated with eroded areas that have deterred agricultural or commercial use. A major threat to these remaining prairie remnants is the encroachment of eastern redcedar (*Juniperus virginiana*) due to suppression of fire.

Preservation and restoration of a prairie habitat can be a complicated and difficult process involving selection and acquisition of the site, assistance from individuals who can provide leadership for the effort, cooperation of a diverse group of people (especially those willing to donate time), development of a management plan, and funding. The following case history provides an overview of recent efforts to preserve and restore a prairie remnant in the Black Belt.

RESTORATION OF OSBORN PRAIRIE IN MISSISSIPPI

SITE SELECTION AND ACQUISITION

Osborn Prairie, also known as 16th Section Prairie (e.g., Brown, this volume; Peacock and Melsheimer, this volume; Schauwecker and Mac-Donald, this volume), encompasses about 72 of the 146 ha of Section 16, Township 19, Range 15 in Oktibbeha County near Osborn, Mississippi (for illustration, see Chapter 14, p. 248). The selection of a restoration site at Osborn Prairie was based on four major considerations. First, the Section 16 land is owned permanently by the Oktibbeha County School Board and, as mandated by the state constitution, is leased at a percentage of its assessed value to generate funds for the school district. Thus, a professional and legally binding contract is present between the owner and the leaseholder. Second, long-term leases for 30 years or more can be established, which ensures continuity with changing membership in the school board. Third, the majority of Osborn Prairie has never been plowed (Sidney McDaniel, personal communication), and degradation of the site has been minimal, primarily from incursion of *Juniperus,* erosion, and dumping of trash. More than 20 species of plants restricted to the Black Belt within Mississippi occur at Osborn Prairie, and eight of these are considered rare in the state (Mississippi Natural Heritage Program 2000). The uniqueness of Osborn Prairie led to its designation as the fourth site in the state to be placed on the Mississippi Natural Areas Registry in 1988 by the Mississippi Nature Conservancy and the Mississippi Department of Wildlife Conservation. Finally, Osborn Prairie is near the city of Starkville and Mississippi State University, which facilitates research, education, and restoration activities by members of these communities.

Sherrill Wiygul and Kay Krans, teachers of biology and social studies, respectively, at Starkville High School, developed a multidisciplinary course in biogeography in the mid-1990s. While searching for locations to take students on field trips, they went on a tour of Osborn Prairie given by Richard Brown, who had been conducting insect surveys at the site with students and other researchers. Wiygul and Krans pursued a lease of the prairie on behalf of Starkville High School to avoid liability issues related to taking high school students on the land. A series of meetings ensued with the Oktibbeha County Board of Education, including a slide presentation by Starkville High School students. The board of education subsequently granted the lease of 24 ha (60 acres) for a period of 40 years at a nominal charge of $1 each year. In addition to providing a site for students' field trips, the lease offered longer-term protection for the site, which was not provided by the nonregulatory Mississippi Natural Areas Registry.

RESTORATION

Following acquisition of the lease, the students erected a fence in front of the property and a gate across the access road to reduce the dumping of trash and prevent entrance of unauthorized vehicles. A sign describing the restoration project was erected at the gate. A major cleanup of construction debris dumped on the site awaits help from the Oktibbeha County Board of Supervisors.

In 1996 the U.S. Fish and Wildlife Service provided a $500 grant to develop a prospectus for site management. Victor Maddox, a member of the Department of Plant and Soil Sciences at Mississippi State University, drafted a restoration plan including a discussion of the existing vegetation, a plant species inventory, a list of flowering times for key prairie species, site maps, and photographs. The plant inventory for the 24-ha site included 218 species, including a rush (*Juncus filipendulus* Buckl.) that occurs at only one other location in Mississippi. In 1997 another 22 species were added, bringing the total to 240 species for the site; additional species continue to be listed. Future lists will include birds and butterflies. This prospectus is used as an educational guide for high school students visiting the site.

The main concern of the restoration plan was to minimize any disturbance to the existing natural-prairie flora and fauna. The local Natural Resources Conservation Service (NRCS, formerly the Soil Conservation Service) offered time and advice regarding soil conservation and other technical information on erosion and site management. The Wildlife Habitat Incentives Program (WHIP) provided funding through the local NRCS office for clearing and burning. Community and student volunteers gave time donations to supply the matching funds required by WHIP. The Mississippi Forestry Commission offered assistance for controlled burning. The funds for this endeavor were acquired through the local NRCS office. To date no burning has been done at the site, in part because of the need for initial clearing of some *Juniperus*.

The Noxubee National Wildlife Refuge provided an in-kind grant for the clearing of *Juniperus* to expand some of the open areas. The plan called for limited clearing because of concerns that extensive change of the landscape might affect air currents and drainage as well as provide opportunities for invasion of exotic plants. A small area of a few hectares was cleared using a shearing blade on a bulldozer. This process reduced soil disturbance by leaving the root systems of the trees intact. Volunteers used a loaned tractor to remove cut trees, minimizing soil damage that would have resulted from the use of heavier equipment.

RECENT DEVELOPMENTS

In February 2000, a local businessman made an offer to lease a portion of the 16th Section Prairie to use as a riding area for all-terrain vehicles (ATVs). Concerned individuals met to form Friends of the Black Belt, a group that would address potential threats of ATVs to the restoration site as well as to adjacent prairie habitat in the 16th Section Prairie. A presentation on the rare plants and animals of Osborn Prairie, given at a meeting of the Oktibbeha County School Board, became a factor in the subsequent decision to reject the application of a lease to develop an ATV riding area. Over several months, Friends of the Black Belt solicited donations to enable a lease of land adjacent to the restoration site. In the meantime, the lease of 24 ha to the Prairie Restoration Project was cancelled because the school board had allowed a minimal annual payment for the lease that was less than the 5 percent of the assessed value, as mandated by the state constitution. Because of the work already invested in the restoration site and the high quality of its prairie habitat, Friends of the Black Belt acquired donations to obtain a new lease on these 24 ha for 30 years.

Future management plans for this site will be made with assistance from the Mississippi Natural Heritage Program. For the immediate future, the cleared area will be monitored to determine the successfulness of prairie flora recolonization as well as to determine any adverse impacts of the clearing. Small portions of the open areas may be burned on a rotational basis, and woody sprouts will be pruned as needed. The restoration site and adjacent prairie will continue to play an important role in research and education for university and secondary schools.

RESEARCH AND EDUCATIONAL ACTIVITIES AT OSBORN PRAIRIE

Osborn Prairie was not new to students and researchers at Mississippi State University. Students in plant taxonomy have used the site as a field laboratory since the 1960s, and its flora were formally described by Leidolf and McDaniel (1998). Research in plant ecology by Evan Weiher and students during the 1990s resulted in two theses (Schauwecker 1996; Forbes 1999) and a dissertation by Schauwecker (in preparation). The Mississippi Entomological Museum began surveys of insects at Osborn Prairie in 1991 with support from the National Science Foundation. This research resulted in the discovery of several species of insects with disjunct distributions from the Great Plains and the description of a new species of moth not known to occur elsewhere in Mississippi (Brown, this volume; MacGown and Schiefer 1992; Wright et al. 1997; Schiefer 1998). Osborn Prairie was a major sampling site for a thesis on macrolepidoptera of the Black Belt (Pollock 2000) and is currently the major site for thesis research on native bees of the Black Belt. In addition, an undergraduate student in the Department of Wildlife and Fisheries is conducting a research project on arthropod productivity and diversity of the prairie.

Following the lease of 24 ha by Kay Krans and Sherrill Wiygul in 1996, 40 high school students enrolled each fall semester in the biogeography course have visited the site biweekly for taxonomic and ecological studies. Beginning in 2002, the course is being offered in the spring semester for an additional 26 students. Among the requirements for the course is a taxonomic field journal, including detailed drawings, measurements, and descriptions of plants (Figure 15.2). Because prairie plants have variable blooming times, the students have several dozen species in their journals by the end of the semester. To better understand how ecologists census organisms, students calculate species diversity indices of plants at several locations on the prairie. To appreciate how moving animals are censused, they calculate the Lincoln Index to arrive at an estimate of animal populations. This field simulation is then applied to how hunting bag limits are set. Historical studies of human and environmental interactions are also covered in the course. An experienced photographer leads the photography unit, and students prepare a photo board or portfolio using prairie plants as subjects. Some students have chosen to work with Joe MacGown, a scientific illustrator at the Mississippi Entomological Museum, to prepare drawings of plants and insects that occur at the prairie. In past years some students' drawings have been used for T-shirt designs. The high school students have also worked with three fifth-grade classes at Rosa Stewart Elementary School: taking students on field trips to the prairie and teaching them how to keep field journals, key out plants, and estimate plant numbers.

FUTURE PRESERVATION OF PRAIRIE
REMNANTS IN THE BLACK BELT

Philip Gosse described seeing prairies of many miles in extent when he visited the Alabama Black Belt in 1838 (Gosse 1993), but these large expanses have been lost during the last two centuries. Natural stands of prairie vegetation still can be found in many small patches on private and public land in the Black Belt of Mississippi, especially in areas where erosion has deterred agricultural use. Some of these stands may be worthy of preserving and restoring, but information on location, size of the remnant, and ownership is lacking. Mississippi has private land conservation programs to protect natural areas, with dedicated natural areas receiving a reduction in property taxes (Center for Wildlife Law, http://ipl.unm.edu/cwl/), but private landowners have placed little emphasis on preserving prairie remnants.

Of the few remaining large remnants, two are in the Tombigbee National Forest in Chickasaw County. One remnant, covering about 202 ha, is burned every 2–3 years, but a second remnant of about 162 ha is not actively managed (District Ranger John Baswell, personal communication 2001). The Department of Wildlife and Fisheries at Mississippi State University is currently involved with restoration projects in the Black Belt. One project involves restoration of native vegetation and bird populations at Black Belt Prairie Experiment Station in

Fig. 15.1. Starkville High School biogeography students conducting studies on the Osborn Prairie.

Noxubee County. Other projects involve game species management through habitat restoration at the Black Prairie Wildlife Management Area in Lowndes County.

The restoration project at Osborn Prairie has been an effort to preserve one of the most biologically unique sites remaining in the Black Belt. The future of Osborn Prairie and other prairie remnants in the Black Belt will depend on wise management practices for maintaining and expanding these natural areas. Most important, preservation will depend on educating students in secondary schools and universities and increasing public awareness of the biological diversity that still remains in these prairie remnants. It is hoped that the case study presented here has provided some ideas for how public education, county, state, and federal agencies, and concerned private citizens can work together to ensure the survival of our nation's fragile natural resources.

Acknowledgments. We thank the Natural Resources Conservation Service and the Mississippi Forestry Commission for their time and advice regarding restoration of this prairie, and the Wildlife Incentives Program and Noxubee Wildlife Refuge for funding and equipment to initiate the restoration. Many individuals have volunteered to work at

Osborn Prairie and provided other assistance. We appreciate the generous donors and Friends of the Black Belt, who, along with members of the Oktibbeha County School District, have ensured that Osborn Prairie will continue to be protected. Foremost, we thank the wonderful students at Starkville High School who contributed their enthusiasm, time, and energy to conserve a piece of the Black Belt Prairie.

16 Priorities for the Future

Planning for Sustainable Multiple Use

THOMAS W. SCHURCH

A HISTORICAL PERSPECTIVE

Planning and sustainability as regarded today are fundamentally similar because of their emphasis on quality of life in natural and built environments. Sustainability related to environmental concerns is a very recent development, dating to the United Nations Brundtland Commission of 1987. However, its development parallels that of planning in the United States from the mid–nineteenth century.

Accurately pinpointing movements or like events spanning long periods of time is often haphazard, and planning and sustainability are not exceptions. Nevertheless, planning's early development, especially as related to natural environments, can be traced to an act of Congress in 1864 establishing a commission charged with preserving Yosemite Valley. The commission, headed by Frederick Law Olmsted, created a management policy as a basis for preserving Yosemite (Fein 1972:39). Through Olmsted's efforts to preserve Yosemite, an example of his early work with linkages to John Muir's founding of the Sierra Club, sustainability and the need for planning began to emerge.

Olmsted's 1858 plan for Central Park predated his Yosemite management policy work and was significant in setting the stage for three very important and closely related developments of the nineteenth century that can be considered an American Renaissance (Botwinick 1979:7). The first of these, the American parks movement, affected virtually every major American city of the time. It was an effort to provide urban populations with some connection to nature (Chadwick 1966: 163). A second development, the city beautiful movement inspired by Chicago's World's Columbian Exposition of 1893, attempted to provide an example of good urban form and quality of life (Wilson 1989:53).

The social reform movement, a third major development concerned with the physical and social well-being of city dwellers, resulted in significant policy initiatives and physical developments pertaining to hygiene, air quality, and water quality (Boyer 1983:23; Hollander et al. 1988). The social reform movement, along with its sister movements regarding parks and urban form, resulted in modern planning. Few cities in the United States, if any, were unaffected by these three major planning developments.

In more recent times planning has been greatly affected by the environmental movement that emerged in the 1960s. The impetus for this movement was twofold. First, a growing environmental awareness was reflected in and fueled by notable written works. Rachel Carson's *Silent Spring* (1962), Peter Blake's *God's Own Junkyard* (1964), William Whyte's *The Last Landscape* (1968), and other books directed attention to alarming conditions in natural or built environments and were critical to a growing discourse. A second impetus inspired by the discourse was centered largely in federal legislation adopted during the period. The Water Quality Act of 1965, the National Environmental Policy Act of 1969, and in the 1970s the Soil and Water Conservation Act, the Safe Water Drinking Act, the Solid Waste Management Act, the Resource Conservation and Recovery Act, the Toxic Substances Control Act, the Surface Mining Control and Reclamation Act, the Clean Air Act, the Coastal Zone Management Act, the Wild and Scenic Rivers Act, and the Flood Disaster Protection Act were part and parcel of the environmental movement.

A direct outgrowth of the flurry of federal legislation was development of similar and related legislation at the state level. Environmental planning developed at all levels of government, engaging environmental planners as specialists with various responsibilities. These include environmental impact assessment, development of environmental land-use plans, preparation and administration of environmental land-use regulations, and the like.

The origins of sustainability are also traceable to nineteenth-century developments and luminaries of the period. George Perkins Marsh is credited with founding the science of ecology; his hallmark book, *Man and Nature: Physical Geography as Modified by Human Action*, published in 1864, coincided with Olmsted's work in Yosemite. In 1878 John Wesley Powell published *Report on the Lands of the Arid Region of the United States*, which advocated environmentally sound, or "sustainable," western settlements. Gifford Pinchot is the individual most widely associated with the conservation movement originating in the nineteenth century. As the first head of the U.S. Forest Service, he advocated the use of scientific management methods in the nation's forests. Of course, as with planning, sustainability is rooted in the environmental movement of the 1960s, during which particular emphasis was placed on the finite nature or vulnerability of energy, soil, water, and air quality. Particularly noteworthy was Robert MacArthur's and Edward O. Wilson's *The Theory of Island Biogeography* (1967), inspired by the work of Charles Darwin. MacArthur and Wilson's theory is also regarded as the basis for conservation biology, a field emphasizing habitat preservation that has gained particular interest in recent years.

RATIONALES AND CHARACTERISTICS OF PLANNING AND SUSTAINABILITY

Justification of planning and sustainability efforts for the blackland prairies requires some understanding of their rationales and characteristics. After all, isn't it possible to "let nature take its course" and to have faith in the leveling effect of the so-called invisible hand with respect to natural environments, land-use planning, and regard for present and future generations? The answer to this rhetorical question is an emphatic no. The refuting of Adam Smith's widely held belief that competition—that is, the market's invisible hand—would preclude the necessity for government intervention is well supported by recent history. Most notable are the Great Depression and the long history of humankind's role in environmental degradation such as deforestation, desertification, alteration of water basins, urbanization, and subsequent soil deterioration, in which market forces were considerable in contributing to rather than correcting significant adversities. Inclusive of economic history as well as that pertaining to social, built, and natural environments, the hard lessons of the past have been major rationales for planning (Levy 1988:295). In short, governmental involvement is needed in guiding human activity to avert catastrophe, whether economic, social, or environmental.

As a largely public-sector endeavor, professional planning is further justified by the concept of public interest, which regards the planner as a neutral public servant not beholden to a private client or the profit incentive. Coupled with rejecting the effects of the hidden hand and the need to safeguard the public interest, planning is further rationalized by the interconnectedness of a global economy, complex social and technological change, and subsequent environmental impacts that are potentially adverse and therefore require direction, regulation, and mitigation. Moreover, planners view such change and its impacts as potentially resulting in externalities or spillovers having substantial effects on third parties not represented in particular actions between two originating parties (Levy 1988:297). Therefore in considering the blackland prairies or any other unique environments in the context of human activities, planning assumes that without a framework to guide change, those areas and adjoining properties where change occurs may be adversely affected and the public interest betrayed.

Planning has various characteristics that are outgrowths of the precepts giving it rationale. In recognizing the inevitability of change and its impacts, planning is characterized by being future oriented and visionary—that is, by having a supportable sense of what is suitable, practical, and feasible with respect to natural, built, and social contexts. Similarly, planning is by nature intentional: forces that cause and affect change can be understood and dealt with in rational terms that serve as a major basis for realizing the means by which desirable ends can be achieved. In this regard, planning is a generalist field that relies on data from a variety of sources: the sciences, law, economics, business interests, public agencies, and the public at large, especially that public which is somehow affected by or contributes to change in the environment. Finally, planning is both physical and policy oriented in that planners, through an informed constituency, can guide or regulate creation of land-use plans dealing specifically with tangible situations, such as a master plan for a nature preserve, cluster housing, or a mixed-use subdivision. Or, through an elaborate process of public participation and review, the planning function might establish a policy framework through which a set of policies, goals, and objectives might guide land use.

Many of the rationales for sustainability are similar to those for planning; they involve the impacts of complex change and the interconnectedness of the myriad factors having to do with built and natural environments. However, the main rationales for sustainability involve two issues. First is the concern about providing for current and future generations relative to the consumption of natural resources and the effects of consumption. Population growth, social equity, and economic prosperity are significant, especially as they relate to the use of finite resources and impacts on habitat (Krizek and Power 1997:7). A second major rationale for sustainability is the moral prerogative for humankind to be stewards of natural resources. The classic argument for this viewpoint lies in Aldo Leopold's idea of a "land ethic" dating to 1933 and in intervening years the rather sizeable literature that has built on Leopold's work (Leopold 1949:239).

The emergence and practice of sustainability are largely derived from the ideas of a land ethic and stewardship where appropriate use of natural resources and application of scientific data and technology are mandatory. Monitoring the impacts of human intervention on natural resources is an important need. Here sustainability relies heavily on input from the natural sciences and a managed approach to natural resources to maximize qualitative habitat improvements and minimize or altogether avoid undesirable environmental and social impacts.

Therefore, significant to a sustainable approach to management of natural resources would be low material and energy throughputs and closed-loop production cycles. In recent years the further emergence of sustainability has resulted in widespread consideration of its basic precepts beyond the natural sciences and into the social sciences, business circles, and all levels of government. Therefore, while sustainability shares planning's characteristic of being visionary as reflected in the work of the various luminaries in the field (see Ehrlich 1968; Leopold 1949; Rifkin 1991), it is rapidly evolving beyond being a conceptual set of constructs to carefully applied practices.

However, recent developments in conservation biology are noteworthy. Planning has become very well developed in its methodologies and processes, formulation of plans and policies, and implementation strategies, whereas sustainability shares some of conservation biology's doctrine of excluding human presence in select environments except as pertains to scientific inquiry (Hascom 1999:10). Unlike sustainability, the planning profession prefers to involve an informed and active constituency as inherent in its concern for the public interest. By virtue of these basic characteristics and distinctions, among others, planning and sustainability are potentially complementary and symbiotic. Therefore, a basic tenet of this paper is that sustainability can greatly benefit by becoming integral to the planning process, especially as related to the various means of implementation discussed below.

Another significant distinction between planning and sustainability is that planning can be bisected into two major concerns. One is referred to as growth management, in which a particular area or community has a growing economy and various associated developments that require regulation, direction, and management. The blackland prairies of Texas that have experienced significant urbanization require growth management, for example, farmland preservation and other forms of open-space preservation and conservation.

The second general planning effort is economic development, which concerns areas and communities that may be economically stagnant or in recession. The blackland prairies of Mississippi and Alabama contrast with those of Texas, for example, in that to be sustainable, adequate economic resources should be applied that are "clean" with respect to the environment and that are reflective of the rich history, culture, and natural milieu of the setting. Types of clean industry are numerous. A case in point is the community of West Point, Mississippi, which over time has developed the Prairie Arts Festival. An arts, crafts, and local food event held one weekend each year, the festival attracts thousands of people who provide a significant influx of revenue to the community with minimal environmental, social, and fiscal impacts on the city. And, of course, it underscores the community's connection with the prairie.

IMPLEMENTATION—PLANNING'S "INVISIBLE WEB"

Key factors in realizing sustainable multiple-use planning in the blackland prairies—or in any other environment, for that matter—are the types and strategies of implementation used in developing and realizing a plan. In planning circles, approaches to developing and realizing (that is, implementing) plans are commonly called the "invisible web," a structure of policies, statutes, ordinances, and similar regulations. Plans themselves—for example, comprehensive plans, so-called precise plans, neighborhood plans, and so forth—are also part of the implementation process, along with the other approaches cited here. Citizens and other users of such plans usually do not associate the plans with the tangible effects they have on people's lives because, at best, the plans are regarded as guidelines for directing future developments. Therefore, implementation in planning is not physical per se, as it would be in building a new parkway, cluster development, or school complex. Instead, it is legalistic, regulatory, and therefore not directly apparent to most people.

The various strands of the invisible web are numerous and limited only by the abilities of officials to create such measures and have them adopted. These strategies are largely implemented at the local level, where government is authorized to engage in planning-related activity by virtue of enabling state legislation. The amount and effectiveness of such legislation varies from state to state, as does the ability and willingness of local governments and constituencies to take advantage of it.

Implementation strategies typically at the disposal of local governments can be categorized as regulatory, incentive in nature, and acquisition based. Private-sector initiatives available at the local level also might be carried out in concert with local governments. Moreover, government at the state and federal levels includes agencies and related sources that are part of the implementation process. Table 16.1 presents various implementation measures and their relationship to levels of government, growth management, and economic development.

REGULATORY MEASURES

The comprehensive plan is a framework at the local level that provides a baseline for regulatory measures and concerns the entire geographic area of a particular city or county. The plan is long range (spanning 20

Table 16.1 Implementation options, strategies, and sources. Implementation strategies comprising the "invisible web" may also affect growth management or economic development involving blackland prairies.

		Local	State	Federal	Growth Management	Economic Development
				APPLICATION (A) or SOURCE (S)		
REGULATORY	Plans	AS	AS	AS	A	A
	Zoning	AS			A	A
	Subdivision Regulations	AS			A	A
	Land Suitability Analysis (LSA)	A	AS	AS	A	
	Environmental Impact Analysis (EIS)	A	AS	AS	A	A
	Endangered Species Act (ESA)	A	A	AS	A	A
	National Biological Survey (NBS)			AS	A	A
INCENTIVES	Density Bonuses	AS			A	A
	Clustering	AS			A	A
	Transfer of Development Rights (TDRs)	AS			A	A
	Grants and Loans	AS	S	S	A	A
	Tax Programs	AS	AS	AS	A	A
	Conservation Reserve Programs	A		S	A	
	Training and Education	AS	S	S	A	A
	Leases	AS			A	A
	Tax Increment Financing (TIFs)	AS				A
	Infrastructure Development	AS	AS	AS	A	A
ACQUISITION	Fee Simple Purchase	AS	AS	AS	A	A
	Easements	AS			A	A
	"Triggers"	AS			A	
	Right of First Refusal	AS			A	
	Impact Fees	AS			A	A
	Land Trades	AS	AS	AS	A	A
PRIVATE SECTOR	Land Trusts	A			A	
	Limited Conservation Development	A				
	Venture Capital	A			A	A
	Interest Subsidies	A				A

(IMPLEMENTATION OPTIONS)

to 30 years) and renewable and is reviewed and updated approximately every five years. Such a comprehensive plan considers social and economic issues, but its essential purpose is to guide physical development of a community. A comprehensive plan can also reflect policy within the community; hence it is a policy statement on which future development and management should be based with respect to amount, quality, location, type, and rate of growth. Plans are typically composed of various elements or parts, such as a central business district element, a housing element, or, in the case of the blackland prairies, a conservation element.

Comprehensive plans provide a base for the two regulatory measures most widely used in planning: zoning ordinances and subdivision standards (Hollander et al. 1988). Zoning was originally adopted in the United States in the 1920s. The Standard Zoning Enabling Act was adopted by the U.S. Department of Commerce in 1926 to regulate height, bulk, setback, and use of land parcels (Kelly 1988:252). These ordinances reacted to severe land-use problems stemming from the Industrial Revolution, when incompatible uses ended up next to each other because there was no regulatory authority. Today's local zoning ordinances too often reflect values and awareness of an earlier period that have precluded compatible mixed uses, created isolation, and encouraged sprawl. Such ordinances require modernizing to deal with more complex concerns—for example, overdependence on cars, concern for environmentally or historically sensitive landscapes, and habitat protection. Zoning-ordinance updating might include restriction of uses in areas containing or adjacent to blackland prairies. Other ordinances might be updated to address vegetation management, tree protection, grading, or the inclusion of buffer areas. The possibilities are numerous and should reflect local needs and conditions. Regardless of improvements made in zoning ordinances, along with the comprehensive plan they are powerful tools in realizing compatible and multiple land use in built environments.

Variations of standard zoning have been developed in recent years to deal with contemporary land-use challenges. Among these are overlay zones, which supplement the standard zoning regulations (Stokes et al. 1989:143). The most common application of overlay zones is floodplain protection, but they also can be applied to sensitive landscapes such as prairies. The use of overlay districts precludes the need to revise regulations for each zoned area. Instead, developers must conform to standards above and beyond those within the basic ordinance to address special situations or needs.

The use of agricultural land and large-lot zoning is another variation that might provide protection of prairie habitat (Toner 1988:118). In this variation, large minimum lot sizes (often 65 ha [160 acres] or larger) are required, where substantial portions of each parcel remain in open space. The assumption is that agricultural land includes relatively undisturbed habitat; in situations where this is not the case, large-lot zoning alone would be recommended.

Performance zoning controls land use for protection of important environmental features. This type of zoning is intended to minimize adverse impacts of development through the measurement and mapping of pertinent environmental features and the permitting of land use, impervious surfaces, and open space accordingly. As for protecting habitat, "performance standards may be expressed in terms of minimum open-space ratios, maximum vegetation disturbance limits," and the like (Stokes et al. 1989:146).

In addition to comprehensive plans and zoning ordinances, subdivision regulations comprise a third major implementation strategy (Ducker 1988:200). Regulation of development can be very significant, ranging from lot sizing, location, and layout variations to street design, lighting, tree planting and other landscaping, grading, erosion control, creation of public amenities such as parks, and the like. With respect to habitat protection, subdivision regulations could limit disturbance by requiring buffering, storm-drainage management, dedication of land for open space, or large lots, thereby limiting population and use densities.

An overall strategy of growth management could employ three approaches to regulating land use that may be of merit in blackland prairie habitats. One is establishment of an urban growth boundary allowing communities to take into account sensitive landscapes and shape land-use patterns through strategic provision or exclusion of urban services (Duerksen et al. 1977:38). A second is capital improvements programming, whereby careful attention is given to the location of infrastructure. In this case communities can protect sensitive habitat by *not* planning or budgeting for roads, water, sewer, and the like in those areas (Duerksen et al. 1977:39; Mantell et al. 1990:183; Stokes et al. 1989:133). This is potentially a very powerful tool that local governments can wield to direct and regulate land use. A third innovative regulatory approach to protecting landscapes is known as "legislatively adopted 'sanctuaries.'" A recently implemented approach, it is useful to localities wishing to avoid encroachment of incompatible uses (Duerksen et al. 1977:38).

None of these regulatory measures can be fully effective in preserving the unique features of blackland prairies without the application of two important tools of environmental planning: land-suitability analysis (LSA) and environmental impact analysis (EIA). LSA is a relatively complex process comprising four steps. First, a classification system for resources in a land area is selected and defined. This system might include data on soils, hydrologic conditions, geology, topography, vegetation, history, and the like. Second, the land area is classified according to the system. Third, a classification system for land use is selected and defined. Finally, each of the classified land uses is compared with the classified land area (Toner 1988:126). This four-step process requires extensive mapping and analysis; matrices are often used to arrive at suitability recommendations. LSA is highly suitable to geographic information systems (GIS) methods and technology, making a complex process somewhat less cumbersome.

As environmental impact assessment is more focused and detailed than LSA, it should naturally follow LSA. EIA may involve a single project site or an entire comprehensive plan. Conceivably it could encompass land areas larger than those addressed in a comprehensive plan. Various methods can be applied, but irrespective of those used, the analysis is built around a six-step framework emanating from the National Environmental Policy Act (NEPA). The framework includes (1) a description of existing conditions; (2) identification of alternatives to a main proposed project; (3) a description of the likely impacts of each alternative; (4) identification of a preferred alternative and the method used in choosing it; (5) a detailed description of the impacts of the preferred alternative; and (6) identification of means to minimize adverse impacts of the preferred alternative (Toner 1988:129).

Unfortunately, government is too often unable or unwilling to adequately implement a comprehensive plan, even when there is a good plan in place. In its place an incremental approach to growth is practiced, with no application of the analysis or assessment that characterizes LSA and EIA. Although portions of the blackland prairies of Texas and most other areas of the country are graphic evidence of what in planning is referred to as *incrementalism*, this does not have to be the case (Allen et al. 1998).

INCENTIVES

Communities unwilling to implement land-use controls may find the use of incentives for habitat protection more to their liking. With careful application, incentives can be at least as effective as land-use controls.

Five types of incentives are possibly applicable to blackland prairies: density bonuses, clustering, transferable development rights (TDRs), grants and loans, and tax programs. Density bonuses are commonly used to encourage developers to adopt certain actions, such as habitat protection, in exchange for the right to develop more real estate than would otherwise be allowed (Duerksen et al. 1977:40).

Clustering or cluster zoning typically requires developers to protect specified areas from encroachment and future development in exchange for grouping buildings and related amenities in certain other areas. The advantage to developers is that minimum–lot size requirements can be waived; there may also be a reduction in infrastructure costs (Duerksen et al. 1977:40; Mantell et al. 1990:9; Stokes et al. 1989:144).

TDRs represent a density transfer whereby the permissible amount of development density is shifted to another, more suitable setting. Communities map "sending" and "receiving" areas, where transfers can take place. The development rights are bought and sold, with pricing determined by the market. A community has the option of making the transfers entirely voluntary, mandatory in both sending and receiving areas, or mandatory in one area and voluntary in the other. TDRs used to protect habitat would limit development densities, thus avoiding or reducing adverse impacts to sensitive areas (Duerksen et al. 1977:40; Mantell et al. 1990:12; Stokes et al. 1989:151).

Another incentive at communities' disposal is the use of loans and grants. Communities can make loans or grants for acquisition and management of important areas for such endeavors as public education, inventories of flora and fauna, and monitoring. Grant programs originating at the local level are unusual, but local governments can apply for grants offered by nonprofit associations and foundations or through state and federal agencies (Duerksen et al. 1977:41; Stokes et al. 1989:178).

Tax credits and use assessments are examples of tax program incentives that can regulate land use. Tax credits can be granted for the value of approved conservation easements in areas where a landowner wishes to preclude or limit real estate development. Current-use assessments, for such cases as agricultural land experiencing development pressures, allow for land-value assessment based on farming activity rather than on the higher values caused by more intensive uses. Such assessments preserve farmland and restrict development (Duerksen et al. 1977:42).

ACQUISITION PROGRAMS

Other implementation strategies that can result in habitat protection are acquisition programs. The two main types of acquisition programs are outright purchase of land, known as fee simple purchase, and purchase of development rights. Where public awareness of special habitats is high, purchases can be funded by separate taxes. The great advantage of fee ownership is that access and use of the land can be controlled. Such controls are important for sensitive landscapes, although they tend to make public ownership more difficult than if the land were privately owned (Duerksen et al. 1977:44).

Fee ownership also allows for sellback or leaseback of the land with restrictions and conditions put in place at the time of public ownership. In the case of farmlands, this approach may be supported by a public wary of taxes and public expenditures (Duerksen et al. 1977:44; Mantell et al. 1990:184). Conversely, there may be some advantage to a public agency that leases land from a property owner. In this case the lease gives the agency the right to management of the property where outright ownership is not possible or desirable (Stokes et al. 1989:177).

Easements can be part of fee simple ownership and tied into a sellback strategy, too. A local government could apply the law to create an easement, which could restrict the uses of a landscape environment. A related option would be establishment of an easement of land purchased by the public entity to protect a critical area and subsequent sellback to a private owner (Mantell et al. 1990:185; Stokes et al. 1989:178).

Related to acquisition programs are purchase "triggers" and rights of first refusal that can tie up property without requiring actual purchase. A purchase trigger gives a potential buyer an exclusive right to purchase property within a specified time. Rights of first refusal are a form of purchase trigger in which a party—for example, a local government—has bought the first right to buy or refuse to buy a land parcel (Duerksen et al. 1977:44).

Land dedications are another acquisition option local governments might exercise. In this case a landowner might convey land to the public voluntarily. Land owned by developers might be transferred to public ownership to mitigate adverse impacts of a proposed development (Duerksen et al. 1977:44).

Impact fees require developers not to dedicate land, but to pay a fee to offset or cover the cost of services and infrastructure otherwise borne by the public. Fees in this case might be used as a source of outright purchase of sensitive lands (Ducker 1988:218).

Finally, land trades can be a viable way for local governments to acquire habitat or other sensitive lands. Publicly owned land that may no longer be needed by the community may provide the basis for trading for desirable land holdings (Duerksen et al. 1977:46).

PRIVATE-SECTOR MEASURES

Trusts and limited conservation development are two ways that special landscapes might be protected through private-sector initiatives. Land trusts are nonprofit organizations that exercise various land-conservation strategies and also own and purchase land. For example, trusts might purchase land in critical areas when the public sector is unable or unwilling to buy it. They might sell or give land holdings to the public sector if strategic and feasible. Trusts may also work with developers who understand that building land-conservation measures into their projects may make for greater profitability (Mantell et al. 1990:141; Stokes et al. 1989:192).

The National Trust for Historic Preservation offers financial assistance programs in the form of grants and loans. Small sums granted to public agencies and nonprofit organizations are available for professional assistance in areas including archaeology, preservation planning, land-use planning, fundraising, and organizational development. Loan programs from the National Trust are available to eligible local governments and nonprofit organizations for projects such as historic-site acquisition and easement purchases.

Limited conservation development is a land-trust variation in which developers and a conservation organization work to protect appropriate open tracts and the like. In addition, nonprofit organizations can engage in limited development of suitable areas of land they own to reduce their expenditures (Duerksen et al. 1977:49; Mantell et al. 1990:187).

Forming partnerships with government to create land trusts or limit development is another realistic conservation option. In this case a community might solicit assistance from organizations active in creation of land trusts, or in identification of areas that should be considered for limited conservation development agreements.

CONSERVATION OPPORTUNITIES AT THE FEDERAL LEVEL

In addition to efforts that originate at the local level, the federal government's role in protecting habitat can be significant. Although there are numerous federal programs available, the Endangered Species Act (ESA), preservation incentives of the Biological Resources Division (formerly the National Biological Service [NBS]) of the U.S. Geological Survey (USGS), and the U.S. Department of Agriculture's (USDA) Environmental Quality Incentives Program (EQIP) are the topics discussed here.

The ESA was originally intended to address rare species smuggling and poaching. However, a 1981 court ruling expanded the scope of the law, asserting that habitat destruction affecting endangered species is also a violation. This ruling is in keeping with Section 7 of the ESA, which "requires the mapping of 'critical habitat' areas that a species needs to survive and the establishment of 'recovery plans' for each listed species" (Stokes et al. 1989:221). In 1982 the act was amended to require preparation and acceptance of a Habitat Conservation Plan (HCP) where endangered species are involved as a partial basis for granting building permits (Duerksen et al. 1977:65).

The idea of maintaining an inventory of national biological resources has been around for a long time: it originated more than 100 years ago with the USDA. Today the Biological Resources Division of the USGS, under the U.S. Department of Interior, helps to alleviate conflicts created at the local level by numerous environmental regulations emanating from all levels of government. The agency attempts to link existing programs with environmental specialists at the federal level who act as nonadvocating sources of information for local-level specialists. This information might range from restoration of degraded environments to identification of ways to preserve biological heritage (National Resource Council in Duerksen et al. 1977:68). An impressive description of this approach and of the former NBS in general may be found in a document titled *Our Living Resources: A Report to the Nation on the Distribution, Abundance, and Health of U.S. Plants, Animals, and Ecosystems* (U.S. Department of Interior 1995).

A preservation incentive known as the Conservation Reserve Program was established at the federal level to offset some of the detrimental effects of farming monoculture. An outgrowth of the 1985 farm bill (7 CFR 704) and the 1990 farm bill (7 CFR 1410), this program includes provisions for payment to farmers for 10-year agreements to voluntarily remove highly erosive land from production (Stokes et al. 1989:219).

The National Park Service (NPS), through the U.S. Department of Interior, oversees two programs with potential for preserving, conserving, and enhancing the blackland prairies, including archaeological resources found there. One program, the National Register of Historic Places, accepts listings of eligible real property having historic significance. The procedure for listing a property can originate locally or at the state level where official nominations can be made to the National Register. Listing a historic property can contribute to planning measures at various levels of government. Listing also makes historic properties eligible for federal income tax benefits when substantial rehabilitation or protection is undertaken. In addition, federal grants are sometimes available to owners for this purpose. The other program operated by NPS is the Historic Landscape Initiative, which promotes responsible preservation practices for properties of various sizes, including those of cultural and archaeological significance. The initiative works in partnership with state and federal agencies, colleges and universities, and professional organizations. It includes programs that offer grants, internships, and assistance to Native American groups seeking to reverse the loss of sites important to tribal culture.

Finally, the EQIP combines the efforts of several USDA programs. The EQIP establishes 5- to 10-year contracts with landowners by providing incentive and cost-sharing payments of up to 75 percent for installation of conservation measures (Duerksen et al. 1977:70).

ECONOMIC DEVELOPMENT

The blackland prairies are located in states that have experienced the rise of the Sun Belt and the economic benefits that both fueled and were fueled by such growth. In recent years many Sun Belt states have been aggressive in the pursuit, development, or use of vocational training and tax incentives, and in the attraction of defense plants and military installations, all of which contributed to great economic growth.

However, economic benefits realized by Sun Belt states have not necessarily been experienced in rural areas; the economic plight of rural
areas in the Southeast is a well-known and chronic problem.

The relationship between sustainability and economic development
is tenuous at best; one need only look at the many examples of developing nations and their struggle to gain economic footholds at the ex-
pense of environmental quality. However, the problems inherent in
these examples do not preclude planning for sustainable land use. Economic stagnation or recession demands that different strategies be employed and economic problems addressed as a partial basis for avoiding
or at least forestalling environmental degradation of prairie habitat.

In Alabama, the combination of a rich cultural heritage and current
economic practices in the blackland prairies may provide clues to how
sustainable land-use planning might be directed. The long history of
Alabama's prairies includes many fascinating dimensions, including
pre-Columbian culture, early French settlement, slavery and the ante-
bellum South, and recent transitions reflecting forest practices, farming, and hunting (Stauffer 1961:486, 497; Tower 1961:479, 482). The
possibility of developing the economy to reflect the premises of cultural tourism within the cultural and historical context of the blackland prairies may be an entirely viable way to sustain sound land-use
practices in the area (Wells in Oates 2000:9). Clearly evident in this
regard is a potential for recreational and educational attractions.

West Point, Mississippi, offers an example of economic development
with positive results and minimal adverse impacts. Its annual Prairie
Arts Festival began in 1980 with just a handful of participants. In recent years the festival has grown into an event with hundreds of artists and craftspeople, live stage events, food vendors, and classic car
displays, all of which attract thousands of visitors to the city (West
Point, Mississippi 2001:1). Various educational and recreational cultural events also contribute to the festival's success, and, as demonstrated by its history, the festival can further evolve to good ends. Although West Point's festival is just one example, it suggests the type
of "clean" economic activity communities can adopt as a basis for educating the public about the blackland prairies.

RESOURCES AVAILABLE AT THE STATE LEVEL

Economic resources vary from state to state, but commonly there are
several resources worth considering. They include financial incentives,
tax incentives, infrastructure development, and other forms of assistance. Financial incentives at the state level typically include grants,
direct loans, leasing programs, equity and venture capital, and tax increment financing. Interest subsidies in the form of direct subsidies
and loan guarantees might also be considered as part of an economic

development strategy promoting cultural tourism (Friedman and Darragh 1988:314).

Tax incentive possibilities are numerous as well. They include job credits, investment credits, research and development credits, sales tax abatements, establishment of empowerment zones, and incentives that reward property donations resulting in easements (Friedman and Darragh 1988:314; Stokes et al. 1989:178).

Infrastructure development resources related to economic growth might include grants, such as those matched at the local level, direct loans from state and local governments, interest subsidies, and development of land and buildings. To promote cultural tourism, a community might establish a "heritage trail" bike path that offers visitors a guided tour and links them to key commercial nodes. Such a venture might be supported by carefully directed infrastructure development (Friedman and Darragh 1988:293).

Nonfinancial forms of assistance are available as well. They include business consulting, aid in site selection, business procurement assistance, and technical support (Friedman and Darragh 1988:318).

RESOURCES AVAILABLE AT THE FEDERAL LEVEL

Federal resources for economic development typically originate with the U.S. Department of Commerce (DOC), the Small Business Administration (SBA), and the Environmental Protection Agency (EPA). The Economic Development Administration within the DOC provides grants for infrastructure development and planning and loan guarantees. The SBA is a source of loan guarantees, direct loans, equity, and technical and educational assistance through the Service Corps of Retired Executives (SCORE). In addition, the EPA provides some planning and construction grants.

CONCLUSIONS

Realizing sustainable land-use planning is a highly laudable and desirable goal. However, none of the ideas discussed in this paper can be implemented unless certain critical conditions are met. First, there must be some form of adequate leadership at the local level. This leadership may take the form of a grassroots environmental organization, a local group associated with a state or national organization, or perhaps business interests concerned about the quality of life in their community. Similarly, communities must have elected and appointed officials who are responsible in their positions of leadership and responsive to issues concerning the state and future of blackland prairies.

Without adequate state-enabling legislation, elected and appointed officials may be hampered from fulfilling their duties to safeguard the public interest. Where this is the case, both the state planning organization (that is, the state chapter of the American Planning Association) and sympathetic legislators must be willing and able to seek the enactment of improved legislation.

Commitment of appropriate resources is also an important ingredient in the realization of sustainable land-use planning measures. Such resources must be provided at the local level. Just as important, however, community officials must solicit and acquire support at the state and federal levels. The types of change needed in blackland prairie environments most likely cannot be accomplished without such support.

Prioritization of the critical conditions necessary for realizing sustainability differs with each location. Nevertheless, an informed, concerned, and involved public is always a high priority in planning efforts. Educational institutions and the local media should be mobilized to inform the public and facilitate the planning process. Other outlets can be explored as well, such as presentations to local service groups, displays at local libraries, and visits to places of employment where sympathetic businesses will allow their employees to attend presentations on the status and future of prairies.

Getting the job of sustainable land-use planning done is a major undertaking that requires strong organizational skills and team effort. Even if the challenge appears daunting or insurmountable at first, the stakes are too high and the rewards too great to avoid making a worthy attempt.

17 Conclusion

Theory and Applications in the Study of Human/Nature Interactions

EVAN PEACOCK AND TIMOTHY SCHAUWECKER

A host of specialized disciplines and subdisciplines of ecology, anthropology, and other fields make the study of human/nature interactions an explicit goal. These include human ecology, behavioral ecology, cultural ecology, historical ecology, "symbolic ecology," "ethnoecology," cultural geography, historical geography, "human ecodynamics," and environmental archaeology. To a lesser extent, the same goal is present within landscape ecology, restoration ecology, agricultural ecology, conservation biology, landscape archaeology, evolutionary ecology, and evolutionary archaeology. Many of these pursuits have arisen only within the last two decades. Why are so many different people trying in so many different ways to understand the interplay between humans and the environment?

There are many answers to that question, as each of the different approaches has its own aims. To some, it is an issue of trying to understand how nature is "constructed" through human cognition and what the philosophical and humanistic implications of such constructions are. Much of the pertinent, recent literature in anthropology and related disciplines has been in this vein (e.g., Biersack 1999a; Ellen and Fukui 1996; Ernst 1999). Other recent concerns are the incorporation of indigenous knowledge into commercial pursuits (as with "ethnopharmocology," for example) and how native peoples may be properly compensated or otherwise involved (e.g., Brosius 1999; Feinsinger 2001; Guruswamy and McNeely 1998; Lewis 2000; Moran 1999; Posey 1999; Simpson et al. 1998). Such issues have been the focus of several recent works and are not addressed in this volume. Ecological pursuits have increasingly focused on conservation, restoration, and sustainability, all considering the human component of ecological function more than has been the case in the past (Bradshaw 1983; Harper 1987;

Packard and Mutel 1997). Such considerations are a part of this present work, as is an avowed concern of many of the approaches listed above: the applicability of the various data sets to decision making in contemporary resource management. Also covered, albeit to a lesser extent, are the long-term implications of those management decisions for the ongoing transformation of our world.

We are faced with trying to merge two different kinds of science. One kind describes and explains observable biophysical phenomena in terms of functional linkages; this is, in essence, an adaptationist, systems approach free of temporal considerations. Systems theory was the hallmark of classic ecology, which stressed relationships between physical conditions and corresponding plant and animal community patterns (e.g., Whittaker 1956) and the homeostatic regulation of natural systems (e.g., Reichle et al. 1975:27-29). Various attempts have been made to redress the shortcomings of systems theory in ecological studies, one result being a growing list of "new ecologies" like those listed above (cf. Botkin 1990; Kottak 1999; Zimmerer 1994). Short-term predictability is evidenced in studies documenting patterns of ecological succession (e.g., Roberts and Richardson 1985; Chapin et al. 1994; Connell and Slatyer 1977; but see Botkin 1993). However, the need for greater temporal depth in ecological studies has become apparent as the role of humans in long-term environmental change is increasingly debated. For example, what anthropogenic factors, if any, have bearing on the oak decline (Stringer et al. 1989)? Recent studies have improved our knowledge of the timing, nature, and scale of the Native American use of fire and its effects on vegetation over the course of several millennia (e.g., Delcourt et al. 1998), and there is some suggestion that human actions over that time span structured what traditionally have been classified as natural, climax forest types (Weakley 1999).

How does one go about adding time to the mix? One way is by incorporating historical data into land-management decision making (e.g., Russell 1997; Sisk 1998), something that can be seen in many of the papers in this volume. Although this is admirable in intent, the results remain limited by the relatively shallow time depth and biases of the historical record. Paleoecology provides another way, but one that is hampered by the retention of essentialist units, whether geological, biological, or archaeological. The inevitable result of the use of such units is that most variability—the stuff of interest—is masked, as change is necessarily seen as transformation from one arbitrary block to the next. Yet another way is to take an evolutionary approach —the other kind of science. Evolutionary theory provides a means of dealing with change through time as a continuum. Change results from natural selection acting on variability. To understand why things look the way they do at any particular time, it is necessary to explore that variability, not compress it into arbitrary units that may become reified. Such reification has happened, for example, with the imposition of ethnographically informed labels like "chiefdom" on the archaeological record (Dunnell 1978; Leonard and Jones 1987). There is a growing body of literature advocating the use of evolutionary theory in archaeology (Dunnell 1980, 1989, 1992; O'Brien 1996; O'Brien and Lyman 2000; Maschner 1996; Teltser 1995) and a growing number of examples of how archaeological data may be structured so that change through time may be viewed without the use of essentialist units (e.g., Peacock 1997; Rafferty 1994; O'Brien et al. 2001). Paleoecologists, paleobiologists, and archaeologists share a need to grapple with time in a nonessentialist fashion. In this regard, the use of uniformitarian assumptions and essentialist units such as species in environmental archaeology and paleoecology, although defensible in relatively short-term studies (Gifford 1981; Peacock and Reese, this volume), deserves a great deal more critical attention.

Evolutionary theory provides a means of understanding how things get to be the way they are; ecological theory provides a means of understanding how those things operate together at any given time. Neither necessarily provides an effective basis for prediction of the long-term consequences of our actions. There are simply too many contingencies to account for (see the papers in Bintliff 1999), as we have learned time and again when dealing with the unintended consequences of our past actions. The removal of stocked fish from high-elevation lakes in the Sierra Nevada to prevent the extinction of an endemic frog species is a good recent example (Daerr 2002). If we cannot predict the biological outcomes of our actions beyond relatively short-term responses, such as the appearance of pioneer species on newly exposed ground, why do we try to restore, or conserve, ecosystems? How can there be such a thing as "ecosystem management"? Isn't it inevitable that change will occur in the long term regardless of efforts to the contrary?

The answer is yes, but there is an overriding rationale that justifies conservation, preservation, and restoration efforts: the need to preserve variability as a buffer against changes too rapid or radical for comfortable human adjustment. We are far too prone to look for shortcuts in the quest for economic gain. The results can be detrimental in economic terms, as with the annual destruction of thousands of hectares of monocultured pine stands by the southern pine beetle. The human costs can be catastrophic, as with the great potato famine of nineteenth-century Ireland. Although the importance of biotic diversity is widely recognized, we continue to ignore the lessons of the past. On the one hand, we seek out and preserve germ plasm from ancient crop varieties in remote parts of the world (Harlan 1992). On the other hand, we genetically alter crops to be able to withstand higher levels of pesticides and herbicides so that we can more effectively kill off anything we do not intend to ship to market. Studies such as those presented in this volume help to reveal the variability underlying past human/nature interactions. It is hoped that they also will help to emphasize why that variability is important and how we go about maintaining it.

The catalyst for understanding comes from neoenvironmental studies. The need for basic field recording, habitat description, assessment of physical parameters, and observations of species' responses to various stimuli is more important now than ever before, as we adapt our management practices to account for mounting human population pressure. Professionals and amateurs alike are accumulating ecological data at increasing rates. Technological innovations such as computers, geographic information systems, and remote sensing are allowing us to explore contemporary natural complexity in ways that were undreamed of just a few decades ago (e.g., D'Erchia 1997; Packard and Mutel 1997). The heuristic value of ecological restoration work has been recognized: in ways that cannot be matched by even the most sophisticated modeling, we learn by doing (e.g., Harper 1987; the papers in Jordan et al. 1987). The more we learn, the more we realize how little we yet know. What is certain at this point is that information is critical. What we choose to do with that information is no less critical.

As we grow more sophisticated in achieving a true, evolutionary perspective on the dual unfolding of culture and nature, we are able to influence policy by presenting research results to an interested public (e.g., Addyman 1992; IJzereef 1992; Fowler 1992; Marquardt 1994), and to better coordinate management decisions to reflect different natural- and cultural-resource needs (e.g., Bell 1992). That alone is reason enough to strive to build the interdisciplinary bridge. The two main difficulties we face are clarity in communication (cf. Peacock 2002) and the appropriateness of our analytical units for the questions being asked. The first may be addressed by efforts such as this volume, which presents the results of many different kinds of studies in the same package, notes the interdisciplinary implications of those studies, and attempts to address a common theme. Other recent publications have been exemplary in these regards (e.g., Egan and Howell 2001; Nicholas 1988b). Addressing the second difficulty is a matter of doing better science. These are not simple or easy goals to reach, but the promise in tackling such issues lies in what we can achieve: better understanding and appreciation of our extraordinary planet and the many cultures and life forms that inhabit it, and a better hope for the world we bequeath to the future.

References Cited

Abrams, M. D., A. K. Knapp, and L. C. Hulbert
  1986   A Ten-Year Record of Aboveground Biomass in a Kansas Tallgrass
          Prairie: Effects of Fire and Topographic Position. *American Journal
          of Botany* 73(10):1509–1515.

Adair, J.
  1930   *Adair's History of the American Indians*, edited by S. C. Williams.
          Promontory Press, New York.

Addyman, P. D.
  1992   The Public Role of Environmental Archaeology: Presentation and
          Interpretation. In *Issues in Environmental Archaeology*, edited by
          N. Balaam and J. Rackham, pp. 63–69. University College, Institute
          of Archaeology, London.

Aiken, W. C.
  1961   Progress in Soil Conservation in the Black Belt Since the Start of
          Soil Conservation Service. *Journal Alabama Academy Sciences* 31:
          493–495.

Allen, C. M.
  1993   Ecological Assessment of the Forest Vegetation of Keiffer Prairie Re-
          search Natural Area. Unpublished report on file, USDA Forest Ser-
          vice Office, Pineville, Louisiana.

Allen, C. M., and M. F. Vidrine
  1989   Wildflowers of the Cajun Prairie. *Louisiana Conservationist* 41:20–25.

Allen, P. M., D. L. Amsbury, P. N. Dolliver, O. T. Hayward, L. C. Nordt, and
          J. C. Yelderman
  1998   *Geography and Geology of the Grand and Black Prairies of Texas.*
          Friends of the Pleistocene, South-Central Cell. Baylor Geological So-
          ciety, Waco.

Anderson, R. C.
  1990   The Historic Role of Fire in the North American Grassland. In *Fire
          in North American Tallgrass Prairies*, edited by S. L. Collins and
          L. L. Wallace, pp. 8–18. University of Oklahoma Press, Norman.

1999   The Indian Southwest, 1580–1830. University of Oklahoma Press,
          Norman.

Anderson, R. C., and M. L. Bowles
1999   Deep-Soil Savannas and Barrens of the Midwestern United States.
          Savannas, Barrens, and Rock Outcrop Plant Communities of North
          America, edited by R. C. Anderson, J. S. Fralish, and J. M. Baskin,
          pp. 155–170. Cambridge University Press, New York.

Anderson, R. C., and K. J. Roberts
1993   Mycorrhizae in Prairie Restoration: Response of Three Little Blue-
          stem (Schizachyrium scoparium) Populations to Mychorrhizal In-
          oculum from a Single Source. Restoration Ecology 1:83–93.

Apfelbaum, S. I., and K. A. Chapman
1997   Ecological Restoration: A Practical Approach. In Ecosystem Manage-
          ment, edited by M. S. Boyce and A. Haney, pp. 301–332. Yale Uni-
          versity Press, New Haven.

Archer, A. F.
1948   Land Snails of the Genus Stenotrema in the Alabama Region. Mu-
          seum Paper 28. Geological Survey of Alabama.

Atkinson, J. R.
1979   A Historic Contact Indian Settlement in Oktibbeha County, Missis-
          sippi. Journal of Alabama Archaeology 25(1):61–82.

1987   Historic Chickasaw Cultural Material: A More Comprehensive Iden-
          tification. Mississippi Archaeology 22(2):32–62.

1992   Archaeological Investigations on the 3 P Section of the Natchez
          Trace Parkway in Mississippi, 1988, 1990, and 1991. National Park
          Service, Southeast Archaeological Center, Tallahassee, Florida.

Atkinson, J. R., and J. D. Elliott, Jr.
1978   A Cultural Resources Survey of Selected Construction Areas in the
          Tennessee-Tombigbee Waterway: Alabama and Mississippi. Report
          submitted to the U.S. Army Corps of Engineers, Mobile, by the De-
          partment of Anthropology, Mississippi State University.

Atwill, L.
1992   Bow Camp. Field and Stream 97(2):37–39.

Axelrod, D. I.
1985   Rise of the Grassland Biome, Central North America. Botanical
          Review 51:163–201.

Baca, K. A., and E. Peacock
1997   The Brogan Mound, a Middle Woodland Site in Clay County, Mis-
          sissippi. In Mounds, Embankments, and Ceremonialism in the
          Midsouth, edited by R. C. Mainfort, Jr., and R. Walling, pp. 12–21.
          Arkansas Archeological Survey Research Series 46, Fayetteville.

Baerreis, D. A.
1973   Gastropods and Archaeology. In Variation in Anthropology: Essays
          in Honor of John C. McGregor, edited by D. W. Lathrap and J. Doug-
          las, pp. 43–54. Illinois Archaeological Survey, Urbana.

1990   Terrestrial Gastropods from the Rainbow Site. In Woodland Cul-
          tures on the Western Prairies: The Rainbow Site Investigations, ed-
          ited by D. W. Benn, pp. 183–192. Office of the State Archaeologist
          Report 18. Iowa City.

Bamforth, D. B.

1988   *Ecology and Human Organization on the Great Plains.* Plenum Press, New York.

Barber, R. J.

1988   The Use of Land Snails from Prehistoric Sites for Paleoenvironmental Reconstruction. In *Holocene Human Ecology in Northeastern North America,* edited by G. P. Nicholas, pp. 11–28. Plenum Press, New York.

Barbour, M. G., J. H. Burk, and W. D. Pitts

1987   *Terrestrial Plant Ecology.* 2nd ed. Benjamin/Cummings Publishing, Menlo Park, California.

Barlow, C.

2000   *The Ghosts of Evolution: Nonsensical Fruit, Missing Partners, and Other Ecological Anachronisms.* With a foreword by Paul Martin. Basic Books, New York.

Baskin, J. M., and C. C. Baskin

1986   Distribution and Geographical/Evolutionary Relationships of Cedar Glade Endemics in Southeastern United States. *Association of Southeastern Biologists Bulletin* 33:138–154.

Baskin, J. M., C. C. Baskin, and E. W. Chester

1994   The Big Barrens Region of Kentucky and Tennessee: Further Observations and Considerations. *Castanea* 59(3):226–254.

Baugh, T. G.

1991   Ecology and Exchange: The Dynamics of Plains-Pueblo Interaction. In *Farmers, Hunters, and Colonists: Interaction Between the Southwest and the Southern Plains,* edited by K. A. Spielmann, pp. 107–127. University of Arizona Press, Tucson.

1998   Regional Polities and Socioeconomic Exchange: Caddoan and Puebloan Interaction. In *The Native History of the Caddo: Their Place in Southeastern Archeology and Ethnohistory,* edited by T. K. Perttula and J. E. Bruseth, pp. 145–174. Texas Archeological Research Laboratory Studies in Archeology 30, Austin.

Beach, T.

1994   The Fate of Eroded Soils: Sediment Sinks and Sediment Budgets of Agrarian Landscapes in Southern Minnesota, 1851–1988. *Annals of the Association of American Geographers* 84:5–28.

Bekele, A.

2001   Spatial Variability and Isotopic Studies of the Prairie-forest Transition Soil in Louisiana. Ph.D. dissertation, Louisiana State University, Baton Rouge.

Bekele, A., and W. H. Hudnall

2000   Soil Spatial Variability and C Stable Isotope Studies on Prairie-Forest Transition in Louisiana. Unpublished report on file, USDA Forest Service Office, Pineville, Louisiana.

Bell, L., and R. S. Weddle

1987   Voyage to the Mississippi through the Gulf of Mexico. In *La Salle, the Mississippi, and the Gulf; Three Primary Documents,* edited by R. S. Weddle, M. C. Morkovsky, and P. Galloway, pp. 225–258. Texas A&M University Press, College Station.

Bell, M.
1990   Sedimentation Rates in the Primary Fills of Chalk-Cut Features.
        In *Experimentation and Reconstruction in Environmental Archae-
        ology*, edited by D. E. Robinson, pp. 237–249. Oxbow Books, Oxford.
1992   The Co-ordination of Environmental and Archaeological Projects.
        In *Issues in Environmental Archaeology*, edited by N. Balaam and
        J. Rackham, pp. 21–33. University College, Institute of Archaeology,
        London.
Bell, R. E.
1984   The Plains Villagers: The Washita River. In *Prehistory of Oklahoma*,
        edited by R. E. Bell, pp. 307–324. Academic Press, New York.
Bergquist, H. R.
1943   Clay County Geology. *Mississippi State Geological Survey, Bulletin* 53.
Bierhorst, J.
1994   *The Ways of the Earth: Native America and the Environment.* William
        Morrow, New York.
Biersack, A.
1999a   The Mount Kare Python and His Gold: Totemism and Ecology in
        the Papua New Guinea Highlands. *American Anthropologist* 101(1):
        68–87.
1999b   Introduction: From the "New Ecology" to the New Ecologies. *Ameri-
        can Anthropologist* 101(1):5–18.
Bintliff, J. (editor)
1999   *Structure and Contingency: Evolutionary Processes in Life and Hu-
        man Society.* Leicester University Press, London.
Blake, G. R.
1965   Bulk Density. In Methods of Soil Analysis, Part 1, edited by C. A.
        Black, pp. 374–390. *Agronomy* 9:374–390.
Blakeman, C. H., Jr.
1975   *Archaeological Investigations in the Upper Central Tombigbee Val-
        ley: 1974 Season.* Report submitted to the National Park Service by
        the Department of Anthropology, Mississippi State University.
1985   An Archaeological Site Survey in Central Oktibbeha County, Mis-
        sissippi: June–July 1975. In *Anthology of Mississippi Archaeology*,
        edited by P. K. Galloway, pp. 118–215. Mississippi Department of
        Archives and History, Jackson.
Blakeslee, D. J.
1975   *The Plains Interband Trade System: An Ethnohistoric and Archaeo-
        logical Investigation.* Ph. D. dissertation, University of Wisconsin–
        Milwaukee. University Microfilms, Ann Arbor.
Bobrowsky, P. T.
1984   The History and Science of Gastropods in Archaeology. *American
        Antiquity* 49(1):77–93.
Bobrowsky, P. T., and T. W. Gatus
1984   Archaeomalacological Significance of the Hall Shelter, Perry County,
        Kentucky. *North American Archaeologist* 5(2):89–110.
Boszhardt, R. F.
2000   Turqouise, Rasps, and Heartlines: The Oneota Bison Pull. In *Mounds*,

Modoc, and Mesoamerica: Papers in Honor of Melvin L. Fowler, edited by S. R. Ahler, pp. 361–373. Illinois State Museum Scientific Papers, vol. 28, Springfield.

Boszhardt, R. F., and J. McCarthy
1999   Oneota End Scrapers and Experiments in Hide Dressing: An Analysis from the Lacrosse Locality. *Midcontinental Journal of Archaeology* 24(2):178–199.

Botkin, D. B.
1990   *Discordant Harmonies.* Oxford University Press, Oxford.
1993   *Forest Dynamics.* Oxford University Press, Oxford.

Botwinick, M.
1979   Foreword. In *The American Renaissance 1876–1917.* Pantheon, New York.

Boudreau, E. H.
1980   *Making the Adobe Brick.* Fifth Street Press, Berkeley.

Bourdo, E. A., Jr.
1956   A Review of the General Land Office Survey and of Its Use in Quantitative Studies of Former Forests. *Ecology* 37:754–768.

Boyer, M. C.
1983   *Dreaming the Rational City: The Myth of American City Planning.* MIT Press, Cambridge.

Bradshaw, A.D.
1983   The Reconstruction of Ecosystems. *Journal of Applied Ecology* 20: 1–17.

Brain, J. P.
1988   The Great Mound Robbery. *Archaeology* 41(3):18–25.

Brain, J. P., and P. Phillips
1996   *Shell Gorgets: Styles of the Late Prehistoric and Protohistoric Southeast.* Peabody Museum Press, Cambridge.

Braun, E. L.
1928   Glacial and Post-Glacial Plant Migrations Indicated by Relic Colonies in Southern Ohio. *Ecology* 9:284–302.

Brent, F. V., Jr.
1973   *Soil Survey of Oktibbeha County, Mississippi.* USDA Soil Conservation Service, Washington, D.C.

Bridges, E. L.
1987   The Coastal Prairie Region of Southeastern Louisiana—An Inventory for Potential Remnant Prairies. Unpublished report on file, Louisiana Natural Heritage Program, Baton Rouge.

Brooks, R. L.
1989   Village Farming Societies. In *From Clovis to Comanchero: Archeological Overview of the Southern Great Plains,* edited by J. L. Hoffman, R. L. Brooks, J. S. Hayes, R. L. Jantz, M. K. Marks, and M. H. Manhein, pp. 71–90. Arkansas Archeological Survey Research Series 35, Fayetteville.

Brosius, J. P.
1999   Green Dots, Pink Hearts: Displacing Politics from the Malaysian Rain Forest. *American Anthropologist* 101(1):36–57.

Brower, A. E.
1974   A List of the Lepidoptera of Maine—Part 1, the Macrolepidoptera. *University of Maine, Life Sciences and Agriculture Experiment Station, Technical Bulletin* 66:1–126.

Brown, A. J.
1894   *History of Newton County from 1834–1894.* Itawamba County Times, Fulton, Mississippi. Republished by Melvin Tingle, Decatur, Mississippi.

Brown, C. A.
1941a   Report on the Flora of the Isolated Prairies in Louisiana. *Proceedings of the Louisiana Academy of Sciences* 5:15.

1941b   Studies on the Isolated Prairies of Louisiana. *American Journal of Botany* 28:16.

1953   Studies on the Isolated Prairies of Louisiana. *Proceedings of the 7th International Botanical Congress, Stockholm, Sweden*, pp. 682–683.

1986   The Uncommon Bodark. *Arkansas Times* 12(9):51–55.

1997   Preliminary Report on the Isolated Prairies of Louisiana. *Proceedings of the Louisiana Academy of Sciences* 60:10–19.

Brown, J. A.
1975   Spiro Art and Its Mortuary Contexts. In *Death and the Afterlife in Pre-Columbian America*, edited by E. P. Benson, pp. 1–32. Dumbarton Oaks Research Library and Collections, Washington, D.C.

1983   Spiroan Exchange Connections Revealed by Sources of Imported Raw Materials. In *Southeastern Natives and Their Pasts: A Collection of Papers Honoring Dr. Robert E. Bell*, edited by D. G. Wyckoff and J. L. Hoffman, pp. 129–162. Studies in Oklahoma's Past No. 11. Oklahoma Archeological Survey, Norman.

1984   Arkansas Valley Caddoan: The Spiro Phase. In *Prehistory of Oklahoma*, edited by R. E. Bell, pp. 241–263. Academic Press, Orlando.

1996   The Spiro Ceremonial Center: the Archaeology of Arkansas Valley Caddoan Culture in Eastern Oklahoma. Memoirs of the Museum of Anthropology 29, vols. 1 and 2. University of Michigan, Ann Arbor.

Brown, J. A., R. A. Kerber, and H. D. Winters
1990   Trade and the Evolution of Exchange Relations at the Beginning of the Mississippi Period. In *The Mississippian Emergence*, edited by B. D. Smith, pp. 251–280. Smithsonian Institution Press, Washington, D.C.

Brues, A. M.
1957   Skeletal Material from the Nagle Site. *Bulletin of the Oklahoma Anthropological Society* 5:101–106.

1958   Skeletal Material from the Horton Site. *Bulletin of the Oklahoma Anthropological Society* 6:27–32.

1959   Skeletal Material from the Morris Site (Ck-39). *Bulletin of the Oklahoma Anthropological Society* 7:63–70.

1962   Skeletal Material from the McLemore Site. *Bulletin of the Oklahoma Anthropological Society* 10:68–78.

Bruseth, J. E., D. E. Wilson, and T. K. Perttula
  1995   The Sanders Site: A Spiroan Entrepot in Texas? *Plains Anthropologist* 40(153):223–236.
Buikstra, J. E.
  1992   Diet and Disease in Late Prehistory. In *Disease and Demography in the Americas,* edited by J. Verano and D. Ubelaker, pp. 87–101. Smithsonian Institution Press, Washington, D.C.
Bunting, M. J., and R. Tipping
  2000   Sorting Dross from Data: Possible Indicators of Post-depositional Assemblage Biasing in Archaeological Palynology. In Human Ecodynamics, edited by G. Bailey, R. Charles, and N. Winder, pp. 63–69. *Symposia of the Association for Environmental Archaeology No. 19.* Oxbow Books, Oxford.
Burch, J. B.
  1962   *How To Know the Eastern Land Snails.* Wm. C. Brown, Dubuque, Iowa.
Burgess, L. H., C. S. Wilson, E. H. McBride, J. L. Anderson, and K. E. Dahms
  1960   Soil Survey of Montgomery County, Alabama. USDA Soil Conservation Service Series 1957, No. 7. Washington, D.C.
Burnett, B. A.
  1990   The Biological Synthesis of the Eastern Portion of Gulf Coastal Plain. In D. A. Story, I. A. Guy, B. A. Burnett, M. D. Freeman, J. C. Rose, D. G. Steele, B. W. Olive, and K. J. Reinhard, *The Archeology and Bioarcheology of the Gulf Coastal Plain,* pp. 385–418. Arkansas Archeological Survey Research Series 38, Fayetteville.
Burton, J. D.
  1973   *Osage-orange . . . an American Wood.* Forest Service Bulletin FS-248. U.S. Department of Agriculture, Washington, D.C.
Butzer, K. W.
  1982   *Archaeology as Human Ecology.* Cambridge University Press, Cambridge.
Caddell, G. M.
  1982a   Plant Remains from the Yarborough Site. In C. Solis and R. Walling, *Archaeological Investigations at the Yarboriough Site (22C1814), Clay County, Mississippi,* pp. 134–140. Report of Investigations 30. Office of Archaeological Research, University of Alabama, Tuscaloosa.
  1982b   *Plant Resources, Archaeological Plant Remains, and Prehistoric Plant-use Patterns in the Central Tombigbee River Valley.* Bulletin of the Alabama Museum of Natural History 7. University of Alabama, Tuscaloosa.
Carey, C.
  2000   Infectious Diseases and Worldwide Declines of Amphibian Populations, with Comments on Emerging Diseases in Coral Reef Organisms and in Humans. *Environmental Health Perspectives* 108, *Supplement* 1:143–150.
Carr, B.
  1993   A Botanical Inventory of Blackland Prairie Openings in Sam Hous-

ton National Forest. Unpublished report on file, Texas Natural Heritage Program, Texas Parks and Wildlife Department. Austin.

Carr, S.
2000   Composition and Structure of Pine-Hardwood Forests of Central and Northwest Louisiana. Unpublished M.S. thesis, Louisiana State University, Baton Rouge.

Carroll, T. B.
1931   *Historical Sketches of Oktibbeha County,* edited by A. B. Butts, A. W. Garner, and F. D. Mellen. Dixie Press, Gulfport, Mississippi.

Catlin, G.
1973   *Notes on the Manners, Customs, and Conditions of the North American Indians.* Dover, New York.

Chadwick, G. F.
1966   *The Park and the Town: Public Landscape in the 19th and 20th Centuries.* F. A. Praeger, New York.

Chapin, F. S., III, L. R. Walker, C. L. Fastie, and L. C. Sharman
1994   Mechanisms of Primary Succession Following Deglaciation at Glacier Bay Alaska. *Ecological Monographs* 64: 149–175.

Chapman, H. D.
1965a   Total Exchangeable Bases. In Methods of Soil Analysis, Part 2, edited by C. A. Black. *Agronomy* 9:901–904. American Society of Agronomy, Madison, Wisconsin.
1965b   Cation-Exchange Capacity. In Methods of Soil Analysis, Part 2, edited by C. A. Black. *Agronomy* 9:900. American Society of Agronomy, Madison, Wisconsin.

Chapman, J., and A. B. Shea
1981   The Archaeobotanical Record: Early Archaic Period to Contact in the Lower Little Tennessee River Valley. *Tennessee Anthropologist* 6:61–84.

Chapman, J., P. A. Delcourt, P. A. Cridlebaugh, A. B. Shea, and H. R. Delcourt
1982   Man-Land Interaction: 10,000 Years of American Indian Impact on Native Ecosystems in the Lower Little Tennessee River Valley, Eastern Tennessee. *Southeastern Archaeology* 1:115–121.

Chatwin, B.
1987   *The Songlines.* Viking Press, New York.

Chester, E. W., B. E. Wofford, J. M. Baskin, and C. C. Baskin
1997   A Floristic Study of Barrens on the Southwestern Pennyroyal Plain, Kentucky and Tennessee. *Castanea* 62:161–172.

Chipman, D. E.
1992   *Spanish Texas, 1519–1821.* University of Texas Press, Austin.

Choate, J. R., J. K. Jones, Jr., and C. Jones
1994   *Handbook of Mammals of the South-Central States.* Louisiana State University Press, Baton Rouge.

Clayton, L. A., V. J. Knight, and E. C. Moore (editors)
1993   *The De Soto Chronicles: The Expedition of Hernando de Soto to North America in 1539–1543.* 2 vols. University of Alabama Press, Tuscaloosa.

Cleland, H. F.
1920   The Black Belt of Alabama. *Geographical Review* 10:375–387.
Cohen, M.
1977   *The Food Crisis in Prehistory.* Yale University Press, New Haven.
Colinvaux, P. A.
1987   The Changing Forests: Ephemeral Communities, Climate and Refugia. *Quarterly Review of Archaeology* 8(1).
Collins, O. B., F. E. Smeins, and D. H. Riskind
1975   Plant Communities of the Blackland Prairie of Texas. In *Prairie: A Multiple View,* edited by M. K. Wali, pp. 75–87. University of North Dakota Press, Grand Forks.
Collins, S. L.
1987   Interaction of Disturbances in a Tallgrass Prairie: A Field Experiment. *Ecology* 68(5):1243–1250.
1992   Fire Frequency and Community Heterogeneity in Tallgrass Prairie Vegetation. *Ecology* 73:2001–2006.
Collins, S. L., and L. L. Wallace (editors)
1990   *Fire in North American Prairies.* University of Oklahoma Press, Norman.
Collins, S. L., A. K. Knapp, J. M. Briggs, J. M. Blair, and E. M. Steinauer
1998   Modulation of Diversity by Grazing and Mowing in Native Tallgrass Prairie. *Science* 280:745–747.
Comas, J.
1960   *Manual of Physical Anthropology.* Charles C. Thomas, Springfield, Illinois.
Connaway, J. M.
1984   *The Wilsford Site (22-Co-516), Coahoma County, Mississippi.* Archaeological Report 14. Mississippi Department of Archives and History, Jackson.
Connell, J. H., and R. O. Slatyer
1977   Mechanisms of Succession in Natural Communities and Their Role in Community Stability and Organisation. *American Naturalist* 111:1119–1144.
Covell, C. V.
1984   *A Field Guide to the Moths of Eastern North America.* Peterson Field Guide Series. Houghton Mifflin, Boston.
Cowan, C. W., and P. J. Watson
1992   *The Origins of Agriculture: An International Perspective.* Smithsonian Institution Press, Washington, D.C.
Cowardin, L. M., V. Carter, F. C. Golet, and E. T. LaRoe
1979   Classification of Wetlands and Deepwater Habitats of the United States. Biological Services Program FWS/OBS-79/31. U.S. Department of the Interior, U.S. Fish and Wildlife Service. Washington, D.C.
Creel, D.
1991   Bison Hides in Late Prehistoric Exchange in the Southern Plains. *American Antiquity* 56(1):40–49.

Cronon, W.

1983   *Changes in the Land: Indians, Colonists, and the Ecology of New England.* Hill and Wang, New York.

Crosby, A. W.

1972   *The Columbian Exchange: Biological and Social Consequences of 1492.* Greenwood Press, Westport, Connecticut.

Crumb, S. E.

1956   *The Larvae of the Phalaenidae.* U.S. Department of Agriculture Technical Bulletin 1135:1–356. Washington, D.C.

Crumley, C. L.

1994   Historical Ecology: A Multidimensional Ecological Orientation. In *Historical Ecology: Cultural Knowledge and Changing Landscapes,* edited by C. L. Crumley, pp. 1–16. School of American Research Press, Santa Fe.

Daerr, E. G.

2002   Rare and Endangered: On the Rebound. *National Parks* 76(1–2):49.

Darby, W.

1816   A Map of the State of Louisiana with Part of the Mississippi Territory. N.p.

1818   *The Emigrant's Guide to the Western and Southwestern States and Territories.* Kirk and Mercein, New York.

Davis, G. B., L. J. Perry, and J. W. Kirkley.

1983   *The Official Military Atlas of the Civil War.* Gramercy Books, New York.

deFrance, S. D., W. F. Keegan, and L. A. Newson

1996   The Archaeobotanical, Bone Isotope, and Zooarchaeological Records from Caribbean Sites in Comparative Perspective. In *Case Studies in Environmental Archaeology,* edited by E. J. Reitz, L. A. Newsom, and S. J. Scudder, pp. 289–304. Plenum Press, New York.

Delcourt, H. R.

1979   Late Quaternary Vegetation History of the Eastern Highland Rim and Adjacent Cumberland Plateau of Tennessee. *Ecological Monographs* 49: 255–280.

1987   The Impact of Prehistoric Agriculture and Land Occupation on Natural Vegetation. *Trends in Ecology and Evolution* 2:39–44.

Delcourt, H. R., and P. A. Delcourt

1991   *Quaternary Ecology: A Paleoecological Perspective.* Chapman and Hall, London.

1997   Pre-Columbian Native American Use of Fire on Southern Appalachian Landscapes. *Conservation Biology* 11(4):1010–1014.

Delcourt, H. R., P. A. Delcourt, G. R. Wilkins, and E. N. Smith, Jr.

1986   Vegetational History of the Cedar Glades Region of Tennessee, Kentucky, and Missouri During the Past 30,000 Years. *Association of Southeastern Biologists Bulletin* 33:128–137.

Delcourt, P. A.

1978   Quaternary Vegetation History of the Gulf Coastal Plain. Unpublished Ph.D. dissertation, University of Minnesota.

Delcourt, P. A., and H. R. Delcourt

1977 The Tunica Hills, Louisiana-Mississippi: Late Glacial Locality for Spruce and Deciduous Forest Species. *Quaternary Research* 7: 218–237.

1987 *Long-Term Forest Dynamics of the Temperate Zone.* Springer-Verlag, New York.

1993 Paleoclimates, Paleovegetation, and Paleofloras During the Late Quaternary. In *Flora of North America North of Mexico,* edited by the Flora of North America Editorial Committee, pp. 71–94. Vol. 1. Oxford University Press, New York.

Delcourt, P. A., H. R. Delcourt, R. C. Brister, and L. E. Lackey

1980 Quaternary Vegetation History of the Mississippi Embayment. *Quaternary Research* 13:111–132.

Delcourt, P. A., H. R. Delcourt, P. A. Cridlebaugh, and J. Chapman

1986 Holocene Ethnobotanical and Paleoecological Record of Human Impact in the Little Tennessee River Valley, Tennessee. *Quaternary Research* 25:330–385.

Delcourt, P. A., H. R. Delcourt, C. R. Ison, W. E. Sharp, and K. J. Gremillion

1998 Prehistoric Human Use of Fire, the Eastern Agricultural Complex, and Appalachian Oak-Chestnut Forests: Paleoecology of Cliff Palace Pond, Kentucky. *American Antiquity* 63(2):263–278.

Denevan, W. M.

1992 The Pristine Myth: The Landscape of the Americas in 1492. *Annals of the Association of American Geographers* 82:369–385.

D'Erchia, F.

1997 Geographic Information Sytems and Remote Sensing Applications for Ecosystem Management. In *Ecosystem Management,* edited by M. S. Boyce and A. Haney, pp. 201–225. Yale University Press, New Haven.

de Richarville, C. D.

1739 Report on the Accounts Furnished by Sr. de Richarville of the War Against the Chickasaws. *Archives des Colonies,* series C13C, vol. 4, ff.202–205. Paris. Translation by P. Galloway, 1986, on file with the National Park Service, Natchez Trace Parkway, Tupelo, Mississippi.

Derrick, S. M., and D. Wilson

1997 Cranial Modeling as an Ethnic Marker among the Prehistoric Caddo. *Bulletin of the Texas Archeological Society* 68:139–146.

DeSelm, H. R.

1988 The Barrens of the Western Highland Rim of Tennessee. In *Proceedings of the First Annual Symposium on the Natural History of Lower Tennessee and Cumberland River Valleys,* edited by D. H. Snyder, pp. 199–219. Clarksville, Tennessee: Austin Peay State University, Center for Field Biology of Land Between the Lakes.

1994 Tennessee Barrens. *Castanea* 59(3):214–225.

DeSelm, H. R., and N. Murdock

1993 Grass Dominated Communities. In *Biodiversity of the Southeastern United States: Upland Terrestrial Communities,* edited by W. H.

Martin, S. G. Boyce, and A. C. Echternacht, pp. 87–141. John Wiley & Sons, New York.

Diamond, D. D.
  1985   Composition, Classification and Species Response Patterns of Remnant Tallgrass Prairies in Texas. *American Midland Naturalist* 113(2):294–311.

Diamond, D. D., and F. E. Smeins
  1988   Gradient Analysis of Remnant True and Upper Coastal Prairie Grasslands of North America. *Canadian Journal of Botany* 66:2152–2161.

Dicken, S. N.
  1935   The Kentucky Barrens. *Bulletin of the Geographical Society of Philadelphia* 33:42–51.

Diggs, G. M., B. L. Lipscomb, and R. J. O'Kennon
  1999   Illustrated Flora of North Central Texas. *Sida, Botanical Miscellany* 16:1–1626.

Dillehay, T.
  1974   Late Quaternary Bison Population Changes on the Southern Plains. *Plains Anthropologist* 19:180–196.

Dimbleby, G.
  1978   *Plants and Archaeology.* Granada Publishing Limited, London.

Dincauze, D. F.
  2000   *Environmental Archaeology: Principles and Practices.* Cambridge University Press, Cambridge.

Dobyns, H. F.
  1992   Native American Trade Centers as Contagious Disease Foci. In *Disease and Demography in the Americas,* edited by J. W. Verano and D. H. Ubelaker, pp. 215–222. Smithsonian Institution Press, Washington, D.C.

Dodd, J. D.
  1968   Grassland Associations in North America. In *Grass Systematics,* edited by F. W. Gould, pp. 322–338. McGraw-Hill, New York.

Drooker, P. B.
  1997   *The View From Madisonville: Protohistoric Western Fort Ancient Interaction Patterns.* Memoirs of the Museum of Anthropology. University of Michigan, Ann Arbor.

Ducker, R.
  1988   Land Subdivision Regulation. In *The Practice of Local Government Planning,* 2nd ed., edited by F. S. So and J. Getzels, pp. 198–250. International City/County Management Association, Washington, D.C.

Duerksen, C. J., D. L. Elliott, N. T. Nobbs, E. Johnson, and J. R. Miller
  1977   *Habitat Protection Planning.* American Planning Association, Chicago.

Dunnell, R. C.
  1978   Archaeological Potentials of Anthropological and Scientific Models of Function. In *Archaeological Essays in Honor of Irving B. Rouse,* edited by R. C. Dunnell and E. S. Hall, Jr., pp. 41–73. Mouton, The Hague.
  1980   Evolutionary Theory and Archaeology. In *Advances in Archaeologi-*

cal Method and Theory, edited by M. B. Schiffer, pp. 35–99. Vol. 3. Academic Press, New York.

1986   Five Decades of American Archaeology. In *American Archaeology Past and Future*, edited by D. J. Meltzer, D. D. Fowler, and J. A. Sabloff, pp. 23–49. Smithsonian Institution Press, Washington, D.C.

1989   Aspects of the Application of Evolutionary Theory in Archaeology. In *Archaeological Thought in America*, edited by C. C. Lamberg-Karlovsky, pp. 35–49. Cambridge University Press, New York.

1990   The Role of the Southeast in American Archaeology. *Southeastern Archaeology* 9(1):11–22.

1992   *Archaeology and Evolutionary Science*. In Quandaries and Quests: Visions of Archaeology's Future, edited by L. Wandsnider, pp. 209–224. Occasional Paper No. 20. Southern Illinois University, Center for Archaeological Investigations.

Du Pratz, M. L. P.

1774   *The History of Louisiana*, edited by J. G. Tregle. American Revolution Bicentennial Commission. Louisiana State University Press, Baton Rouge.

Dyksterhuis, E. J.

1946   The Vegetation of the Fort Worth Prairie. *Ecological Monographs* 16:1–29.

Early, A. M.

1993   Finding the Middle Passage: The Spanish Journey from the Swamplands to Caddo Country. In *The Expedition of Hernando de Soto West of the Mississippi, 1541–1543*, edited by G. A. Young and M. P. Hoffman, pp. 68–77. University of Arkansas Press, Fayetteville.

2000a   The Caddo and the Forest. In Forest Farmsteads: A Millennium of Human Occupation at Winding Stair in the Ouachita Mountains, edited by A. M. Early, pp. 94–110. Arkansas Archeological Survey Research Series 57, Fayetteville.

2000b   The Caddos of the Trans-Mississippi South. In *Indians of the Greater Southeast: Historical Archaeology and Ethnohistory*, edited by B. G. McEwan, pp. 122–141. University Press of Florida, Gainesville.

Egan, D., and E. A. Howell (editors)

2001   *The Historical Ecology Handbook*. Island Press, Washington, D.C.

Ehrlich, P.

1968   *The Population Bomb*. Ballantine Books, New York.

Eichlin, T. D., and W. D. Duckworth

1988   Sesioidea. Sesiidae. In *The Moths of America North of Mexico*, 5.1, edited by R. B. Dominick et al., pp. 1–176. Wedge Entomological Research Foundation, Washington, D.C.

Elias, T. S.

1987   *The Complete Trees of North America*. Gramercy Books, New York.

Ellen, R.

1989   *Environment, Subsistence, and System: The Ecology of Small-Scale Social Formations*. Cambridge University Press, Cambridge.

Ellen, R., and K. Fukui (editors)

1996   *Redefining Nature*. Berg, Oxford.

Emerson, T. E., and R. E. Hughes
2000   Figurines, Flint Clay Sourcing, the Ozark Highlands, and Cahokian
        Acquisition. *American Antiquity* 65(1):79–101.

Ernst, T. M.
1999   Land, Stories, and Resources: Discourse and Entification in Ona-
        basulu Modernity. *American Anthropologist* 101(1):88–97.

Evans, J. G.
1972   *Land Snails in Archaeology.* Seminar Press, New York.

Ewers, J. C.
1954   The Indian Trade of the Upper Missouri Before Lewis and Clark: An
        Interpretation. *Missouri Historical Society Bulletin* 10(4):429–446.
1955   *The Horse in Blackfoot Indian Culture: With Comparative Material
        from Other Western Tribes.* Bureau of American Ethnology Bulletin
        No. 159. Smithsonian Institution, Washington, D.C.

Farney, D.
1980   The Tallgrass Prairie: Can It Be Saved? *National Geographic* 157(1):
        37–61.

Featherman, A.
1872   Report of Botanical Survey of Southwest and Northwest Louisiana,
        Made During the Year 1871, to the Board of Supervisors of the Loui-
        siana State University. New Orleans, 103–161. N.p.

Featherstonhaugh, G. W.
1844   *Excursion Through the Slave States.* Harper and Bros, New York.

Fein, A.
1972   *Frederick Law Olmsted and the American Environmental Tradition.*
        George Braziller, New York.

Feinsinger, P.
2001   *Designing Field Studies for Biodiversity Conservation.* Island Press,
        Washington, D.C.

Fernald, C. H.
1896   *The Crambidae of North America.* Massachusetts Agricultural Col-
        lege, Amherst.

Finklestein, J. J.
1940   The Norman Site Excavations Near Wagoner, Oklahoma. *The Okla-
        homa Prehistorian* 3(3):12–15.

Fisher-Carroll, R. L.
1997   Sociopolitical Organization at Upper Nodena (3MS4) from a Mortu-
        ary Perspective. Unpublished M.A. thesis, University of Arkansas.

Fleming, T. H.
1979   Life-History Strategies. In *Ecology of Small Mammals,* edited by
        D. M. Stoddart, pp. 1–61. Chapman and Hall, London.

Flores, D. L. (editor)
1984   *Jefferson and Southwestern Exploration: The Freeman and Custis
        Accounts of the Red River Expedition of 1806.* University of Okla-
        homa Press, Norman.
1985   *Journal of an Indian Trader: Anthony Glass and the Texas Frontier,
        1790–1810.* College Station: Texas A&M University Press.

1991   Bison Ecology and Bison Diplomacy: The Southern Plains from 1800 to 1850. *Journal of American History* 78:465–485.

Fogel, R. W.
1989   *Without Consent or Contract: The Rise and Fall of American Slavery.* W. W. Norton, New York.

Forbes, S. P.
1999   Community Properties Along Biomass Gradients in Blackland Prairies. Unpublished M.S. thesis, Mississippi State University.

Forbes, W. T. M.
1948   The Lepidoptera of New York and Neighboring States. Part II. Geometridae, Sphingidae, Notodontidae, Lymantriidae. *Cornell University Agricultural Experiment Station Memoir* 274:1–263.

1954   The Lepidoptera of New York and Neighboring States. Part III. Noctuidae. *Cornell University Agricultural Experiment Station Memoir* 329:1–433.

1960   The Lepidoptera of New York and Neighboring States. Part IV. Agaristidae through Nymphalidae Including Butterflies. *Cornell University Agricultural Experiment Station Memoir* 371:1–188.

Ford, R. I.
1972   Barter, Gift, or Violence: An Analysis of Tewa Intertribal Exchange. In *Social Exchange and Interaction,* edited by E. M. Wilmsen, pp. 21–45. Anthropological Papers No. 46. Museum of Anthropology, University of Michigan, Ann Arbor.

Forshey, C. G.
1845   Description of Some Artificial Mounds on Prairie Jefferson, Louisiana. *American Journal of Science and Arts* 49:39–42.

Foster, D. R., T. Zebryk, P. Schoonmaker, and A. Lezberg
1992   Post-Settlement History of Human Land-Use and Vegetation Dynamics of a *Tsuga canadensis* (Hemlock) Woodlot in Central New England. *Journal of Ecology* 80:733–786.

Foster, S., and J. A. Duke
1990   *Peterson Field Guide to Eastern/Central Medicinal Plants.* Houghton Mifflin, New York.

Foster, W. C. (editor)
1998   *The La Salle Expedition to Texas.* Texas State Historical Association, Austin.

Foti, T. L.
1974   Natural Divisions of Arkansas. In *Arkansas Natural Area Plan,* pp. 11–34. Arkansas Department of Planning, Little Rock.

1989   Blackland Prairies of Southwestern Arkansas. *Proceedings of the Arkansas Academy of Science* 43: 23–28.

1990   The Vegetation of Saratoga Landing Blackland Prairie. *Proceedings of the Arkansas Academy of Science* 44:40–43.

Foti, T. L., M. Blaney, X. Li, and K. G. Smith
1994   A Classification System for the Natural Vegetation of Arkansas. *Proceedings of the Arkansas Academy of Science* 48:50–63.

Fowler, M. L.
1997   *The Cahokia Atlas: A Historical Atlas of Cahokia Archaeology.* Uni-

versity of Illinois at Urbana–Champaign, Studies in Archaeology 2, Urbana.

Fowler, P. J.

1992   Responsibility to the Public. In *Issues in Environmental Archaeology*, edited by N. Balaam and J. Rackham, pp. 85–88. University College, Institute of Archaeology, London.

Fox, B. J.

1999   The Genesis and Development of Guild Assembly Rules. In *Ecological Assembly Rules: Perspectives, Advances, Retreats*, edited by E. Weiher and P. Keddy, pp. 23–57. Cambridge University Press, Cambridge.

Fox, B. J., and J. H. Brown

1993   Assembly Rules for Functional Groups in North American Desert Rodent Communities. *Oikos* 67:358–370.

1995   Reaffirming the Validity of the Assembly Rule for Functional Groups or Guilds. *Oikos* 73:125–132.

Freitag, R.

1969   A Revision of the Species of the Genus *Evarthrus* LeConte (Coleoptera: Carabidae). *Quaestiones entomologicae* 5:89–212.

Frey, D. G.

1953   Regional Aspects of the Late-Glacial and Postglacial Pollen Succession of Southeastern North Carolina. *Ecological Monographs* 23: 289–313.

Friedman, S. B., and A. J. Darragh

1988   Economic Development. In *The Practice of Local Government Planning*, 2nd ed., edited by F. S. So and J. Getzels, 287–329. International City/County Management Association, Washington, D.C.

Friends of the Pleistocene South-Central Cell

1998   *Geography and Geology of the Grand and Black Prairies of Texas.* Baylor Geological Society, Waco.

Fritz, G. J.

1990   Multiple Pathways to Farming in Precontact Eastern North America. *Journal of World Prehistory* 4(4):387–431.

Frost, C. C., J. Walker, and R. K. Peet

1986   Fire-Dependent Savannas and Prairies of the Southeast: Original Extent, Preservation Status and Management Problems. In *Wilderness and Natural Areas in the Eastern United States: A Management Challenge*, edited by D. L. Kulhavy and R. N. Conner, 348–357. Stephen J. Austin State University, School of Forestry, Center for Applied Studies, Nacogdoches, Texas.

Futato, E. M.

1989   *An Archaeological Overview of the Tombigbee River Basin, Alabama and Mississippi.* Report of Investigations 59. Division of Archaeology, University of Alabama, Tuscaloosa.

Galloway, P. K.

1992   The Unexamined Habitus: Direct Historic Analogy and the Archaeology of the Text. In *Representations in Archaeology*, edited by J.-C.

Gardin and C. S. Peebles, pp. 178–195. Indiana University Press, Bloomington.

1994 Prehistoric Population of Mississippi: A First Approximation. *Mississippi Archaeology* 29(2):44–71.

2000 Archaeology from the Archives: The Chambers Excavations at Lyon's Bluff, 1934–35. *Mississippi Archaeology* 35(1):23–90.

Garber, M. C.

1973 *Soil Survey of Lee County, Mississippi.* USDA Soil Conservation Service, Washington, D.C.

Gardner, P. S.

1997 The Ecological Structure and Behavioral Implications of Mast Exploitation Strategies. In *People, Plants, and Landscapes: Studies in Paleoethnobotany,* edited by K. J. Gremillion, pp. 161–178. University of Alabama Press, Tuscaloosa.

Gaudreau, D. C.

1988 The Distributions of Late Quaternary Forest Regions in the Northeast: Pollen Data, Physiography, and the Prehistoric Record. In *Holocene Human Ecology in Northeastern North America,* edited by G. P. Nicholas, pp. 215–256. Plenum Press, New York.

Gavin, D.

1843 Journal of Major David Gavin's Horseback Ride, St. George to Mississippi and Return, 1843. Typescript in Lauderdale County, Department of Archives and History, Meridian, Mississippi.

Gezon, L. L

1999 Of Shrimps and Spirit Possession: Toward a Political Ecology of Resource Management in Northern Madagascar. *American Anthropologist* 101(1):58–67.

Gibson, J. L.

1999 *Poverty Point: A Terminal Archaic Culture of the Lower Mississippi Valley.* Department of Culture, Recreation, and Tourism, Anthropological Series 7, Baton Rouge.

Gifford, D. P.

1981 Taphonomy and Paleoecology: A Critical Review of Archaeology's Sister Disciplines. In *Advances in Archaeological Method and Theory,* edited by M. B. Schiffer, pp. 365–438. Vol. 4. Academic Press, New York.

Giliberti, J. A.

1999 *Phase II Testing and Phase III Data Recovery of Site 22OK908, Oktibbeha County, Mississippi.* Report submitted to Mississippi Department of Transportation by Brockington and Associates, Bay St. Louis, Mississippi.

Gordon, K. L., and J. B. Wiseman, Jr.

1989 *Bienville National Forest Prairie Survey.* Department of Wildlife Conservation, Mississippi Natural Heritage Program, Museum of Natural Science, Technical Report. No. 7, Jackson.

Gosse, P. H.

1993 *Letters from Alabama: Chiefly Relating to Natural History,* edited by H. H. Jackson. University of Alabama Press, Tuscaloosa. Originally published in 1859. Morgan and Chase, London.

Goudie, A.

2000   *The Human Impact on the Natural Environment.* 5th ed. MIT Press, Cambridge.

Goulet, H.

1998   Sawflies (Hymenoptera: Symphyta). In I. M. Smith, *Assessment of Species Diversity in the Mixedwood Plains Ecozone.* http://eqb-dqe. cciw.ca/eman/reports/publications/Mixedwood/intro.html. Available on CD-ROM from the Eastern Cereal and Oilseed Research Centre, Agriculture Canada, K. W. Neatby Building, Central Experimental Farm, Ottawa, Ontario K1A 0C6.

Grace, J. B.

1998   Can Prescribed Fire Save the Endangered Coastal Prairie Ecosystem from Chinese Tallow Invasion? *Endangered Species Update* 15:70–76.

Graham, A., and C. Heimsch

1960   Pollen Studies of Some Texas Peat Deposits. *Ecology* 41:785–790.

Gramly, R. M.

1977   Deerskins and Hunting Territories: Competition for a Scarce Resource of the Northeastern Woodlands. *American Antiquity* 42(4): 601–605.

Gray, B.

1993   *Cultural Resources Survey of Proposed Relocation of U.S. Highway 82, Mississippi Highway 25 and Mississippi Highway 12 at Starkville, Oktibbeha County, Mississippi.* Mississippi Department of Transportation, Jackson.

Gray, B., P. J. Carr, and C. Jenkins

1997   *Supplement to Cultural Resources Survey of Proposed Relocation of U.S. Highway 82, Mississippi Highway 25 and Mississippi Highway 12 at Starkville, Oktibbeha County, Mississippi.* Mississippi Department of Transportation, Jackson.

Grayson, D. K.

1991a   The Small Mammals at Gatecliff Shelter: Did People Make a Difference? In *Beamers, Bobwhites, and Blue Points: Tributes to the Career of Paul W. Parmalee,* edited by J. R. Purdue, W. E. Klippel, and B. W. Styles, pp. 99–100. Illinois State Museum Scientific Papers, vol. 23, and the University of Tennessee, Department of Anthropology Report of Investigations No. 52.

1991b   The Biogeographic History of Small Mammals in the Great Basin: Observations on the Last 20,000 years. *Journal of Mammalogy* 68: 359–375.

Gregory, H. F.

1992   The Louisiana Tribes: Entering Hard Times. In *Indians of the Southeastern United States in the Late 20th Century,* edited by J. A. Paredes, pp. 162–182. University of Alabama Press, Tuscaloosa.

Gremillion, K. J.

1993   Paleoethnobotany. In *The Development of Southeastern Archaeol-*

ogy, edited by J. K. Johnson, pp. 132–159. University of Alabama Press, Tuscaloosa.

1997   (editor) *People, Plants, and Landscapes: Studies in Paleoethnobotany.* University of Alabama Press, Tuscaloosa.

Griffin, J. B.

1952   Prehistoric Cultures of the Central Mississippi Valley. In *Archeology of Eastern United States,* edited by J. B. Griffin, pp. 226–238. University of Chicago Press, Chicago.

1961   Relationships Between the Caddoan Area and the Mississippi Valley. *Bulletin of the Texas Archeological Society* 31:27–43.

1985   Changing Concepts of the Prehistoric Mississippian Cultures of the Eastern United States. In *Alabama and the Borderlands, from Prehistory to Statehood,* edited by E. R. Badger and L. A. Clayton, pp. 40–63. University of Alabama Press, Tuscaloosa.

Griffith, W. J.

1954   The Hasinai Indians of East Texas as Seen by Europeans, 1687–1772. *Philological and Documentary Studies* 2(3):41–168. Middle American Research Institute, Tulane University, New Orleans.

Grime, J. P.

1979   *Plant Strategies and Vegetation Processes.* John Wiley & Sons, New York.

1993   Ecology Sans Frontiers. *Oikos* 69:385–392.

Grimm, E. C., and G. L. Jacobson, Jr.

1992   Fossil-Pollen Evidence for Abrupt Climate Changes during the Past 18,000 Years in Eastern North America. *Climate Dynamics* 6:179–184.

Grimm, W. C.

1966   *The Book of Trees.* Stackpole, Harrisburg, Pennsylvania.

Grossman, D. H., K. L. Goodin, and C. L. Reuss

1994   *Rare Plant Communities of the Conterminous United States: An Initial Survey.* Nature Conservancy, Arlington, Virginia.

Grossman, D. H., D. Faber-Langendoen, A. S. Weakley, M. Anderson, P. Bourgeron, R. Crawford, K. Goodin, S. Landaal, K. Metzler, K. D. Patterson, M. Pyne, M. Reid, and L. Sneddon

1998   *International Classification of Ecological Communities: Terrestrial Vegetation of the United States. Vol. I. The National Vegetation Classification System: Development, Status, and Applications.* Nature Conservancy, Arlington, Virginia.

Guillory, C. M., E. D. Scott, C. Corkern, M. A. Marino, and E. Williams

1997   *Soil Survey of Sabine Parish, Louisiana.* U.S. Department of Agriculture, Soil Conservation Service, Washington, D.C.

Guruswamy, L. D., and J. A. McNeely (editors)

1998   *Protection of Global Biodiversity: Converging Strategies.* Duke University Press, Durham.

Hamilton, K. G. A.

1998   "Short-horned" Bugs (Homoptera—Auchenorrhyncha). In I. M. Smith, *Assessment of Species Diversity in the Mixedwood Plains Ecozone.* http://eqb-dqe.cciw.ca/eman/reports/publications/Mixed-

wood/intro.html. Available on CD-ROM from the Eastern Cereal
and Oilseed Research Centre, Agriculture Canada, K. W. Neatby
Building, Central Experimental Farm, Ottawa, Ontario K1A 0C6.

Hamm, J.

1989   *Bows and Arrows of the Native Americans; A Complete Step-by-Step Guide to Wooden Bows, Sinew-backed Bows, Composite Bows, Strings, Arrows, and Quivers.* Lyon's and Burford, New York.

1992   Traditional Choices. *Field and Stream* 97(6):24–25.

Hansen, A., A. Gallant, J. Rotella, and D. Brown

1998   Natural and Human Drivers of Biodiversity in the Greater Yellowstone Ecosystem. In *Perspectives on the Land Use History of North America: A Context for Understanding our Changing Environment*, edited by T. D. Sisk, pp. 61–69. Biological Science Report USGS/BRD/BSR-1998-0003. U.S. Geological Survey, Biological Resources Division.

Hardcastle, R.

1992   Osage Flat Bow. In *The Traditional Bowyer's Bible, vol. 1*, edited by J. Hamm, pp. 131–148. Lyon's and Burford, New York.

Hardesty, D. L., and D. D. Fowler

2001   Archaeology and Environmental Changes. In *New Directions in Anthropology and Environment*, edited by C. L. Crumley, pp. 72–89. Altamira Press, Walnut Creek, California.

Hardwick, D. F.

1996   *A Monograph to the North American Heliothentinae (Lepidoptera: Noctuidae).* Almonte, Ontario: Privately published by D. Hardwick.

Harlan, J. R.

1992   *Crops and Man.* 2nd ed. American Society of Agronomy, Crop Science Society of America, Madison, Wisconsin.

Harper, J. L.

1987   The Heuristic Value of Ecological Restoration. In *Restoration Ecology*, edited by W. R. Jordan III, M. E. Gilpin, and J. D. Aber, pp. 35–45. Cambridge University Press, Cambridge.

Harper, L.

1857   *Preliminary Report on the Geology and Agriculture of the State of Mississippi.* E. Barksdale, State Printer, Jackson.

Harper, R. M.

1943   Forests of Alabama. *Geological Survey of Alabama Monograph* 10:1–230.

Hart, B. L., and G. D. Lester

1993   Natural Community and Sensitive Species Assessment on Fort Polk Military Reservation. Unpublished report on file, Louisiana Department of Wildlife and Fisheries, Baton Rouge.

Hartnett, D. C., K. R. Hickman, and L. E. F. Waller

1996   Effects of Bison Grazing, Fire, and Topography on Florisitic Diversity in Tallgrass Prairie. *Journal of Range Management* 49:413–420.

Hascom, G.

1999   Visionaries or Dreamers. *High Country News* 31(8):1, 8–11.

Hattenbach, M. J., D. Zollner and S. Simon
  2000   Arkansas Blackland Ecosystem Assessment. Unpublished report
          submitted to Arkansas Natural Heritage Commission from the Na-
          ture Conservancy. Little Rock.
Hayward, G. F., and J. Phillipson
  1979   Community Structure and Functional Role of Small Mammals in
          Ecosystems. In *Ecology of Small Mammals,* edited by D. M. Stod-
          dart, pp. 135–212. Chapman and Hall, London.
Headland, T. N.
  1997   Revisionism in Ecological Anthropology. *Current Anthropology*
          38(4):605–609.
Heikens, A. L., K. A. West, and P. A. Robertson
  1994   Short-Term Response of Chert and Shale Barrens Vegetation to Fire
          in Southwestern Illinois. *Castanea* 59(3):274–285.
Heinrich, C.
  1923   Revision of the North American Moths of the Subfamily Eucosminae
          of the Family Olethreutidae. *Bulletin of the United States National
          Museum* 123:1–298.
Hetz, M. W., and F. G. Werner
  1979   Insects Associated with Roots of Some Rangeland Compositae in
          Southern Arizona. *Southwestern Entomologist* 4:285–288.
Hickerson, N. P.
  1994   *The Jumanos: Hunters and Traders of the South Plains.* University
          of Texas Press, Austin.
Hilgard, E. W.
  1860   *Report on the Geology and Agriculture of the State of Mississippi.*
          E. Barksdale, State Printer, Jackson.
Hill, R. T.
  1901   *Geography and Geology of the Black and Grand Prairies, Texas.* U.S.
          Geological Survey, 21st Annual Report, Part 7. Washington, D.C.
Hinton, J. L.
  1951   The Terrestrial Shell-Bearing Mollusca of the Black Belt of Alabama.
          Unpublished M.S. thesis, University of Alabama, Tuscaloosa.
Hirth, K. G.
  1978   Interregional Trade and the Formation of Prehistoric Gateway Com-
          munities. *American Antiquity* 43(1):35–45.
Hodder, I., and C. Orton
  1976   *Spatial Analysis in Archaeology.* Cambridge University Press, Cam-
          bridge.
Hodges, R. W.
  1971   Sphingoidea. In *The Moths of America North of Mexico,* 21, edited
          by R. B. Dominick et al., pp. 1–158. W. Classey, London.
  1986   Gelechioidea. Gelechiidae (part). In *The Moths of America North of
          Mexico,* 7.1, edited by R. B. Dominick et al., pp. 1–195. Wedge En-
          tomological Research Foundation, Washington, D.C.
Hoffman, R. S., and J. K. Jones, Jr.
  1970   Influence of Late-Glacial and Post-Glacial Events on the Distribu-
          tion of Recent Mammals on the Northern Great Plains. In *Pleisto-*

cene and Recent Environments of the Central Great Plains, edited by W. Dort, Jr., and J. K. Jones, Jr., pp. 355–394. Special Publication 3, University of Kansas, Department of Geology. University Press of Kansas, Lawrence.

Hogue, S. H.

2000 Burial Practices, Mortality, and Diet in East-Central Mississippi: A Case Study from Oktibbeha County. *Southeastern Archaeology* 19(1):84–104.

Hogue, S. H., and W. Erwin

1993 A Preliminary Analysis of Diet Change Using Small Burial Samples from Three Sites in Mississippi. *Mississippi Archaeology* 28(1):1–19.

Hogue, S. H., and E. Peacock

1995 Environmental and Osteological Analysis at the South Farm Site (220K543), a Mississippian Farmstead in Oktibbeha County, Mississippi. *Southeastern Archaeology* 14(1):31–45.

Hogue, S. H., A. Boyd, and J. Jacobson

1995 A Secondary Burial from the Rolling Hills Subdivision in Starkville, Mississippi: Osteological and Archaeological Interpretations. *Mississippi Archaeology* 30(1):1–22.

Hollander, E. L., L. S. Pollock, J. D. Reckinger, and F. Beal

1988 General Development Plans. In *The Practice of Local Government Planning,* 2nd ed., edited by F. S. So and J. Getzels, pp. 60–91. International City/County Management Association, Washington, D.C.

Homoya, M. A.

1994 Indiana Barrens: Classification and Description. *Castanea* 59(3): 204–213.

Howden, H. F.

1966 Some Possible Effects of the Pleistocene on the Distributions of North American Scarabaeidae (Coleoptera). *Canadian Entomologist* 98:1177–1190.

Howe, H. F.

1994 Managing Species Diversity in Tallgrass Prairie: Assumptions and Implications. *Conservation Biology* 8(3):691–704.

1995 Succession and Fire Season in Experimental Prairie Plantings. *Ecology* 76(6):1917–1925.

Hrdy, S. B.

1999 *Mother Nature: A History of Mothers, Infants, and Natural Selection.* Pantheon Books, New York.

Hubbell, S. P., R. B. Foster, S. T. O'Brien, K. E. Harms, R. Condit, B. Wechsler, S. J. Wright, and S. Loo de Lao

1999 Light-Gap Disturbances, Recruitment Limitation, and Tree Diversity in a Neotropical Forest. *Science* 283:554–557.

Hubricht, L.

1985 The Distributions of the Native Land Mollusks of the Eastern United States. *Fieldiana: Zoology,* n.s., no. 24.

Hudson, C.

1976 *The Southeastern Indians.* University of Tennessee Press, Knoxville.

1979   (editor) *Black Drink: A Native American Tea.* University of Georgia
        Press, Athens.

1993   Reconstructing the De Soto Expedition Route West of the Missis-
        sippi River: Summary and Contents. In *The Expedition of Hernando
        de Soto West of the Mississippi, 1541–1543,* edited by G. A. Young
        and M. P. Hoffman, pp. 143–154. University of Arkansas Press,
        Fayetteville.

1997   *Knights of Spain, Warriors of the Sun: Hernando de Soto and the
        South's Ancient Chiefdoms.* University of Georgia Press. Athens.

Hunt, T. L., and P. V. Kirch

1997   The Historical Ecology of Ofu Island, American Samoa, 3000 B.P. to
        the Present. In *Historical Ecology of the Pacific Islands: Prehistoric
        Environmental and Landscape Change,* edited by P. V. Kirch and
        T. L. Hunt, pp. 105–123. Yale University Press, New Haven.

Huston, M. A.

1979   A General Hypothesis of Species Diversity. *American Naturalist*
        113:81–101.

Hutchens, A. R.

1991   *Indian Herbology of North America.* Shambahala, Boston.

Hutchison, M. D.

1994   The Barrens of the Midwest: An Historical Perspective. *Castanea*
        59(3):195–203.

Hyatt, P. E.

1999   Conservation Assessment for Prairies and Associated Rare Plant Spe-
        cies of the Kisatchie National Forest. Unpublished report on file,
        USDA Forest Service Office, Pineville, Louisiana.

IJzereef, G. F.

1992   The Presentation of Environmental Archaeology in "Archeon": A
        Plan for an Archaeological Theme Park in The Netherlands. In *Issues
        in Environmental Archaeology,* edited by N. Balaam and J. Rackham,
        pp. 71–84. University College, Institute of Archaeology, London.

Inglis, J. T. (editor)

1993   *Traditional Ecological Knowledge: Concepts and Cases.* Interna-
        tional Development Research Centre, Ottawa.

Ingold, J. L.

2000   Birds of the Keiffer Prairies, Kisatchie National Forest, Winn Ranger
        District, Winnfield, Louisiana. Unpublished report on file, USDA
        Forest Service Office, Pineville, Louisiana.

Innis, D. Q.

1997   *Intercropping and the Scientific Basis of Traditional Agriculture.* In-
        termediate Technology Publications, London.

Irving, R. S., S. Brenholts, and T. Foti

1980   Composition and Net Primary Productivity of Native Prairies in Ar-
        kansas. *American Midland Naturalist* 103:298–309.

Isenberg, A. C.

2000   *The Destruction of the Bison: An Environmental History, 1750–
        1920.* Cambridge University Press, Cambridge.

Jackson, A. T., M. S. Goldstein, and A.D. Krieger
2000 *The 1931 Excavations at the Sanders Site, Lamar County, Texas; Notes on the Fieldwork, Human Osteology, and Ceramics.* University of Texas at Austin, Texas Archeological Research Laboratory, Archival Series 2.

Jackson, D. D.
1962 *Letters of the Louis and Clark Expedition with Related Documents 1783–1854.* University of Illinois Press, Urbana.

Janis, C.
1975 The Evolutionary Strategy of the Equidae and the Origins of Rumen and Cecal Digestion. *Evolution* 30:757–774.

Janzen, D. H.
1986 Chihuahuan Desert Nopaleras: Defaunated Big Mammal Vegetation. *Annual Review of Ecology and Systematics* 17:595–636.

Janzen, D. H., and P. S. Martin
1982 Neotropical Anachronisms: The Fruits the Gompotheres Ate. *Science* 215(1):19–27.

Jenkins, N.J.
1981 *Gainesville Lake Area Ceramic Description and Chronology.* Report of Investigations 12. Office of Archaeological Research, University of Alabama, Tuscaloosa.

1982 *Archaeology of the Gainesville Lake Area: Synthesis.* Report of Investigations 23. Office of Archaeological Research, University of Alabama, Tuscaloosa.

Jenkins, N.J., and R. A. Krause
1986 *The Tombigbee Watershed in Southeastern Prehistory.* University of Alabama Press, Tuscaloosa.

Jennings, J. D.
1941 Chickasaw and Earlier Indian Cultures of Northeast Mississippi. *Journal of Mississippi History* 3:155–226.

1947 (editor) Nutt's Trip to the Chickasaw Country. *Journal of Mississippi History* 9:34–61.

Johnson, C. W.
1951 Protein as a Factor in the Distribution of the American Bison. *Geographical Review* 41:330–331.

Johnson, J. K.
1990 Cedar Glades and Protohistoric Settlement: A Reply to Peacock and Miller. *Mississippi Archaeology* 25(2):58–62.

1993 (editor) *The Development of Southeastern Archaeology.* University of Alabama Press, Tuscaloosa.

1996 The Nature and Timing of the Late Prehistoric Settlement of the Black Prairie in Northeast Mississippi: A Reply to Hogue, Peacock, and Rafferty. *Southeastern Archaeology* 15(2):244–248.

1997 Stone Tools, Politics, and the Eighteenth-Century Chickasaw in Northeast Mississippi. *American Antiquity* 62(2):215–230.

2000 The Chickasaws. In *Indians of the Greater Southeast: Historical Archaeology and Ethnohistory,* edited by B. G. McEwan, pp. 85–121. University Press of Florida, Gainesville.

Johnson, J. K., H. K. Curry, J. R. Atkinson, and J. T. Sparks
   1984   *Cultural Resources Survey in the Line Creek Watershed, Chicka-
           saw, Clay, and Webster Counties, Mississippi.* Report submitted to
           Soil Conservation Service by Center for Archaeological Research,
           University of Mississippi.
Johnson, J. K., P. K. Galloway, and W. Belokon
   1989   Historic Chickasaw Settlement Patterns in Lee County, Mississippi:
           A First Approximation. *Mississippi Archaeology* 24(2):45–52.
Johnson, J. K., G. R. Lehmann, J. R. Atkinson, S. L. Scott, and A. Shea
   1991   *Protohistoric Chickasaw Settlement Patterns and the De Soto Route
           in Northeast Mississippi.* Report submitted to the National Endow-
           ment for the Humanities by The Center for Archaeological Research,
           University of Mississippi.
Johnson, J. K., S. L. Scott, J. R. Atkinson, and A. B. Shea
   1994   Late Prehistoric/Protohistoric Settlement and Subsistence on the
           Black Prairie: Buffalo Hunting in Mississippi? *North American Ar-
           chaeologist* 15(2):167–179.
Johnson, J. K., and J. T. Sparks
   1986   Protohistoric Settlement Patterns in Northeastern Mississippi. In
           The Protohistoric Period in the Mid-South, edited by D. H. Dye and
           R. C. Brister, pp. 64–87. Archaeological Report 18. Mississippi De-
           partment of Archives and History, Jackson.
Johnson, R. G., and R. C. Anderson
   1986   The Seed Bank of a Tallgrass Prairie in Illinois. *American Midland
           Naturalist* 115(1):123–130.
Jones, A. S., and E. G. Patton
   1966   Forest, "Prairie," and Soils in the Black Belt of Sumter County, Ala-
           bama, in 1832. *Ecology* 47(1):75–80.
Jones, S. B., Jr.
   1971   A Virgin Prairie and a Virgin Loblolly Pine Stand in Central Missis-
           sippi. *Castanea* 36:223–225.
Jordan, T. G.
   1973   Pioneer Evaluation of Vegetation in Frontier Texas. *Southwestern
           Historical Quarterly* 76:233–254.
Jordan, W. R., III, M. E. Gilpin, and J. D. Aber
   1987   *Restoration Ecology.* Cambridge University Press, Cambridge.
Joyce, A. A.
   1988   Early/Middle Holocene Environments in the Middle Atlantic Region.
           In *Holocene Human Ecology in Northeastern North America,* edited
           by G. P. Nicholas, pp. 185–214. Plenum Press, New York.
Jurney, D. H.
   1994   The Original Distribution of Bois D'Arc. Part 1: Texas. *Caddoan Ar-
           cheology Newsletter* 5(2):6–13.
Jurney, D. H., and W. Young
   1995   Southwestern Pottery and Turquoise in Northeastern Texas. *Cad-
           doan Archeology Newsletter* 6(2):15–28.
Kaila, L.
   1996   Revision of the Nearctic Species of *Elachista* I. The *Tetragonella*

Group (Lepidoptera: Elachistidae). *Entomologica Scandinavica* 27: 217–238.

Kaplan, C.

1998   Investigating Occupation Span at a Mississippian Homestead, Oktibbeha County, Mississippi. Paper presented at the 19th Mid-South Archaeological Conference, Memphis, Tennessee.

Kaye, J. M.

1974   Pleistocene Sediment and Vertebrate Fossil Associations in the Mississippi Black Belt: A Genetic Approach. Unpublished Ph.D. dissertation, Louisiana State University.

Kazmann, R. G.

1972   *Modern Hydrology.* Harper and Row, New York.

Kelly, E. D.

1988   "Zoning." In *The Practice of Local Government Planning,* 2nd ed., edited by F. S. So and J. Getzels. International City/County Management Association, Washington, D.C.

Kelly, J. E.

1991   Cahokia and Its Role as a Gateway Center in Interregional Exchange. In *Cahokia and the Hinterlands: Middle Mississippian Cultures in the Midwest,* edited by T. E. Emerson and R. B. Lewis, pp. 61–80. Urbana: University of Illinois Press.

Kelly, R. L.

1998   Foraging and Sedentism. In Seasonality and Sedentism: Archaeological Perspectives from Old and New World Sites, edited by T. R. Rocek and O. Bar-Yosef, pp. 9–23. *Harvard University, Peabody Museum of Archaeology and Ethnology, Bulletin* 6:9–23.

Kelso, G. K., D. Ritchie, and N. Misso

2000   Pollen Record Preservation Processes in the Salem Neck Sewage Plant Shell Midden (19-ES-471). *Journal of Archaeological Science* 27(3):235–240.

Kent, M., and P. Coker.

1992   *Vegetation Description and Analysis.* John Wiley & Sons, West Sussex, England.

Kerber, J. E.

1997   *Lambert Farm: Public Archaeology and the Canine Burials Along Narragansett Bay.* Harcourt Brace, Fort Worth, Texas.

King, J. E.

1973   Late Pleistocene Palynology and Biogeography of the Western Missouri Ozarks. *Ecological Monographs* 43:539–565.

King, J. E., and W. H. Allen

1977   A Holocene Vegetation Record from the Mississippi River Valley, Southeastern Missouri. *Quaternary Research* 8:307–323.

King, M. E., and J. S. Gardner

1981   The Analysis of Textiles from the Spiro Mound, Oklahoma. In The Research Potential of Anthropological Museum Collections, edited by A.-M. Cantwell, J. B. Griffin, and N. A. Rothschild, pp. 123–129. *Annals of the New York Academy of Science* 376.

Kline, V. M., and E. A. Howell

1987   Prairies. In *Restoration Ecology,* edited by W. R. Jordan, III, M. E. Gilpin, and J. D. Aber, pp. 75–83. Cambridge University Press, Cambridge.

Klippel, W. E., and W. B. Turner

1991   Terrestrial Gastropods from Glade Sere and the Hayes Shell Midden in Middle Tennessee. In *Beamers, Bobwhites, and Blue-Points: Tributes to the Career of Paul W. Parmalee,* edited by J. R. Purdue, W. E. Klippel, and B. W. Styles, pp. 177–188. Illinois State Museum Scientific Papers No. 23, Springfield.

Klute, A.

1965   Laboratory Measurement of Hydraulic Conductivity of Saturated Soil. In Methods of Soil Analysis. Part 1, edited by C. A. Black. *Agronomy* 9:214–215. American Society of Agronomy, Madison, Wisconsin.

Knapp, A. K., and T. R. Seastedt

1998   Introduction: Grasslands, Konza Prairie and Long-Term Ecological Research. In *Grassland Dynamics: Long-Term Ecological Research in Tallgrass Prairie,* edited by A. K. Knapp, J. M. Briggs, D. C. Hartnett and S. L. Collins. Oxford University Press, New York.

Knight, V. J., Jr., and V. P. Steponaitis

1998   A New History of Moundville. In *Archaeology of the Moundville Chiefdom,* edited by V. J. Knight Jr., and V. P. Steponaitis, pp. 1–25. Smithsonian Institution Press, Washington, D.C.

Knox, J. C.

1976   Concept of the Graded Stream. In *Theories of Landform Development,* edited by W. N. Melhorn and R. C. Flemal, pp. 169–198. Allen and Unwin, London.

Komarek, E. V.

1964   The Natural History of Lightning. *Proceedings of the Tall Timbers Fire Ecology Conference* 3:139–183.

1965   Fire Ecology—Grasslands and Man. *Proceedings of the Tall Timbers Fire Ecology Conference* 4:169–220.

1968   Lightning and Lightning Fires as Ecological Forces. *Proceedings of the Tall Timbers Fire Ecology Conference* 8:169–197.

1974   Effects of Fire in Temperate Forest and Related Ecosytems: Southeastern United States. In *Fire and Ecosystems,* edited by T. T. Kozlowski and C. Ahlgren, pp. 251–277. Academic Press, New York.

Kottak, C. P.

1999   The New Ecological Anthropology. *American Anthropologist* 101(1): 23–35.

Krech, S., III

1999   *The Ecological Indian.* W. W. Norton, New York.

Krieger, A.D.

1946   *Culture Complexes and Chronology in Northern Texas with Extensions of Puebloan Dating to the Mississippi Valley.* University of Texas Publication 4640, Austin.

Krizek, K. J., and J. Power
  1997   *A Planner's Guide to Sustainable Development.* American Planning
          Association, Chicago.
Kucera, C. L.
  1992   Tall-Grass Prairie. In *Ecosystems of the World: Natural Grasslands,*
          edited by R. T. Coupland, pp. 227–268. Vol. 8a. Elsevier, Amsterdam.
Kuchler, A. W.
  1964   *Potential Natural Vegetation of the Conterminous United States.*
          American Geographical Society Special Publication 36.
Kuttruff, J. T.
  1993   Mississippian Period Status Differentiation Through Textile Analy-
          sis: A Caddoan Example. *American Antiquity* 58(1):125–145.
Ladd, D.
  1997   Vascular Plants of Midwestern Tallgrass Prairies. In *The Tallgrass
          Restoration Handbook for Prairies, Savannas, and Woodlands,* ed-
          ited by S. Packard and C. F. Mutel, pp. 351–399. Island Press, Covelo,
          California.
Lafferty, R. H., III
  1994   Prehistoric Exchange in the Lower Mississippi Valley. In *Prehistoric
          Exchange Systems in Eastern North America,* edited by T. G. Baugh
          and J. E. Ericson, pp. 117–213. Plenum Press, New York.
Lafontaine, J. D.
  1982   Biogeography of the Genus *Euxoa* (Lepidoptera: Noctuidae) in North
          America. *Canadian Entomologist* 114:1–53.
  1998   Butterflies and Moths (Lepidoptera). In I. M. Smith, *Assessment of
          Species Diversity in the Mixedwood Plains Ecozone.* http://eqb-dqe.
          cciw.ca/eman/reports/publications/Mixedwood/intro.html. Available
          on CD-ROM from the Eastern Cereal and Oilseed Research Centre,
          Agriculture Canada, K. W. Neatby Building, Central Experimental
          Farm, Ottawa, Ontario K1A 0C6.
Lance, R.
  2000   Status Report on *Crataegus harbisonii* and *Crataegus ashei,* Har-
          bison Hawthorn and Ashe Hawthorn. The North Carolina Arbore-
          tum, Asheville, North Carolina. 83 pp. Report prepared for the U.S.
          Fish and Wildlife Service, Mississippi Field Office, Jackson.
Landmarks: Louisiana
  2001   *Nature Conservancy* (March/April):29.
Langston, J. M.
  1927   A New Species of *Phyllophaga* from Mississippi. *Annals of the En-
          tomological Society of America* 20:221–223.
Larson, L. H.
  1971   Archaeological Implications of Social Stratification at the Etowah
          Site, Georgia. In Approaches to the Social Dimensions of Mortuary
          Practices, edited by J. A. Brown, pp. 58–67. Society for American Ar-
          chaeology Memoir No. 25. Washington, D.C.
Laubin, R., and G. Laubin
  1980   *American Indian Archery.* University of Oklahoma Press, Norman.

Leidolf, A., and S. McDaniel
  1998   A Floristic Study of Black Prairie Plant Communities at Sixteen Section Prairie, Oktibbeha County, Mississippi. *Castanea* 63:51–62.
Leonard, R. D., and G. T. Jones
  1987   Elements of an Inclusive Evolutionary Model for Archaeology. *Journal of Anthropological Archaeology* 6:199–219.
Leopold, A.
  1949   *A Sand County Almanac.* Oxford University Press, New York.
Leopold, D. J., W. C. McComb, and R. N. Muller
  1998   *Trees of the Central Hardwood Forests of North America: An Identification and Cultivation Guide.* Timber Press, Portland, Oregon.
Leveau, P.
  1999   The Integration of Archaeological, Historical and Paleoenvironmental Data at the Regional Scale: The Vallée de Baux, Southern France. In *Environmental Reconstruction in Mediterranean Landscape Archaeology,* edited by P. Leveau, F. Trément, K. Walsh, and G. Barker, pp. 181–205. Oxbow Books, Oxford.
Levy, J. M.
  1988   *Contemporary Urban Planning.* Prentice Hall, Englewood Cliffs, New Jersey.
Lewis, M. D. K.
  1995   Burial Customs and Physical Types. In *The Prehistory of the Chickamauga Basin in Tennessee,* vol. 1, by T. M. N. Lewis and M. D. K. Lewis, compiled and edited by Lynne P. Sullivan. University of Tennessee Press, Knoxville.
Lewis, W. H.
  2000   Ethnopharmacology and the Search for New Therapeutics. In *Biodiversity and Native America,* edited by P. E. Minnis and W. J. Elisens, pp. 74–96. University of Oklahoma Press, Norman.
Lippert, R. D., and H. Hopkins
  1950   Study of Viable Seeds in Various Habitats in Mixed Prairie. *Transactions of the Kansas Academy of Science* 53:355–364.
Lockett, S. H.
  1969   *Louisiana As It Is: A Geographical and Topographic Description of the State,* edited by L. C. Post. Louisiana State University Press, Baton Rouge.
Logan, W. N.
  1903   *The Geology of Oktibbeha County.* Geological and Industrial Survey of Mississippi, Report 1. Rand, McNally, Chicago.
Lolley, T.
  1992   Prehistoric Settlement Pattern Change in Central Oktibbeha County, Mississippi. Paper presented at the 49th Annual Meeting, Southeastern Archaeological Conference, Little Rock, Arkansas.
Louisiana Natural Heritage Program
  1998   Natural Plant Communities in Louisiana. Unpublished report on file, Louisiana Department of Wildlife and Fisheries, Baton Rouge.
  1999   Rare Plant Species of Louisiana. Unpublished report on file, Louisiana Department of Wildlife and Fisheries, Baton Rouge.

Lowe, E. N.
1911   *A Preliminary Study of Soils of Mississippi.* Nashville: Brandon
        Printing Company.
1915   Misssissippi, Its Geology, Geography, Soils, and Mineral Resources.
        Mississippi State Geological Survey, Bulletin No. 12.
1921   Plants of Mississippi: A List of Flowering Plants and Ferns. *Missis-
        sippi State Geological Survey, Bulletin* 17:1–292.

Lowe, J. J., and M. J. C. Walker
1997   *Reconstructing Quaternary Environments.* Longman Group, Ltd.,
        Essex.

Lyman, R. L.
1994   *Vertebrate Taphonomy.* Cambridge University Press, Cambridge.
1996   Applied Zooarchaeology: The Relevance of Faunal Analysis to Wild-
        life Management. *World Archaeology* 28(1):110–125.

Lynott, M. J.
1980   Prehistoric Bison Populations of Northcentral Texas. *Bulletin of the
        Texas Archeological Society* 50:89–101.

Lynott, M. J., T. W. Boutton, J. E. Price, and D. E. Nelson
1986   Stable Isotope Evidence for Maize Agriculture in Southeast Missouri
        and Northeast Arkansas. *American Antiquity* 51:51–65.

MacGown, M. W., and T. L. Schiefer
1992   Disjunct Distribution and a New Record for an Anthophorid Bee,
        Xenoglossodes albata (Hymenoptera: Anthophoridae), in Southeast-
        ern United States. *Entomological News* 103:81–82.

Macrander, A. M., and W. R. Telle
1989   Environmental Description. In *An Archaeological Overview of the
        Tombigbee River Basin, Alabama and Mississippi,* by E. M. Futato,
        pp. 15–56. Report of Investigations 59. Division of Archaeology.
        University of Alabama, Tuscaloosa.

MacRoberts, B. R., and M. H. MacRoberts
1995   Vascular Flora of Two Calcareous Prairie Remnants on the Kisatchie
        National Forest, Louisiana. *Phytologia* 78:18–27.
1996a   The Floristics of Calcareous Prairies on the Kisatchie National For-
        est, Louisiana. *Phytologia* 81:35–43.
1996b   Report on the Keiffer Prairies. Unpublished report on file, USDA For-
        est Service Office, Pineville, Louisiana.
1997   Historical Notes on Louisiana Prairies: Changes in Prairie Flora in
        Half a Century. *Phytologia* 82:65–72.

MacRoberts, D. T., B. R. MacRoberts, and M. H. MacRoberts
1997   A Floristic and Ecological Interpretation of the Freeman and Custis
        Red River Expedition of 1806. *Bulletin of the Museum of Life Sci-
        ences* 12:1–26.

MacRoberts, M. H., and B. R. MacRoberts
1993   Vascular Flora of Sandstone Outcrop Communities in Western Loui-
        siana, with Notes on Rare and Noteworthy Species. *Phytologia* 75:
        463–480.
1995   Noteworthy Vascular Plant Collections on the Kisatchie National
        Forest, Louisiana. *Phytologia* 78:291–313.

1997a   Former Distribution of Prairies in Northern Louisiana. *Phytologia* 82:315–325.

1997b   Prairie Report and Management Statement: Winn Ranger District. Unpublished report on file, USDA Forest Service Office, Pineville, Louisiana.

MacRoberts, M. H., B. R. MacRoberts, and D. C. Moore

1997   Introduction and Notes to Clair Brown's "Preliminary Report on the Isolated Prairies of Lousiana." *Proceedings of the Louisiana Academy of Science* 60:1–9.

MacRoberts, M. H., B. R. MacRoberts, and L. M. Stacey

1997   Historical Notes on Louisiana Prairies: Size Changes in a Century and a Half. *Phytologia* 83:102–108.

Mantell, M. A., S. F. Harper, and L. Propst

1990   *Creating Successful Communities: A Guidebook to Growth Management Strategies.* Island Press, Washington, D.C.

MARIS (Mississippi Automated Resources Information System)

1998   www.maris.state.ms.us.

Marquardt, W. H.

1994   The Role of Archaeology in Raising Environmental Consciousness: An Example from Southwest Florida. In *Historical Ecology,* edited by C. L. Crumley, pp. 203–221. School of American Research Press, Santa Fe.

Marsh, G. P.

1965   *Man and Nature: Physical Geography as Modified by Human Action.* Belknap Press of Harvard University, Cambridge.

Marshall, R. A.

1977   Lyon's Bluff Site (220K1) Radiocarbon Dated. *Journal of Alabama Archaeology* 23:53–57.

1986   The Protohistoric Component at the Lyon's Bluff Site Complex, Oktibbeha County, Mississippi. In The Protohistoric Period in the Mid-South: 1500–1700, edited by D. H. Dye and R. C. Brister, pp. 82–88. Archaeological Report 18. Mississippi Department of Archives and History, Jackson.

Martin, A. C., and W. D. Barkley

1961   *Seed Identification Manual.* University of California Press, Berkeley.

Maschner, H. D. G.

1996   (editor) *Evolutionary Archaeologies.* Plenum Press, New York.

Mason, O. T.

1972   *North American Indian Bows, Arrows and Quivers.* Carl J. Pugliese, Yonkers, New York.

Masters, L. A.

1997   Monitoring Vegetation. In *The Tallgrass Restoration Handbook for Prairies, Savannas, and Woodlands,* edited by S. Packard and C. F. Mutel, pp. 279–301. Island Press, Covelo, California.

Mayr, E.

1949   The Species Concept: Semantics Versus Semantics. *Evolution* 3:371–372.

1987   The Ontological Status of Species: Scientific Progress and Philosophical Terminology. *Biology and Philosophy* 2:145–166.

1998   *This Is Biology: The Science of the Living World.* Belknap Press of
         Harvard University, Cambridge.
McCarty, K., M. Magai, C. A. Evans, S. Smith, and L. Larson
1999   Fall, Winter, and Spring Burning: Comparing the Differences in a
         Study at Prairie State Park. Jefferson City: Missouri Department of
         Natural Resources, Division of State Parks.
McDaniel, S., and D. T. Carraway
1995   Guide to the Vegetation of the Tallahalla Wildlife Management
         Area, Bienville National Forest. Mississippi State University, Insti-
         tute for Botanical Exploration, Starkville.
McDermott, J. F. (editor)
1963   The Western Journals of Dr. George Hunter: 1796–1805. *Transac-
         tions of the American Philosophical Society,* n.s., 53(4):1–133.
McGuire, W. W.
1834   On the Prairies of Alabama. *American Journal of Science* 26:93–98.
McInnis, N. C.
1997   Barksdale Air Force Base Threatened and Endangered Species and
         Natural Areas Survey. Unpublished report on file, Nature Conser-
         vancy, Baton Rouge.
Mead, J. I.
1991   Late Pleistocene and Holocene Molluscan Faunas and Environmental
         Changes in Southeastern Arizona. In *Beamers, Bobwhites, and Blue-
         Points: Tributes to the Career of Paul W. Parmalee,* edited by J. R.
         Purdue, W. E. Klippel, and B. W. Styles, pp. 215–226. Illinois State
         Museum Scientific Papers No. 23, Springfield.
Merchant, C.
1989   *Ecological Revolutions.* Chapel Hill: University of North Carolina
         Press.
Merrill, R. K., J. J. Sims, Jr., D. E. Gann, and K. J. Liles
1985   Newton County Geology and Mineral Resources. Bulletin 126. Mis-
         sissippi Department of Natural Resources, Jackson.
Miller, M. W.
1998   Doing Prairie Restoration. *Conservation Biology* 12(1):250–258.
Milner, G. R.
1998   *The Cahokia Chiefdom.* Smithsonian Institution Press, Washing-
         ton, D.C.
Minnis, P. E., and W. J. Elisens (editors)
2000   *Biodiversity and Native America.* University of Oklahoma Press,
         Norman.
Mississippi Natural Heritage Program
2000   *Special Plant and Animal List.* Museum of Natural Science, Missis-
         sippi Department of Wildlife, Fisheries & Parks, Jackson.
Mohr, C.
1901   *Plant Life of Alabama.* Brown Printing Company, Montgomery, Ala-
         bama.
Monette, J. W.
1824–   Papers, hand-written drafts of chapters of a projected 6-volume work
1851   to be called the Valley of the Mississippi. Original at Clements Li-
         brary, Manuscript Collection, University of Michigan, Ann Arbor.

Moore, A. (editor)
  1988   *Nairne's Muskhogean Journals: The 1708 Expedition to the Missis-
          sippi River.* University Press of Mississippi, Jackson.
Moore, W. H.
  1969   *Geologic Map of Mississippi.* Mississippi Geological Survey, Jackson.
Moorehead, W. K. (editor)
  1932   *Etowah Papers: Exploration of the Etowah Site in Georgia.* Yale Uni-
          versity Press, New Haven.
Moran, K.
  1999   Toward Compensation: Returning Benefits from Ethnobotanical Drug
          Discovery to Native Peoples. In *Ethnoecology,* edited by V. D. Naz-
          area, pp. 249–262. University of Arizona Press, Tucson.
Moran, L. P.
  1995   Soil and Ecology of Prairie Remnants in the Jackson Prairie Region
          of Mississippi. Unpublished M.S. thesis, Mississippi State Univer-
          sity.
Moran, L. P., D. E. Pettry, R. E. Switzer, S. T. McDaniel, and R. G. Wieland
  1997   Soils on Native Prairie Remnants in the Jackson Prairie Region of
          Mississippi. Mississippi Agricultural and Forestry Experiment Sta-
          tion, Bulletin 1067. Mississippi State University, Jackson.
Morris, M. W., C. T. Bryson, and R. C. Warren
  1993   Rare Vascular Plants and Associated Plant Communities from the
          Sand Creek Chalk Bluffs, Oktibbeha County, Mississippi. *Castanea*
          58:250–259.
Muckle, R. J.
  1994   Differential Recovery of Mollusk Shell from Archaeological Sites.
          Journal of Field Archaeology 21(1):129–131.
Muller, J. D.
  1984   Review of *Pre-Columbian Shell Engravings from the Craig Mound
          at Spiro, Oklahoma.* Vols. 1–6, by P. Phillips and J. A. Brown. *Ameri-
          can Antiquity* 49(3):669–670.
  1987   Salt, Chert, and Shell: Mississippian Exchange and Economy. In *Spe-
          cialization, Exchange, and Complex Societies,* edited by E. M. Braun-
          fiel and T. K. Earle, pp. 10–21. Cambridge University Press, Cambridge.
  1997   *Mississippian Political Economy.* Plenum Press, New York.
Murphree, L. C.
  1957   *Soil Survey of Newton County, Mississippi.* USDA Soil Conserva-
          tion Service, Washington, D.C.
Murphree, L. C., and K. H. Miller
  1976   *Soil Survey of Clay County, Mississippi.* USDA Soil Conservation
          Service, Washington, D.C.
Myers, M. W.
  1948   *Geography of the Mississippi Black Prairie.* Ph.D. dissertation, Clark
          University, Worcester, Massachusetts.
Nabhan, G.
  1995   Cultural Parallax in Viewing North American Habitats. In *Reinvent-
          ing Nature? Responses to Postmodern Deconstruction,* edited by
          M. Soule and G. Lease, pp. 87–102. Island Press, Washington, D.C.

Nance, J.
  1832   Letter between James Nance and his father Elder George Nance. Col-
          lection of Jack Elliot, Mississippi Department of Archives and His-
          tory, Mississippi State University Field Office, Mississippi State
          University, Jackson.
National Oceanic and Atmospheric Administration
  1999   Climatological Data Annual Summary. U.S. Department of Com-
          merce. Washington, D.C.
Nature Conservancy
  1996   *Conservation by Design.* Nature Conservancy, Arlington, Virginia.
Nazarea, V. D.
  1999   (editor). *Ethnoecology.* University of Arizona Press, Tucson.
Nelson, J. C., R. E. Sparks, L. DeHaan, and L. Robinson
  1998   Presettlement and Contemporary Vegetation Patterns along Two
          Navigation Reaches of the Upper Mississippi River. In *Perspectives
          on the Land Use History of North America: A Context for Under-
          standing Our Changing Environment,* edited by T. D. Sisk, pp. 51–
          60. Biological Science Report USGS/BRD.BSR-1998-0003. U.S. Geo-
          logical Survey, Biological Resources Division.
Neuman, R. W.
  1983   The Buffalo in Southeastern United States Post-Pleistocene Prehis-
          tory. In *Southeastern Natives and Their Pasts: A Collection of Pa-
          pers Honoring Dr. Robert E. Bell,* edited by D. G. Wyckoff and J. L.
          Hoffman, pp. 261–280. Studies in Oklahoma's Past No. 11. Okla-
          homa Archeological Survey, Norman.
  1984   *An Introduction to Louisiana Archaeology.* Louisiana State Univer-
          sity Press, Baton Rouge.
Nicholas, G. P.
  1988a   Human Behavior and Holocene Ecology. In *Holocene Human Ecology
          in Northeastern North America,* edited by G. P. Nicholas, pp. 1–7.
          Plenum Press, New York.
  1988b   (editor) *Holocene Human Ecology in Northeastern North America.*
          Plenum Press, New York.
Nicholson, R. A., and T. P. O'Conner
  2000   (editors), *People as an Agent of Environmental Change,* pp. 81–91.
          Symposia of the Association for Environmental Archaeology No. 16.
          Oxbow Books, Oxford.
Norman, H. J.
  1991   Guarding Copenhagen Hills. *Forest and People* 41(4):4–9.
Noss, R.
  1997   Endangered Major Ecosystems of the United States. *Wild Earth*
          7(2):43.
Nuttall, T.
  1980   *A Journal of Travels into the Arkansas Territory During the Year 1819,*
          edited by Savoie Lottinville. University of Oklahoma Press, Norman.
Oates, S. M.
  2000   An Analysis of Cultural Tourism and Its Role in Museums and Heri-
          tage Sites. Unpublished M.A. thesis, University of Oklahoma.

O'Brien, M. J.
  1996   *Paradigms of the Past: The Story of Missouri Archaeology.* University of Missouri Press, Columbia.
  2001   Archaeology, Paleoecosystems, and Ecological Restoration. In *The Historical Ecology Handbook,* edited by D. Egan and E. A. Howell, pp. 29–53. Island Press, Washington, D.C.
O'Brien, M. J., and R. L. Lyman
  2000   *Applying Evolutionary Archaeology: A Systematic Approach.* Kluwer Academic/Plenum Publishers, New York.
O'Brien, M. J., J. Darwent, and R. L. Lyman
  2001   Cladistics is Useful for Reconstructing Archaeological Phylogenies: Paleoindian Points from the Southeastern United States. *Journal of Archaeological Science* 28(10):1115–1136.
Ojima, D. S., W. J. Parton, D. S. Schimel, and C. E. Owensby
  1990   Simulated Impacts of Annual Burning on Prairie Ecosystems. In *Fire in North American Tallgrass Prairies,* edited by S. L. Collins and L. L. Wallace, pp. 118–132. University of Oklahoma Press, Norman.
Old, S. M.
  1969   Microclimate, Fire and Plant Production in an Illinois Prairie. *Ecology* 39:355–384.
Olson, D. L.
  1995   *Shared Spirits: Wildlife and Native Americans.* NorthWord Press, Minocqua, Wisconsin.
Owen, D. D.
  1860   *Second Report of a Geological Reconnoissance [sic] of the Middle and Southern Counties of Arkansas Made During the Years 1859 and 1860.* Johnson and Yerkes, State Printers, Little Rock.
Owen, O. S.
  1980   *Natural Resource Conservation, An Ecological Approach.* MacMillan, New York.
Owsley, D. W.
  1989   The History of Bioarcheological Research in the Southern Great Plains. In *From Clovis to Comanchero: Archeological Overview of the Southern Great Plains,* edited by J. L. Hofman, R. L. Brooks, J. S. Hayes, D. W. Owsley, R. L. Jantz, M. K. Marks, and M. H. Manhein, pp. 126–136. Arkansas Archeological Survey Research Series 35, Fayetteville.
Owsley, D. W., and K. L. Bruwelheide
  1996   Bioarcheological Research in Northeastern Colorado, Northern Kansas, Nebraska, and South Dakota. In *Archeology and Paleoecology of the Central Plains,* edited by J. L. Hoffman, pp. 150–203. Arkansas Archeological Survey Research Series 48, Fayetteville.
Owsley, D. W., and R. L. Jantz
  1989   A Systematic Approach to the Skeletal Biology of the Southern Plains. In *From Clovis to Comanchero: Archeological Overview of the Southern Great Plains,* edited by J. L. Hoffman, R. L. Brooks, J. S. Hayes, D. W. Owsley, R. L. Jantz, M. K. Marks, and M. H. Manhein,

pp. 137–156. Arkansas Archeological Survey Research Series 35, Fayetteville.

Packard, S.

1997   Interseeding. In *The Tallgrass Restoration Handbook for Prairies, Savannas, and Woodlands,* edited by S. Packard and C. F. Mutel, pp. 163–192. Island Press, Covelo, California.

Packard, S., and C. F. Mutel (editors)

1997   *The Tallgrass Restoration Handbook for Prairies, Savannas, and Woodlands.* Island Press, Covelo, California.

Packard, S., and L. M. Ross

1997   Restoring remnants. In *The Tallgrass Restoration Handbook for Prairies, Savannas, and Woodlands,* edited by S. Packard and C. F. Mutel, pp. 63–88. Island Press, Covelo, California.

Parfit, M.

1993   Water. *National Geographic* 184(5A):5–17.

Patterson, P.

1990   *An Archaeological Reconnaissance of Selected Areas of the Black Prairie Region of West Central Alabama.* A report submitted to the Alabama De Soto Commission by the Division of Archaeology, University of Alabama.

Pauketat, T. R.

1992   The Reign and Ruin of the Lords of Cahokia: A Dialectic of Dominance. In *Lords of the Southeast: Social Inequality and the Native Elites of Southeastern North America,* edited by A. W. Barker and T. R. Pauketat, pp. 31–51. American Anthropological Association, Archeological Papers No. 3.

Payne, C., and J. F. Scarry

1998   Town Structure at the Edge of the Mississippian World. In *Mississippian Towns and Sacred Places: Searching for an Architectural Grammar,* edited by R. B. Lewis and C. Stout, pp. 22–48. University of Alabama Press, Tuscaloosa.

Peacock, E.

1992   Some Additional Notes on Forest Reconstruction in the Black Belt. *Mississippi Archaeology* 27(1):1–18.

1993   Reconstructing the Black Belt Environment Using Leaf Impressions in Daub. *Southeastern Archaeology* 12(2):148–154.

1995   Test Excavations at an Upland Mississippian Site in Oktibbeha County, Mississippi. *Mississippi Archaeology* 30(2):1–20.

1996   Tchula Period Sites on the Holly Springs National Forest, North-Central Mississippi. In *Proceedings of the 14th Annual Mid-South Archaeological Conference,* edited by R. Walling, C. Wharey, and C. Stanley. Special Publications 1:13–23. Panamerican Consultants, Memphis.

1997   Woodland Ceramic Affiliations and Settlement Pattern Change in the North Central Hills of Mississippi. *Midcontinental Journal of Archaeology* 22:237–261.

1998a   Historical and Applied Perspectives on Prehistoric Land Use in Eastern North America. *Environment and History* 4(1):1–29.

1998b   A Heritage Resources Survey in Compartments 74, 75, 76 and 77, Ackerman Unit, Tombigbee National Forest, Choctaw and Winston Counties, Mississippi. USDA Forest Service report on file, Mississippi Department of Archives and History, Jackson.

2000   Assessing Bias in Archaeological Shell Assemblages. *Journal of Field Archaeology* 27(2):183–196.

2002   Review of *Biodiversity and Native America*, edited by P. E. Minnis and W. J. Elisens. *American Antiquity* 67(2):382–383.

Peacock, E., and S. Chapman

2001   Taphonomic and Biogeographic Data from a Plaquemine Shell Midden on the Ouachita River, North Louisiana. *Southeastern Archaeology* 20(1):44–55.

Peacock, E., and W. F. Miller

1990   Protohistoric Settlement Patterns in Northeast Mississippi and the Cedar Glade Hypothesis. *Mississippi Archaeology* 25(2):45–57.

Peacock, E., and J. E. Rafferty

1996   Settlement Pattern Continuity and Change in the Mississippi Black Prairie: A Response to Johnson. *Southeastern Archaeology* 15(2):249–253.

Peacock, E., and M. Reynolds

2001   Remote Sensing at Lyon's Bluff, a Mississippian Mound and Village Site in Oktibbeha County, Mississippi. Paper presented at the 58th Annual Meeting, Southeastern Archaeological Conference, Chattanooga, Tennessee.

Peattie, D. C.

1953   *A Natural History of Western Trees.* Houghton Mifflin, Boston.

Peech, M. L.

1965a   Hydrogen Activity. In *Methods of Soil Analysis. Part 2. Agronomy* 9:914–926, edited by C. A. Black.

1965b   Exchange Acidity: Barium Chloride-Triethanolamine Method. In Methods of Soil Analysis. Part 2. *Agronomy* 9:910–911, edited by C. A. Black.

Peech, M. L., L. A. Dean, and J. F. Reed

1947   *Methods of Soil Analysis for Soil Fertility Investigations.* USDA Circular 757.

Peregrine, P. N.

1992   *Mississippian Evolution: A World-System Perspective.* Prehistory Press, Monographs in World Archaeology 9, Madison, Wisconsin.

Peterson, D. A.

1989   A History of Excavations and Interpretations of Artifacts from the Spiro Mounds Site. In *The Southeastern Ceremonial Complex: Artifacts and Analysis*, edited by P. K. Galloway, pp. 114–121. University of Nebraska Press, Lincoln.

Phillips, P., and J. A. Brown

1978   *Pre-Columbian Shell Engravings from the Craig Mound at Spiro, Oklahoma.* Peabody Museum Press, Cambridge.

Pianka, E. R.

1988   *Evolutionary Ecology.* Harper and Row, New York.

Pilsbry, H. A.

1939–   *Land Mollusca of North America (North of Mexico)*. 2 vols., 4 parts.
1948   Academy of Natural Sciences of Philadelphia Monographs 3.

Plog, F. T.

1974   *The Study of Prehistoric Change*. Academic Press, New York.

Pohl, M. D., and P. Bloom

1996   Prehistoric Maya Farming in the Wetlands of Northern Belize: More
         Data from Albion Island and Beyond. In *The Managed Mosaic: An-
         cient Maya Agriculture and Resource Use*, edited by S. L. Fedick,
         pp. 145–164. University of Utah Press, Salt Lake City.

Pollock, D.

2000   The Macrolepidoptera of the Mississippi Black Belt. Unpublished
         M.S. thesis, Mississippi State University.

Poole, R. D., Jr.

1990   A 5 percent Random Sample Survey in North Oktibbeha County,
         Mississippi. Ms. on file, Mississippi Department of Archives and
         History, Jackson.

Poole, R. W.

1995   Noctuoidea, Noctuidae (part). In *The Moths of America North of
         Mexico* 26.1, edited by R. B. Dominick et al., pp. 1–249. Wedge En-
         tomological Research Foundation, Washington, D.C.

Pope, S.

1962   *Bows and Arrows*. University of California Press, Berkeley.

Posey, D. A.

1999   Safeguarding Traditional Resource Rights of Indigenous Peoples. In
         Ethnoecology, edited by V. D. Nazarea, pp. 217–229. University of
         Arizona Press, Tucson.

Post, L. C.

1940   The Rice Country of Southwestern Louisiana. *Geographical Review*
         30:574–590.

Powell, J. A., and N. S. Obraztsov

1977   *Cudonigera:* A New Genus for Moths Formerly Assigned to *Choris-
         toneura houstonana* (Tortricidae). *Journal of the Lepidopterists So-
         ciety* 31:119–123.

Powell, J. W.

1878   *Report on the Lands of the Arid Region of the United States*. Gov-
         ernment Printing Office. 45th Cong. 2nd Sess. H. R. Exec. Doc. 73.
         Washington, D.C.

Powers, J.

1987   Restoration Practice Raises Questions. In *Restoration Ecology*, ed-
         ited by W. R. Jordan, III, M. E. Gilpin, and J. D. Aber, pp. 85–87.
         Cambridge University Press, Cambridge.

Prentice, I. C., P. J. Bartlein, and T. Webb III

1991   Vegetation and Climate Change in Eastern North America since the
         Last Glacial Maximum. *Ecology* 72(6):2038–2056.

Quarterman, E.

1950   Major Plant Communities of Tennessee Cedar Glades. *Ecology* 31:
         234–254.

1986   Biota, Ecology, and Ecological History of Cedar Glades. Introduction. *Association of Southeastern Biologists Bulletin* 33:124–127.

Quinn, D. B. (editor)

1979   *The Expedition of Hernando de Soto and His Successor, Luis de Moscoso, 1538–1543.* Arno Press, New York.

Rabinowitz, D.

1981   Buried Viable Seeds in a North American Tallgrass Prairie: The Resemblance of Their Abundance and Composition to Dispersing Seeds. *Oikos* 36:191–195.

Radford, A. E.

1948   The Vascular Flora of the Olivine Deposits of North Carolina and Georgia. *Journal of the Elisha Mitchell Scientific Society* 64:45–106.

Radford, A. E., H. E. Ahles, and C. R. Bell

1968   *Manual of the Vascular Flora of the Carolinas.* University of North Carolina Press, Chapel Hill.

Rafferty, J.

1978   *Cultural Resource Reconnaissance and Project-Oriented Survey, Noxubee National Wildlife Refuge, Mississippi.* Report submitted to Interagency Archeological Services, Atlanta, by the Department of Anthropology, Mississippi State University.

1985   The Archaeological Record on Sedentariness: Recognition, Development, and Implications. In *Advances in Archaeological Method and Theory* 8, edited by M. B. Schiffer, pp. 113–156. Academic Press, New York.

1994   Gradual or Step-Wise Change: The Development of Sedentary Settlement Patterns in Northeast Mississippi. *American Antiquity* 59: 405–425.

1995   A Seriation of Historic Period Aboriginal Pottery from Northeast Mississippi. *Journal of Alabama Archaeology* 41:180–207.

1996   Continuity in Woodland and Mississippian Settlement Patterning in Northeast Mississippi. *Southeastern Archaeology* 15:230–243.

1998   Tracking Change in Pottery Temper through Late Prehistory in the Tombigbee Valley. Paper presented at the 63rd Annual Meeting, Society for American Archaeology, Seattle, Washington.

2001   Short-Term Sedentary Settlement on the Black Prairie, Northeast Mississippi. Paper presented at the 58th Annual Meeting, Southeastern Archaeological Conference, Chattanooga, Tennessee.

2002   Woodland Period Settlement Patterning in the Northern Coastal Plain of Alabama, Mississippi, and Tennessee. In *The Woodland Southeast,* edited by D. G. Anderson and R. C. Mainfort, Jr. University of Alabama Press, Tuscaloosa.

Rafferty, J., and S. H. Hogue

1998   Phase II Archaeological Testing, 22Ok904, Oktibbeha County, Mississippi. Preliminary report submitted to the Mississippi Department of Transportation, Jackson, by the Cobb Institute of Archaeology, Mississippi State University.

1999   *Test Excavations at Six Sites in Oktibbeha County, Mississippi.* Report submitted to Mississippi Department of Transportation by Cobb Institute of Archaeology, Mississippi State University.

Rafferty, J., and E. Peacock
2000   Absolute Dating and Style-Based Ceramic Chronologies in the Lower Mid-South. Paper presented at the 65th Annual Meeting of the Society for American Archaeology, Philadelphia.

Rankin, H. T.
1974   Black Belt Prairie, Montgomery County, Alabama, and Vicinity. *Auburn University Agricultural Experiment Station, Bulletin* 454.

Rankin, H. T., and E. D. Davis
1971   Woody Vegetation in the Black Belt Prairie of Montgomery County, Alabama, 1845–46. *Ecology* 52(4):716–719.

Ratcliffe, B. C.
1991   The Scarab Beetles of Nebraska. *Bulletin of the University of Nebraska State Museum* 12:1–333.

Redclift, M.
1991   The Multiple Dimensions of Sustainable Development. *Geography* 76:36–42.

Redman, C. L.
1999   *Human Impact on Ancient Environments.* University of Arizona Press, Tucson.

Reese, M. C.
2000   Analyses of Various Methods Used to Quantify Historical Plant Assemblages in East-Central Mississippi. Unpublished M.S. thesis, Mississippi State University.

Reichle, D. E., R. V. O'Neill, and W. F. Harris
1975   Principles of Energy and Material Exchange in Ecosystems. In *Unifying Concepts in Ecology,* edited by W. H. van Dobben and R. H. Lowew-McConnell, pp. 27–43. Dr W. Junk B. V., The Hague.

Reitz, E. J.
1993   Zooarchaeology. In *The Development of Southeastern Archaeology,* edited by J. K. Johnson, pp. 109–131. University of Alabama Press, Tuscaloosa.

Reitz, E. J., and E. S. Wing
1999   *Zooarchaeology.* Cambridge University Press, Cambridge.

Reitz, E. J., L. A. Newsom, and S. J. Scudder
1996   Issues in Environmental Archaeology. In *Case Studies in Environmental Archaeology,* edited by E. J. Reitz, L. A. Newsom, and S. J. Scudder, pp. 3–16. Plenum Press, New York.

Richards, L. A.
1949   Methods of Measuring Soil Moisture Tension. *Soil Science* 68:95–112.
1954   (editor) *Diagnosis and Improvement of Saline and Alkali Soils.* Salinity Laboratory Handbook No. 60. U.S. Department of Agriculture, Washington, D.C.

Rifkin, J.
1991   *Biosphere Politics: A New Consciousness for a New Century.* Harper, San Francisco.

Riley, C. L.

1971 Early Spanish-Indian Communication in the Greater Southwest. *New Mexico Historical Review* 46(4):285–314.

1975 The Road to Hawikuh: Trade and Trade Routes to Cibola-Zuni During Late Prehistoric and Early Historic Times. *Kiva* 41(2):137–159.

1978 Pecos and Trade. In *Across the Chichimec Sea: Papers in Honor of J. Charles Kelley,* edited by C. L. Riley and B. C. Hedrick, pp. 53–64. Southern Illinois University Press, Carbondale.

1987 *The Frontier People: The Greater Southwest in the Historic Period.* University of New Mexico Press, Albuquerque.

Rindge, F. H.

1949 A Revision of the Geometrid Moths Formerly Assigned to *Drepanulatrix* (Lepidoptera). *Bulletin of the American Museum of Natural History* 94:235–298.

1971 A Revision of the Moth Genus *Lytrosis* (Lepidoptera, Geometridae). *American Museum Novitates* 2474:1–21.

Rindos, D.

1984 *The Origins of Agriculture: An Evolutionary Perspective.* Academic Press, New York.

Riser, P. G.

1986 Preservation Status of True Prairie Grasslands and Ecological Concepts Relevant to Management of Prairie Preserves. In *Wilderness and Natural Areas in the Eastern United States: A Management Challenge,* edited by D. L. Kulhavy and R. N. Conner, pp. 339–344. Stephen J. Austin State University, School of Forestry, Center for Applied Studies, Nacogdoches, Texas.

Robbins, W. W., J. P. Harrington, and B. Freire-Marreco

1916 *Ethnobotany of the Tewa.* Bureau of American Ethnology Bulletin No. 55. Smithsonian Institution, Washington, D.C.

Roberts, J.

1979 *The Arkansas Blackland Region.* Report submitted to the Arkansas Natural Heritage Commission. Arkansas Department of Natural Heritage, Little Rock.

Roberts, M. R., and C. J. Richardson

1985 Forty-one Years of Population Change and Community Succession in Aspen Forests on Four Soil Types, Northern Lower Michigan, U.S.A. *Canadian Journal of Botany* 63:1641–1651.

Robertson, P. A., and A. L. Heikens

1994 Fires Frequency in Oak-Hickory Forests of Southern Illinois. *Castanea* 59(3):286–291.

Rogers, J. D.

1996 Markers of Social Integration: The Development of Centralized Authority in the Spiro Region. In *Political Structure and Change in the Prehistoric Southeastern United States,* edited by J. F. Scarry, pp. 53–68. University Press of Florida, Gainesville.

Rogers, S. L.

1975 *Artificial Deformation of the Head: New World Examples of Ethnic*

Mutilation and Its Consequences. San Diego Museum of Man, San Diego.

Rohrbaugh, C. L.

1982 *Spiro and Fort Coffee Phases: Changing Cultural Complexes of the Caddoan Area.* Ph.D. dissertation, University of Wisconsin–Madison. University Microfilms, Ann Arbor.

Romans, Bernard

1999 *A Concise Natural History of East and West Florida,* edited by K. E. H. Braund. Originally published in 1775. University of Alabama Press, Tuscaloosa.

Rose, J. C., M. K. Marks, and L. L. Tieszen

1991 Bioarchaeology and Subsistence in the Central and Lower Portions of the Mississippi Valley. In *What Mean These Bones? Studies in Southeastern Bioarchaeology,* edited by M. L. Powell, P. S. Bridges, and A. M. W. Mires, pp. 7–21. University of Alabama Press, Tuscaloosa.

Rosenberg, M.

1998 Cheating at Musical Chairs: Territoriality and Sedentism in an Evolutionary Context. *Current Anthropology* 39:653–681.

Ross, H. H.

1970 The Ecological History of the Great Plains: Evidence from Grassland Insects. In *Pleistocene and Recent Environments of the Central Great Plains,* edited by W. Dort, Jr., and J. K. Jones, pp. 225–240. University of Kansas, Department of Geology, Special Publication No. 3. University Press of Kansas, Lawrence.

Rostlund, E.

1957 The Myth of a Natural Prairie Belt in Alabama: An Interpretation of Historical Records. *Annals of the Association of American Geographers* 47:392–411.

Rowland, D. (editor)

1930 *Life, Letters and Papers of William Dunbar.* Mississippi Historical Society, Jackson.

Rowland, D., and A. G. Sanders

1927 *Mississippi Provincial Archives, French Dominion, 1729–1740.* Vol. 1. Mississippi Department of Archives and History, Jackson.

Rowland, D., A. G. Sanders, and P. K. Galloway

1984 *Mississippi Provincial Archives, French Dominion, 1729–1748.* Vol. 4. Louisiana State University Press, Baton Rouge.

Rucker, M. D.

1974 *Archeological Survey and Test Excavations in the Upper-Central Tombigbee River Valley: Aliceville-Columbus Lock and Dam and Impoundment Areas, Alabama and Mississippi.* Report submitted to National Park Service by Department of Anthropology, Mississippi State University.

Ruhl, D. L.

1987 Impression in and on Daub: a Preliminary Look at Some Burned Clay from Three Mission Sites in *La Florida.* Paper presented at the

44th Annual Southeastern Archaeological Conference, Charleston, South Carolina.

Russell, E. W. B.
1997   *People and the Land Through Time.* Yale University Press, New Haven.

Sahlins, M. D.
1968   *Tribesmen.* Prentice Hall, Englewood Cliffs, New Jersey.

Salmón, E.
2000   *Iwígara:* a Raramuri Cognitive Model of Biodiversity and Its Effects on Land Management. In *Biodiversity and Native America,* edited by P. E. Minnis and W. J. Elisens, pp. 180–203. University of Oklahoma Press, Norman.

Samson, F. B., and F. L. Knopf (editors)
1996   *Prairie Conservation.* Island Press, Covelo, California.

Sargent, C. S.
1884   *The Forests of North America.* Government Printing Office, Washington, D.C.

Saucier, R. T.
1974   Quaternary Geology of the Lower Mississippi Valley. Arkansas Archeological Survey Research Series 6, pp. 1–26. Fayetteville.

Sauer, C. O.
1980   *Seventeenth Century North America.* Turtle Island, Berkeley.

Saunders, J. W., R. D. Mandel, R. T. Saucier, E. T. Allen, C. T. Hallmark, J. K. Johnson, E. H. Jackson, C. M. Allen, G. L. Stinger, D. S. Frink, J. K. Feathers, S. Williams, K. J. Gremillion, M. F. Vidrine, and R. Jones
1997   A Mound Complex in Louisiana at 5400–5000 Years Before the Present. *Science* 277:1796–1799.

Schaeffer, J. B.
1954   The Nagle Site, Ok-4. *Bulletin of the Oklahoma Anthropological Society* 5:93–99.

Schambach, F. F.
1993a   Some New Interpretations of Spiroan Culture History. In *Archaeology of Eastern North America: Papers in Honor of Stephen Williams,* edited by J. B. Stoltman, pp. 187–230. Archaeological Report No. 25. Mississippi Department of Archives and History, Jackson.

1993b   Spiroan Entrepots at and Beyond the Western Border of the Trans-Mississippi South. *Caddoan Archeology Newsletter* 4(2):11–26.

1995   A Probable Spiroan Entrepot in the Red River Valley in Northeast Texas. *Caddoan Archeology Newsletter* 6(1):9–25.

1997   Continuing the Discussion of the Spiroans and Their Entrepots: A Reply to Brooks's Critique of My New Paradigm for the Archeology of the Arkansas Valley. *Caddoan Archeology* 7(4):17–46.

1999a   Deconstructing the "Sanders Focus" and the "Sanders Phase": A Reply to Perttula Regarding the Taxonomy and Significance of the So-Called Sanders Focus or Sanders Phase Pottery of Northeast Texas and Southeast Oklahoma. *Caddoan Archeology* 9(3/4):3–55.

1999b   The End of the Trail: Reconstruction of the Route of Hernando de Soto's Army Through Southwest Arkansas and Northeast Texas. In

*The Expedition of Hernando de Soto West of the Mississippi, 1541–
1543*, edited by G. A. Young and M. P. Hoffman, pp. 78–105. University of Arkansas Press, Fayetteville.

1999c   Spiro and the Tunica: A New Interpretation of the Role of the Tunica
in the Culture History of the Southeast and the Southern Plains,
A.D. 1100–1750. In *Arkansas Archeology: Essays in Honor of Dan
and Phyllis Morse*, edited by R. C. Mainfort, Jr., and M. D. Jeter,
pp. 169–224. University of Arkansas Press, Fayetteville.

2000a   The Significance of the Sanders Site in the Culture History of the
Mississippi Period Southeast and the Southern Plains. In *The 1931
Excavations at the Sanders Site, Lamar County Texas; Notes on the
Field Work, Human Osteology, and Ceramics*, by A. T. Jackson,
M. S. Goldstein, and A. Krieger, pp. 1–7. Texas Archeological Research Laboratory Archival Series 2. University of Texas, Austin.

2000b   Spiroan Traders, the Sanders Site, and the Plains Interaction Sphere:
A Reply to Bruseth, Wilson, and Perttula. *Plains Anthropologist*
45(171):7–33.

2001   A Preliminary Report on the 2001 Investigations by the Arkansas
Archeological Survey and the Arkansas Archeological Society at the
Grandview Prairie Wildlife Management Area, Hempstead County,
Southwest Arkansas. *Arkansas Archeological Survey Field Notes*
301, July/August 2001:5–11.

Schauwecker, T. J.
1996   A Comparison of Blackland Prairie Relicts in Arkansas and Mississippi. Unpublished M.S. thesis, Mississippi State University.

Schiefer, T. L.
1998   Disjunct Distribution of Cerambycidae (Coleoptera) in the Black Belt
Prairie and Jackson Prairie in Mississippi and Alabama. *Coleopterists' Bulletin* 52:278–284.

Schmitz, D. W., D. L. Wax, and J. W. Pote
1999   Influence of Water Availability on Settlement Patterns. In *Proceedings of the Mississippi Water Resources Conference, Water Resources
Research Institute, Mississippi State University*, edited by B. J.
Daniel, pp. 153–156.

Schuster, M., and S. McDaniel
1974   A Vegetative Analysis of a Black Prairie Relict Site near Aliceville,
Alabama. *Journal of the Mississippi Academy of Sciences* 19:153–
159.

Scott, S.
1982   Yarborough Site Faunal Remains. In *Archaeological Investigations
at the Yarborough Site (22CL814), Clay County, Mississippi*, by
C. Soling and R. Walling, pp. 140–152. Report of Investigations 30.
Office of Archaeological Research, University of Alabama, Tuscaloosa.

1983   Analysis, Synthesis, and Interpretation of Faunal Remains from the
Lubbub Creek Archaeological Locality. In *Prehistoric Agricultural
Communities in West Central Alabama, Vol. 2: Studies of Material
Remains from the Lubbub Creek Archaeological Locality*, edited by

C. S. Peebles, pp. 272–390. Museum of Anthropology, University of Michigan, Ann Arbor.

Shands, W. E., and J. S. Hoffman (editors)
1987   *The Greenhouse Effect, Climate Change, and U.S. Forests.* Conservation Foundation, Washington, D.C.

Shantz, H. L., and R. Zon
1924   Natural Vegetation (Map). In Atlas of American Agriculture. Washington, D.C., p. 5.

Shaw, J. H., and M. Lee
1997   Relative Abundance of Bison, Elk, and Pronghorn on the Southern Plains, 1806–1857. *Plains Anthropologist* 42(159):163–172.

Sheehan, M. C.
1982   Report on Pollen Analyses for the Yarborough Site (22CI814). In C. Solis and R. Walling, Archaeological Investigations at the Yarborough Site (22CI814), Clay County, Mississippi, pp. 133–134. Report of Investigations 30. Office of Archaeological Research, University of Alabama, Tuscaloosa.

Sibley, J.
1832   Letter to General H. Dearborn, April 5,1805. In *Documents, Legislative and Executive of the Congress of the United States,* edited by W. Lowrie and M. S. C. Clarke, pp. 725–731. American State Papers, Class II, Indian Affairs Vol. 4. Washington, D.C.

Simberloff, D., L. Stone, and T. Dayan
1999   Ruling Out a Community Assembly Rule: The Method of Favored States. In *Ecological Assembly Rules: Perspectives, Advances, Retreats,* edited by E. Weiher and P. Keddy, pp. 58–74. Cambridge University Press, Cambridge.

Simmons, I. G.
1999   History, Ecology, Contingency, Sustainability. In *Structure and Contingency: Evolutionary Processes in Life and Human Society,* edited by J. Bintliff, pp. 118–131. Leicester University Press, London.

Simpson, R. D., R. A. Sedjo, and J. W. Reid
1998   The Commercialization of Indigenous Genetic Resources as Conservation and Development Policy. In *Protection of Global Biodiversity: Converging Strategies,* edited by L. D. Guruswamy and J. A. McNeely, pp. 129–146. Duke University Press, Durham.

Sims, P. L., and P. G. Risser
2000   Grasslands. In *North American Terrestrial Vegetation,* edited by M. G. Barbour and W. D. Billings, pp. 324–356. Cambridge University Press, New York.

Sisk, T. D. (editor)
1998   *Perspectives on the Land Use History of North America: A Context for Understanding Our Changing Environment.* Biological Science Report USGS/BRD/BSR-1998-0003. U.S. Geological Survey, Biological Resources Division.

Smeins, F. E., and D. D. Diamond
1988   Grasslands and Savannahs of East Central Texas: Ecology, Preservation Status and Management Problems. In *Wilderness and Natural*

Areas in the Eastern United States: A Management Challenge, edited by D. L. Kulhavy and R. N. Conner, pp. 381–394. Stephen F. Austin State University, Nacogdoches, Texas.

Smeins, F. E., D. D. Diamond, and C. W. Hanselka

1992   Coastal Prairie. In *Ecosystems of the World: Natural Grasslands,* edited by R. T. Coupland, pp. 269–290. Vol. 8a. Elsevier, Amsterdam.

Smith, B. D.

1975   Middle Mississippi Exploitation of Animal Populations. Museum of Anthropology Anthropological Papers No. 57. University of Michigan, Ann Arbor.

1978   Variation in Mississippian Settlement Patterns. In *Mississippian Settlement Patterns,* edited by B. D. Smith, pp. 479–503. Academic Press, New York.

1986   The Archaeology of the Southeastern United States: From Dalton to deSoto, 10,500–500 B.P. *Advances in World Archaeology* 5:1–92.

1990   (editor) *The Mississippian Emergence.* Smithsonian Institution Press, Washington, D.C.

1992   *Rivers of Change: Essays on Early Agriculture in Eastern North America.* Smithsonian Institution Press, Washington, D.C.

Smith, J. L., and J. V. Perino

1981   Osage Orange (*Maclura pomifera*): History and Economic Uses. *Economic Botany* 35(1):24–41.

Smith, L. M., N. M. Gilmore, R. P. Martin, and G. D. Lester

1989   Keiffer Calcareous Prairie/Forest Complex: A Research Report and Preliminary Management Plan. Unpublished report on file, Department of Wildlife and Fisheries, Baton Rouge.

Solis, C., and R. Walling

1982   Archaeological Investigations at the Yarborough Site (22CL814), Clay County, Mississippi. Report of Investigations 30. Office of Archaeological Research, University of Alabama, Tuscaloosa.

Somers, P.

1986   (editor) Symposium: Biota, Ecology, and Ecological History of Cedar Glades. *Association of Southeastern Biologists Bulletin* 33:124–215.

Speth, J. D.

1991   Some Unexplored Aspects of Mutualistic Plains-Pueblo Food Exchange. In *Farmers, Hunters, and Colonists,* edited by K. A. Spielmann, pp. 18–35. University of Arizona Press, Tucson.

Spielmann, K. A.

1983   Late Prehistoric Exchange Between the Southwest and Southern Plains. *Plains Anthropologist* 28(102):257–272.

1991   *Farmers, Hunters, and Colonists: Interaction Between the Southwest and the Southern Plains.* University of Arizona Press, Tucson.

Spielmann, K. A., M. J. Shoeninger, and K. Moore

1990   Plains-Pueblo Interdependence and Human Diet at Pecos Pueblo, New Mexico. *American Antiquity* 55(4):745–765.

Stahl, P. W.

1996   Holocene Biodiversity: An Archaeological Perspective from the Americas. *Annual Review of Anthropology* 25:105–126.

Stauffer, J. M.
1961   Historical Aspects of Forest and Vegetation of the Black Belt. *Journal of the Alabama Academy of Sciences* 32:485-492.

Stein, J. K., and A. R. Linse (editors)
1993   *Effects of Scale on Archaeological and Geoscientific Perspectives.* Geological Society of America Special Paper 283.

Stephenson, D. J., Jr.
1999   A Practical Primer on Intellectual Property Rights in a Contemporary Ethnoecological Context. In *Ethnoecology,* edited by V. D. Nazarea, pp. 230-248. University of Arizona Press, Tucson.

Stephenson, L. W., and W. H. Monroe
1940   The Upper Cretaceous Deposits. *Mississippi Geological Survey Bulletin* 40:1-296.

Stephenson, L. W., W. N. Logan, and G. A. Waring
1928   *The Ground-Water Resources of Mississippi.* U.S. Geological Survey, Water Supply Paper 576. Washington, D.C.

Steponaitis, V. P.
1986   Prehistoric Archaeology in the Southeastern United States, 1970-1985. *Annual Review of Anthropology* 15:363-404.

Stewart, T. D.
1941   The Circular Type of Cranial Deformation in the United States. *American Journal of Physical Anthropology* 28:343-351.

Stokes, S. N., E. Watson, and S. Mastran
1989   *Saving America's Countryside.* Johns Hopkins University Press, Baltimore.

Stoltman, J. B. (editor)
1991   *New Perspectives on Cahokia: Views from the Periphery.* Monographs in World Archaeology 2. Prehistory Press, Madison, Wisconsin.

Stone, L., T. Dayan, and D. Simberloff
1996   Community-Wide Patterns Unmasked: The Importance of Species' Differing Geographical Ranges. *American Naturalist* 148:997-1015.

Stringer, J. W., T. W. Kimmerer, J. C. Overstreet, and J. P. Dunn
1989   Oak Mortality in Eastern Kentucky. *Southern Journal of Applied Forestry* 13(2):86-91.

Stubbs, J. D., Jr.
1983   A report presenting the results of archaeological survey in Lee County, Mississippi, June, 1981 to June, 1983. Manuscript on file, Mississippi Department of Archives and History, Jackson.

Swanton, J. R.
1942   Source Material on the History and Ethnology of the Caddo Indians. Bureau of American Ethnology Bulletin No. 132. Smithsonian Institution, Washington, D.C.

Taitt, D.
1772   The Journal of a Journey through the Creek Country, 1772. In *Travels in the American Colonies,* edited by N. D. Mereness, pp. 493-565. Antiquarian Press, New York, 1961.

Teltser, P. A. (editor)
1995   *Evolutionary Archaeology: Methodological Issues.* University of Arizona Press, Tucson.

Theler, J. L.

n.d.   Paleoenvironmental Interpretation from the Burnham Site Gastro-
          pods. Ms. in possession of the author.

Thomas, R. D.

1986   Survey of Former Prairies in North Louisiana. Unpublished report
          on file, Louisiana Natural Heritage Program, Baton Rouge.

Tiffany, J. A.

1991   The Western Prairie Peninsula. In *Cahokia and the Hinterlands:
          Middle Mississippian Cultures in the Midwest,* edited by T. E. Emer-
          son and R. B. Lewis, pp. 183–192. University of Illinois Press, Ur-
          bana.

Timme, S. L.

1989   *Wildflowers of Mississippi.* University Press of Mississippi, Jackson.

Toner, W.

1988   Environmental Land Use Planning. In *The Practice of Local Govern-
          ment Planning,* 2nd ed., edited by F. S. So and J. Getzels. Interna-
          tional City/County Management Association, Washington, D.C.

Tower, J. A.

1961   The Changing Black Belt—A Geographical Review. *Journal of the
          Alabama Academy of Science* 32:479–485.

Transeau, E. N.

1935   The Prairie Peninsula. *Ecology* 16:423–437.

Trinkley, M.

1999   Paleoethnobotanical Samples. In J. Rafferty and S. H. Hogue, *Test
          Excavations at Six Sites in Oktibbeha County, Mississippi,* pp. 193–
          210. Report submitted to Mississippi Department of Transportation
          by Cobb Institute of Archaeology, Mississippi State University.

Turgeon, D. D., J. F. Quinn, Jr., A. E. Bogan, E. V. Coan, F. G. Hochberg, W. G.
          Lyons, P. M. Mikkelsen, R. J. Neves, C. F. E. Roper, G. Rosenberg,
          B. Roth, A. Scheltema, F. G. Thompson, M. Vecchione, and J. D. Wil-
          liams

1998   *Common and Scientific Names of Aquatic Invertebrates from the
          United States and Canada: Mollusks.* 2nd ed. American Fisheries
          Society Special Publication 26. Bethesda, Maryland.

Turner, C. L., J. M. Blair, R. J. Schartz, and J. C. Neel

1997   Soil N and Plant Responses to Fire, Topography, and Supplemental
          N in Tallgrass Prairie. *Ecology* 78:1832–1843.

Turner, R. L., J. E. van Kley, L. S. Smith, and R. E. Evans

1999   *Ecological Classification System of the National Forests and Adja-
          cent Areas of the West Gulf Coastal Plain.* Nature Conservancy,
          Nacogdoches, Texas.

Tyndall, R. W.

1994   Conifer Clearing and Prescribed Burning Effects to Herbaceous
          Layer Vegetation on a Maryland Serpentine "Barren." *Castanea*
          59(3):255–273.

United Nations Educational, Scientific, and Cultural Organization (UNESCO)

1973   International Classification and Mapping of Vegetation. Paris, France:
          United Nations Educational, Scientific, and Cultural Organization.

United States Department of Agriculture

1982   General Soil Map of Arkansas. University of Arkansas, Fayetteville.

United States Department of Commerce

1992   Monthly Station Normals of Temperature, Precipitation, and Heating and Cooling Degree Days 1961–90. *National Oceanic and Atmospheric Administration, National Climatic Data Center, Climatography of the United States No. 81*. Asheville, North Carolina.

United States Department of Interior

1995   *Our Living Resources: A Report to the Nation on the Distribution, Abundance, and Health of U.S. Plants, Animals, and Ecosystems.* United States Department of Interior, Washington, D.C.

United States Forest Service

1980   Harrell Prairie Hill Botanical Area: Designation and Management as a Botanical Area. Code FSM 2362.43. U.S. Forest Service, Bienville National Forest.

1989   *Procambarus barbinger. U.S. Fish and Wildlife Service and U.S. Forest Service Memorandum of Understanding No. 14-16-0004-89-936.* U.S. Department of Interior, Fish and Wildlife Service, Regional Office, Atlanta.

United States Geological Survey

1993   Geological Map of Arkansas. Arkansas Geological Commission, Little Rock.

van Gelder, B., and P. O'Keefe

1995   *The New Forester.* Intermediate Technology Publications, London.

Varner, J. G., and J. J. Varner

1951   *The Florida of the Inca.* University of Texas Press, Austin.

Vavrek, M. C.

2000   Quantitative Assessment of Keiffer Prairie Plant Populations for Effective Management. Unpublished report on file, USDA Forest Service Office, Pineville, Louisiana.

Vigne, J. D., and H. Valladas

1996   Small Mammal Fossil Assemblages as Indicators of Environmental Change in Northern Corsica During the Last 2500 Years. *Journal of Archaeological Science* 23(2):199–215.

Voget, F. W.

1974   *Osage Indians I: Osage Research Report.* Garland, New York.

Wackerman, A. E.

1929   Why Prairies in Arkansas and Louisiana. *Journal Forestry* 27:726–734.

Waggoner, G. S.

1975   *Eastern Deciduous Forest, Volume 1: Southeastern Evergreen and Oak-Pine Region.* Government Printing Office, Washington, D.C.

Wailes, B. L. C.

1854   *Report on the Agriculture and Geology of Mississippi.* Mississippi State Legislature. E. Barksdale, State Printer, Jackson.

Walker, B.

1928   *The Terrestrial Shell-Bearing Mollusca of Alabama.* Miscellaneous

Publication No. 18. Museum of Zoology, University of Michigan, Ann Arbor.

Walsh, K.
1999   Mediterranean Landscape Archaeology and Environmental Reconstruction. In *Environmental Reconstruction in Mediterranean Landscape Archaeology*, edited by P. Leveau, F. Trément, K. Walsh, and G. Barker, pp. 1–8. Oxbow Books, Oxford.

Walthall, J. A.
1981   *Galena and Aboriginal Trade in Eastern North America*. Illinois State Museum Scientific Papers No. 17, Springfield.

Ward, H. T.
1965   Correlation of Mississippian Sites and Soil Types. *Southeastern Archaeological Conference Bulletin* 3:42–48.

Warner, S. R.
1926   Distribution of Native Plants and Weeds on Certain Soil Types in Eastern Texas. *Botanical Gazette* 82:345–372.

Waselkov, G. A.
1997   Changing Strategies of Indian Field Location in the Early Historic Southeast. In *People, Plants, and Landscapes: Studies in Paleoethnobotany*, edited by K. J. Gremillion, pp. 179–194. University of Alabama Press, Tuscaloosa.

Watson, P. J.
1990   Trend and Tradition in Southeastern Archaeology. *Southeastern Archaeology* 9(1):43–54.

Watts, W. A.
1973   The Vegetation Record of a Mid-Wisconsin Interstadial in Northwest Georgia. *Quaternary Research* 3:257–268.
1975   A Late Quaternary Record of Vegetation from Lake Annie, South-Central Florida. *Geology* 3:344–346.
1980a   The Late Quaternary Vegetation History of the Southeastern United States. *Annual Review of Ecology and Systematics* 11:387–409.
1980b   Late-Quaternary Vegetation History at White Pond on the Inner Coastal Plain of South Carolina. *Quaternary Research* 13:187–199.

Watts, W. A., and R. C. Bright
1968   Pollen, Seed, and Mollusk Analysis of a Sediment Core from Pickeral Lake, Northeastern South Dakota. *Geological Society of America Bulletin* 79:855–876.

Watts, W. A., and H. E. Wright, Jr.
1966   Late-Wisconsin Pollen and Seed Analysis from the Nebraska Sandhills. *Ecology* 47:202–210.

Weakley, A.
1999   Fire Exclusion in the Eastern Ecoregions of the United States and Canada. In T. H. Ricketts, E. Dinerstein, D. M. Olson, C. J. Loucks, W. Eichbaum, D. DellaSala, K. Kavanagh, P. Hedao, P. T. Hurley, K. M. Carney, R. Abell, and S. Walters, *Terrestrial Ecoregions of North America: A Conservation Assessment*, pp. 73–75. Island Press, Washington, D.C.

Weakley, A. S., K. D. Patterson, S. Landall, and M. Pyne
  1999 *International Classification of Ecological Communities: Terrestrial Vegetation of the Southeastern United States, Ecoregion 41.* Nature Conservancy, Chapel Hill, North Carolina.
Weaver, J. E.
  1954 *The North American Prairie.* Johnson Publication, Lincoln, Nebraska.
  1968 *Prairie Plants and Their Environments: A Fifty-Year Study in the Midwest.* University of Nebraska Press, Lincoln.
Weaver, J. E., and T. J. Fitzpatrick
  1934 The Prairie. *Ecological Monographs* 4:109–295.
Webb, C. H., and R. R. McKinney
  1975 Mounds Plantation (16CD12), Caddo Parish, Louisiana. *Louisiana Archaeology* 2:39–127.
Webb, T., III
  1988 Eastern North America. In *Vegetation History*, edited by B. Huntley and T. Webb, pp. 385–414. Kluwer, Dordrecht, Netherlands.
Wedel, M. M.
  1981 The Deer Creek Site, Oklahoma: A Wichita Village Sometimes Called Ferdinandina, An Ethnohistorian's View. Oklahoma City: *Oklahoma Historical Society, Series in Anthropology Number 5.*
  1982 The Indian They Called Turco. In *Pathways to Plains Prehistory: Anthropological Perspectives of Plains Natives and Their Pasts. Papers in Honor of Robert E. Bell*, edited by D. G. Wyckoff and J. Hoffman, pp. 153–162. Oklahoma Anthropological Society Memoir No. 3. Norman.
Weiher, E., and P. A. Keddy
  1995 Assembly Rules, Null Models, and Trait Dispersion: New Questions from Old Patterns. *Oikos* 74:159–164.
  1999 Assembly Rules as General Constraints on Community Assembly. In *Ecological Assembly Rules: Perspectives, Advances, Retreats*, edited by E. Weiher and P. Keddy, pp. 58–74. Cambridge University Press, Cambridge.
Welch, P. D.
  1991 *Moundville's Economy.* University of Alabama Press, Tuscaloosa.
Wells, P. V.
  1970a Historical Factors Controlling Vegetation Patterns and Floristic Distributions in the Central Plains Region of North America. In *Pleistocene and Recent Environments of the Central Great Plains*, edited by W. Dort, Jr., and J. K. Jones, pp. 211–221. University of Kansas, Department of Geology, Special Publication No. 3. University Press of Kansas, Lawrence.
  1970b Postglacial Vegetational History of the Great Plains. *Science* 167:1574–1582.
Weniger, D.
  1996 Catalpa (*Catalpa Bignonioides, Bignoniaceae*) and Bois d'Arc (*Maclura Pomifera, Moraceae*) in Early Texas Records. *SIDA* 17(1):231–242.

West, E.

1998   *The Contested Plains: Indians, Goldseekers, and the Rush to Colorado.* University Press of Kansas, Lawrence.

West Point, Mississippi

2001   "22nd Annual Prairie Arts Festival," West Point, Mississippi, June 16, 2000, 2 pp., February 22, 2001. http://www.wpnet.org/prairie.html.

Whitehead, D. R.

1967   Studies of Full-Glacial Vegetation and Climate in the Southeastern United States. In *Quaternary Paleoecology,* edited by E. J. Cushing and H. E. Wright, Jr., pp. 237–248. Yale University Press, New Haven.

Whitehead, D. R., and M. C. Sheehan

1985   Holocene Vegetational Changes in the Tombigbee River Valley, Eastern Mississippi. *American Midland Naturalist* 113:122–137.

Whitney, G. G.

1994   *From Coastal Wilderness to Fruited Plain.* Cambridge University Press, New York.

Whittaker, R. H.

1956   Vegetation of the Great Smoky Mountains. *Ecological Monographs* 26:1–26.

1975   *Communities and Ecosystems.* MacMillan, New York.

Whyte, T. R.

1991   Small-Animal Remains in Archaeological Pit Features. In *Beamers, Bobwhites, and Blue Points: Tributes to the Career of Paul W. Parmalee,* edited by J. R. Purdue, W. E. Klippel, and B. W. Styles, pp. 163–176. Illinois State Museum Scientific Papers, vol. 23, and the University of Tennessee, Department of Anthropology Report of Investigations No. 52.

Wieland, R. G.

1991   Jackson Prairie: Myth or Reality? *Newsletter of the Mississippi Museum of Natural Science* 8(3):3.

2000   Vegetation composition of clay barrens (prairie openings) of the Jackson Prairie region of central Mississippi. Paper presented at the Blackland Prairies of the Gulf Coastal Plain: Culture, Nature, and Sustainability Conference, May 19–20, Mississippi State University, Starkville.

Wieland, R., and L. Weeks

1990   Field Survey of Forest/Prairie Boundary. Unpublished report on file, Mississippi Museum of Natural Science, Jackson.

Wieland, R. G., K. L. Gordon, J. B. Wiseman, and D. S. Elsen

1991   Agencies inventory and restore prairie openings in Bienville National Forest (Mississippi). *Restoration and Management Notes* 9(2):105–106.

Wilbanks, T. J.

1994   "Sustainable Development" in Geographic Perspective. *Annals of the Association of American Geographers* 84(4):541–556.

Wilcox, D. R.

1991   Changing Contexts of Pueblo Adaptations, A.D. 1250–1600. In *Farm-*

ers, Hunters, and Colonists: Interaction Between the Southwest and the Southern Plains, edited by K. A. Spielmann, pp. 128–154. University of Arizona Press, Tucson.

Williams, G. I., Jr.
1993   Environmental Setting. In Caddoan Saltmakers in the Ouachita Valley: The Hardaman Site, edited by A. M. Early, pp. 15–28. Arkansas Archeological Survey Research Series 43, Fayetteville.

Williams, S.
1981   The Mississippians. Symbols 1:11.

Wilson, D.
1993   Incidence of Degenerative Joint Disease Among the Sanders Site (41LR2) Population. Paper presented at the 35th Caddo Conference, Norman, Oklahoma.

Wilson, E. O.
1992   The Diversity of Life. Harvard University Press, Cambridge.

Wilson, J. B.
1995a   Null Models for Assembly Rules: The Jack Horner Effect is More Insidious than the Narcissus Effect. Oikos 74:543–544.
1995b   Fox and Brown's Random Data Sets Are Not Random. Oikos 72:139–143.
1999   Assembly Rules in Plant Communities. In Ecological Assembly Rules: Perspectives, Advances, Retreats, edited by E. Weiher and P. Keddym, pp. 130–164. Cambridge University Press, Cambridge.

Wilson, S. D., and J. M. Shay
1990   Competition, Fire, and Nutrients in a Mixed-Grass Prairie. Ecology 71:1959–1967.

Wilson, T. H.
1981   Natural History of the Black Belt Prairie. Journal of the Alabama Academy of Science 52:10–19.

Wilson, W. H.
1989   The City Beautiful Movement. Johns Hopkins University Press, Baltimore.

Winberry, J. J.
1979   The Osage Orange, a Botanical Artifact. Pioneer America 11(3):134–141.

Winterhalder, B.
1990   Open Field, Common Pot: Harvest Variability and Risk Avoidance in Agricultural and Foraging Societies. In Risk and Uncertainty in Tribal and Peasant Economies, edited by E. Cashdan, pp. 67–87. Westview Press, Boulder, Colorado.

Wittfogel, K.
1957   Oriental Despotism. Yale University Press, New Haven.

Wolf, E. R.
1999   Cognizing "Cognized Models." American Anthropologist 101(1):19–22.

Wright, D. J., R. L. Brown, and L. D. Gibson
1997   A New Species of Phaneta, with Taxonomic Diagnoses and Seasonal

and Geographical Data on Four Related Species (Tortricidae). *Journal of the Lepidopterists Society* 51:119–127.

Wyckoff, D. G.
  1980   *Caddoan Adaptive Strategies in the Arkansas Basin, Eastern Oklahoma.* Ph.D. dissertation, Washington State University.

Young, J. A., and C. G. Young
  1992   *Seeds of Woody Plants in North America.* Discorides Press, Portland, Oregon.

Yuan, T. L.
  1959   Determination of Exchangeable Aluminum in Soils by a Titration Method. *Soil Science* 88:164–167.

Zimmerer, K. S.
  1994   Human Geography and the "New Ecology": The Prospect and Promise of Integration. *Annals of the Association of American Geographers* 84(1):108–125.

Zutter, C.
  1999   Congruence or Concordance in Archaeobotany: Assessing Micro- and Macro-botanical Data Sets from Icelandic Middens. *Journal of Archaeological Science* 26(7):833–844.

Contributors

Richard Brown is a moth taxonomist and director of the Mississippi Entomological Museum at Mississippi State University. His faunistic and biogeographic research on Lepidoptera has focused on species occurring in unique habitats, especially grasslands, in the southeastern United States.

Dean Elsen is the wildlife biologist for the Bienville Ranger District in east-central Mississippi. His job entails management of the largest population of red-cockaded woodpeckers in the state, prairie restoration, prescribed burning, and deer and turkey management. He is especially interested in landscape archaeology and how Native American fires and activities shaped the coastal plains.

Tom Foti earned an M.S. in botany from the University of Arkansas (Fayetteville). Since 1985 he has worked as plant community ecologist and chief of research for the Arkansas Natural Heritage Commission. He has published a number of scientific papers and books on Arkansas vegetation and environment, including the relationship of people to the natural environment. He has studied blackland prairies of Arkansas since 1972 and has produced two publications on the subject. Currently he is coauthor of a book in preparation on the vegetation of Arkansas, with Edward E. Dale, professor emeritus of the Department of Biology, UAF.

Meryl Hattenbach received a B.A. in anthropology (1993) and an M.S. in environmental science from Ohio State University (1996). From 1997 to 1999 she worked for the University of Florida as a contractor on a state-funded grant to the Nature Conservancy of Florida, coordinating a groundcover restoration project on longleaf pine sandhills. She worked for the National Park Service from 1999 to 2000 in the fire-effects monitoring program at Indiana Dunes National Lakeshore. Since 2000 Meryl has been a field ecologist with the Nature Conservancy of Arkansas.

S. Homes Hogue is an associate professor of anthropology and Cobb Institute of Archaeology senior research associate at Mississippi State University. Her research focuses on prehistoric and protohistoric bioarchaeology and evolution in the southeastern United States. She is particularly interested in dietary reconstruction, health, and disease.

Lynn Stacey Jackson received a B.S. in wildlife and fisheries science from the University of Tennessee, Knoxville, in 1987 and an M.S. in wildlife ecology from Mississippi State University, Starkville, in 1989. She has been employed as a wildlife biologist with the U.S. Forest Service since 1989, when she began her career on the DeSoto National Forest. In 1991 she transferred to the Kisatchie National Forest in Louisiana, where she has been involved in red-cockaded woodpecker management as well as prairie and bog restoration.

Kay Krans is a 1971 graduate of the University of Wisconsin at Stevens Point, where she earned a B.S. in secondary education/history and political science. She obtained a master's degree in secondary education/reading at Mississippi State University. For the past several years she has team-taught a course at Starkville High School that centers on the science and history of land use of the Mississippi Black Prairie. She and Sherrill Wiygul obtained a National Geographic Society grant to create the course and to lease 24 ha of blackland prairie in Oktibbeha County, Mississippi, for preservation and education.

John MacDonald is interested in plant taxonomy and phytogeography of the southeastern United States, with emphasis on floras of Mississippi and Alabama. A biological consultant, he is currently working on a Ph.D. in botany at Mississippi State University.

Barbara R. MacRoberts and Michael H. MacRoberts trained as anthropologists (Berkeley 1968) with postdoctoral education in ethology (Oxford 1972). The MacRobertses worked in the sociology of knowledge and interbehavioral psychology before turning to botany. Centered on the West Gulf Coastal Plain, they focus their efforts on the conservation of rare plant communities. They are self-employed (Bog Research).

Victor Maddox holds a B.S. in horticulture with a minor in botany from Southeast Missouri State University, an M.S. in agronomy from Mississippi State University, and a Ph.D. in agronomy with a minor in biological sciences (plant taxonomy) from Mississippi State University (MSU). He is employed as a research associate in the Plant and Soil Sciences Department at MSU. His current research interests involve the use of native tallgrasses in golf-course natural areas.

Rebecca Melsheimer received her B.A. in anthropology from Mississippi State University in 2001. Currently she is attending the University of New Mexico, working toward an M.A. and eventually a Ph.D. in anthropology. Her research focuses on examining how environmental changes affect human subsistence practices and, ultimately, how these changes biologically affect people themselves.

Louis P. Moran received a B.S. in agricultural science from Tennessee State University (1993), an M.S. in soil science from Mississippi State University in 1995, and a Ph.D. in soil science from Iowa State University (2002). His doctoral dissertation presented research on spatial variability, hydrology, and carbon dynamics in restored prairie-wetland complexes in Iowa. Currently he is a lab technician in the Soil Survey Laboratory at Iowa State University's Department of Agronomy. His research interests include the spatial variability and impact of restoration practices on soils of restored ecosystems, such as wetlands and prairies.

Evan Peacock is an assistant professor of anthropology with the Department of Sociology, Anthropology, and Social Work, and a senior research associate with the Cobb Institute of Archaeology, Mississippi State University (MSU). He holds a B.A. in anthropology from MSU, an MSc. in environmental archaeology and paleoeconomy from the University of Sheffield, England, and a Ph.D. in archaeology from Sheffield. He has worked as an archaeologist in the private sector and with the U.S. Forest Service. His research interests include pre-industrial human environmental impact and the application of paleoenvironmental data to contemporary resource management.

David Pettry is Giles Professor Emeritus of Plant and Soil Sciences at Mississippi State University. He received B.S and M.S. degrees from the University of Florida and a Ph.D. from Virginia Polytechnic Institute and State University. His research has focused on pedology, soil-environmental relationships, remote sensing, and soil-health issues. He has collaborated in multidisciplinary studies in North America, Central America, Europe, Asia, and Africa. He is a Fellow of the American Society of Agronomy and the Soil and Water Conservation Society of America.

Janet Rafferty is professor of anthropology and senior research associate at the Cobb Institute of Archaeology, Mississippi State University. Her main research interests are settlement-pattern change and application of evolutionary theory to archaeology.

Mary Celeste Reese received a B.S. in biological sciences from the Mississippi University for Women in 1992 and an M.S. in biological sciences with an emphasis in historical ecology from Mississippi State University in 2000. Currently she is an instructor in the Biological Sciences Department at MSU, teaching the courses Plant Biology and Plants and Humans. She is also starting a plant nursery business called Native Roots Nursery, specializing in native trees and shrubs for habitat-restoration projects and ornamental landscaping.

Frank F. Schambach (Ph.D., Harvard University) began studying the archaeology of the Blackland Prairie of northeastern Texas in 1993. He has been the Arkansas Archeological Survey's district archaeologist for southwestern Arkansas since 1968.

Timothy Schauwecker received a Ph.D. in 2001 from Mississippi State University, where his research focused on restoration issues in blackland prairie settings. Currently he is a principal consultant with Land Restoration Associates, San Diego, California.

Darrel W. Schmitz is professor of geology in the Department of Geosciences at Mississippi State University. His research specialty is hydrogeology including engineering geology applications. Dr. Schmitz earned degrees from Mississippi State University, the University of Mississippi, and Texas A&M University. Before obtaining his Ph.D. from Texas A&M and entering academia at MSU in 1990, Dr. Schmitz spent more than ten years in industry.

Thomas Schurch is an associate professor at the University of Oklahoma, where he serves as director of the Division of Landscape Architecture. His research interests are sustainable urban design, meaning in the built environment, and approaches to implementation through planning and policy. He earned a Ph.D. in urban design and planning at the University of Washington and a master's degree in landscape architecture at California State Polytechnic University, Pomona.

Scott Simon holds a B.S. in biology from the University of Wisconsin–Madison and an M.S. from the University of Illinois. He is employed by the Nature Conservancy of Arkansas. As director of conservation, he is responsible for coordinating partnership conservation programs in areas of significant biodiversity in Arkansas.

Richard Switzer holds a B.A. in microbiology from Mississippi State University and an M.S. in microbiology from North Carolina State University. Currently he is a biological science technician with the USDA Agricultural Research Service, where his research in the Waste Management and Forage Research Unit involves finding environmentally friendly ways to dispose of waste products generated by commercial agriculture.

Charles L. Wax, a professor of geography in the Department of Geosciences at Mississippi State University, is state climatologist for Mississippi. He holds M.S. and Ph.D. degrees in geography–climatology from Louisiana State University. His research interests include agricultural climatology and water resources.

Ronald Wieland is a vegetation ecologist/botanist with the Mississippi Department of Wildlife, Fisheries and Parks, Museum of Natural Science, Natural Heritage Program, 2148 Riverside Drive, Jackson, MS 39202. He manages the tracking list for special plants of Mississippi and develops the state list of ecological communities.

Sherrill Wiygul attended the University of Southwestern Louisiana and Louisiana State University, where she earned a B.A. in history. She did graduate work in English at Tulane University and taught freshman composition at Mississippi State University (MSU) for more than a decade. In the mid-1980s she earned an M.S. in zoology at MSU and began teaching biology at Starkville High School. She team-teaches a course in biogeography in which high school students study prairie and hardwood forest ecology.

Douglas Zollner, an ecologist with the Nature Conservancy, currently serves as national fire restoration coordinator in Lakewood, Colorado. He received a B.S. in watershed management from the University of Arizona and an M.S. in the ecology of arid lands from Texas Tech University. He spent the 1980s working in conservation overseas, mostly in eastern and southern Africa. Zollner has been working with fire ecology and ecological restoration for the past twenty years.

Index

16th Section Prairie, MS, 31, 34, 37, 39, 41, 255, 257. *See also* Osborn Prairie
22CL764 site, MS, 189
22OK578 site, MS, 187
22OK694 site, MS, 189
22OK904 site, MS, 31–38, 41–43
22OK942 site, MS, 189
Adair, James, 3, 70
Alstonian stadial, 14
Anacoco Prairie, 82
Andropogon gerardii. See big bluestem
animal licks, 117, 142, 144
Annona chalk, 114, 116
Appalachian Mountains, 14, 29
archaeobotany, 29, 49, 54–56, 64–65, 67–73, 75–79
Archaic period, 167, 170
Arkansas Post, 23
Arkansas River Valley, 23–24, 214–215, 222, 227, 230, 232
Atlantic Coastal Plain, 14, 19, 21

barrens, 11, 25, 146, 148–149, 157, 162
Barrier Islands, 16
beads, 216, 218, 221, 225
bearing trees, 99, 102, 105, 106
Bertram's Prairie, LA, 82

Bienville National Forest, MS, 148–149, 239–245
big bluestem, 1, 86, 95, 107, 117, 121–122, 128, 130, 132, 149, 155
biodiversity, 87, 97, 110–111, 149–150, 152, 162–163, 241, 243, 250, 253, 258–260, 281
bison, 2, 4, 15, 84, 214–215, 217–220, 225–227, 230–231, 233–234
Black Belt, AL and MS, 2–6, 11–13, 15–25, 30–31, 34, 37, 42–50, 53, 59–62, 69, 107–108, 195–196, 201, 255–261
black drink, 216
Blackfoot Indians, 227
Blackland Prairie, TX, 223–226, 229–230, 232–236
blackland prairies, 264, 268–271, 275–278; of Alabama, 2, 3, 4, 11, 13, 88, 107–108, 190, 225, 259, 266, 276; of Arkansas, 2, 4, 6, 11, 81, 86, 88, 94–131, 134–143; of Georgia, 2; of Louisiana, 2, 4, 6, 80, 81–90, 92; of Mississippi, 2, 4, 11, 17, 20, 37, 56, 42, 81, 86, 88, 107–108, 146–155, 155–159, 162–163, 167, 169, 188, 190, 211, 239–245, 247, 255–259, 266–267, 276; of Texas, 2, 4, 11, 81, 83, 86,

88, 107–108, 213, 220, 225–226,
229, 234, 266
Black Prairie, MS, 2, 5–6, 30, 41, 49–
50, 56, 64, 67–68, 71, 88, 147–
148, 167–170, 174, 188, 190, 195–
199, 201–207, 210–211, 260
Blake, Peter, 263
bois d'arc, 96, 135, 142, 144, 227,
232. *See also* Osage orange
bone-tempered, 176, 179–184
Bossier Parish, LA, 84, 89, 91
Brogan mound and village site, MS,
173, 175, 177
Brown, C. A., 88, 90, 93
Brundtland Commission, 262
buffalo. *See* bison

Caddo Indians, 98, 100, 224–228,
230, 232–233, 235; sites, 100, 106
Caddo Prairie, LA, 82, 89, 92
Cahokia site, IL, 213, 215, 217
Caldwell Parish, LA, 91
camel, 15
Capaha, province of, 218
carbon isotopes, 55, 189
Carex cherokeensis, 108, 115–120,
122–127, 129–136, 138, 142,
149, 155
Carson, Rachel, 263
Casqui, province of, 218
Catahoula Prairie, LA, 82
cedar. *See* eastern redcedar
Central Basin, 25
Central Plains, 14, 15, 21
Chickasaw County, MS, 16, 31, 34,
37, 40–41, 190, 197, 204, 206, 259
Chickasaw Indians, 70, 167, 200, 210
Choctaw County, MS, 202
Clark County, AR, 115–116, 118–
119, 121, 126–127, 129, 131–132,
134–135, 137, 143
Clarke County, MS, 239
Clay County, MS, 16, 42, 49, 67,
167–171, 173, 177, 185–188, 190,
192, 197, 206
Clean Air Act, 263
Clovis points, 84
coastal plain. *See* Gulf Coastal Plain

Coastal Zone Management Act, 263
Coldwater Prairie, LA, 87
Coligua, province of, 218
Columbus Prairie, AR, 104, 118–
119, 134
coneflower, 19, 108, 115–117, 149,
153, 158
Coronado, Francisco Vázquez de,
217–218, 232
crayfish, 244
Cretaceous, 3, 5, 12, 30, 94, 107,
139, 195, 201, 203, 247
culture history, 5, 28, 171

Dalea spp. See prairie clover
Dallas County, AL, 19
d'Artaguette, Diron, 200
daub, 67–79, 169
deer, 16, 31
de Los Rios, Domingo Teran, 233
Demopolis chalk, 12–13, 15, 168,
192, 247
de Richarville, Sieur Claude
Drouet, 200
Desmanthus illinoensis, 116–117,
119, 122–123, 149, 154, 159–160
de Soto, Hernando, 146, 217, 218,
219, 222, 232
DeSoto Parish, LA, 92
Du Pratz, Le Page, 100–101
Durand Oak Prairie, MS, 150–152,
155–157, 162

eastern redcedar, 11, 13, 19, 25, 30–
32, 34, 37, 40–42, 90, 96, 106,
108, 114, 116–123, 125, 127–128,
144, 149, 241, 243–244, 247, 253,
255–257
Eastern Woodlands, 27–28
Echinacea spp, 89, 114–116, 120–
125, 130–134, 138–139, 158, 160.
See also coneflower
Edwards Plateau, TX, 106
Endangered Species Act, 88, 244, 274
environmental archaeology, 28–29,
32, 45, 64–66, 279, 281
environmental possibilism, 28, 44
Eocene, 147, 239

essentialism, 29, 43–44, 281
Etowah site, GA, 213, 215
Eureka Church Prairie, MS, 150–
152, 156–157, 162
evolutionary archaeology, 29,
279, 281

Farmdalian interstadial, 14
Featherman, Americus, 81–82
Featherstonhaugh, George W., 100
fiber-tempered, 170–172, 176,
178–184
Five Acre Prairie, MS, 150–152, 155–
157, 162
Flatwoods, 192
Flood Disaster Protection Act, 263
flotation, 33, 55, 69
fossil shells, 3, 44, 47, 86, 241
fossil shell-tempered, 44, 170–171,
176, 178–184, 190
Freeman-Custis expedition, 83, 84

gamma grass, 95, 107, 117
Gap Analysis Programs (GAP), 112
Gatecliff Shelter, 50
Gavin, Major David, 201–202
General Land Office (GLO) sur-
veys, 13, 82, 90, 96–99, 101–
102, 104–106
Geographic Information Systems
(GIS), 270
Gilbert site, TX, 220, 234
Glass, Anthony, 234–235
gorgets, 216, 225
Gosse, Philip, 259
Grand Prairie, TX, 11, 24, 220, 229
Grandview Prairie, AR, 104–106,
114–116, 118–119, 121, 124, 126–
127, 129, 131–132, 134, 136
Grant Parish, LA, 82, 90
grazing, 2, 15, 24, 234, 241, 244–246
Great Basin, 20, 50
Great Lakes, 15
Great Plains, 12, 14–17, 19–25, 214,
218–224, 227, 231, 233, 235–236,
254, 258
grog-tempered, 170, 176, 178–184
Gulf Coast, 17, 21–22, 81, 216

Gulf Coastal Plain, 2, 7, 11, 14–
15, 19, 94, 97–98, 103, 107, 113–
115, 117–118, 120–121, 123, 125–
126, 128–129, 132–133, 136–137,
139, 141
Gulf Formational period, 168, 171,
173, 175–176, 184, 186–188

Hancock County, MS, 17
Handy Brake National Wildlife Ref-
uge, LA, 92
Harrell Prairie Hill, MS, 150–152,
155–163, 240, 242, 244–245
Harrison County, MS, 17
Hasinai Indians, 227, 232–233
Hempstead County, AR, 98, 100,
115, 117–119, 121–122, 124, 126–
127, 129, 131–132, 134–135, 137,
139–140, 143
Herman mound and village site,
MS, 173, 175
Highland Rim, 25
Hinds County, MS, 239
Historic period, 15, 30–35, 37–38,
41, 43, 83, 89, 167, 195–196, 199,
201–202, 210, 219, 227, 232
Hohokam, 194
Holocene, 28, 66, 75–76, 228
Horton site, OK, 222
Howard County, AR, 98, 115, 117–
119, 121, 124, 126–127, 129, 134–
135, 137, 140, 143
Hypsithermal, 15

Illinoian glacial stage, 24
Indiangrass, 95, 107, 108, 115, 117,
125, 155

Jackson County, MS, 17
Jackson group, 147, 239–240
Jackson Prairie, MS, 6, 12, 17, 19,
21–22, 146–150, 152–153, 156–
157, 162–163, 239, 241, 244
Jasper County, MS, 147, 239
Jefferson, Thomas, 102
Jefferson Prairie, LA, 84–85
Jennings, Jesse, 3, 200

Johnson, Jay, 31, 169
Josey Farm site, MS, 49, 50, 54–63
Jumanos, 220, 232–233
Juniperus virginiana. See eastern
    redcedar

K5OH Prairie, LA, 87
Kadohadacho Indians, 232–233
Keiffer prairies, LA, 85–86, 88–90, 92
Kemper County, MS, 16, 204
Kisatchie National Forest, LA, 90–93

La Harpe's Post, 226
La Salle Parish, LA, 82
Laurentide ice sheet, 14
Lee County, MS, 16, 188, 190, 197
Leopold, Aldo, 265
Lewis, Meriwether, 235
Liatris spp., 108, 114, 116, 120, 122–
    123, 125, 128, 138, 153, 251–252
limestone-tempered, 176, 179–184
little bluestem, 1–2, 13, 86, 95, 107–
    108, 113–115, 117, 119–122, 124–
    125, 128, 130–132, 134, 138–139,
    149, 155, 158, 247, 251–252
Little River County, AR, 94, 115,
    117–118, 121, 126–127, 129, 134–
    135, 137, 139–140, 143
Little Tennessee River valley, 29
Lockett, S. H., 81, 84
Louisiana Purchase, 102
Lowndes County, MS, 16, 20, 197,
    201, 203, 206, 260
Lubbub Creek archaeological locality,
    AL, 50–53, 55–56, 58–62
Lyon's Bluff site, MS, 55, 67, 71,
    173, 187, 189

MacArthur, Robert, 264
Maclura pomifera. See Osage orange
Madison County, MS, 239
mammoth, 15
Marengo County, AL, 190
Marsh, George Perkins, 263
mastodon, 15
McNairy County, TN, 25
megafauna, 228–229, 235

Midway group, 192
Milam Prairie, LA, 87
Miller I phase, 170–171, 175, 177,
    186–187
Miller II phase, 170–171, 175,
    186–187
Miller III phase, 170–171, 175,
    186–187
Mississippian period, 30–31, 42, 44,
    49, 51–52, 54–56, 58, 60–61, 68–
    69, 71, 167, 169–171, 173–175,
    177, 180, 185–190, 192, 212–217,
    219, 221–222, 225–227, 229–232
Mississippi embayment, 11
Mississippi River valley, 14, 25,
    212, 214, 218, 227, 231–232, 235
Monroe County, AL, 20
Monroe County, MS, 197, 206
Morehouse Parish, LA, 92
Morris site, OK, 220, 222
Mounds Plantation site, LA, 220, 227
Moundville site, AL, 213, 215
Muir, John, 262
mussel shell-tempered, 169–171,
    176, 178–184, 187, 190, 192, 225

Nagle site, OK, 213, 220–222, 224–
    225, 230
Nairne, Thomas, 2
Natchez Trace, 167
Natchitoches Parish, LA, 86, 88,
    91–92
National Environmental Policy Act,
    263, 271
National Trust for Historic Preserva-
    tion, 273
Native Americans, 67, 93; agricul-
    ture and cultivation, 23, 28, 30–
    33, 43–44, 48–58, 61–62, 68, 73,
    75–78, 84, 99–101, 135, 168, 189–
    190, 213, 222; cultures, 1, 84,
    275–276; environmental impact,
    27, 29–30, 32, 43–44, 48, 51–52,
    56, 58, 61, 75–76, 78–79; fire use,
    2, 28, 32, 48, 76, 84, 100–101,
    242, 280; lifeways, 6, 32, 48, 54,
    62, 69–70, 84, 220–222, 225;
    mounds, 31–32, 71, 78, 84–85,

106, 169, 173, 177, 187–188, 214–216, 225 settlement patterns, 6, 29, 31–32, 43, 68, 101, 168–173, 175, 177, 185, 187–193, 198, 200, 210

Natural Heritage programs, 83, 88–89, 92–93, 97, 103–107, 110, 146, 256, 258

Nature Conservancy, 83, 91, 93, 102–107, 110, 255

Neptunia lutea, 12, 87, 107, 114, 116, 122, 154, 160

Nevada County, AR, 115, 117–118, 126, 129, 134–135, 137

New Archaeology, 28

Newton County, MS, 147, 150–151, 239, 241

Nodena phase, 218

North Central Hills, 192, 202, 210

Noxubee County, MS, 197, 201, 203–204, 206, 260

Noxubee Wildlife Refuge, MS, 257

Nutt, Rush, 3, 200

Nuttall, Thomas, 234–235

Oktibbeha County, MS, 13, 16–17, 20, 31, 34, 37, 39, 41–42, 54, 56, 167–171, 173, 177, 185–188, 190–193, 197, 202–204, 206, 247–248, 255–257

Olmsted, Frederick Law, 262–263

Omaha Indians, 227

Osage Indians, 233–234

Osage orange, 18, 19, 22–24, 123, 126–127, 133–135, 137, 226–232, 234–236, 247. *See also* bois d'arc

Osborn Prairie, MS, 13, 17, 20, 31, 37, 247–248, 255–258, 260–261. *See also* 16th Section Prairie

Ouachita Mountains, 98, 100, 214–215, 226

Ozark Mountains, 14, 214–215

Pacaha, province of. *See* Capaha, province of

Packton Prairies, LA, 90

paleoethnobotany. *See* archaeobotany

Paleo-Indian period, 170

Pawnee Indians, 227, 233

peccary, 16

Pickens County, AL, 50

Pinchot, Gifford, 263

Pineywoods, 81

Pleistocene, 15, 21–22, 43, 76, 84, 228–229, 235, 239

pollen, 14, 15, 23, 29, 64, 66–69, 73–79

Pontotoc County, MS, 188

Pontotoc Hills, 16

post oak, 12, 129, 131, 144

Powell, John Wesley, 263

Prairie Bluff chalk, 168, 192

prairie clover, 12, 20, 96, 103, 107–108, 114–115, 117, 120–122, 124–125, 131, 134, 139, 149, 154, 157–160, 251–252

Prairie De Anne, AR, 100

Prairie de Cote, LA, 81

Prairie De Roane, AR, 99, 100

prairie peninsula, 15, 25

processual archaeology, 28–29

Protohistoric period, 30, 32–37, 41–43, 167–171, 173–175, 177, 183, 185–190, 192–193

Quaternary period, 14

radiocarbon dates, 68, 169, 187, 227

Rankin County, MS, 239

Ratibida Prairie, LA, 87

Ratibida spp. See coneflower

Rector's Prairie, LA, 91

Red River valley, 23, 217, 223–224, 227–228, 232–235

Resource Conservation and Recovery Act, 263

Rocky Mountains, 1–2, 23

Romans, Bernard, 200

Rudbeckia spp., 18, 103, 108, 113–114, 116, 120–122, 130, 134, 149, 153, 159–160

Safe Water Drinking Act, 263

Sanders site, TX, 23, 220–232, 234–235

sand-tempered, 170–172, 176, 178–184
Sangamon interglacial, 16
Saratoga chalk, 114, 116
Saratoga Landing Black Prairie, AR,
    104–105, 121–122
Schizachyrium scoparium. See little
    bluestem
Scott County, MS, 147, 150–151, 239
Selma group, 12, 192, 247
Sevier County, AR, 115, 117–118,
    126–127, 129, 132, 134–135, 137,
    140, 143
shortgrass prairie, 2, 162, 219, 221
shrink-swell clays, 55, 86, 114,
    116, 118–119, 124–125, 127,
    130, 132, 138
Sierra Club, 262
Silphium laciniatum, 12, 95, 116–
    117, 120, 122, 134, 152
sloth, 15
Smith County, MS, 147, 150–151, 239
Soil and Water Conservation Act, 263
Sorghastrum nutans, 86, 115–117,
    120–122, 124, 127–132, 134, 138,
    155, 158. *See also* Indiangrass
South Farm site, MS, 55, 189
Spiroan Indians, 23, 214–215, 217–
    218, 220–221, 223–227, 229–232
Spiro site, OK, 213, 215–225, 227–
    228, 230–232, 235
springs, 192–193, 195–196, 199–
    202, 210
Standard Zoning Enabling Act, 269
Sumter County, AL, 13
Surface Mining Control and Recla-
    mation Act, 263
sustainability, 5, 262–267, 276–279
sustainable development, 5, 276–278

Taitt, David, 3
tallgrass prairie, 2, 11, 83–84, 86–
    87, 89, 107, 155, 157, 162, 190,
    213, 219, 221, 225, 233–234,
    246, 254
Tancock's Prairie, LA, 82
Tennessee-Tombigbee Waterway, 167
Terre Noire Blackland Prairie,
    AR, 106

Tertiary, 14–15, 86, 94
Tewa Indians, 227, 232
thermoluminescence dates, 71
Tombigbee National Forest, 37, 259
Tombigbee River valley, 78, 169, 170
Tonti, Henri de, 233
Toxic Substances Control Act, 263
Tula, province of, 219, 222–232, 232
Tunica Hills, 14, 25
Tunica Indians, 232, 234

uniformitarianism, 29, 66, 281
Union County, MS, 188
United Nations Educational, Scien-
    tific, and Cultural Organization
    (UNESCO), 110

Vernon Parish, LA, 81, 91
vertisols, 147, 163

Walls phase, 225
Water Quality Act, 263
Wayne County, MS, 239
whelk, 216, 225
Whyte, William, 263
Wichita Indians, 233–234
Wild and Scenic Rivers Act, 263
Wilson, Edward O., 264
Winn Parish, LA, 86, 88, 90
Wisconsin glacial stage, 14, 16, 21,
    23–25
witness trees, 102. *See also* bearing
    trees
Womack site, TX, 220, 234
Woodland period, 30, 44, 51, 54, 60,
    78, 169–171, 173–175, 177, 179,
    185, 187–190, 192
Woods County, OK, 43
Wybark site, OK, 220, 231

Yaqui Indians, 227
Yarborough site, MS, 49–50, 54–62,
    67–70, 72–79
Yazoo Basin, 232
Yazoo County, MS, 239

zooarchaeology, 28, 48–63, 66, 78